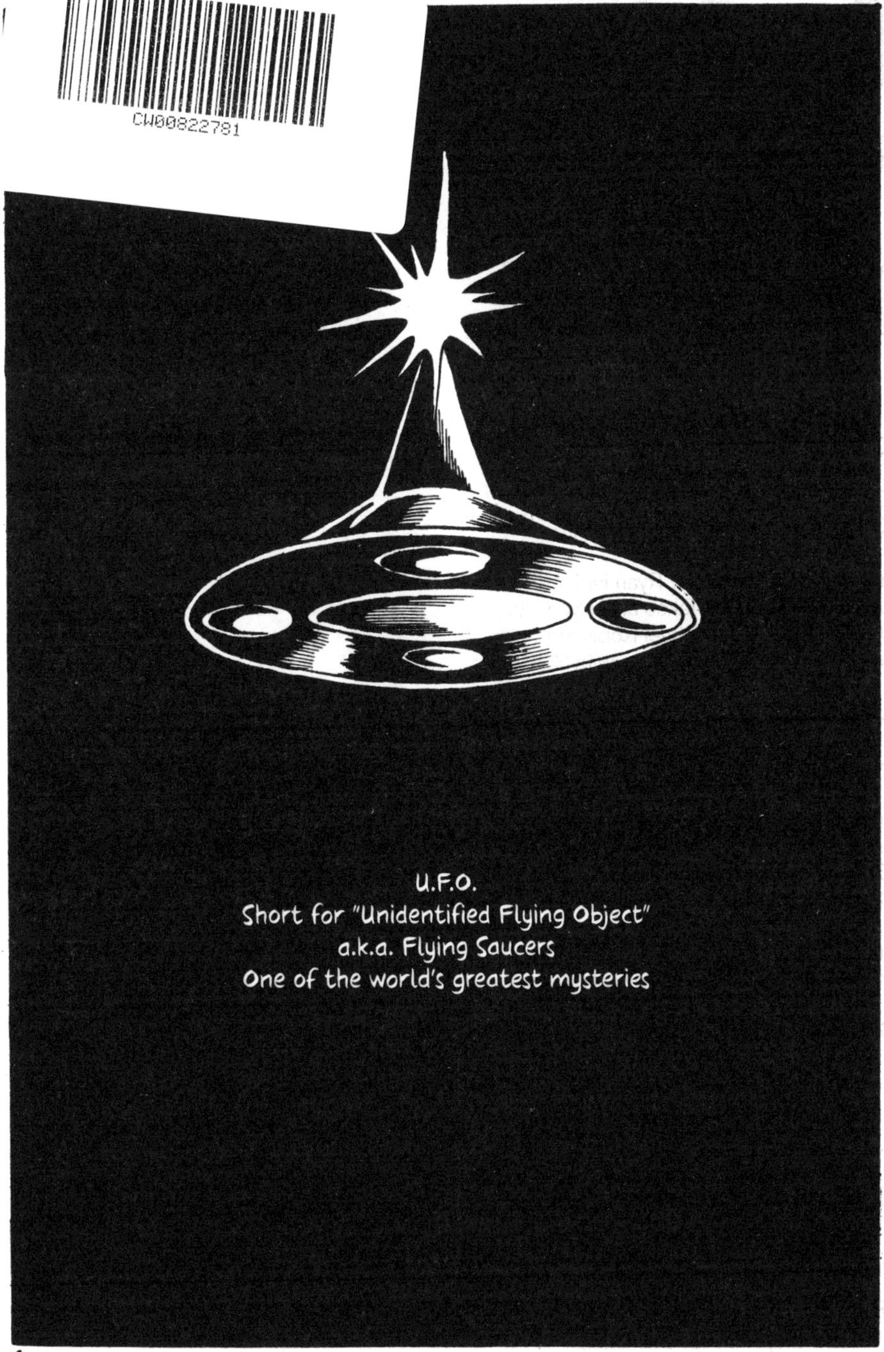
U.F.O.
Short for "Unidentified Flying Object"
a.k.a. Flying Saucers
One of the world's greatest mysteries

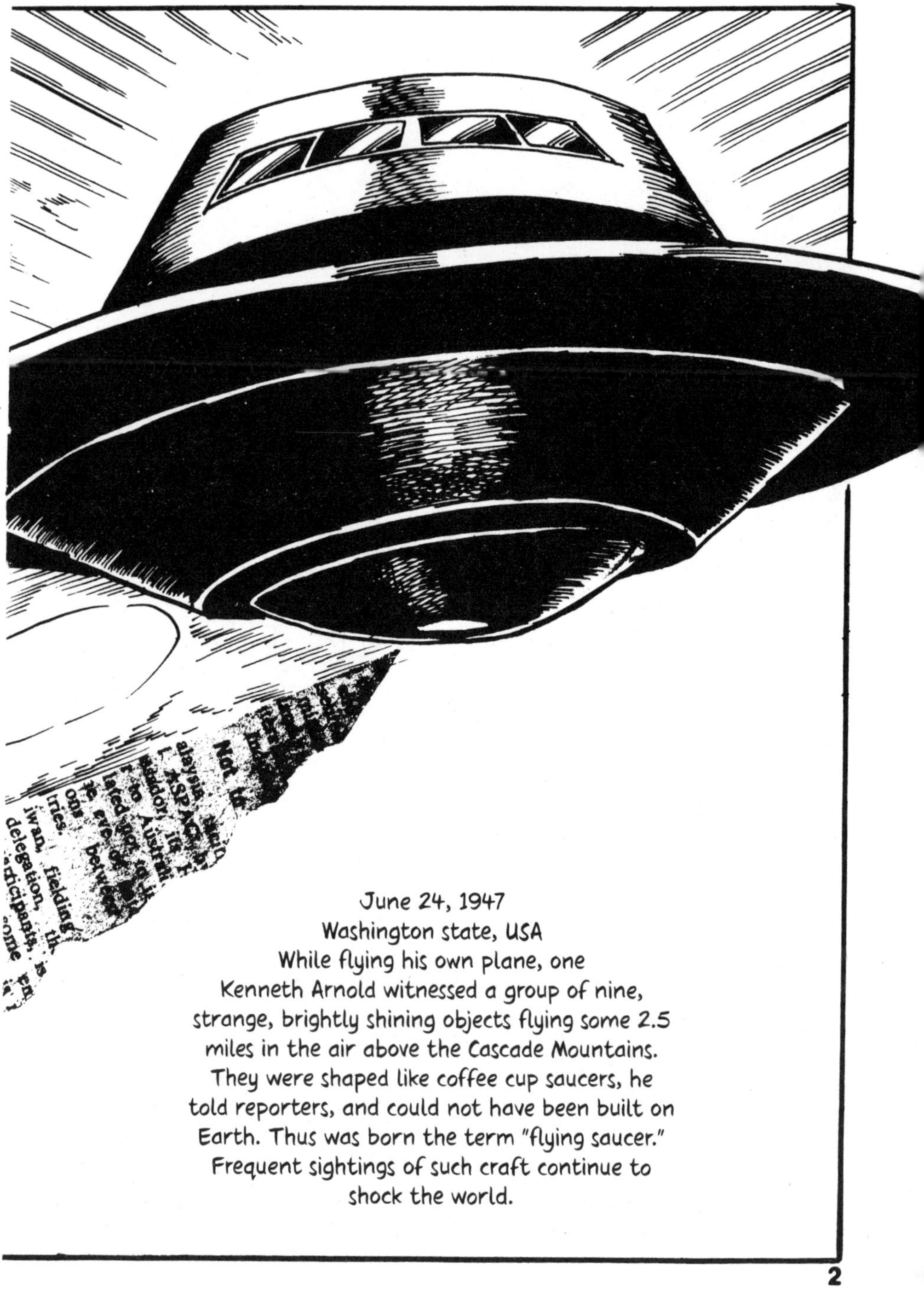
June 24, 1947
Washington state, USA
While flying his own plane, one
Kenneth Arnold witnessed a group of nine,
strange, brightly shining objects flying some 2.5
miles in the air above the Cascade Mountains.
They were shaped like coffee cup saucers, he
told reporters, and could not have been built on
Earth. Thus was born the term "flying saucer."
Frequent sightings of such craft continue to
shock the world.

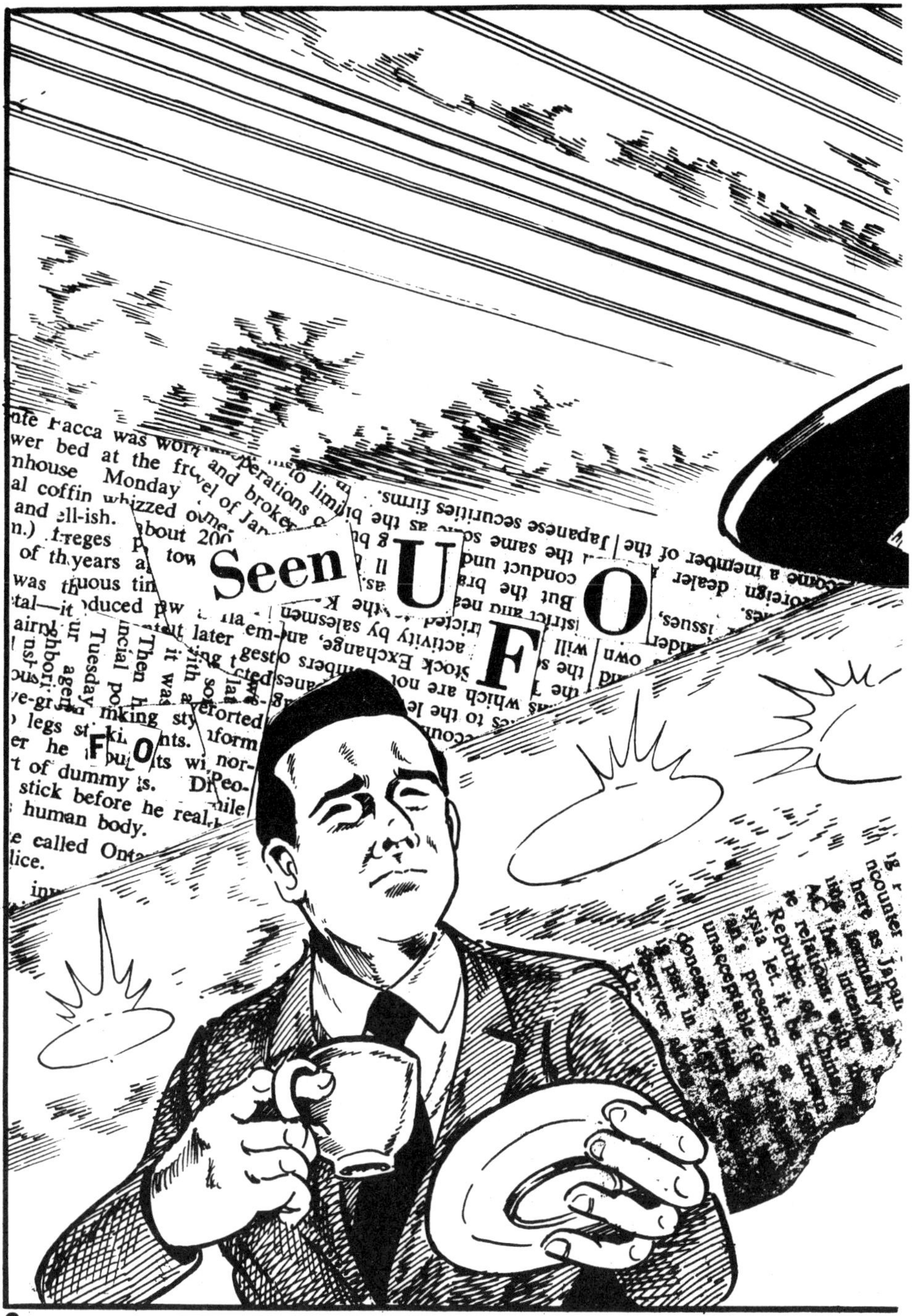
Seen
U
O
F
F O

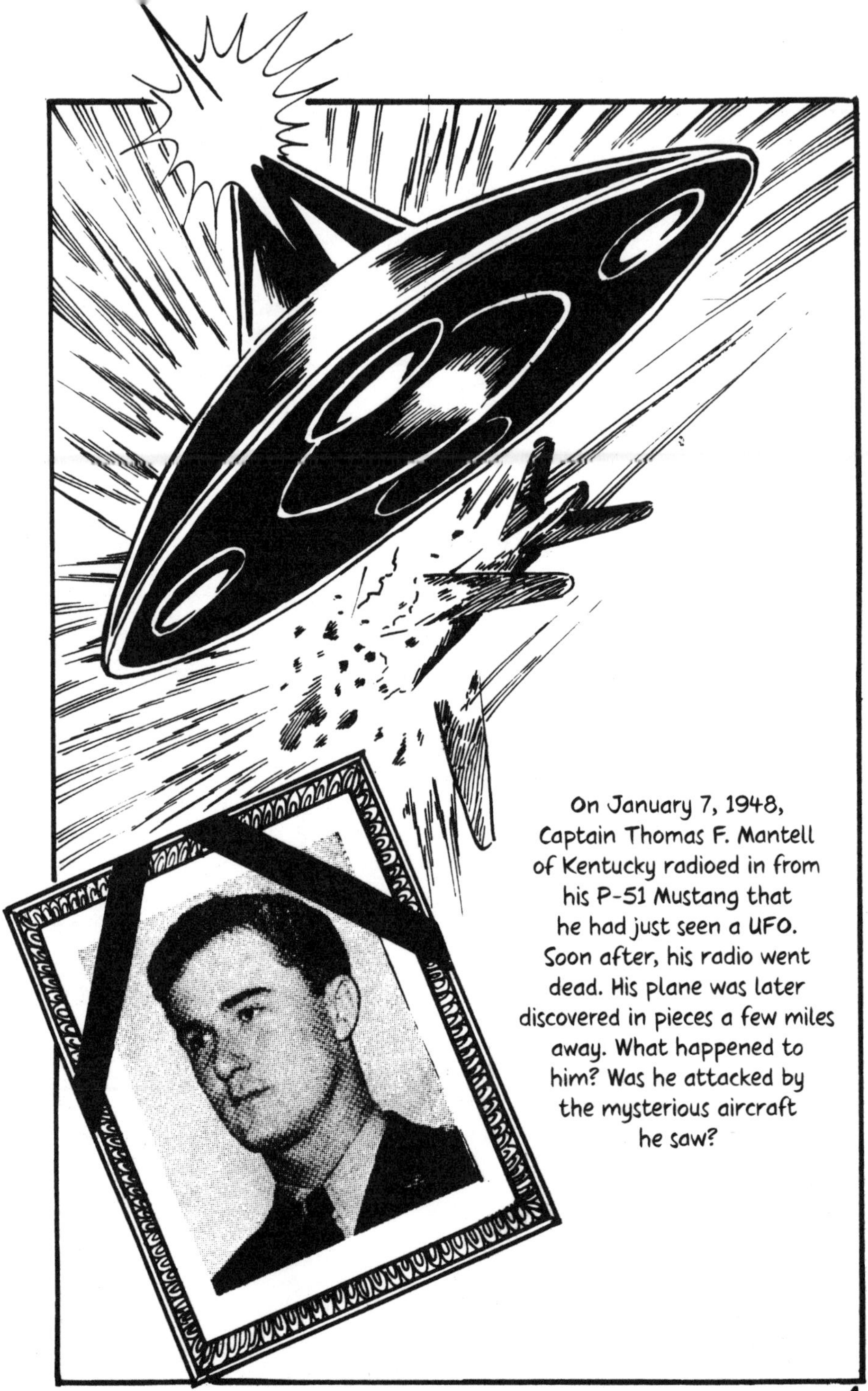
On January 7, 1948, Captain Thomas F. Mantell of Kentucky radioed in from his P-51 Mustang that he had just seen a UFO. Soon after, his radio went dead. His plane was later discovered in pieces a few miles away. What happened to him? Was he attacked by the mysterious aircraft he saw?

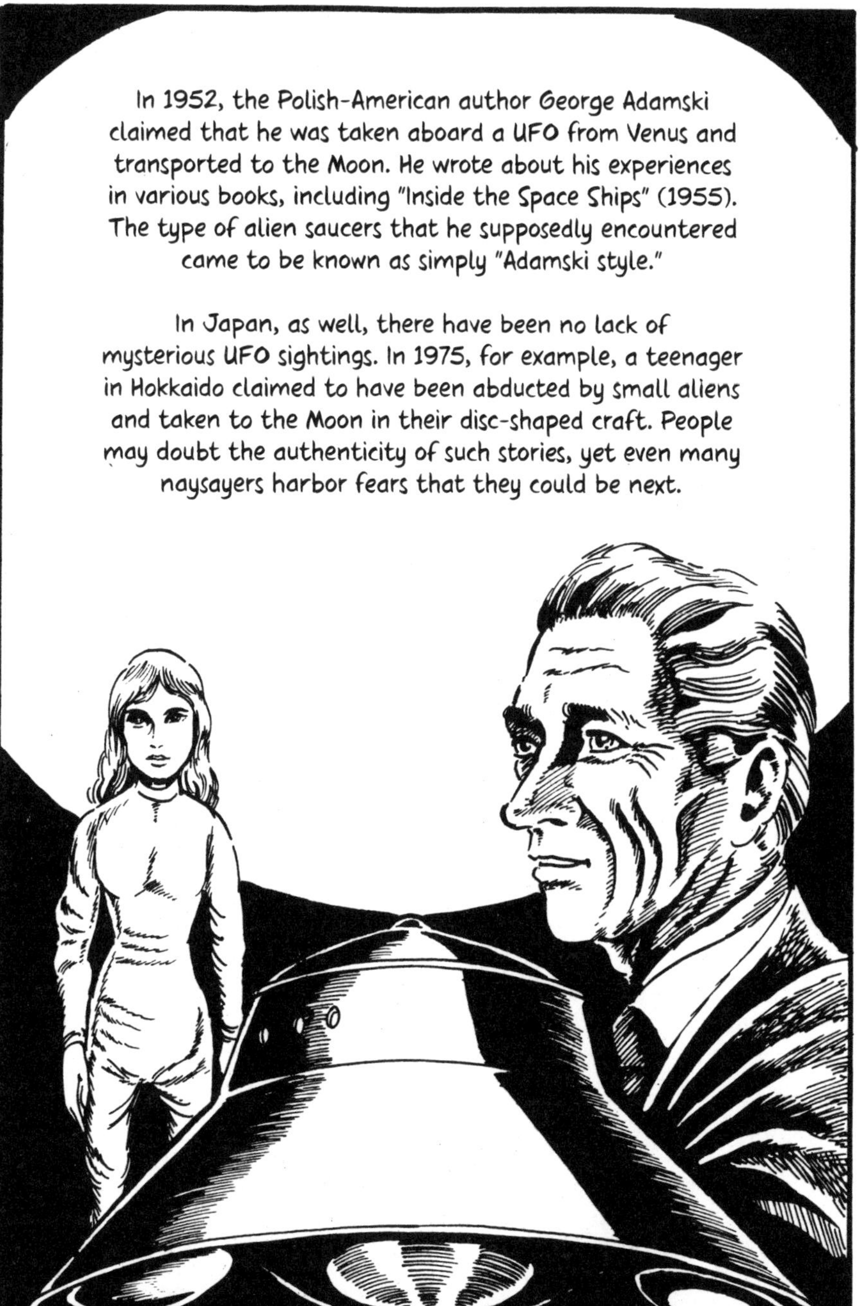
In 1952, the Polish-American author George Adamski claimed that he was taken aboard a UFO from Venus and transported to the Moon. He wrote about his experiences in various books, including "Inside the Space Ships" (1955). The type of alien saucers that he supposedly encountered came to be known as simply "Adamski style."
In Japan, as well, there have been no lack of mysterious UFO sightings. In 1975, for example, a teenager in Hokkaido claimed to have been abducted by small aliens and taken to the Moon in their disc-shaped craft. People may doubt the authenticity of such stories, yet even many naysayers harbor fears that they could be next.

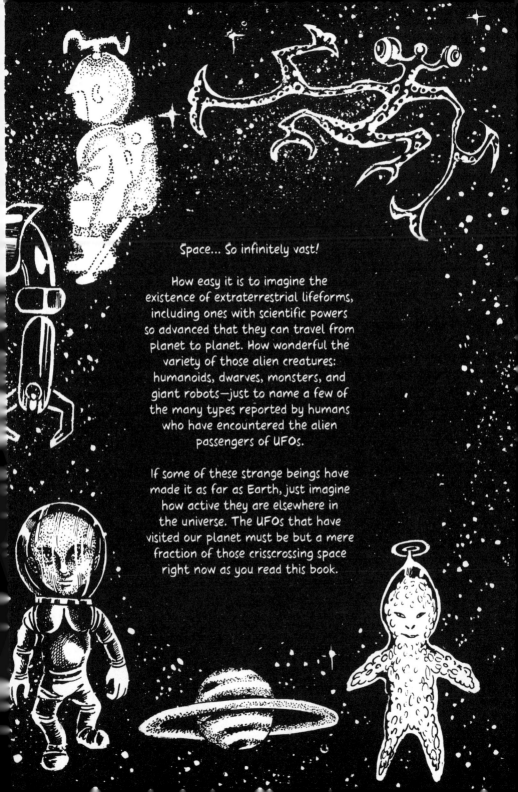

Space... So infinitely vast!

How easy it is to imagine the existence of extraterrestrial lifeforms, including ones with scientific powers so advanced that they can travel from planet to planet. How wonderful the variety of those alien creatures: humanoids, dwarves, monsters, and giant robots—just to name a few of the many types reported by humans who have encountered the alien passengers of UFOs.

If some of these strange beings have made it as far as Earth, just imagine how active they are elsewhere in the universe. The UFOs that have visited our planet must be but a mere fraction of those crisscrossing space right now as you read this book.

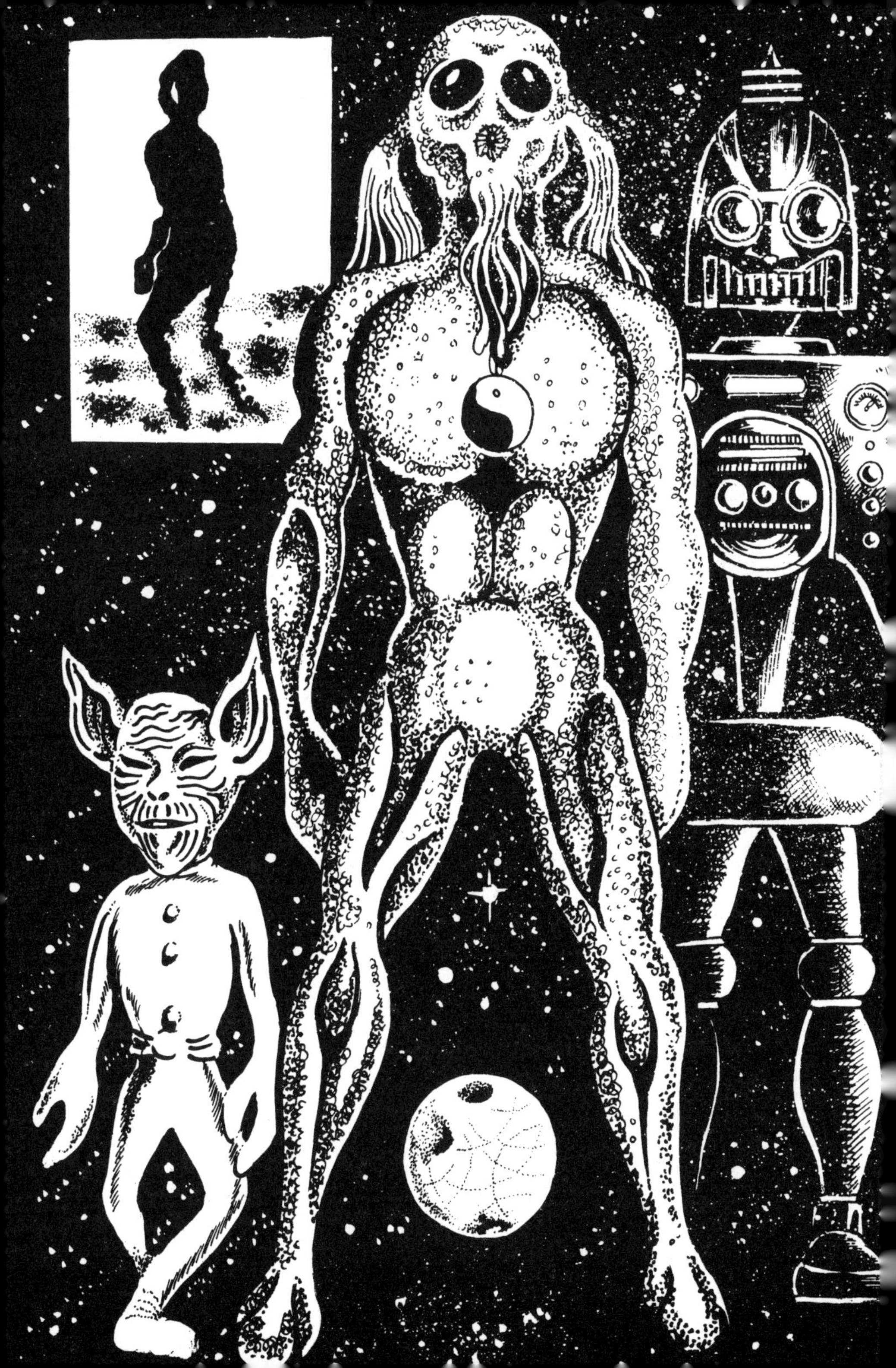

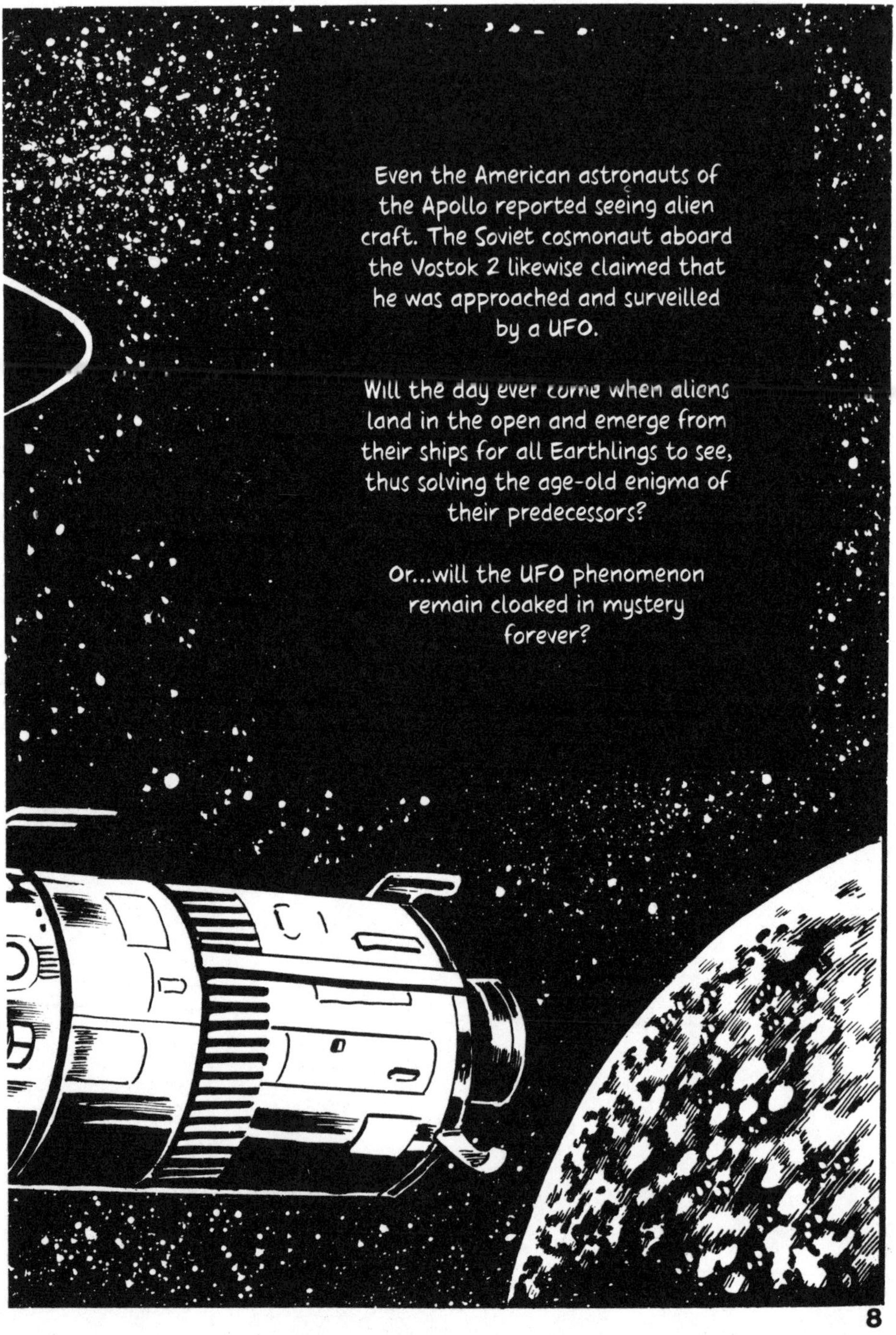
Even the American astronauts of the Apollo reported seeing alien craft. The Soviet cosmonaut aboard the Vostok 2 likewise claimed that he was approached and surveilled by a UFO.
Will the day ever come when aliens land in the open and emerge from their ships for all Earthlings to see, thus solving the age-old enigma of their predecessors?
Or...will the UFO phenomenon remain cloaked in mystery forever?

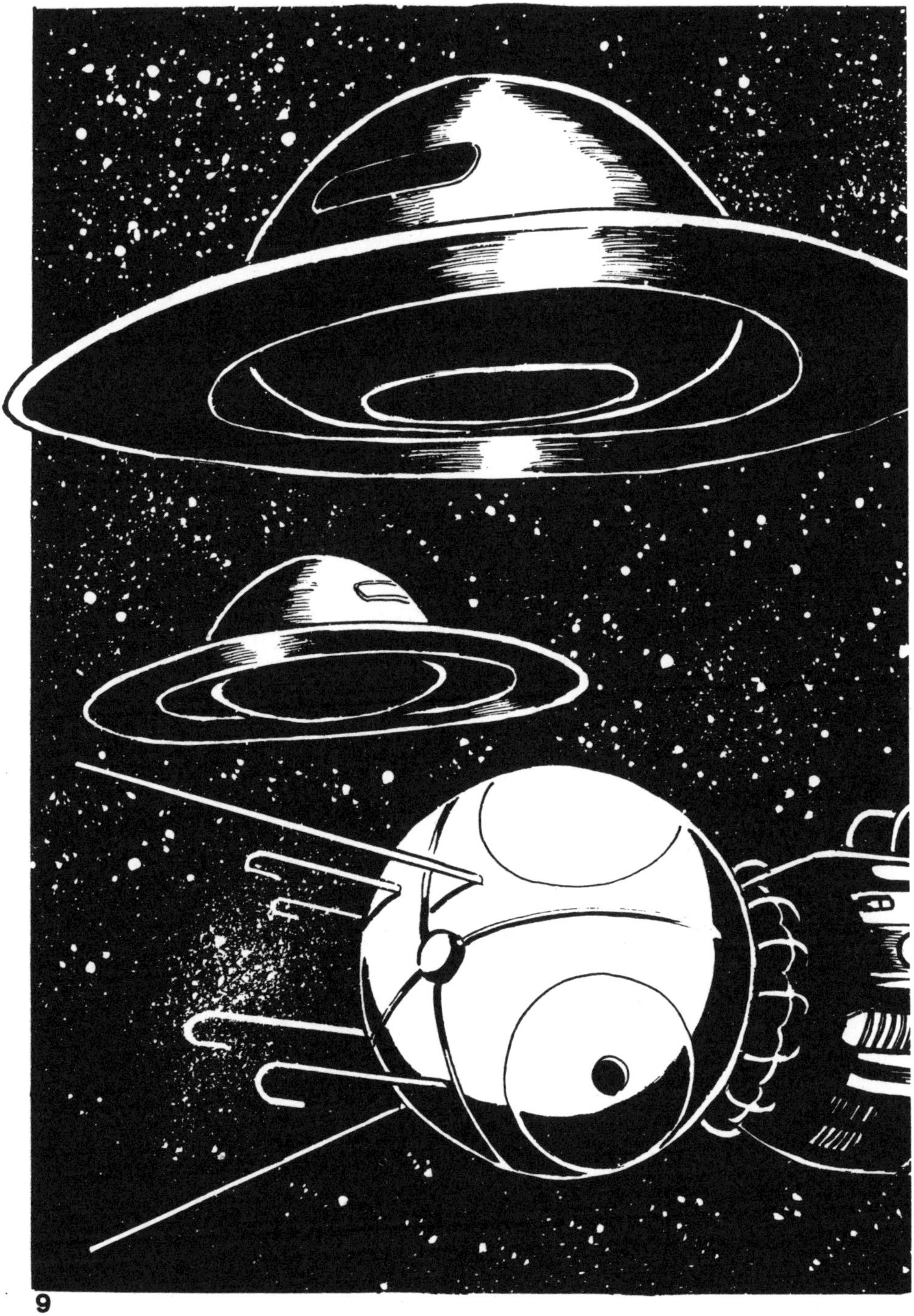

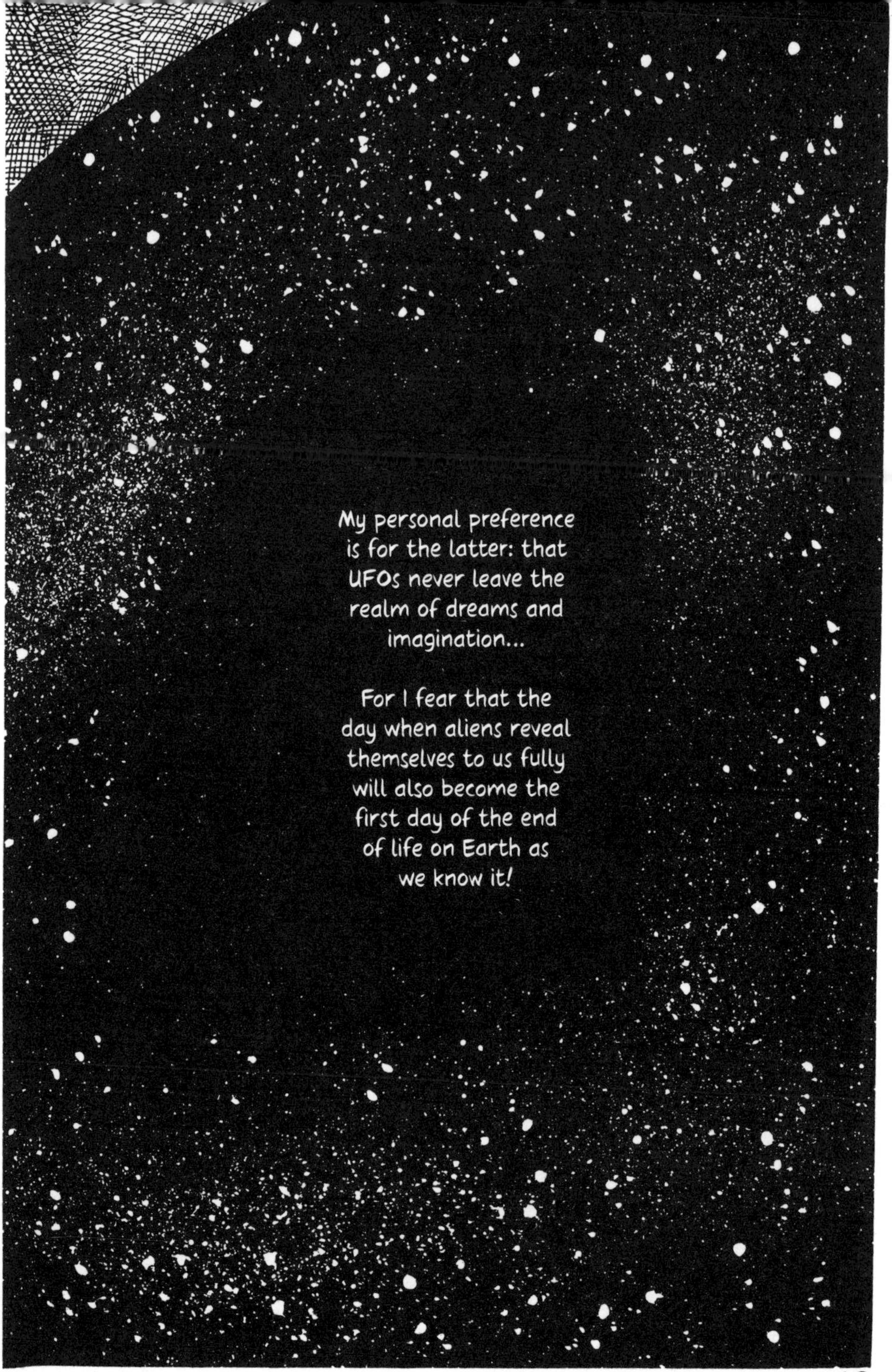
My personal preference is for the latter: that UFOs never leave the realm of dreams and imagination...
For I fear that the day when aliens reveal themselves to us fully will also become the first day of the end of life on Earth as we know it!

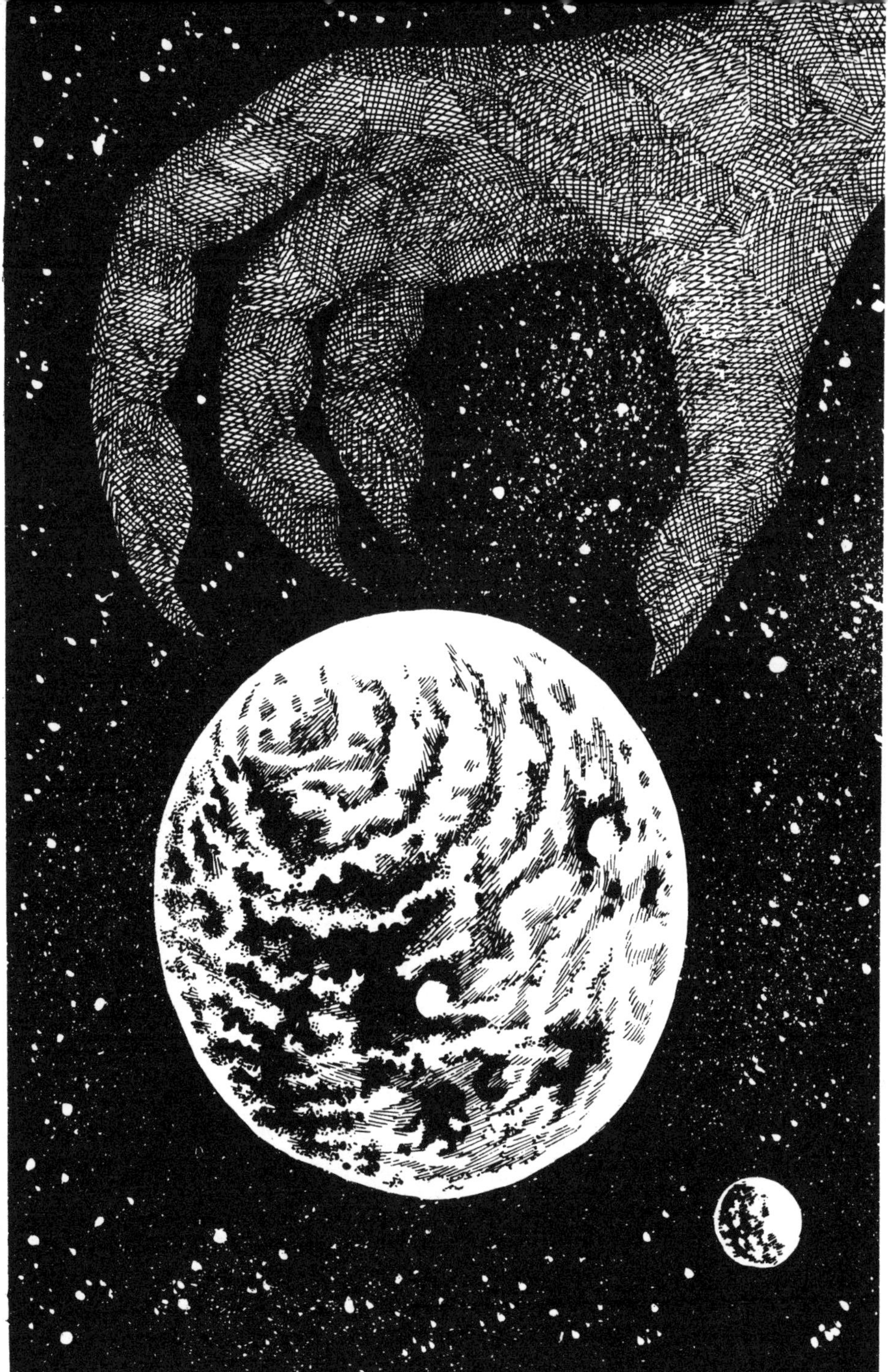

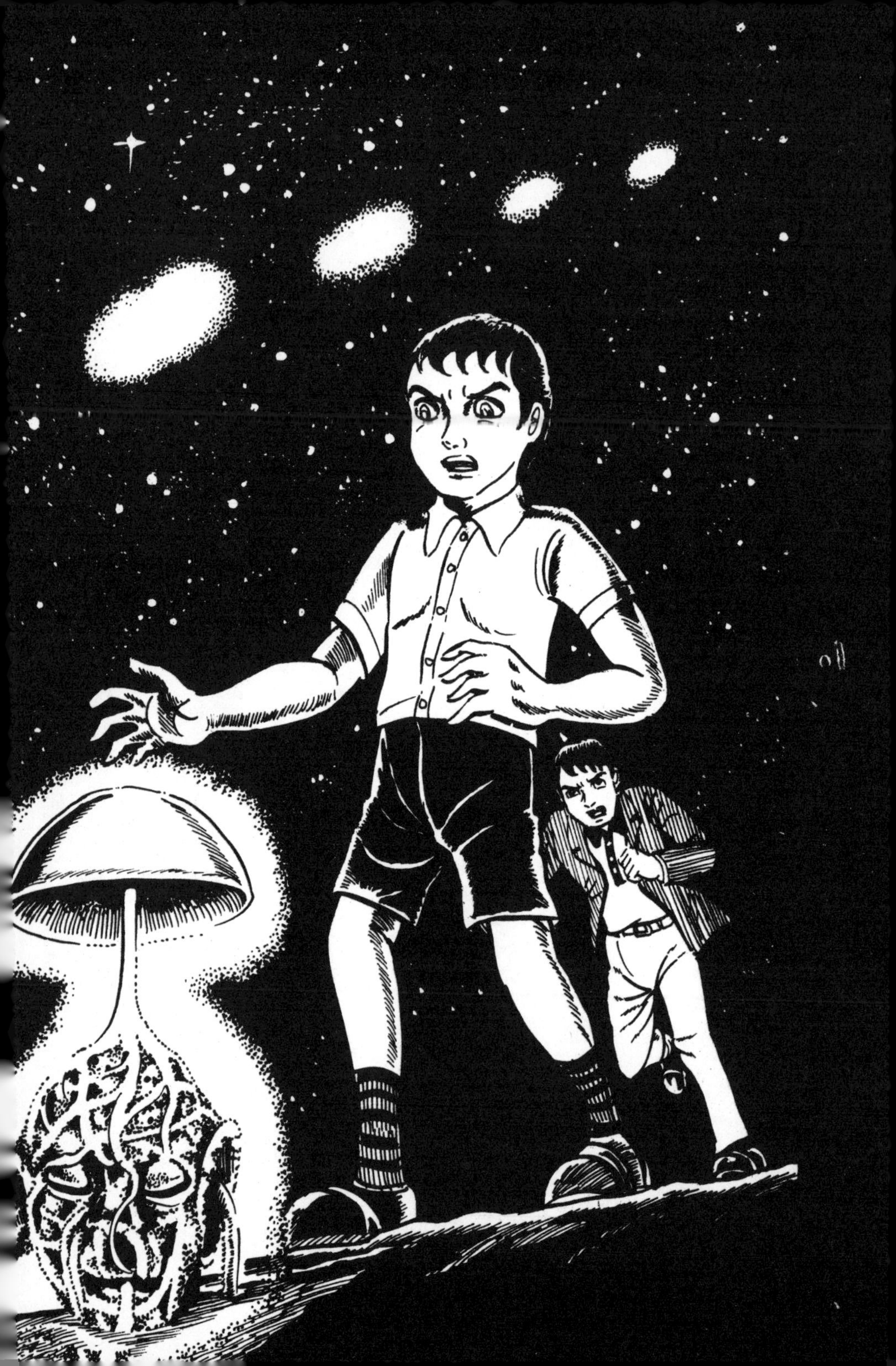

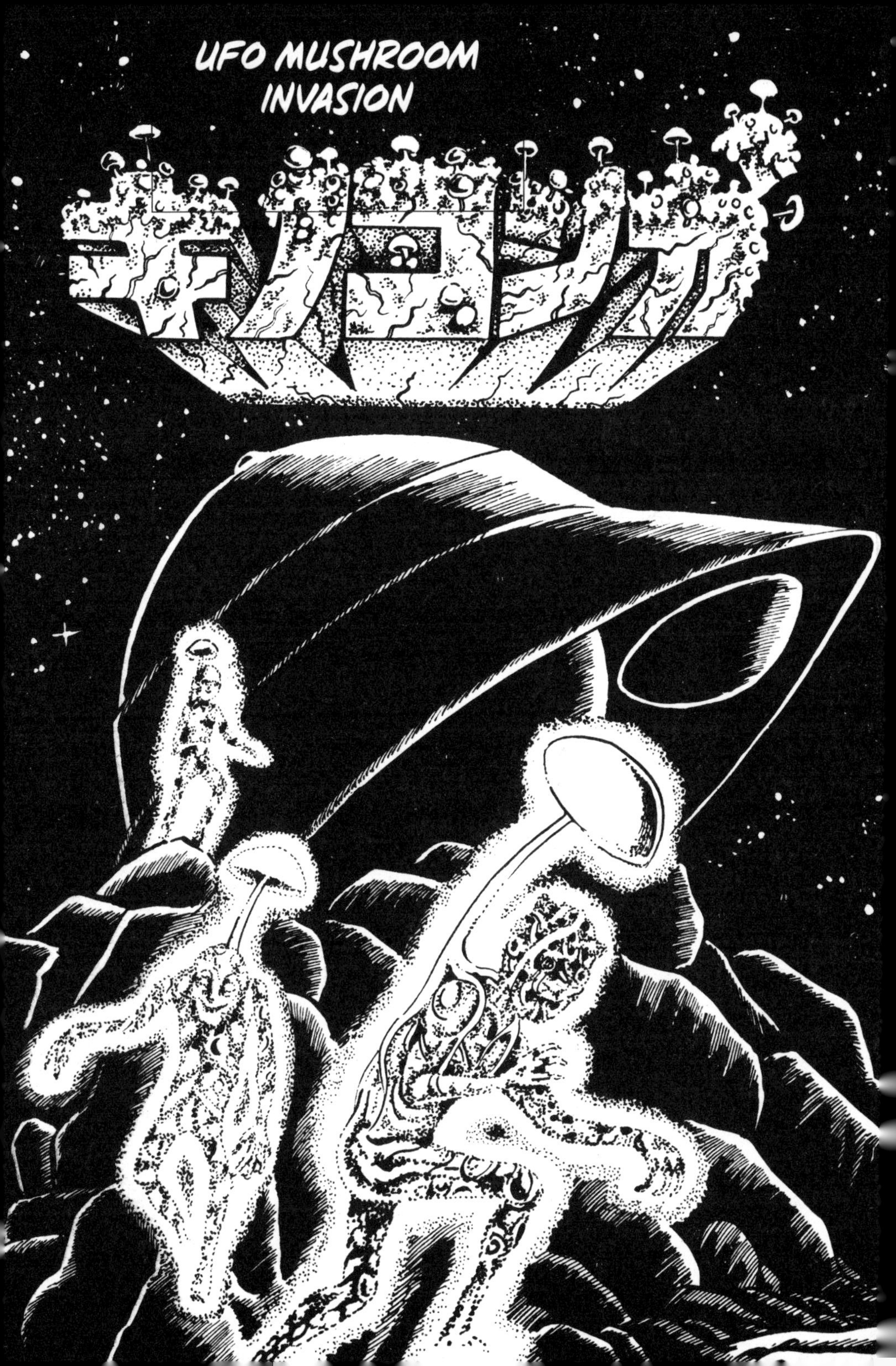
UFO MUSHROOM
INVASION

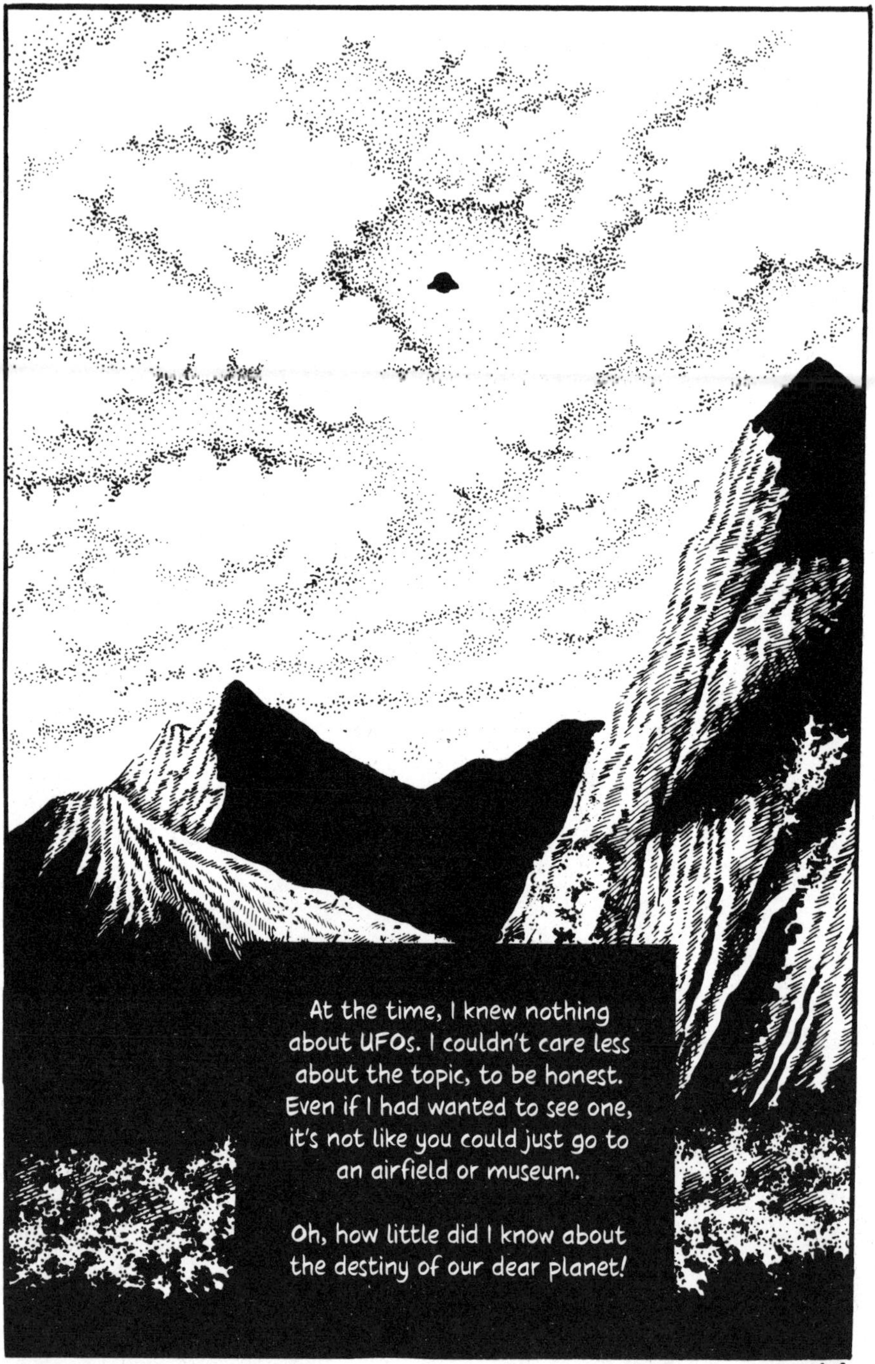
At the time, I knew nothing about UFOs. I couldn't care less about the topic, to be honest. Even if I had wanted to see one, it's not like you could just go to an airfield or museum.
Oh, how little did I know about the destiny of our dear planet!

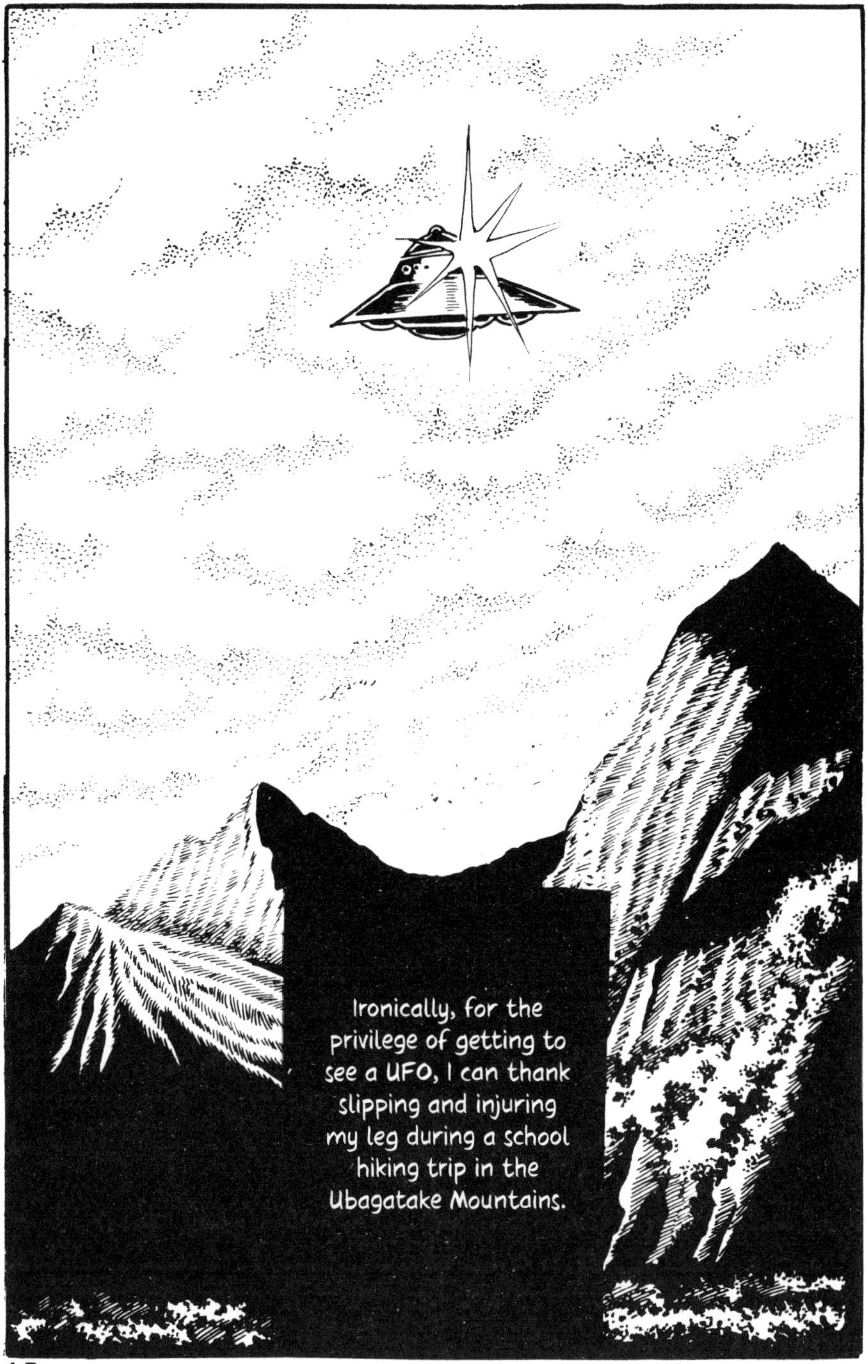
Ironically, for the privilege of getting to see a UFO, I can thank slipping and injuring my leg during a school hiking trip in the Ubagatake Mountains.

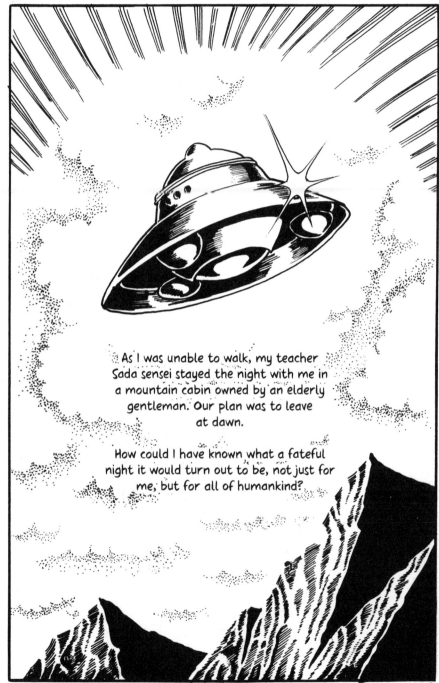

As I was unable to walk, my teacher Sada sensei stayed the night with me in a mountain cabin owned by an elderly gentleman. Our plan was to leave at dawn.

How could I have known what a fateful night it would turn out to be, not just for me, but for all of humankind?

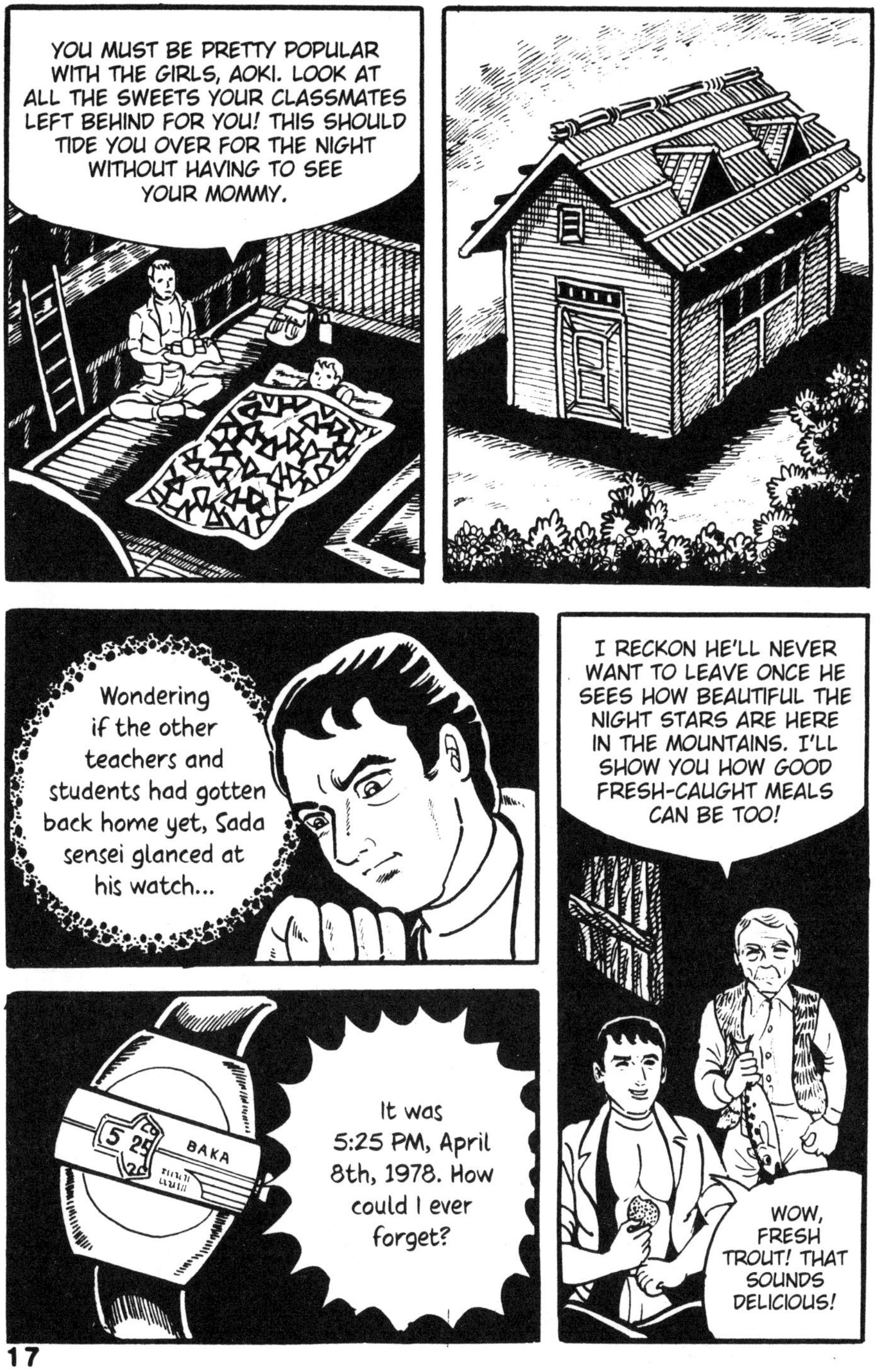
YOU MUST BE PRETTY POPULAR WITH THE GIRLS, AOKI. LOOK AT ALL THE SWEETS YOUR CLASSMATES LEFT BEHIND FOR YOU! THIS SHOULD TIDE YOU OVER FOR THE NIGHT WITHOUT HAVING TO SEE YOUR MOMMY.
Wondering if the other teachers and students had gotten back home yet, Sada sensei glanced at his watch...
BAKA
It was 5:25 PM, April 8th, 1978. How could I ever forget?
I RECKON HE'LL NEVER WANT TO LEAVE ONCE HE SEES HOW BEAUTIFUL THE NIGHT STARS ARE HERE IN THE MOUNTAINS. I'LL SHOW YOU HOW GOOD FRESH-CAUGHT MEALS CAN BE TOO!
WOW, FRESH TROUT! THAT SOUNDS DELICIOUS!

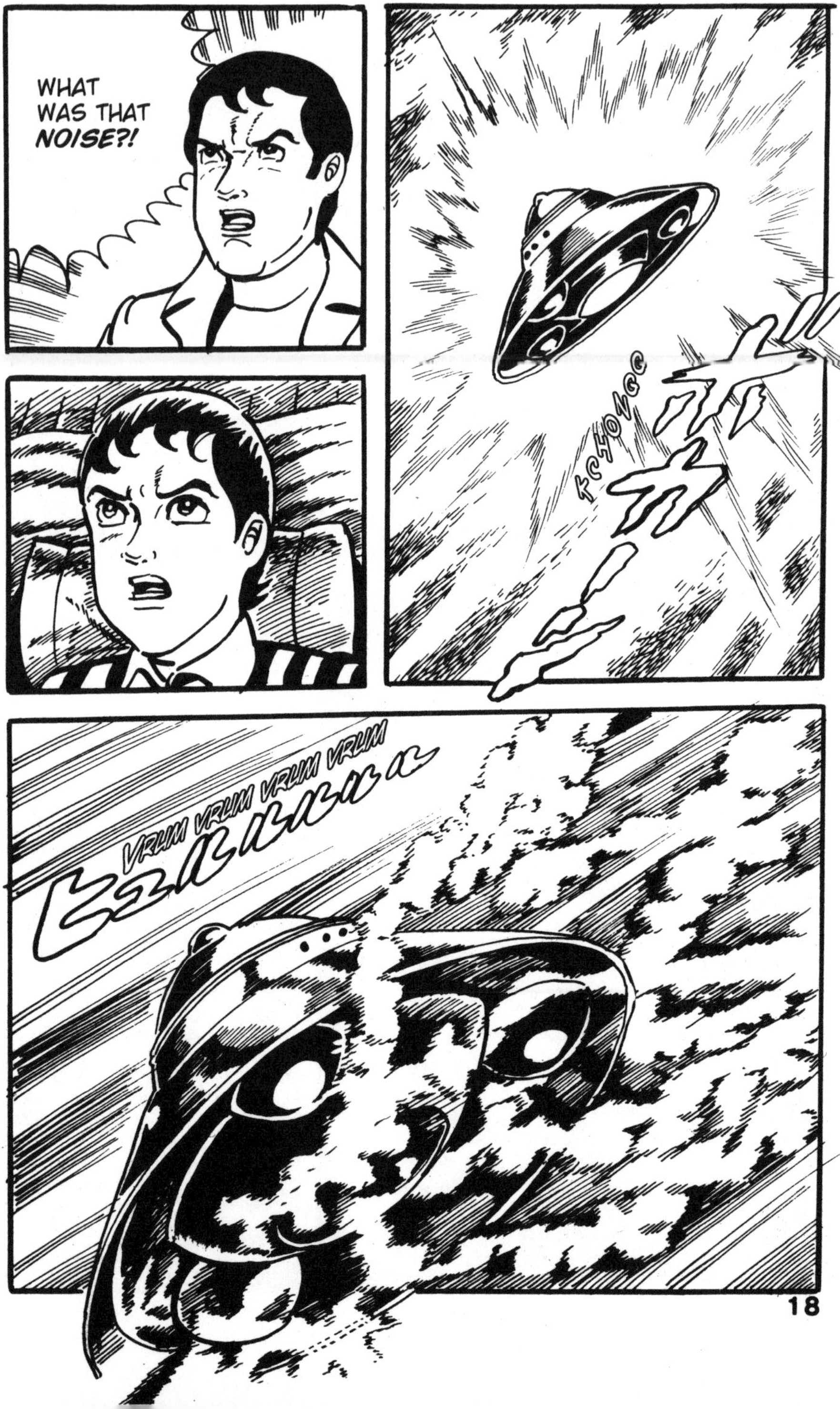
TCHONG
WHAT WAS THAT NOISE?!
VRUM VRUM VRUM VRUM VRUM

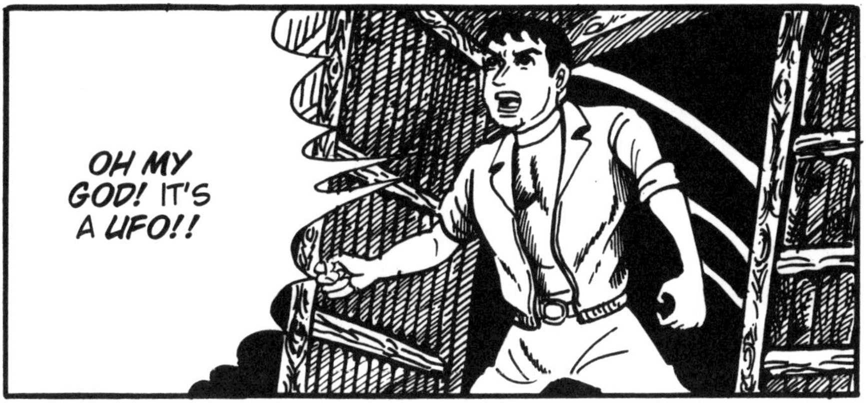
OH MY GOD! IT'S A UFO!!
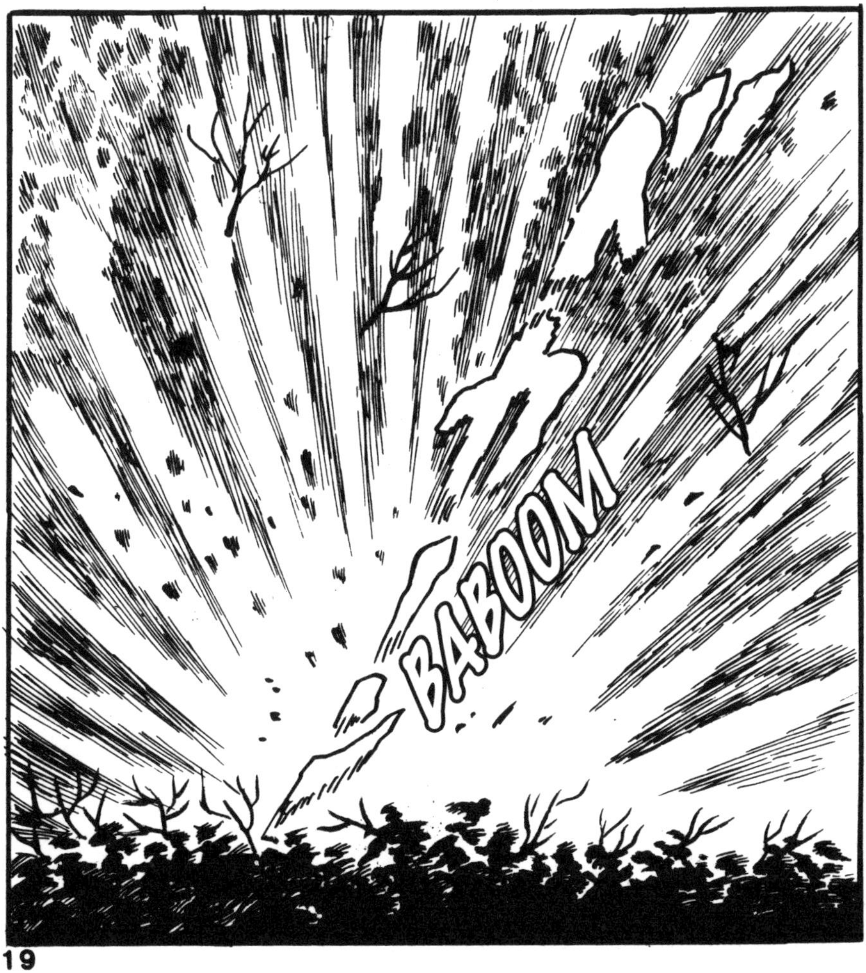
BABOOM

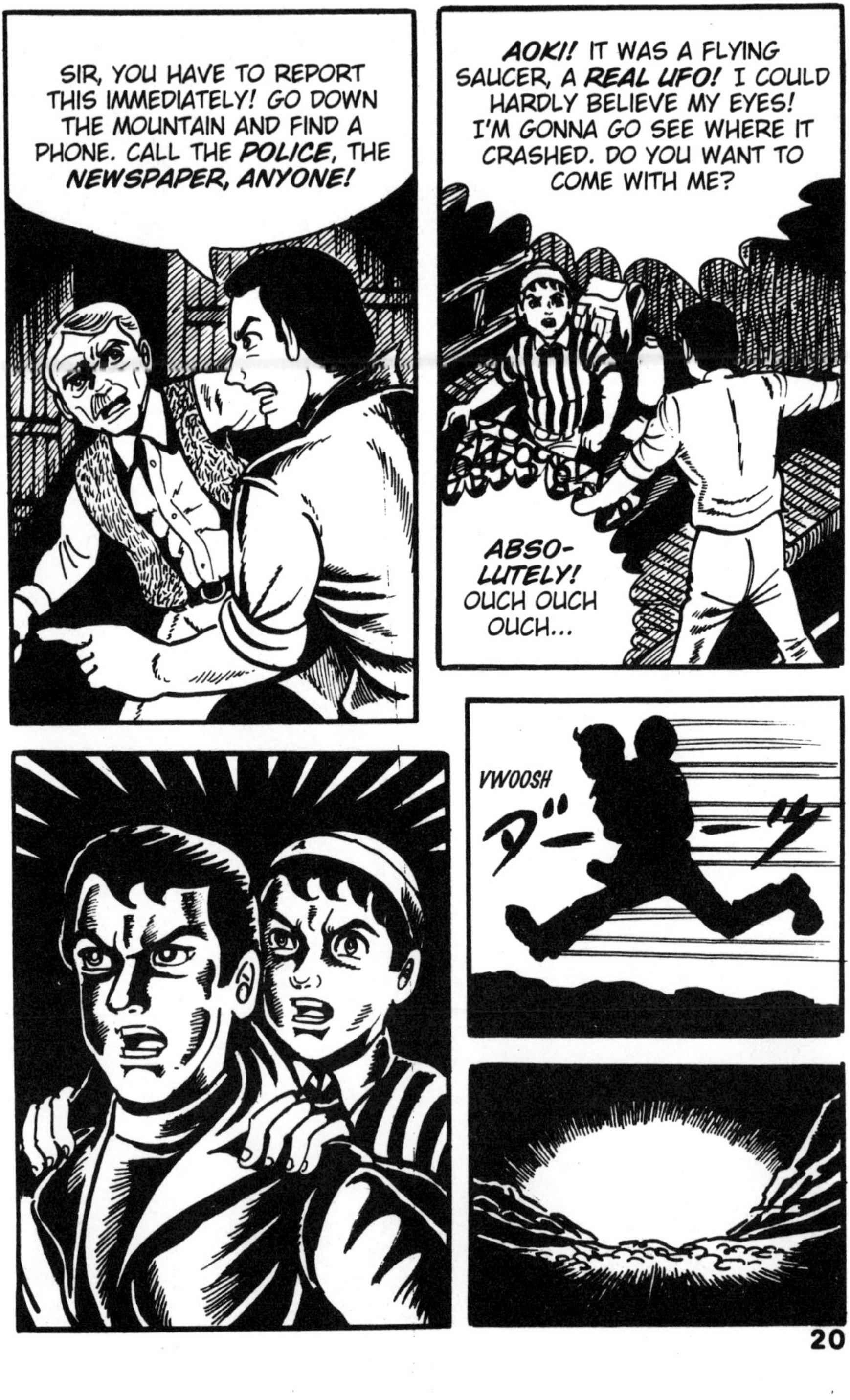
AOKI! IT WAS A FLYING SAUCER, A REAL UFO! I COULD HARDLY BELIEVE MY EYES! I'M GONNA GO SEE WHERE IT CRASHED. DO YOU WANT TO COME WITH ME?
ABSO-LUTELY! OUCH OUCH OUCH...
SIR, YOU HAVE TO REPORT THIS IMMEDIATELY! GO DOWN THE MOUNTAIN AND FIND A PHONE. CALL THE POLICE, THE NEWSPAPER, ANYONE!
VWOOSH
ダーッ

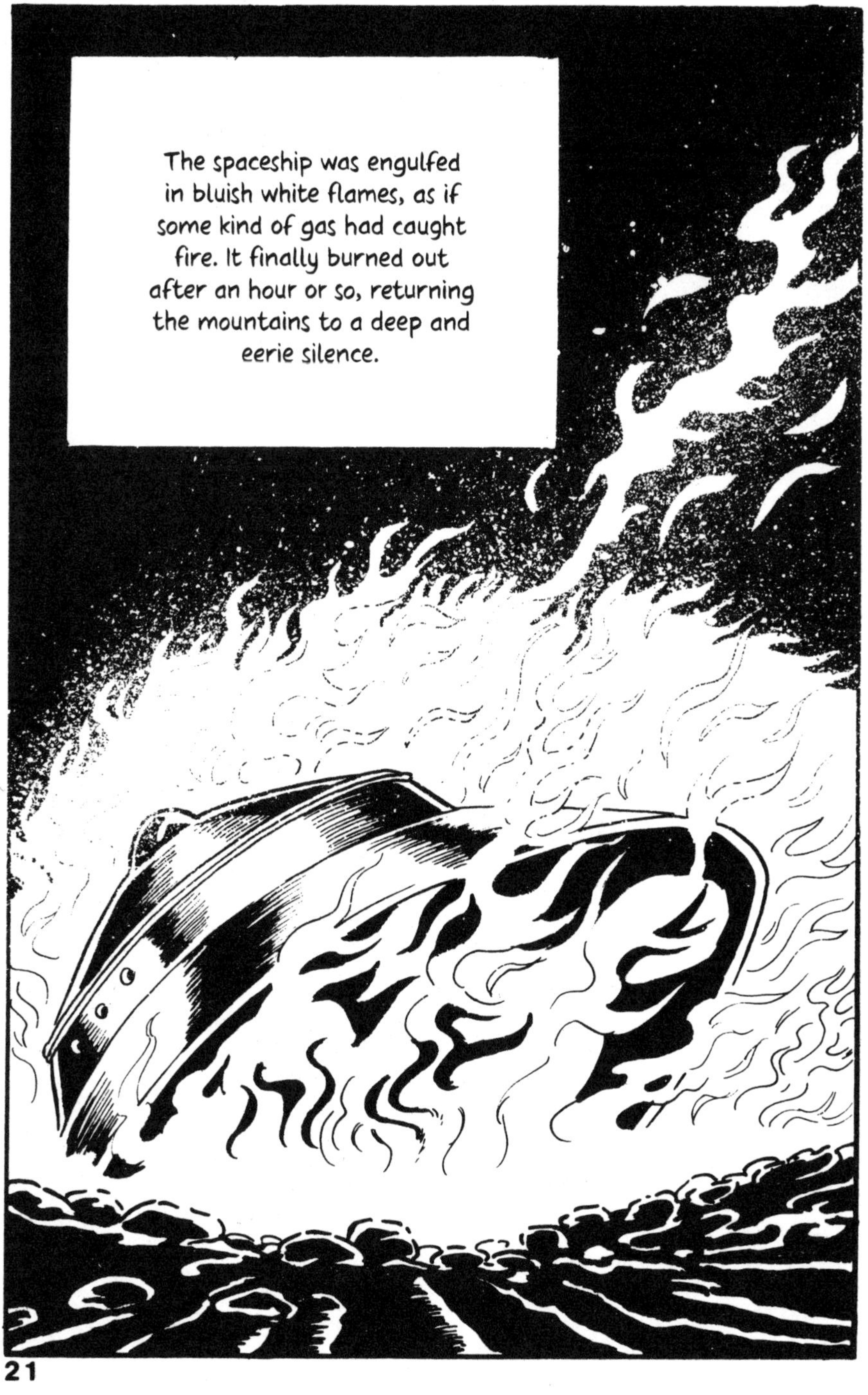
The spaceship was engulfed in bluish white flames, as if some kind of gas had caught fire. It finally burned out after an hour or so, returning the mountains to a deep and eerie silence.

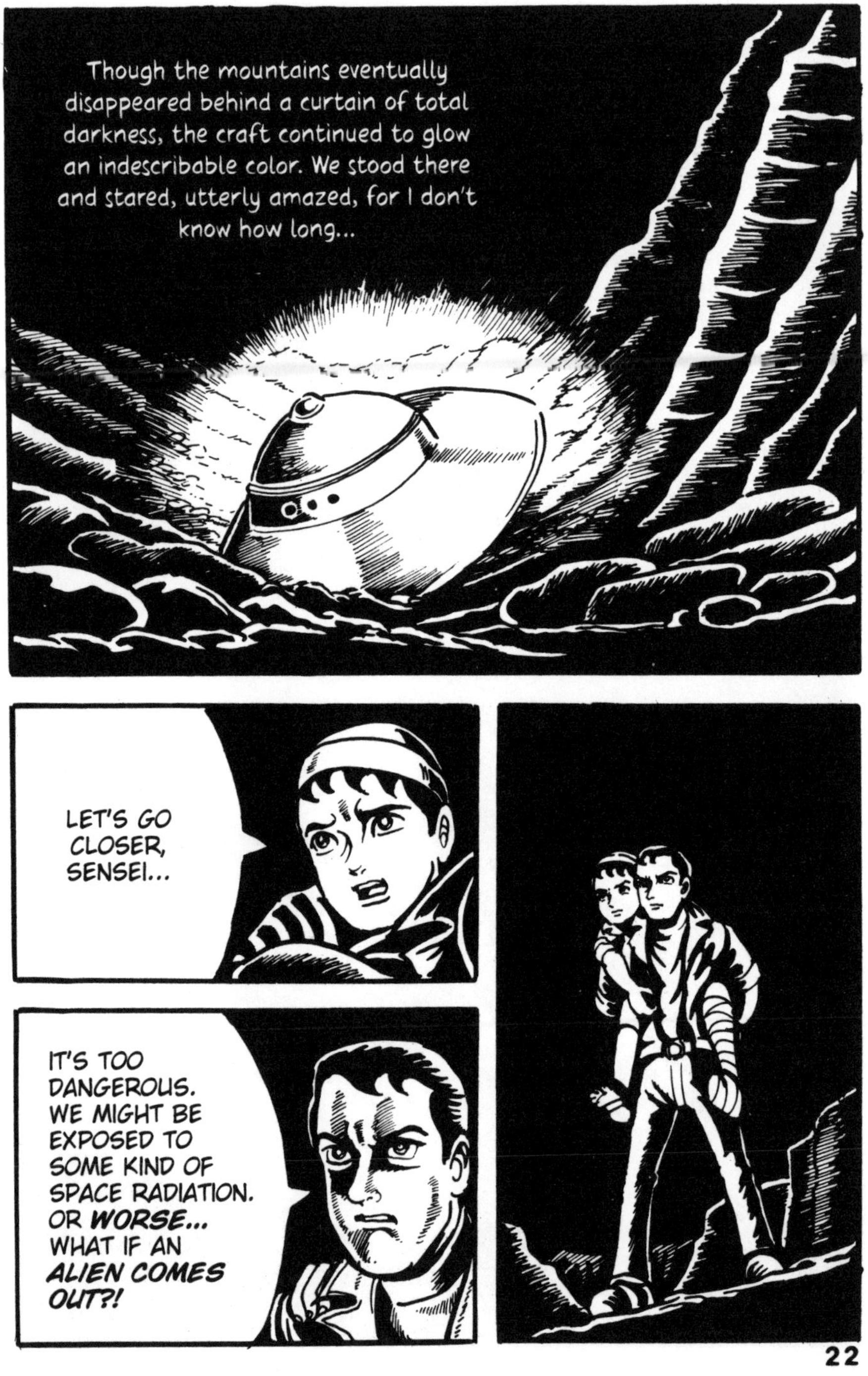
Though the mountains eventually disappeared behind a curtain of total darkness, the craft continued to glow an indescribable color. We stood there and stared, utterly amazed, for I don't know how long...
LET'S GO CLOSER, SENSEI...
IT'S TOO DANGEROUS. WE MIGHT BE EXPOSED TO SOME KIND OF SPACE RADIATION. OR WORSE... WHAT IF AN ALIEN COMES OUT?!

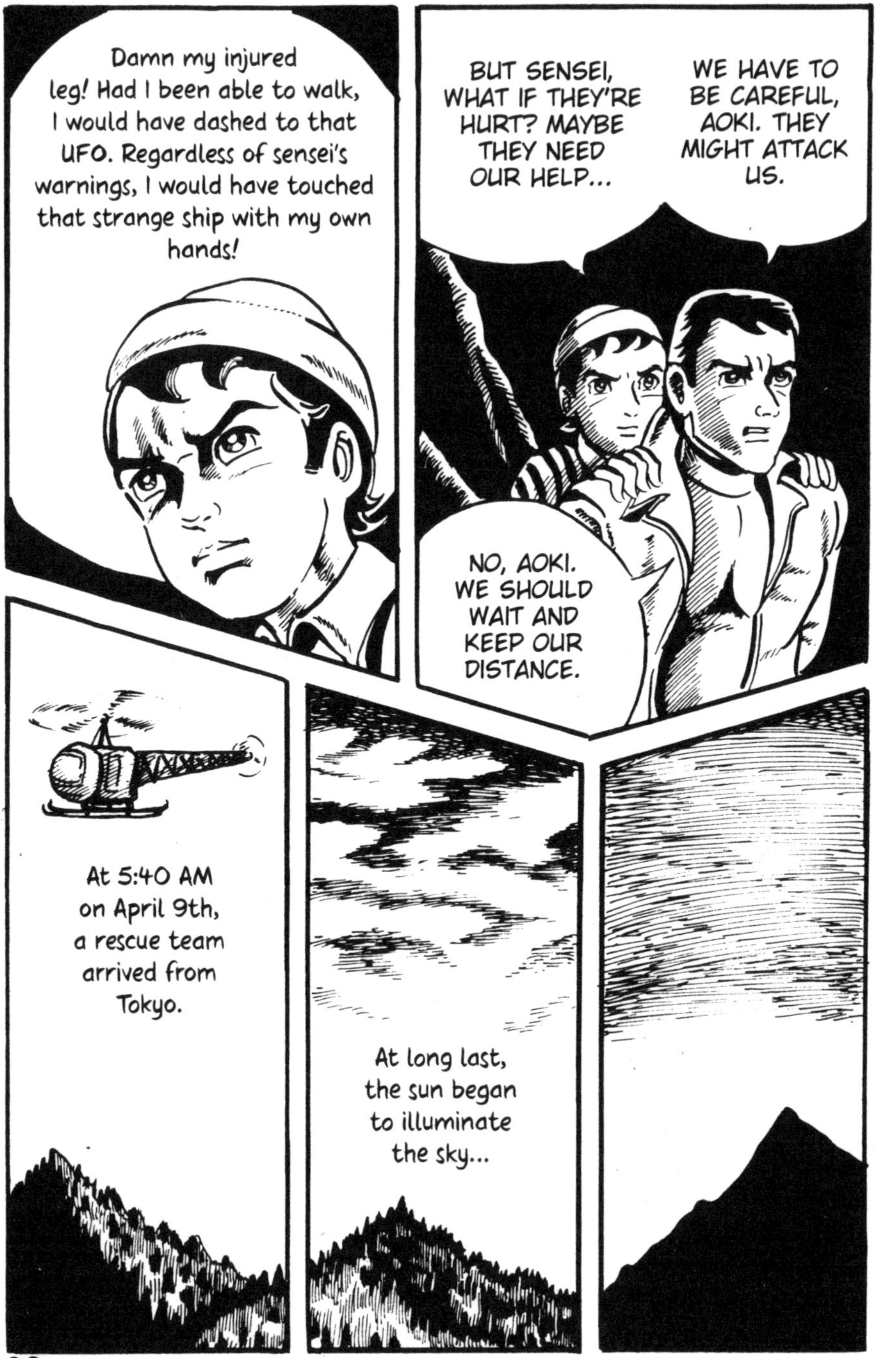
WE HAVE TO BE CAREFUL, AOKI. THEY MIGHT ATTACK US.
BUT SENSEI, WHAT IF THEY'RE HURT? MAYBE THEY NEED OUR HELP...
NO, AOKI. WE SHOULD WAIT AND KEEP OUR DISTANCE.
Damn my injured leg! Had I been able to walk, I would have dashed to that UFO. Regardless of sensei's warnings, I would have touched that strange ship with my own hands!
At long last, the sun began to illuminate the sky...
At 5:40 AM on April 9th, a rescue team arrived from Tokyo.

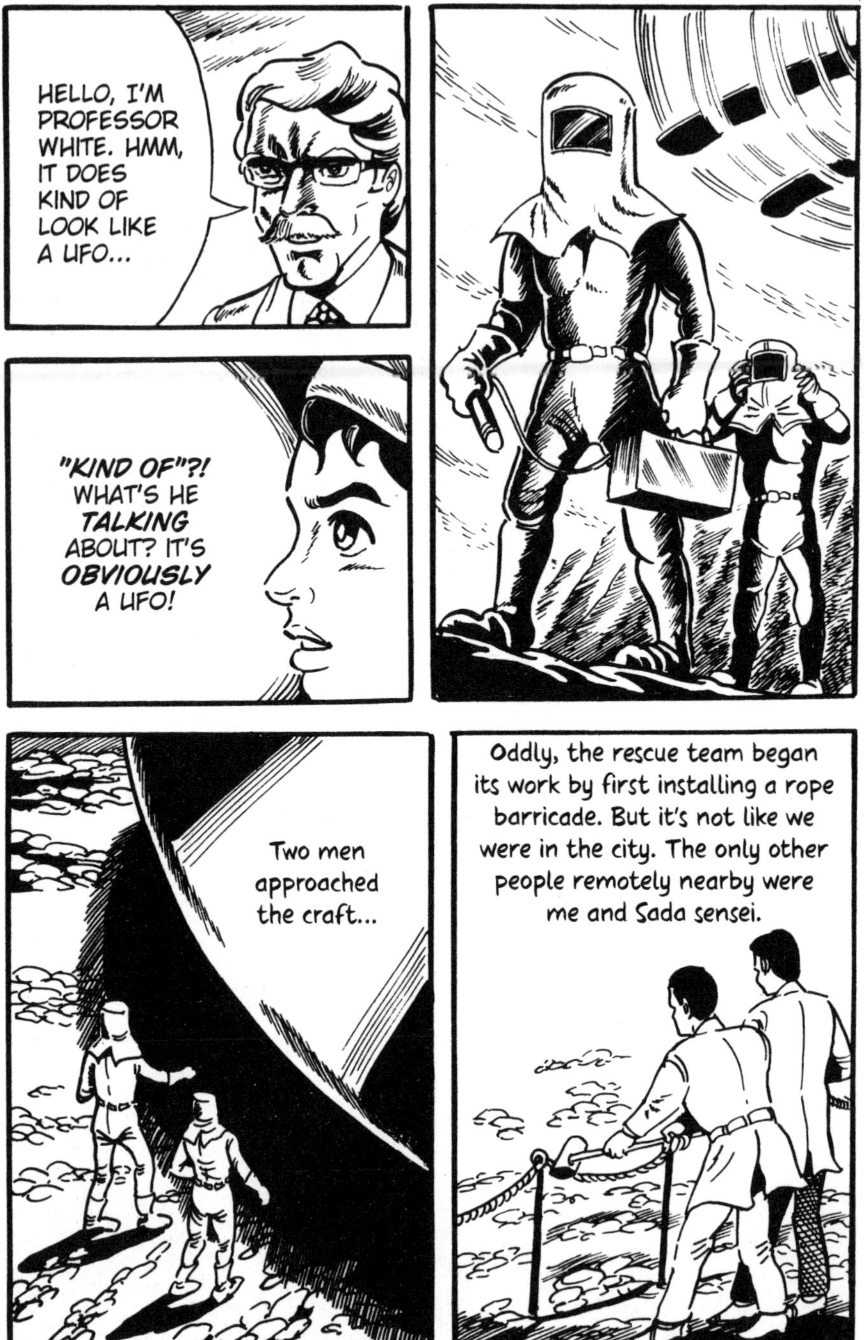

HELLO, I'M PROFESSOR WHITE. HMM, IT DOES KIND OF LOOK LIKE A UFO...
"KIND OF"?! WHAT'S HE TALKING ABOUT? IT'S OBVIOUSLY A UFO!
Oddly, the rescue team began its work by first installing a rope barricade. But it's not like we were in the city. The only other people remotely nearby were me and Sada sensei.
Two men approached the craft...

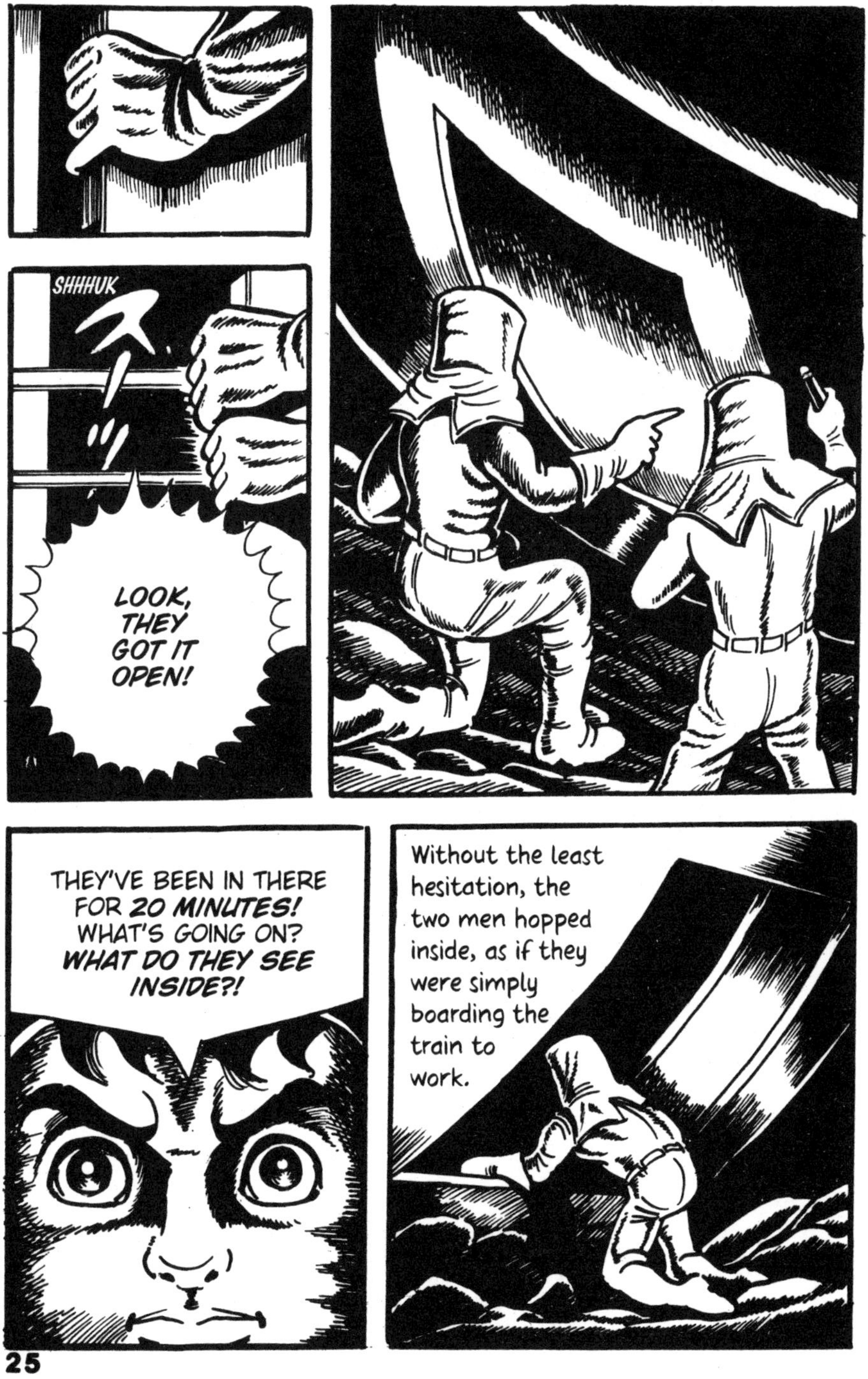
SHHHUK
LOOK, THEY GOT IT OPEN!
Without the least hesitation, the two men hopped inside, as if they were simply boarding the train to work.
THEY'VE BEEN IN THERE FOR **20 MINUTES!** WHAT'S GOING ON? ***WHAT DO THEY SEE INSIDE?!***

Upon emerging, they got a stretcher from the tent and carried it back to the ship.

OH MY GOD! THERE'S SOMETHING UNDER THE SHEET!

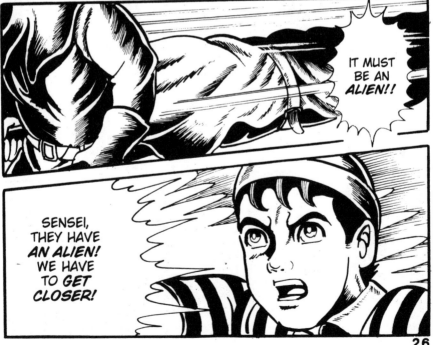

IT MUST BE AN *ALIEN!!*

SENSEI, THEY HAVE *AN ALIEN!* WE HAVE TO *GET CLOSER!*

26

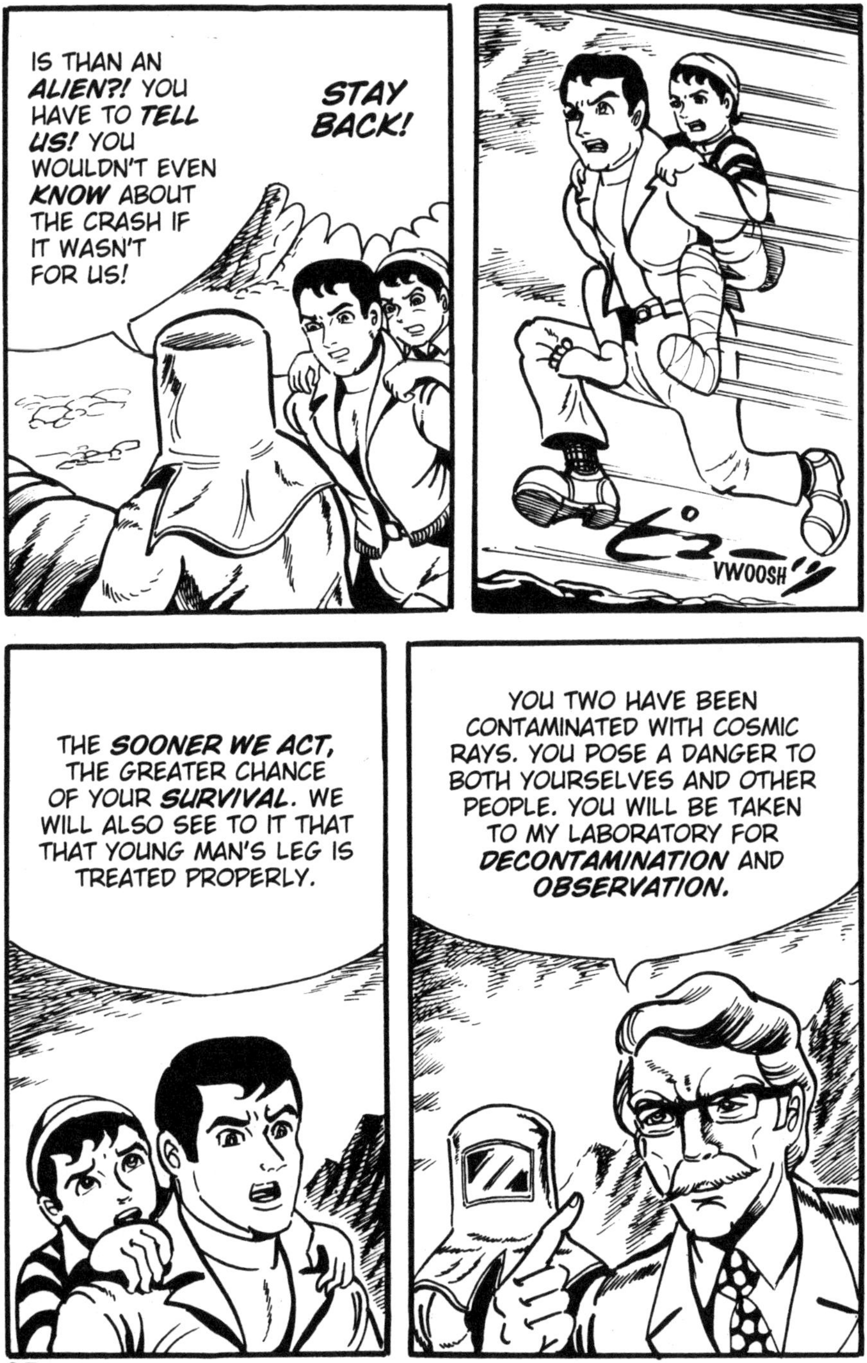
VWOOSH
STAY BACK!
IS THAN AN ALIEN?! YOU HAVE TO TELL US! YOU WOULDN'T EVEN KNOW ABOUT THE CRASH IF IT WASN'T FOR US!
YOU TWO HAVE BEEN CONTAMINATED WITH COSMIC RAYS. YOU POSE A DANGER TO BOTH YOURSELVES AND OTHER PEOPLE. YOU WILL BE TAKEN TO MY LABORATORY FOR DECONTAMINATION AND OBSERVATION.
THE SOONER WE ACT, THE GREATER CHANCE OF YOUR SURVIVAL. WE WILL ALSO SEE TO IT THAT THAT YOUNG MAN'S LEG IS TREATED PROPERLY.

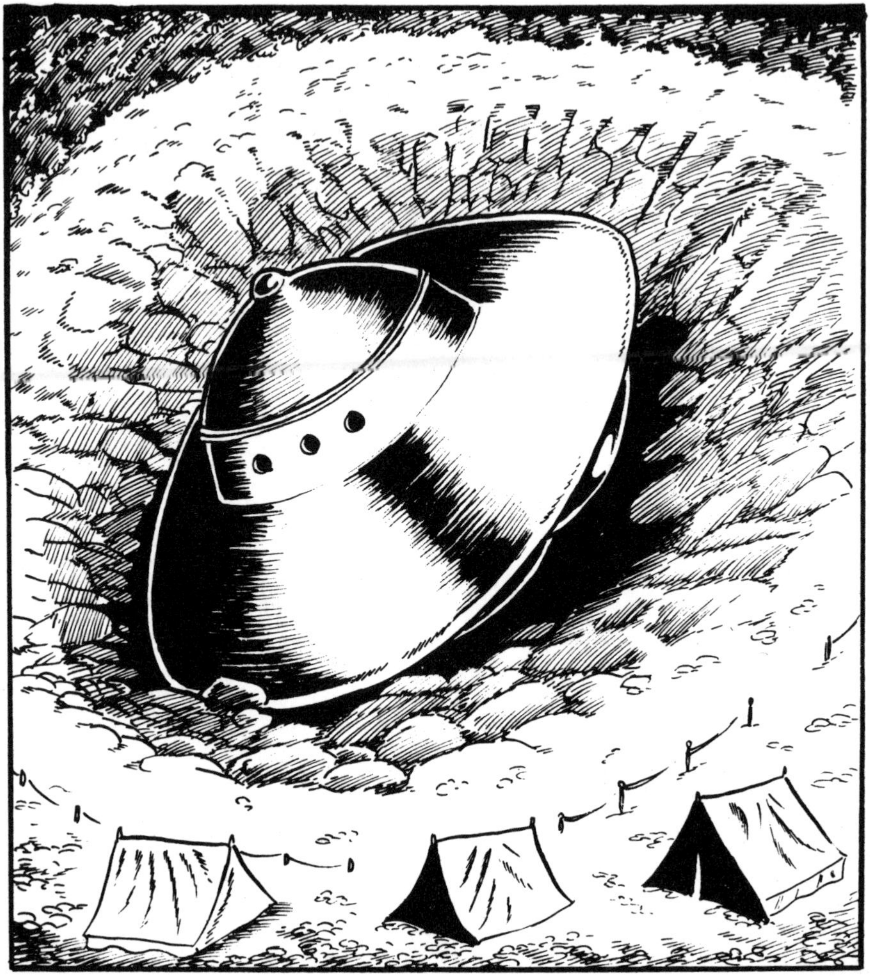

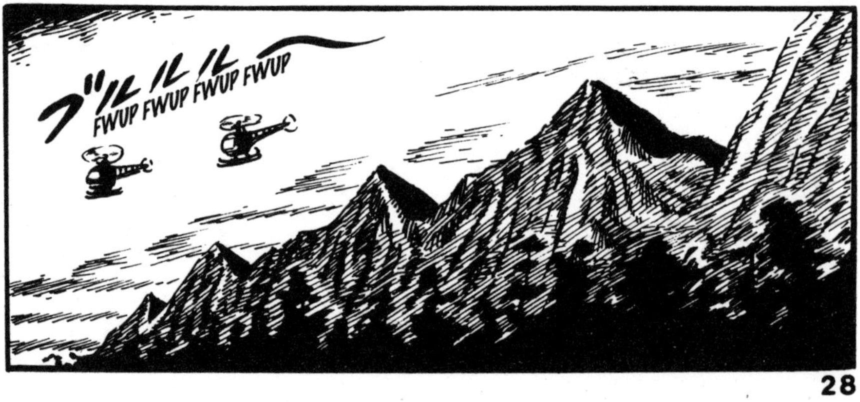
ブルルル
FWUP FWUP FWUP FWUP

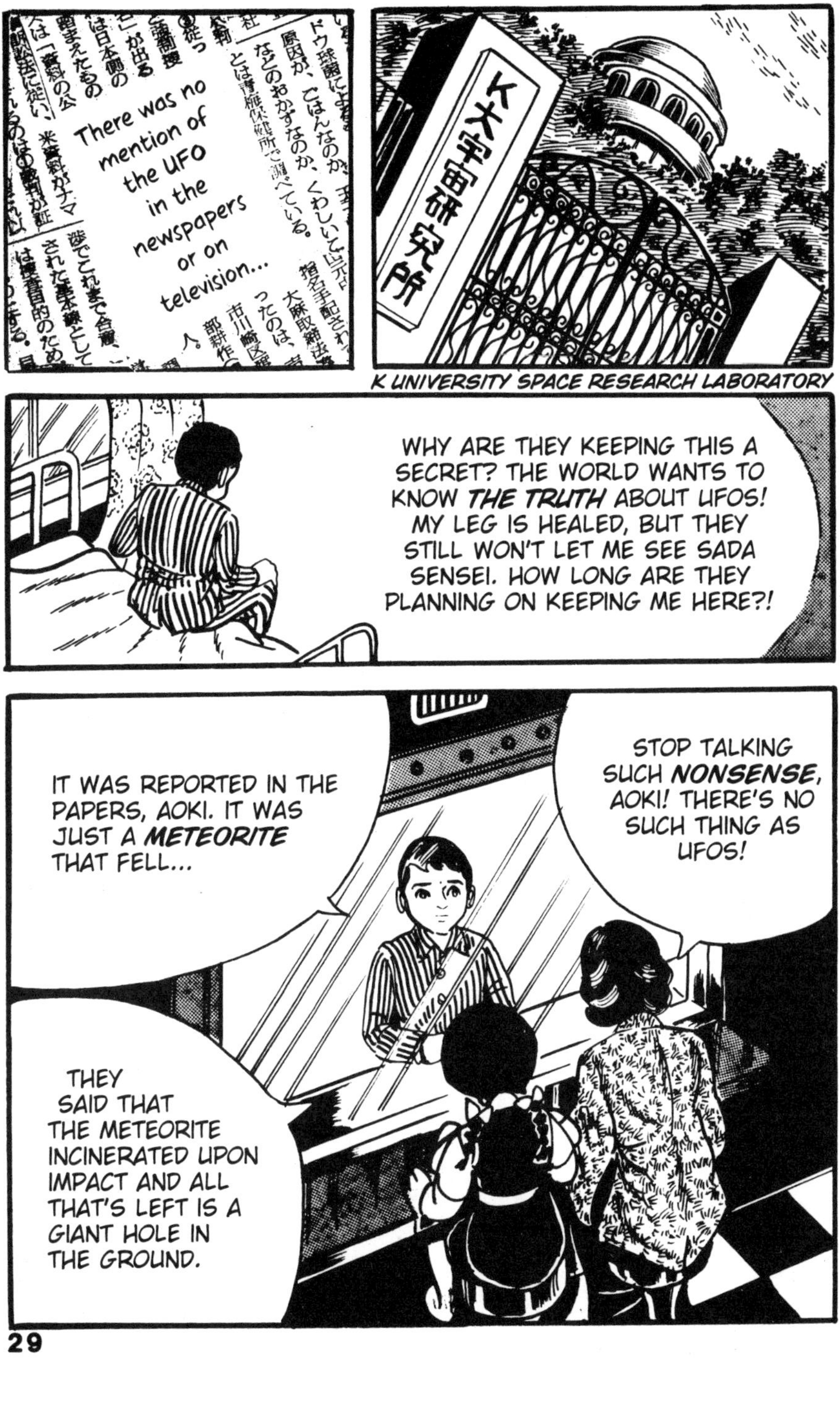
K UNIVERSITY SPACE RESEARCH LABORATORY
There was no mention of the UFO in the newspapers or on television...
WHY ARE THEY KEEPING THIS A SECRET? THE WORLD WANTS TO KNOW ***THE TRUTH*** ABOUT UFOS! MY LEG IS HEALED, BUT THEY STILL WON'T LET ME SEE SADA SENSEI. HOW LONG ARE THEY PLANNING ON KEEPING ME HERE?!
STOP TALKING SUCH ***NONSENSE***, AOKI! THERE'S NO SUCH THING AS UFOS!
IT WAS REPORTED IN THE PAPERS, AOKI. IT WAS JUST A ***METEORITE*** THAT FELL...
THEY SAID THAT THE METEORITE INCINERATED UPON IMPACT AND ALL THAT'S LEFT IS A GIANT HOLE IN THE GROUND.

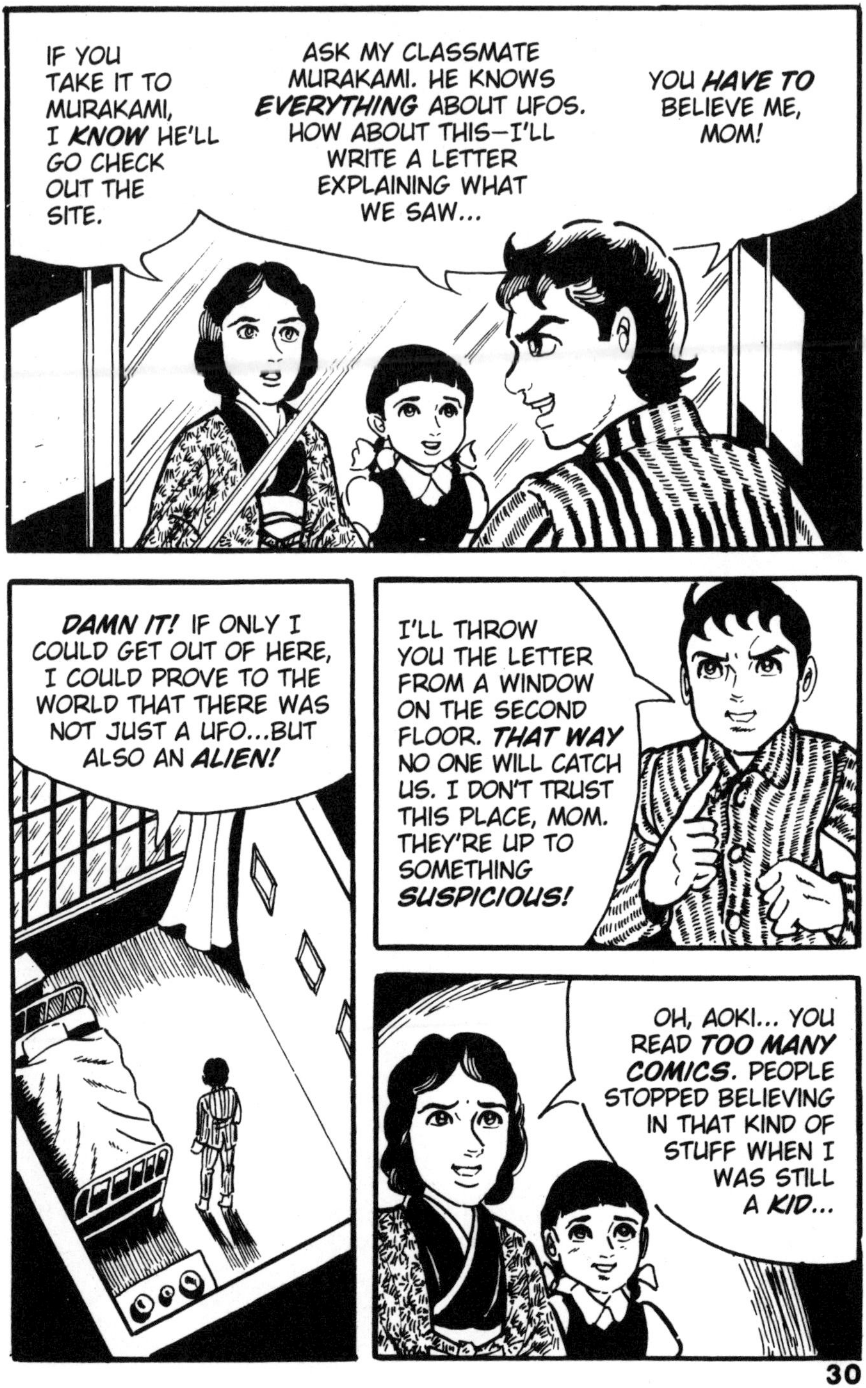
YOU HAVE TO BELIEVE ME, MOM!
ASK MY CLASSMATE MURAKAMI. HE KNOWS EVERYTHING ABOUT UFOS. HOW ABOUT THIS—I'LL WRITE A LETTER EXPLAINING WHAT WE SAW...
IF YOU TAKE IT TO MURAKAMI, I KNOW HE'LL GO CHECK OUT THE SITE.
I'LL THROW YOU THE LETTER FROM A WINDOW ON THE SECOND FLOOR. THAT WAY NO ONE WILL CATCH US. I DON'T TRUST THIS PLACE, MOM. THEY'RE UP TO SOMETHING SUSPICIOUS!
OH, AOKI... YOU READ TOO MANY COMICS. PEOPLE STOPPED BELIEVING IN THAT KIND OF STUFF WHEN I WAS STILL A KID...
DAMN IT! IF ONLY I COULD GET OUT OF HERE, I COULD PROVE TO THE WORLD THAT THERE WAS NOT JUST A UFO...BUT ALSO AN ALIEN!

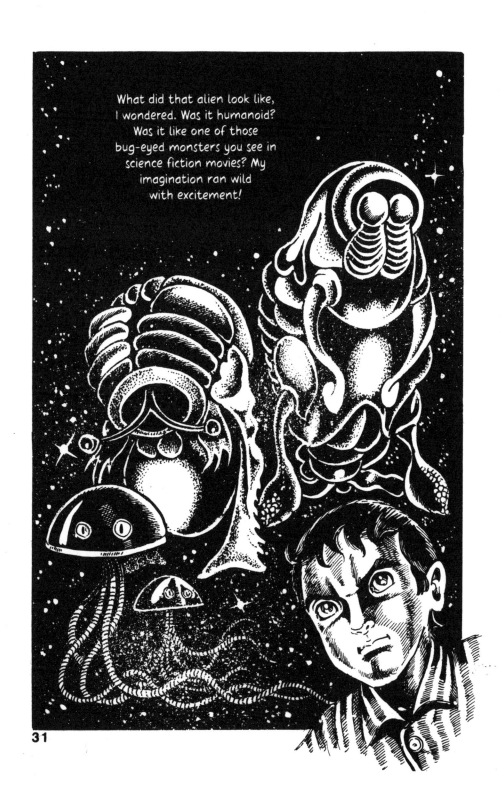

What did that alien look like, I wondered. Was it humanoid? Was it like one of those bug-eyed monsters you see in science fiction movies? My imagination ran wild with excitement!

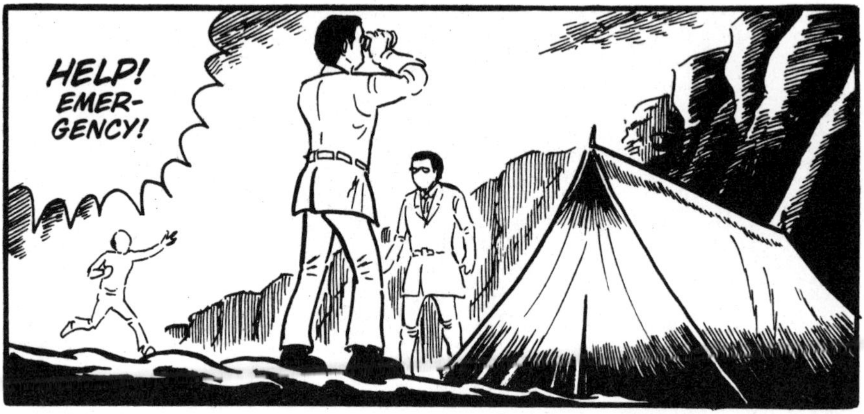
HELP! EMERGENCY!

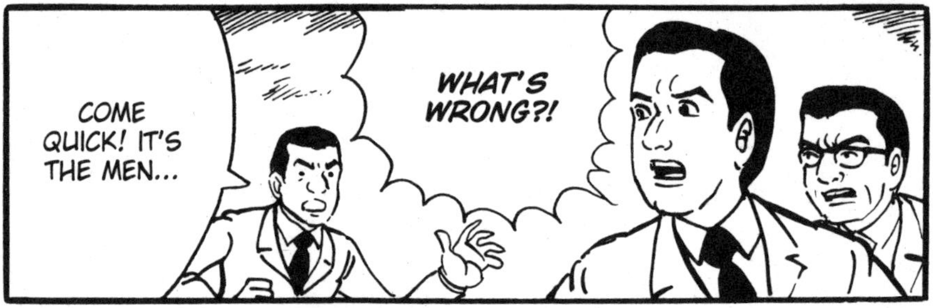
WHAT'S WRONG?!
COME QUICK! IT'S THE MEN...

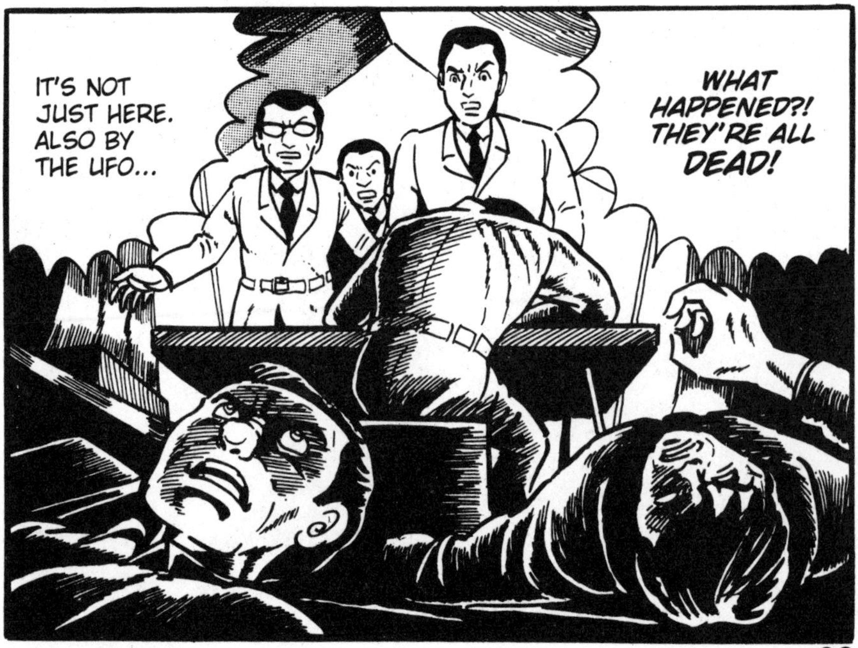
WHAT HAPPENED?! THEY'RE ALL DEAD!
IT'S NOT JUST HERE. ALSO BY THE UFO...

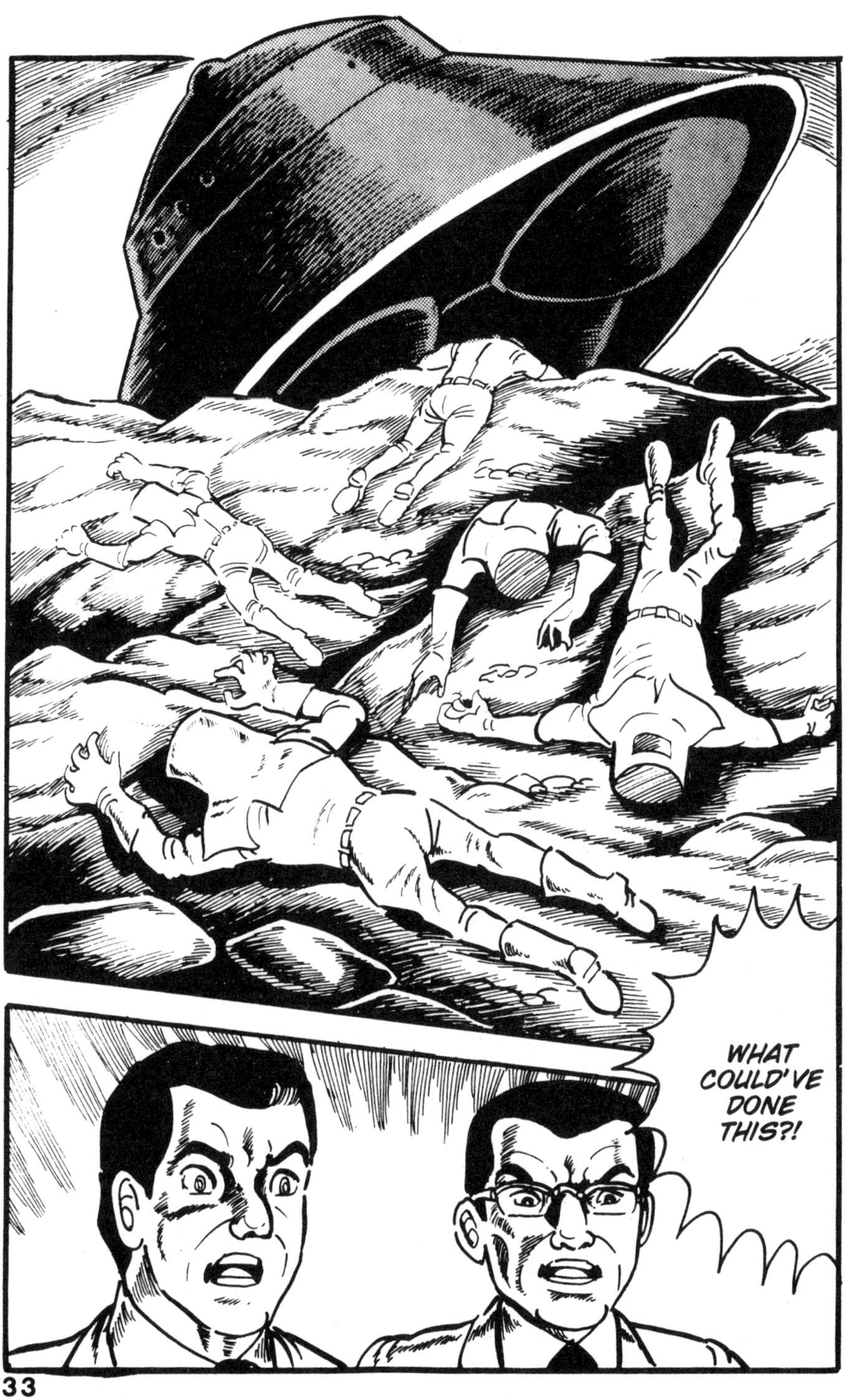
WHAT COULD'VE DONE THIS?!

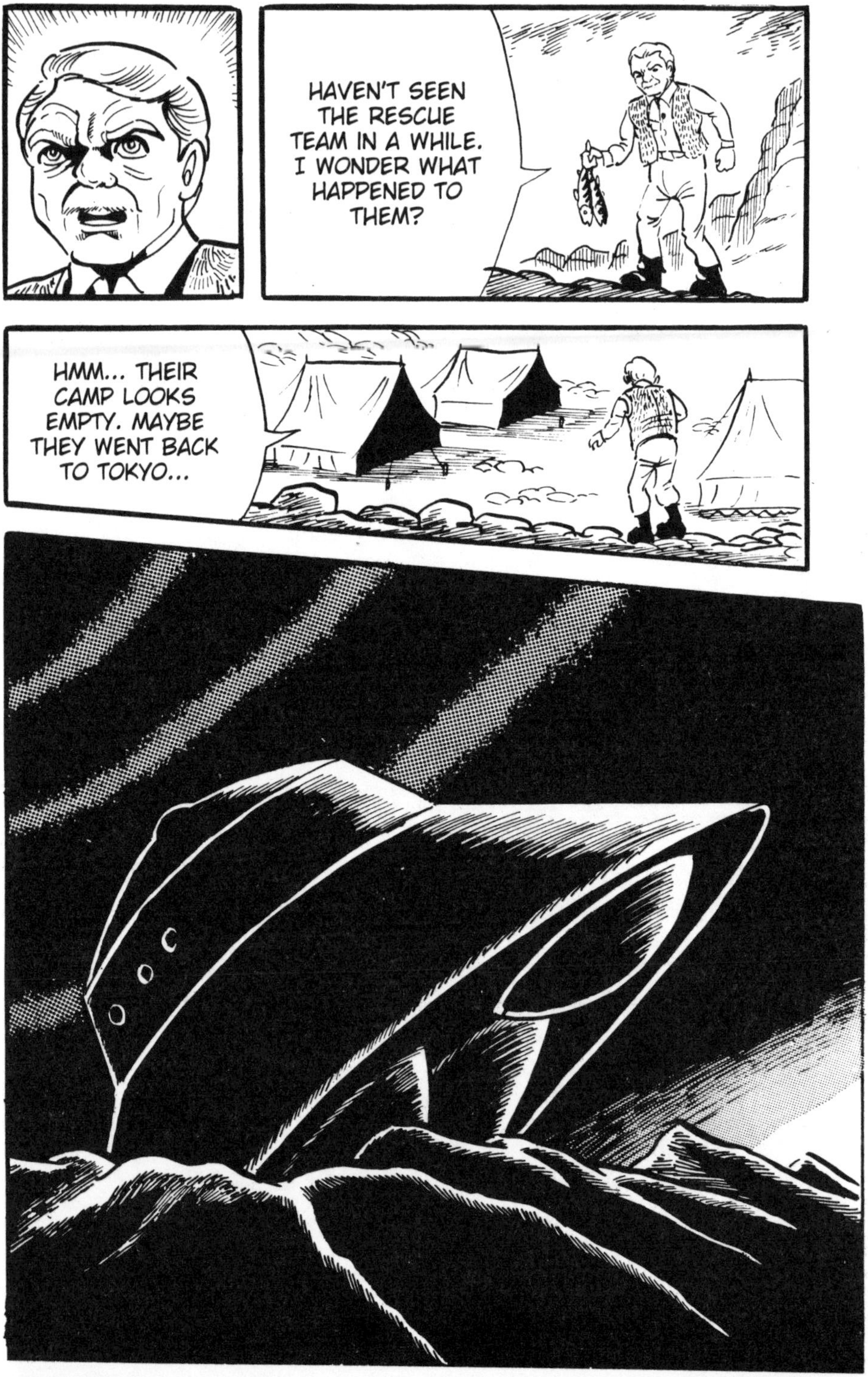
HAVEN'T SEEN THE RESCUE TEAM IN A WHILE. I WONDER WHAT HAPPENED TO THEM?
HMM... THEIR CAMP LOOKS EMPTY. MAYBE THEY WENT BACK TO TOKYO...

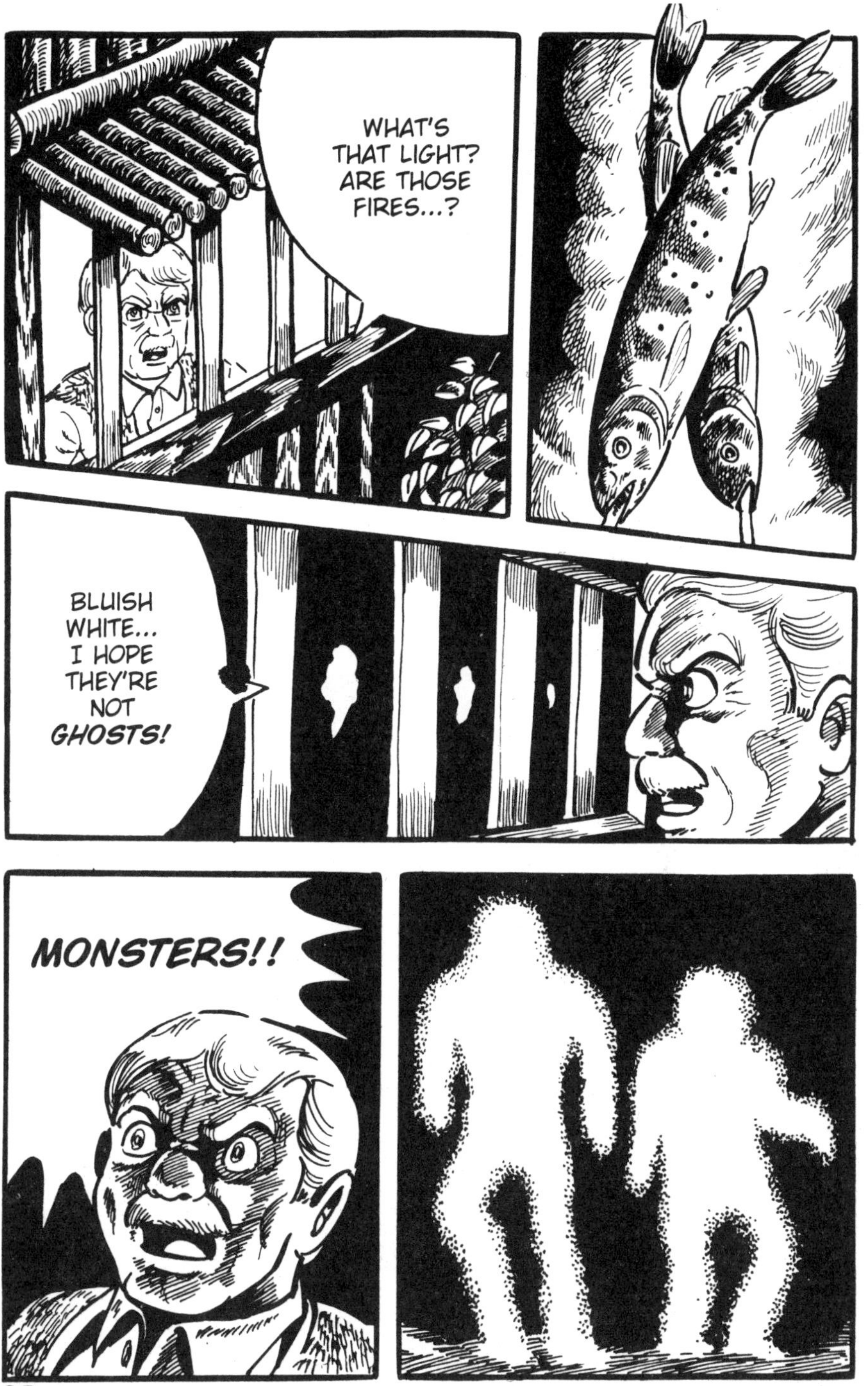
WHAT'S THAT LIGHT? ARE THOSE FIRES...?
BLUISH WHITE... I HOPE THEY'RE NOT GHOSTS!
MONSTERS!!

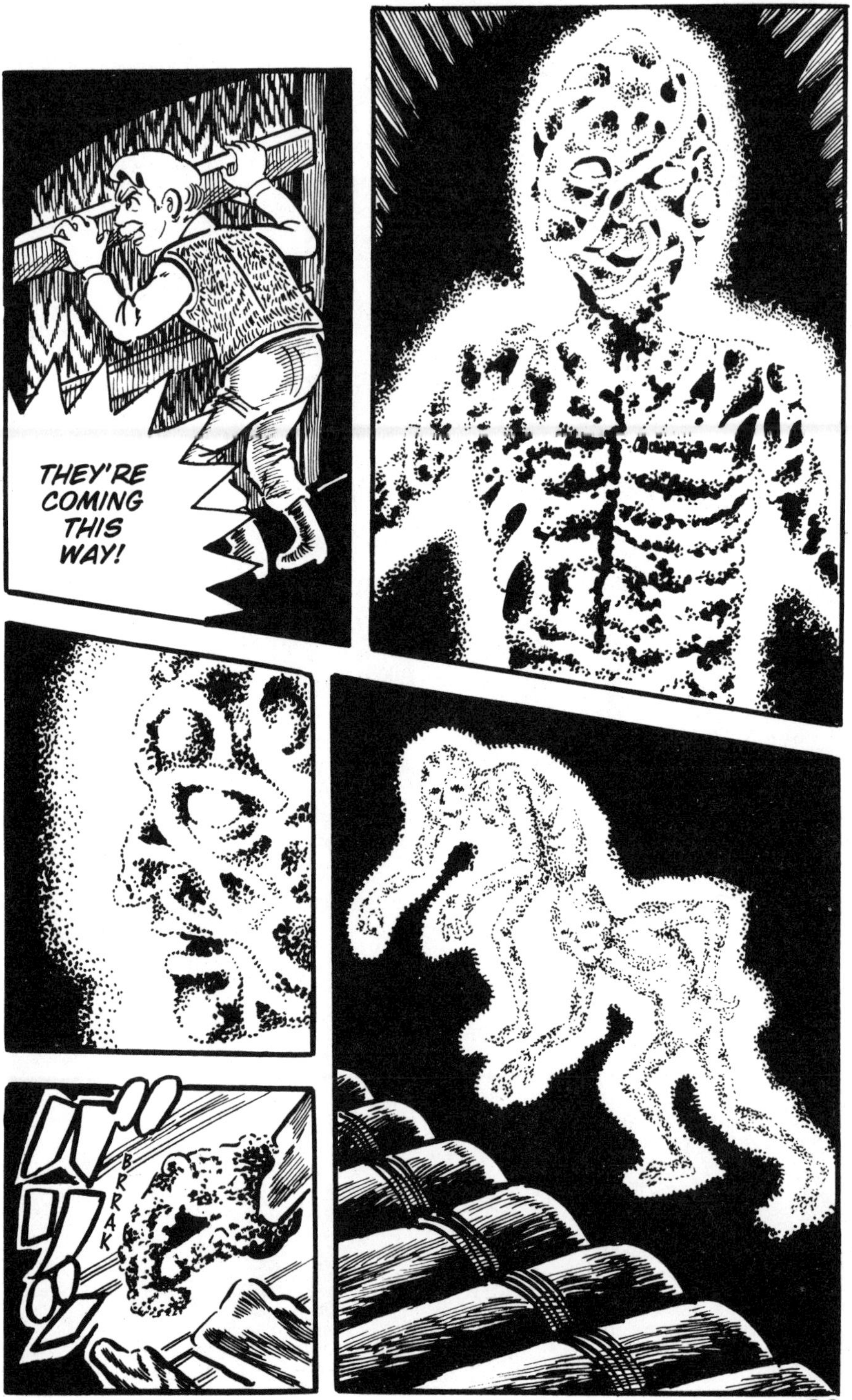
THEY'RE COMING THIS WAY!
BRRAK

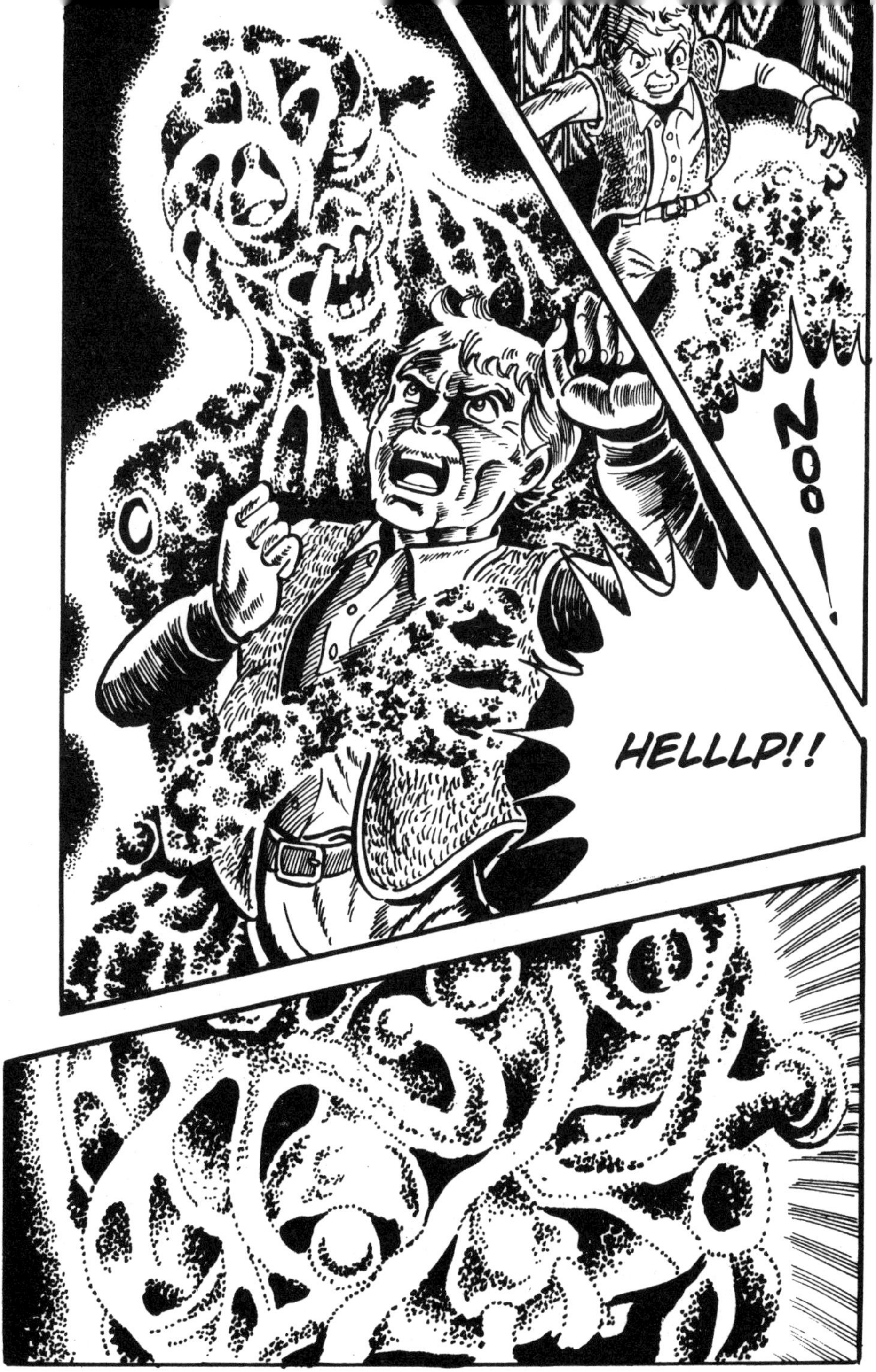
NOO!
HELLLP!!

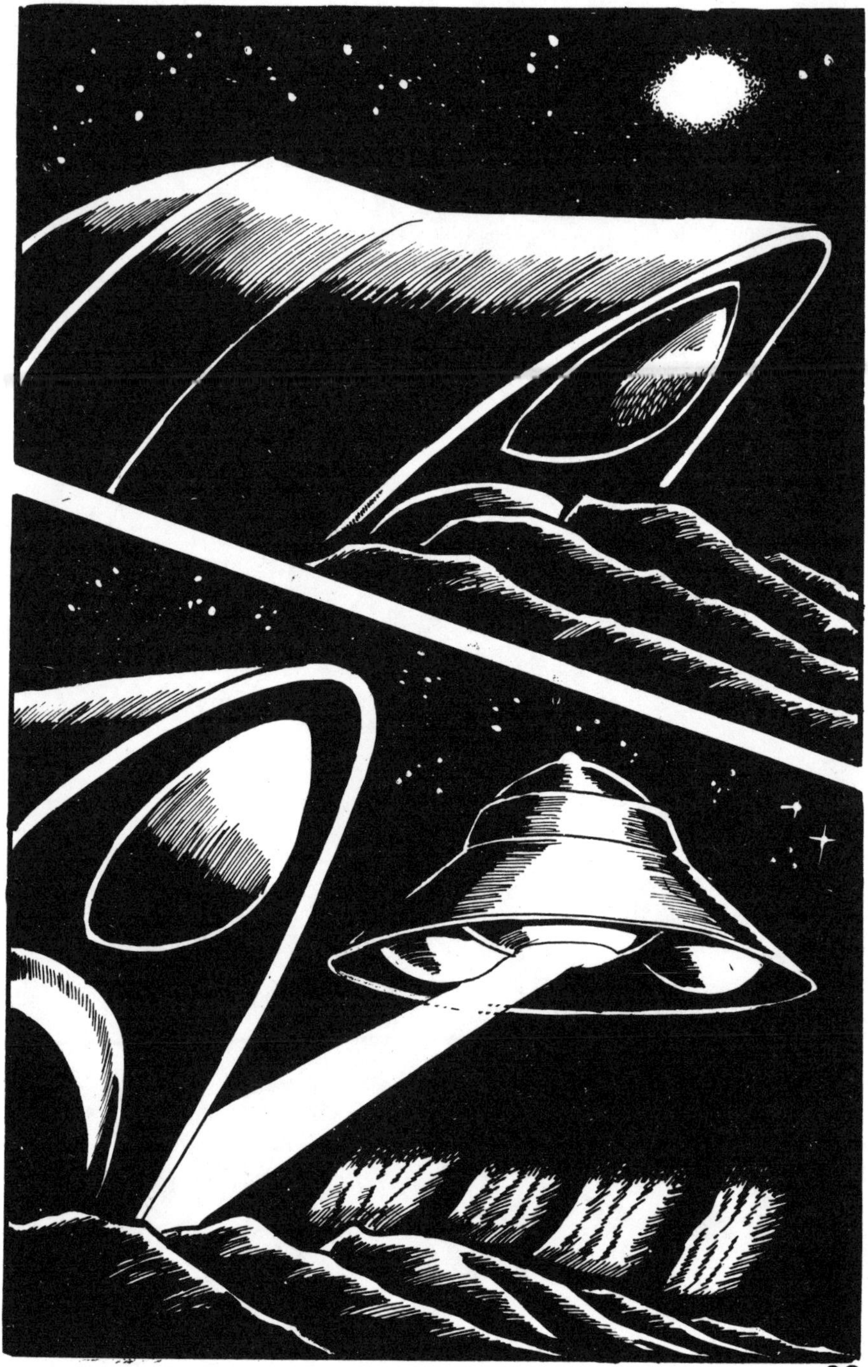

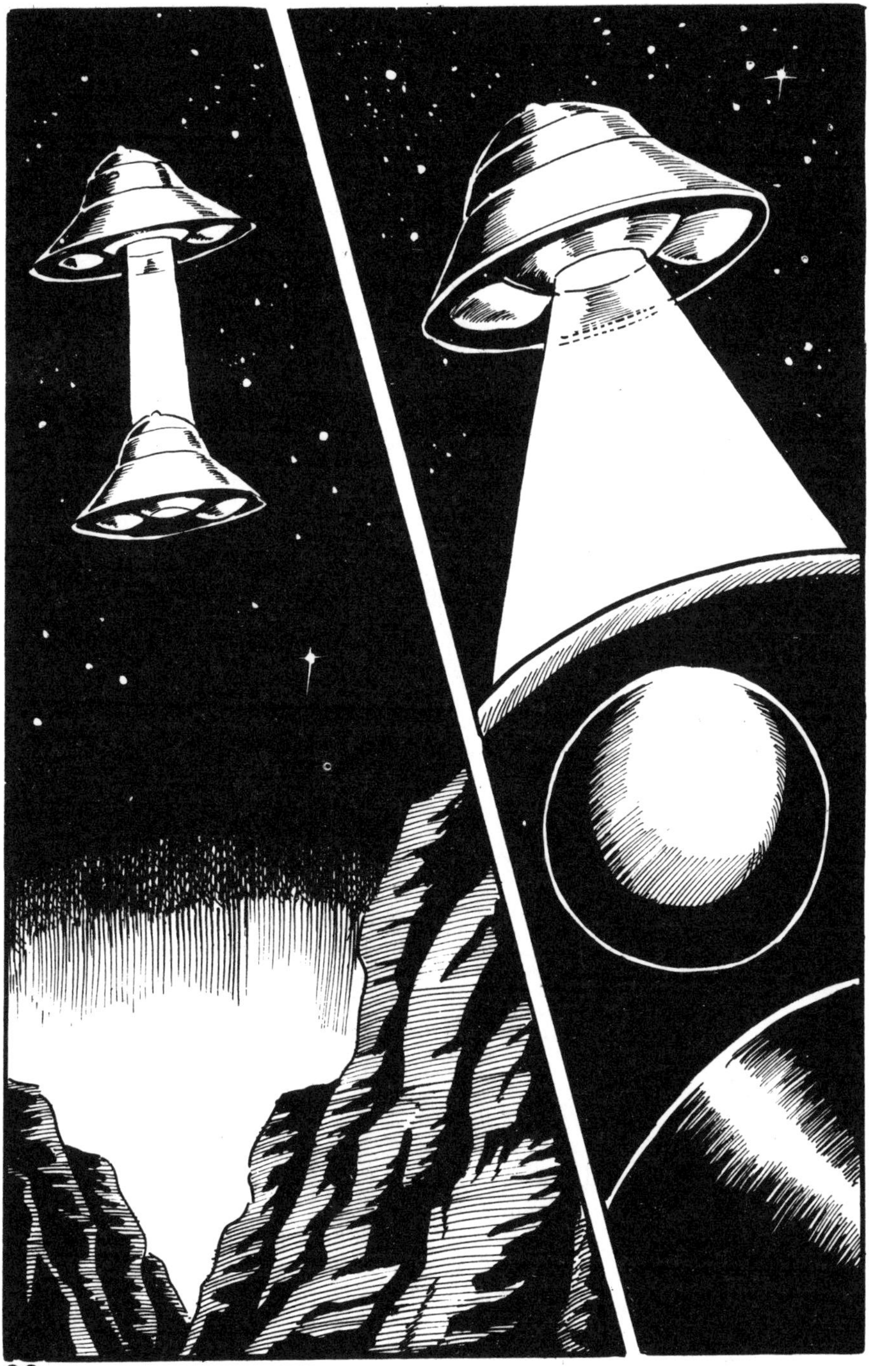

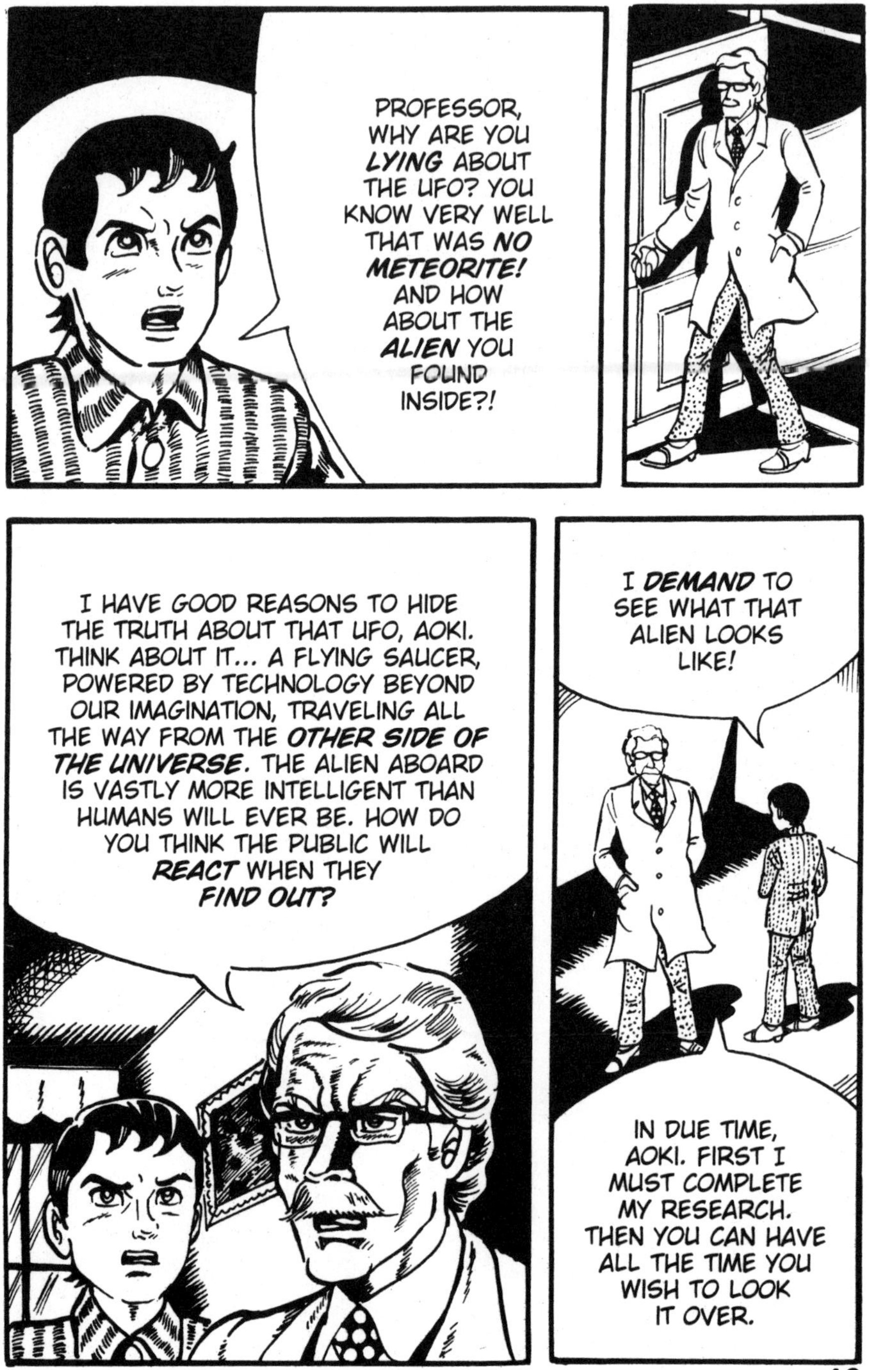
PROFESSOR, WHY ARE YOU LYING ABOUT THE UFO? YOU KNOW VERY WELL THAT WAS NO METEORITE! AND HOW ABOUT THE ALIEN YOU FOUND INSIDE?!
I HAVE GOOD REASONS TO HIDE THE TRUTH ABOUT THAT UFO, AOKI. THINK ABOUT IT... A FLYING SAUCER, POWERED BY TECHNOLOGY BEYOND OUR IMAGINATION, TRAVELING ALL THE WAY FROM THE OTHER SIDE OF THE UNIVERSE. THE ALIEN ABOARD IS VASTLY MORE INTELLIGENT THAN HUMANS WILL EVER BE. HOW DO YOU THINK THE PUBLIC WILL REACT WHEN THEY FIND OUT?
I DEMAND TO SEE WHAT THAT ALIEN LOOKS LIKE!
IN DUE TIME, AOKI. FIRST I MUST COMPLETE MY RESEARCH. THEN YOU CAN HAVE ALL THE TIME YOU WISH TO LOOK IT OVER.

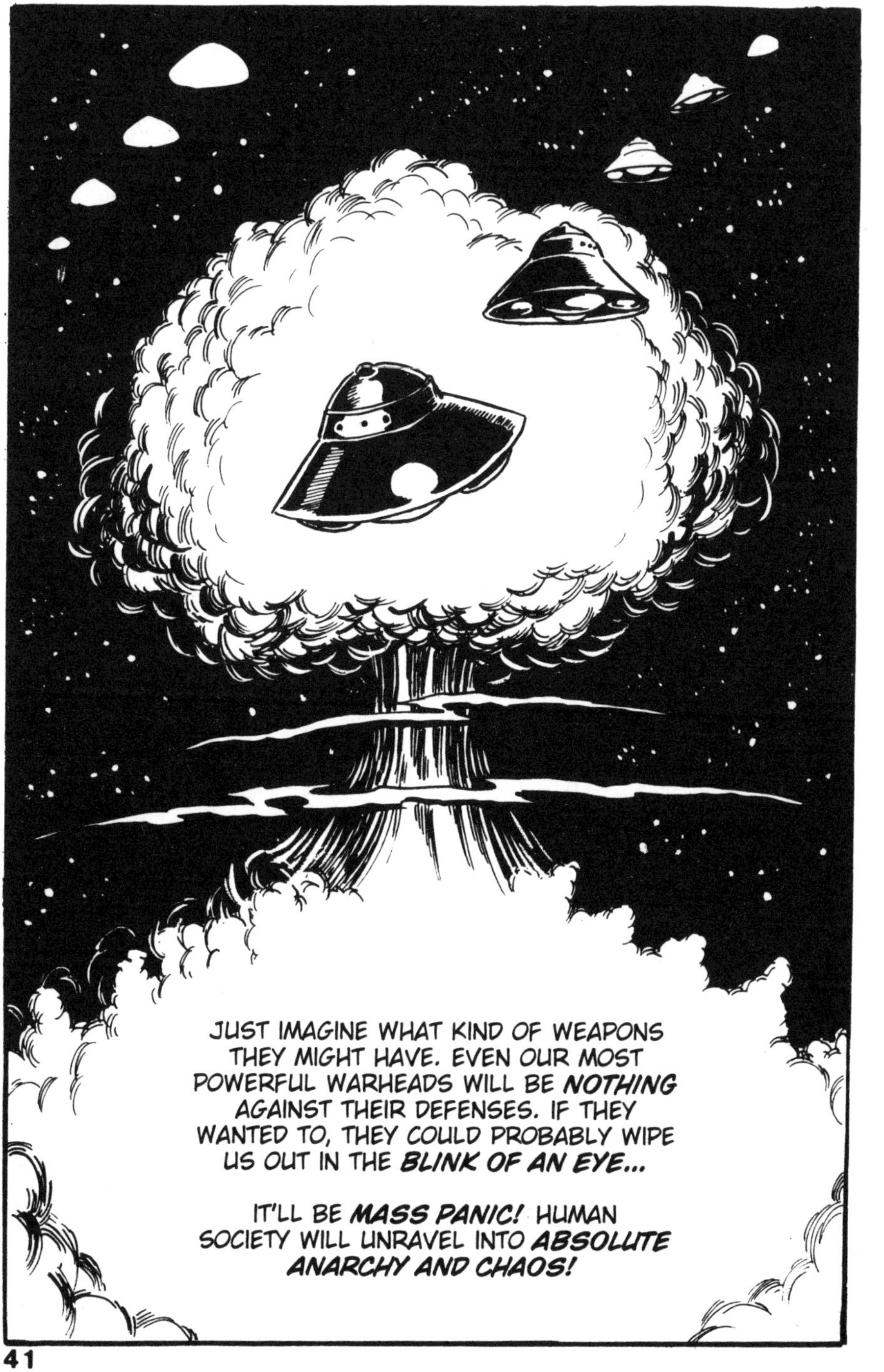
JUST IMAGINE WHAT KIND OF WEAPONS THEY MIGHT HAVE. EVEN OUR MOST POWERFUL WARHEADS WILL BE NOTHING AGAINST THEIR DEFENSES. IF THEY WANTED TO, THEY COULD PROBABLY WIPE US OUT IN THE BLINK OF AN EYE...
IT'LL BE MASS PANIC! HUMAN SOCIETY WILL UNRAVEL INTO ABSOLUTE ANARCHY AND CHAOS!

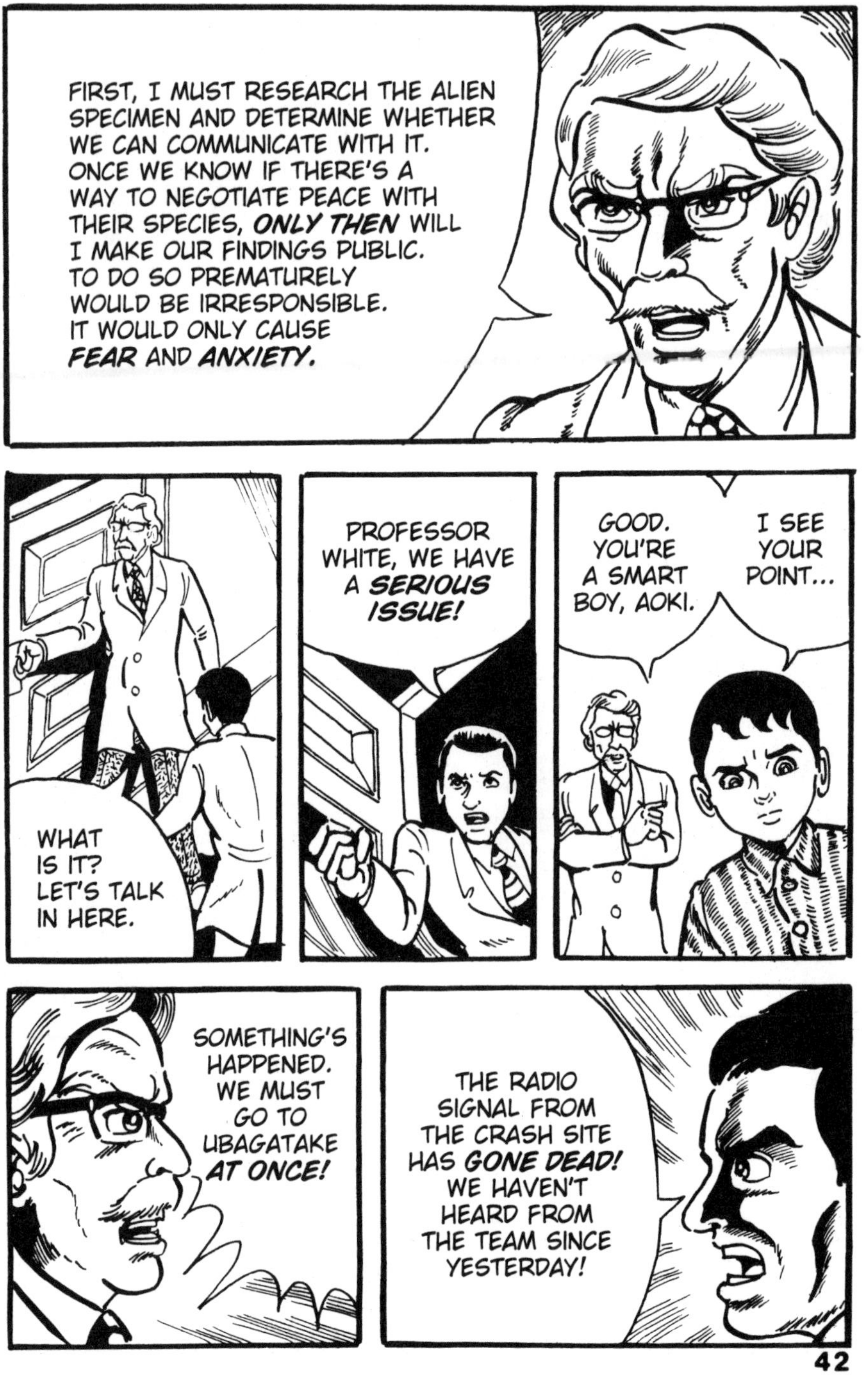
FIRST, I MUST RESEARCH THE ALIEN SPECIMEN AND DETERMINE WHETHER WE CAN COMMUNICATE WITH IT. ONCE WE KNOW IF THERE'S A WAY TO NEGOTIATE PEACE WITH THEIR SPECIES, ONLY THEN WILL I MAKE OUR FINDINGS PUBLIC. TO DO SO PREMATURELY WOULD BE IRRESPONSIBLE. IT WOULD ONLY CAUSE FEAR AND ANXIETY.
I SEE YOUR POINT...
GOOD. YOU'RE A SMART BOY, AOKI.
PROFESSOR WHITE, WE HAVE A SERIOUS ISSUE!
WHAT IS IT? LET'S TALK IN HERE.
THE RADIO SIGNAL FROM THE CRASH SITE HAS GONE DEAD! WE HAVEN'T HEARD FROM THE TEAM SINCE YESTERDAY!
SOMETHING'S HAPPENED. WE MUST GO TO UBAGATAKE AT ONCE!

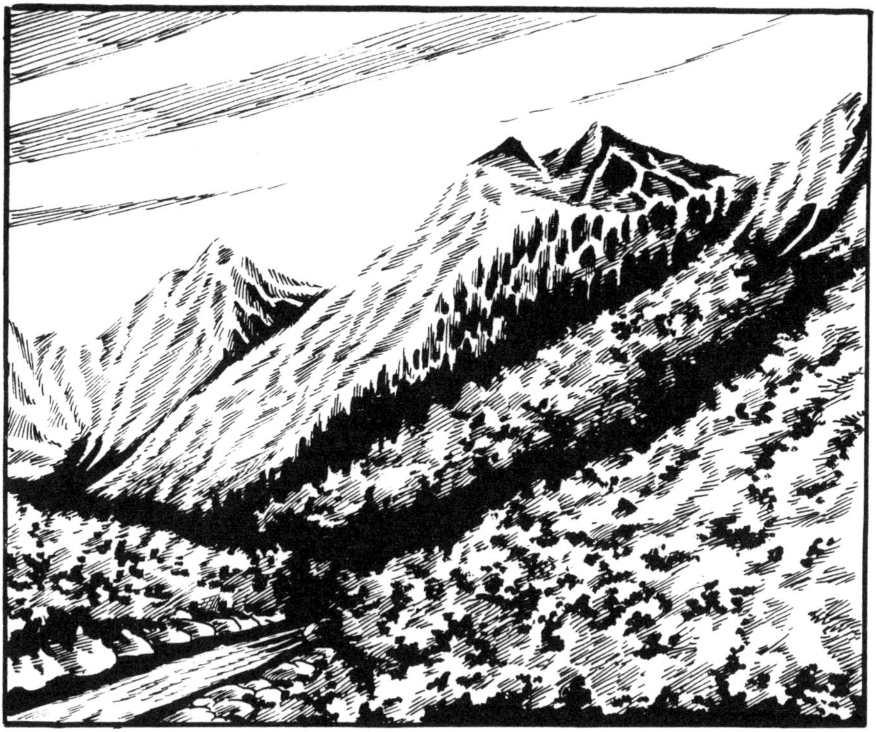

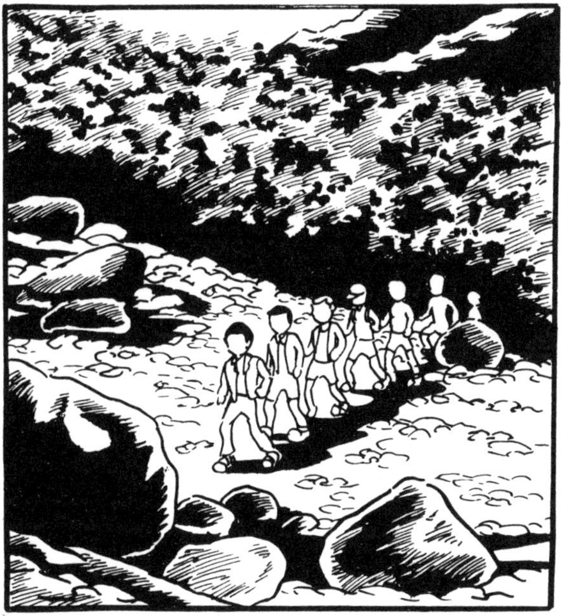

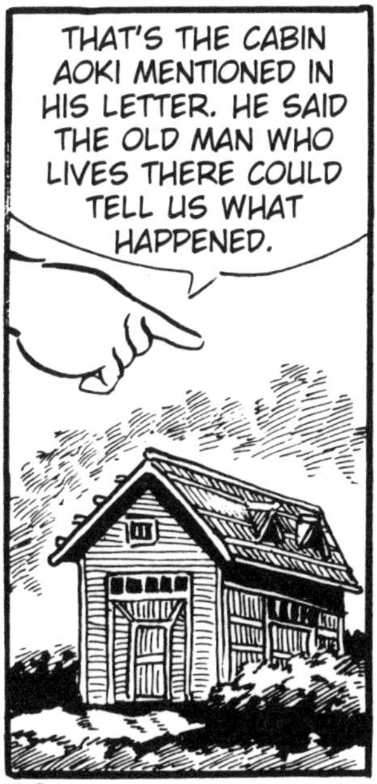
THAT'S THE CABIN AOKI MENTIONED IN HIS LETTER. HE SAID THE OLD MAN WHO LIVES THERE COULD TELL US WHAT HAPPENED.

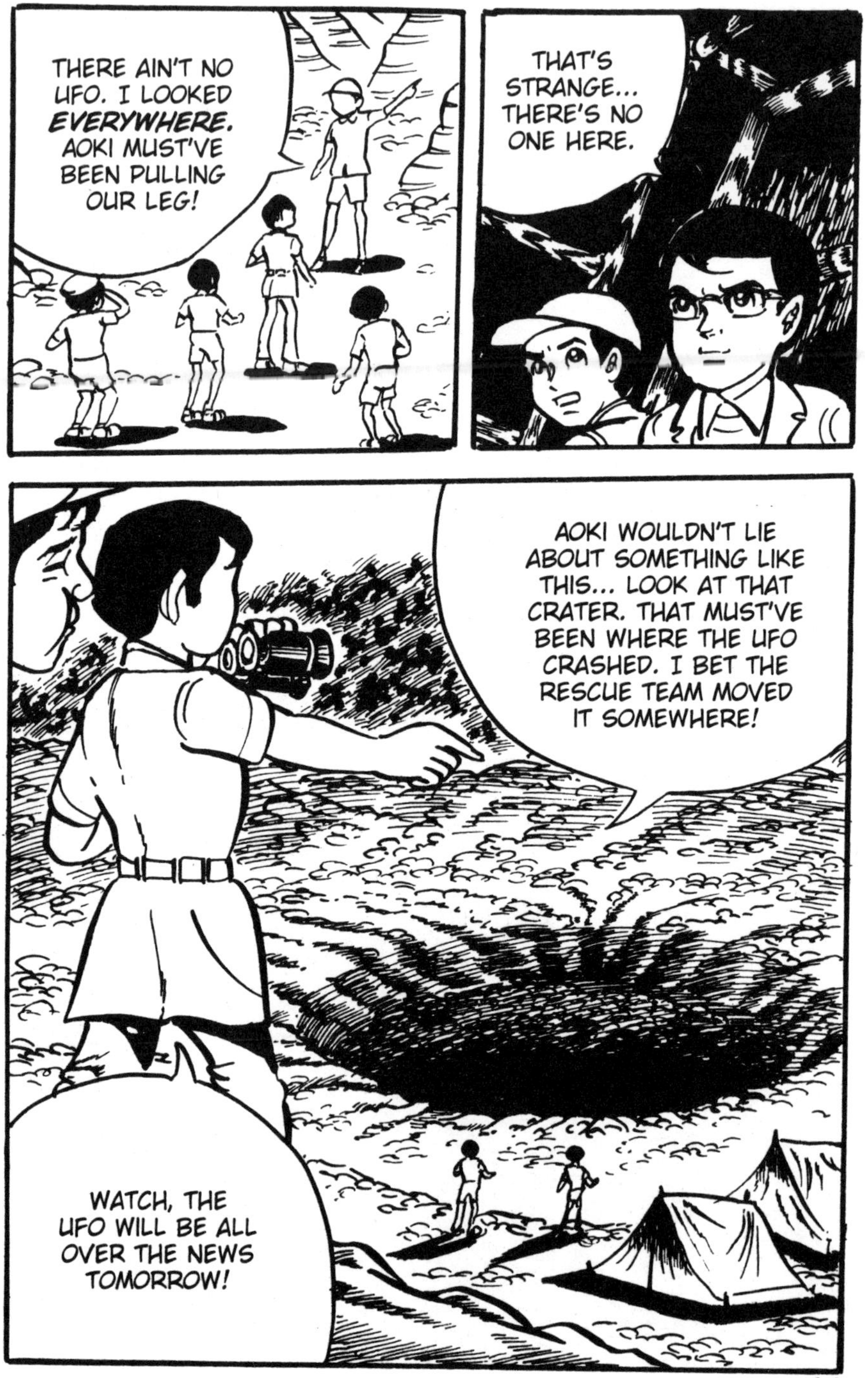
THAT'S STRANGE... THERE'S NO ONE HERE.
THERE AIN'T NO UFO. I LOOKED **EVERYWHERE.** AOKI MUST'VE BEEN PULLING OUR LEG!
AOKI WOULDN'T LIE ABOUT SOMETHING LIKE THIS... LOOK AT THAT CRATER. THAT MUST'VE BEEN WHERE THE UFO CRASHED. I BET THE RESCUE TEAM MOVED IT SOMEWHERE!
WATCH, THE UFO WILL BE ALL OVER THE NEWS TOMORROW!

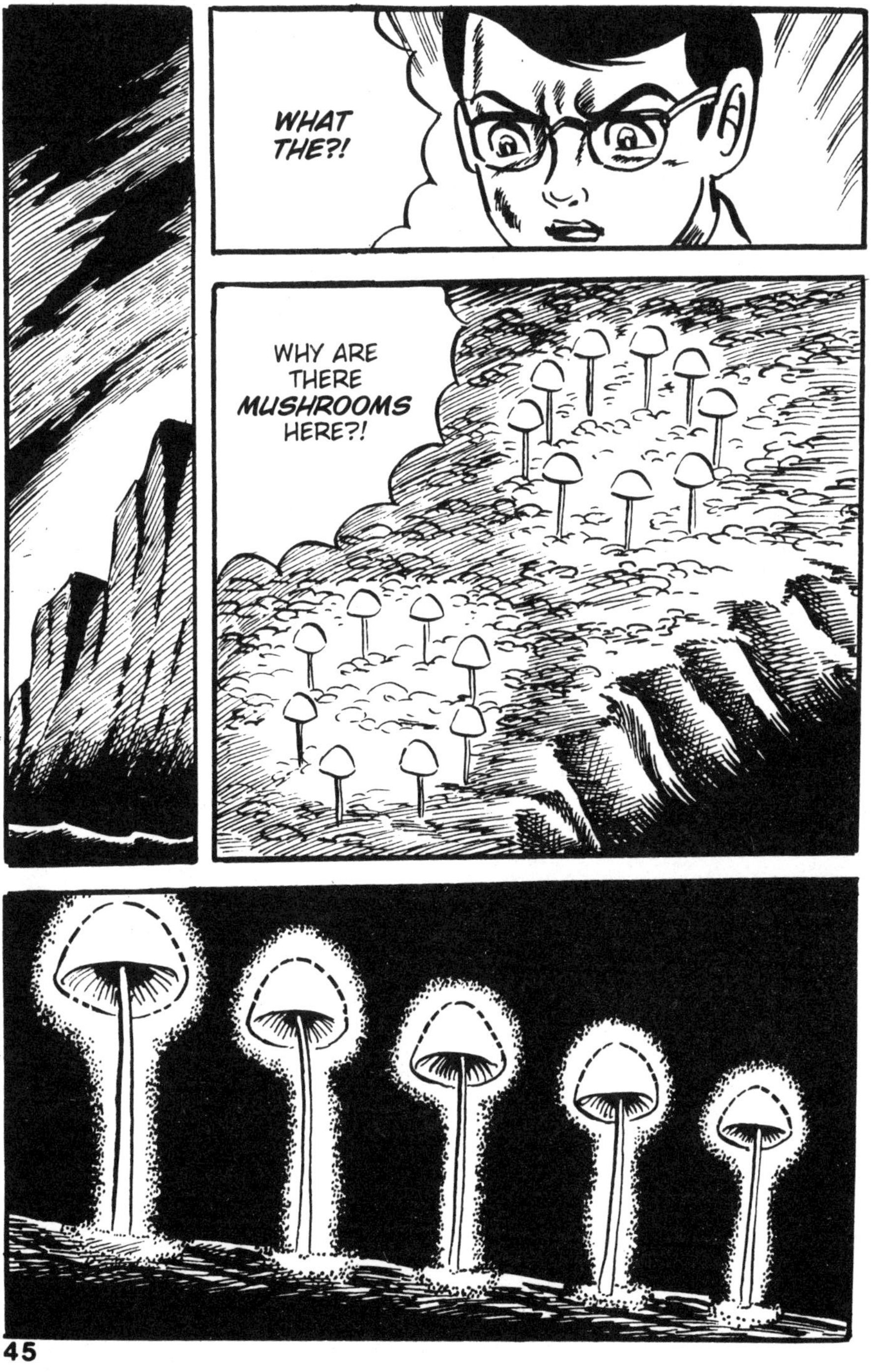
WHAT THE?!
WHY ARE THERE MUSHROOMS HERE?!

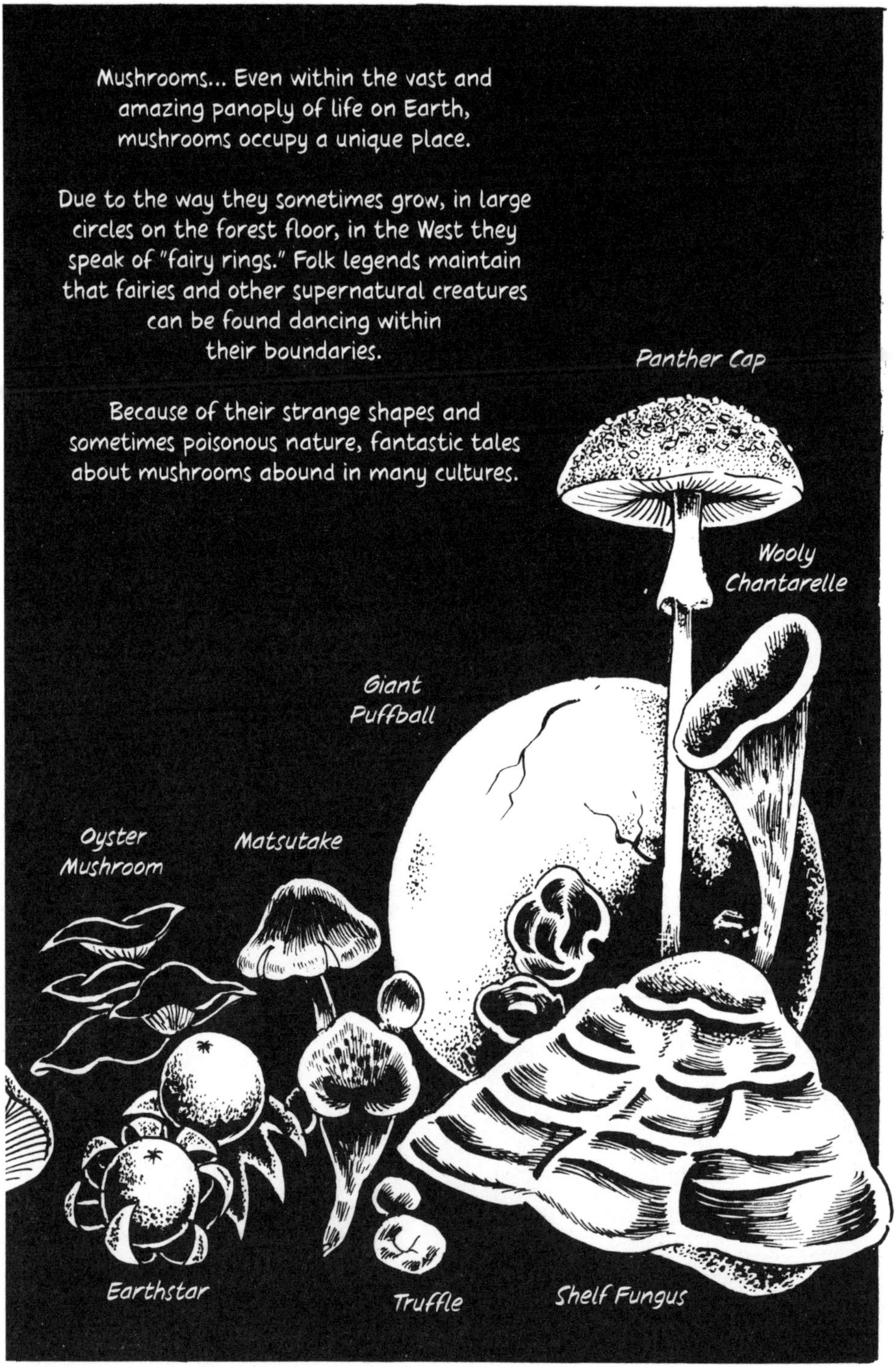
Mushrooms... Even within the vast and amazing panoply of life on Earth, mushrooms occupy a unique place.
Due to the way they sometimes grow, in large circles on the forest floor, in the West they speak of "fairy rings." Folk legends maintain that fairies and other supernatural creatures can be found dancing within their boundaries.
Because of their strange shapes and sometimes poisonous nature, fantastic tales about mushrooms abound in many cultures.
Panther Cap
Wooly Chantarelle
Giant Puffball
Oyster Mushroom
Matsutake
Earthstar
Truffle
Shelf Fungus

The famous Japanese poet Matsuo Basho is said to have died from the consumption of poisonous mushrooms. Large mushrooms were even reportedly found sprouting around his deathbed.

In the 15th century, the samurai lord Ota Dokan grew white mushrooms in the garden of Edo Castle, disconcerting visitors due to their resemblance to a woman's pale thighs. A few days later, after being summoned to court, Dokan was found murdered in his bathtub. White mushrooms have been considered a bad omen in Japan ever since.

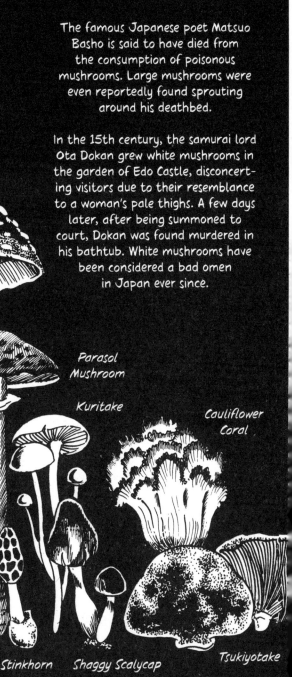

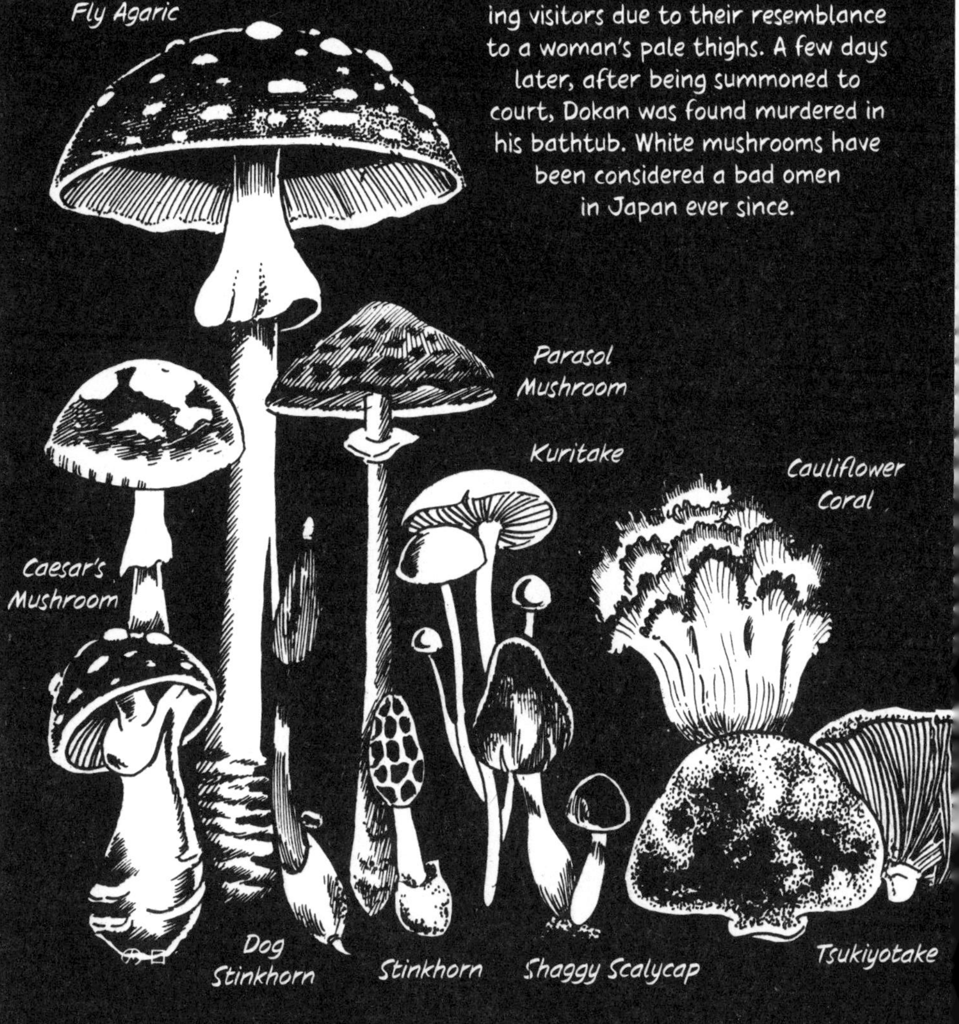
Fly Agaric
Parasol Mushroom
Kuritake
Cauliflower Coral
Caesar's Mushroom
Dog Stinkhorn
Stinkhorn
Shaggy Scalycap
Tsukiyotake

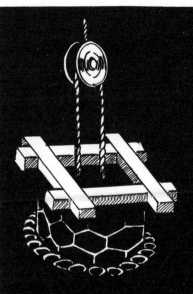

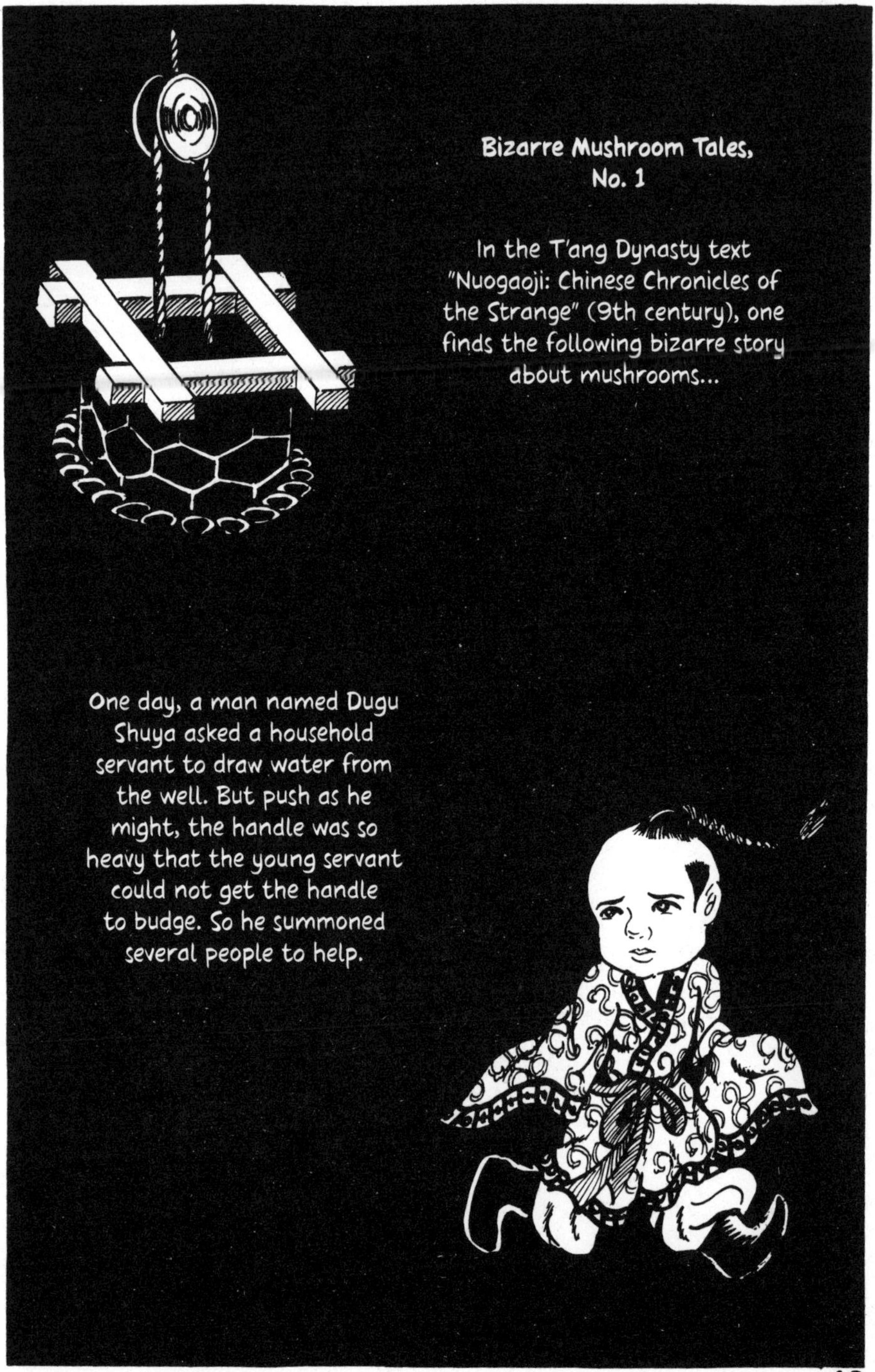

**Bizarre Mushroom Tales,
No. 1**

In the T'ang Dynasty text
"Nuogaoji: Chinese Chronicles of
the Strange" (9th century), one
finds the following bizarre story
about mushrooms...

One day, a man named Dugu
Shuya asked a household
servant to draw water from
the well. But push as he
might, the handle was so
heavy that the young servant
could not get the handle
to budge. So he summoned
several people to help.

48

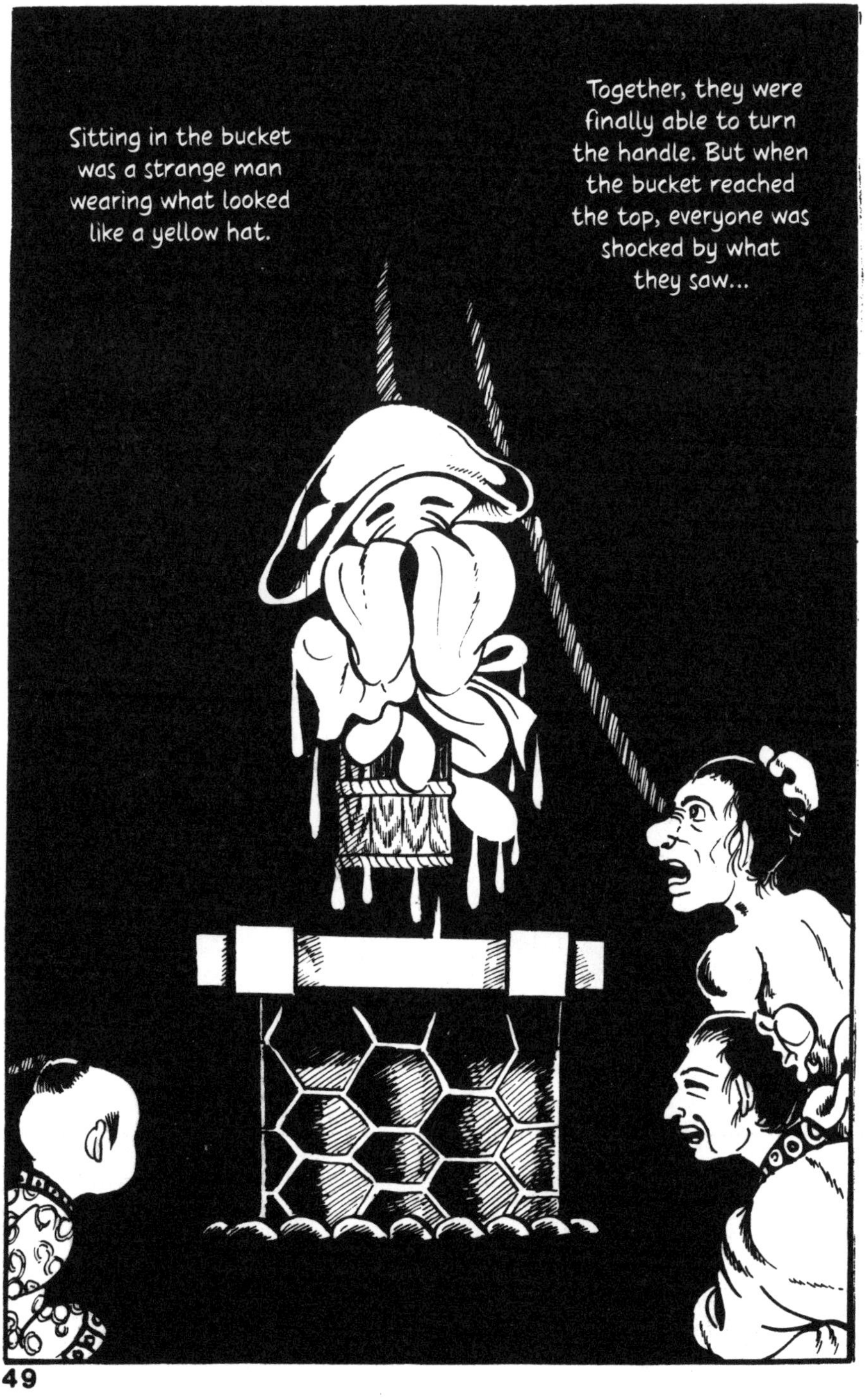
Together, they were finally able to turn the handle. But when the bucket reached the top, everyone was shocked by what they saw...
Sitting in the bucket was a strange man wearing what looked like a yellow hat.

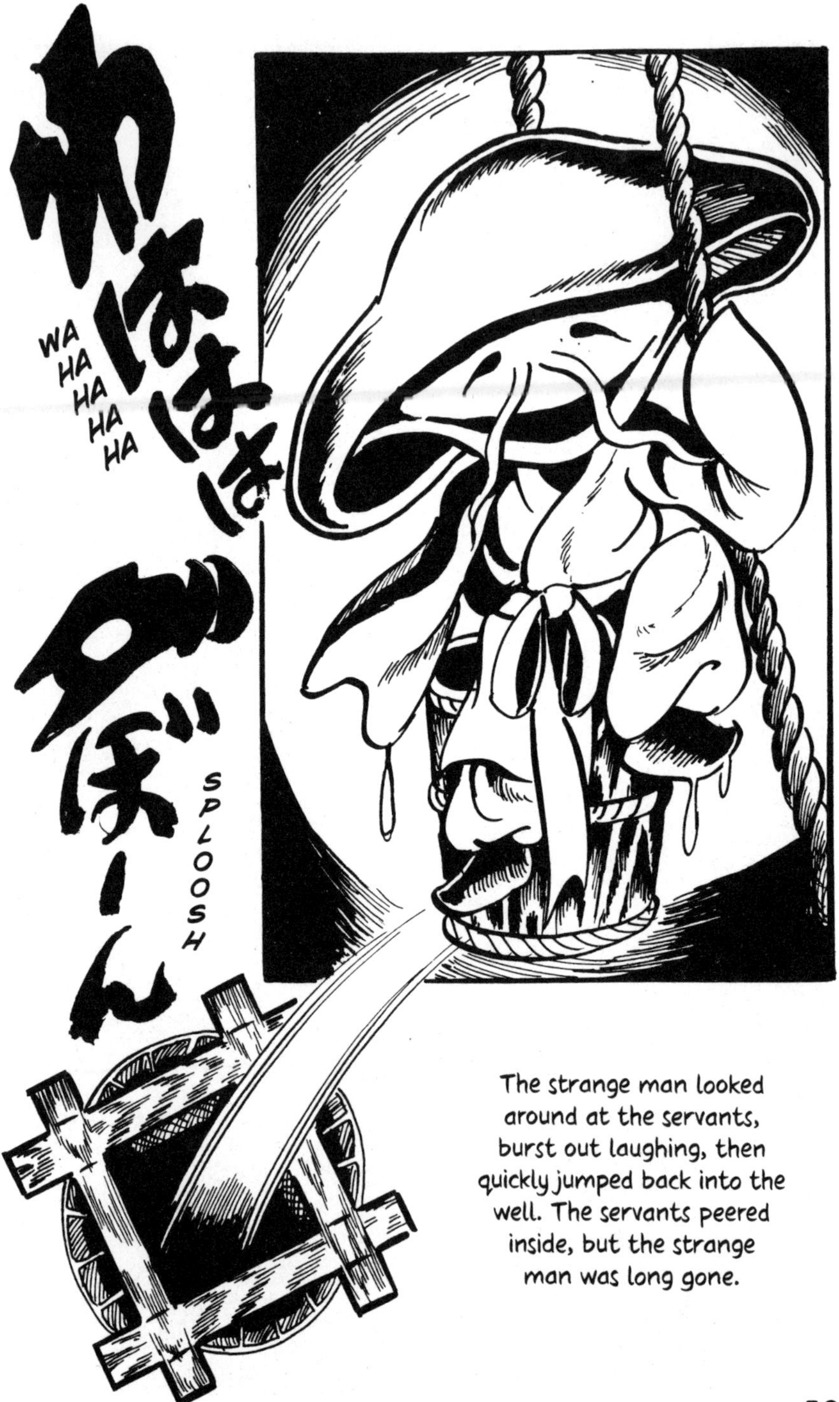
WA HA HA HA HA
SPLOOSH

The strange man looked around at the servants, burst out laughing, then quickly jumped back into the well. The servants peered inside, but the strange man was long gone.

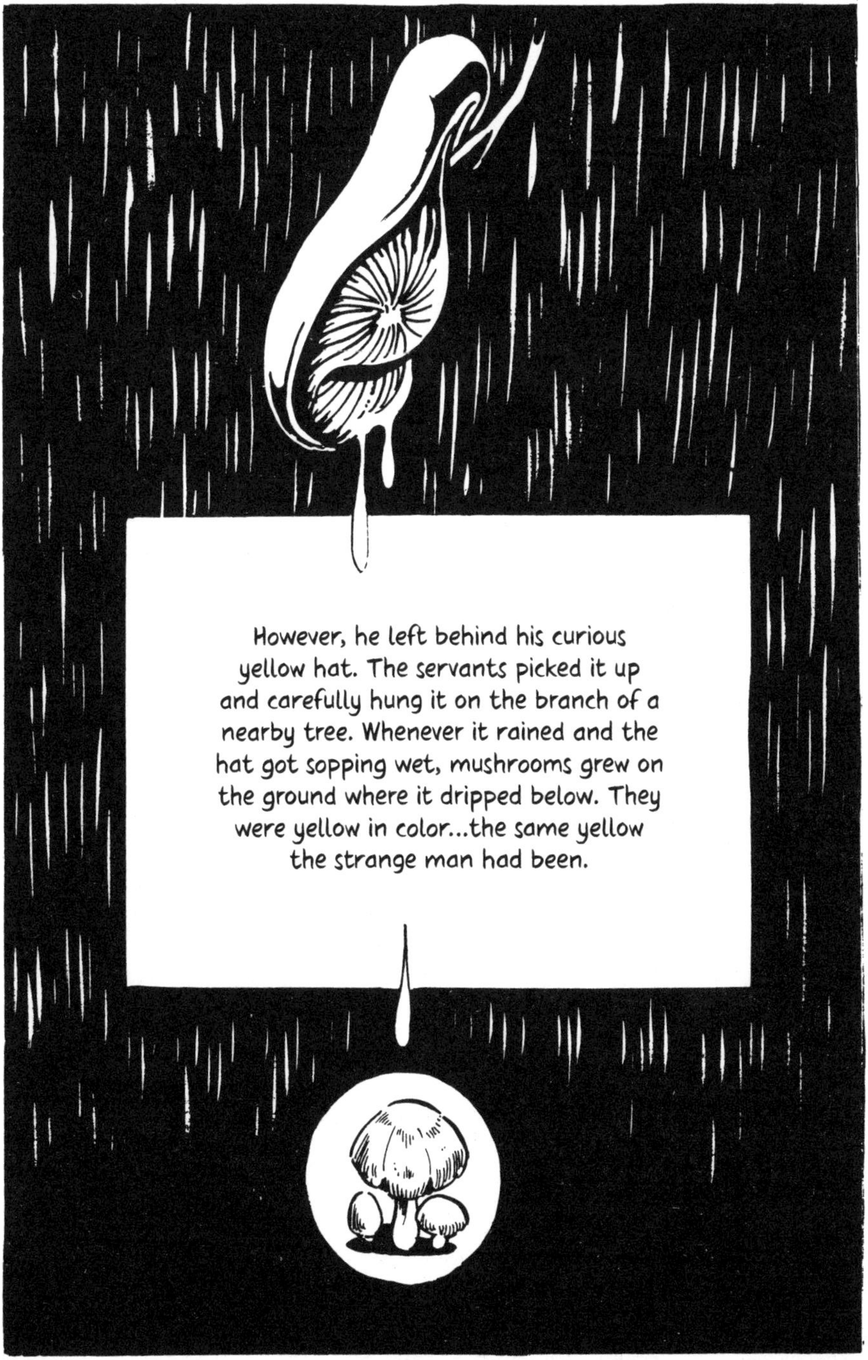
However, he left behind his curious yellow hat. The servants picked it up and carefully hung it on the branch of a nearby tree. Whenever it rained and the hat got sopping wet, mushrooms grew on the ground where it dripped below. They were yellow in color...the same yellow the strange man had been.

adapted from the translation by Carrie E. Reed, "Chinese Chronicles of the Strange" (2001)

Bizarre Mushroom Tales, No. 2

In China, there once was a monk named Huihong. When he died and was buried, the surrounding trees all withered and legions of mushrooms sprung from his grave. A villager ate one and was delighted by the taste, inspiring his fellows to follow suit. No matter how many they ate, the mushrooms kept growing and growing without end. Little did they know that they were actually consuming the monk's flesh and blood. In punishment for a life of receiving alms despite not truly believing in Buddhism, the monk had been reborn as mushrooms.

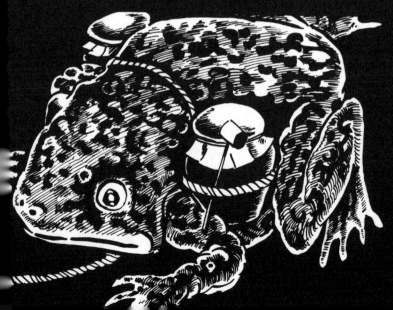

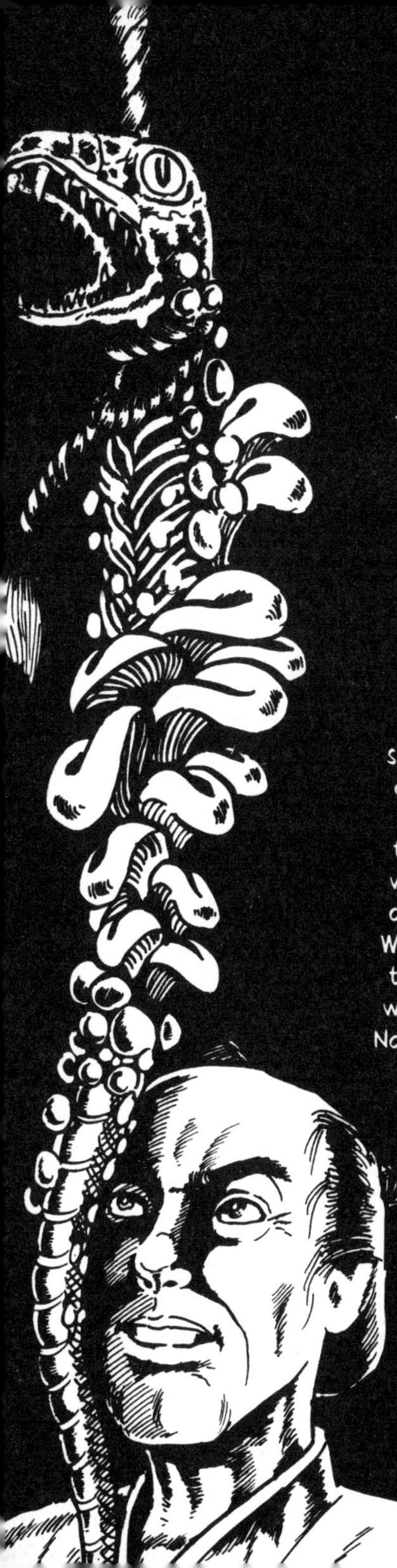

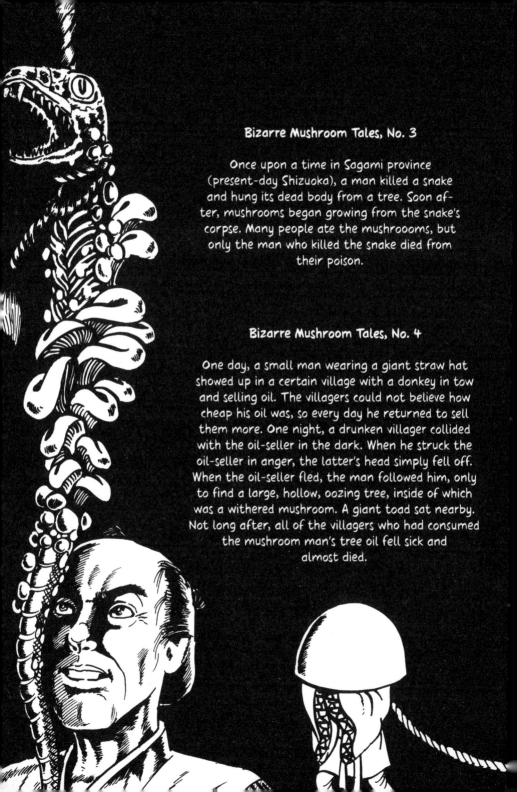

Bizarre Mushroom Tales, No. 3

Once upon a time in Sagami province (present-day Shizuoka), a man killed a snake and hung its dead body from a tree. Soon after, mushrooms began growing from the snake's corpse. Many people ate the mushroooms, but only the man who killed the snake died from their poison.

Bizarre Mushroom Tales, No. 4

One day, a small man wearing a giant straw hat showed up in a certain village with a donkey in tow and selling oil. The villagers could not believe how cheap his oil was, so every day he returned to sell them more. One night, a drunken villager collided with the oil-seller in the dark. When he struck the oil-seller in anger, the latter's head simply fell off. When the oil-seller fled, the man followed him, only to find a large, hollow, oozing tree, inside of which was a withered mushroom. A giant toad sat nearby. Not long after, all of the villagers who had consumed the mushroom man's tree oil fell sick and almost died.

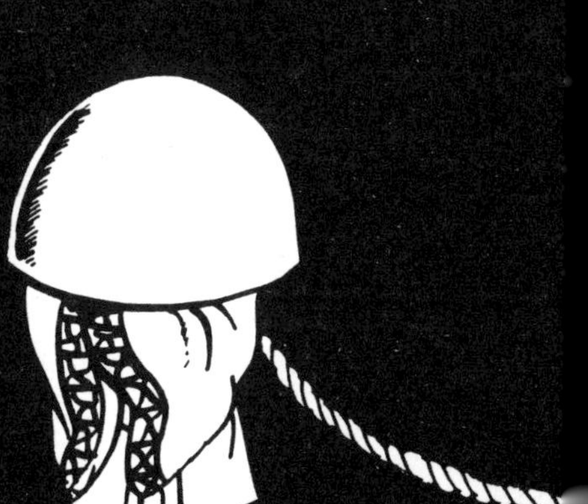

In Japan, there is no lack of strange tales about mushrooms. In the famous "A Collection of Tales from Uji" (13th century), there is a story about Shinomura village in Tanba province, where so many mushrooms grew that no one knew what to do with them all. One night, all of Shinomura's residents saw the same dream. In that dream, some twenty or thirty monks with scraggly, unshaved heads appeared to the dreamer and announced, "We have served well these many years, but our connection to this village has ended and now we must depart." Sure enough, the following year not a single mushroom could be found in the mountains.

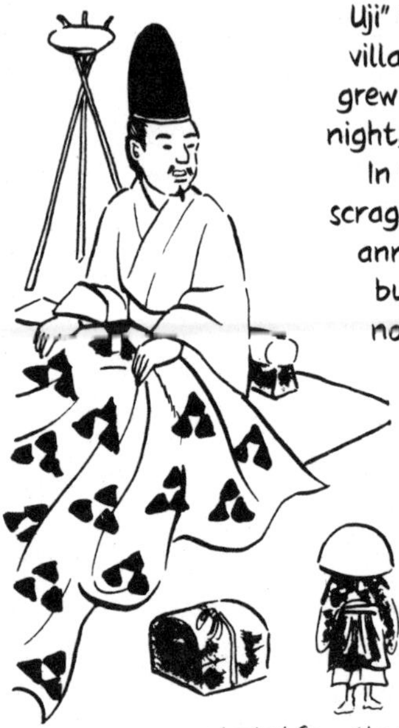

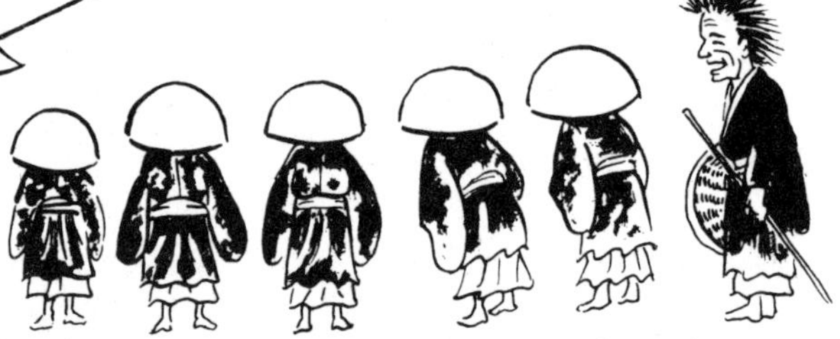

adapted from the translation by D.E. Mills, "A Collection of Tales from Uji" (1970)
**monks who led impure lives were said to be reborn as mushrooms*

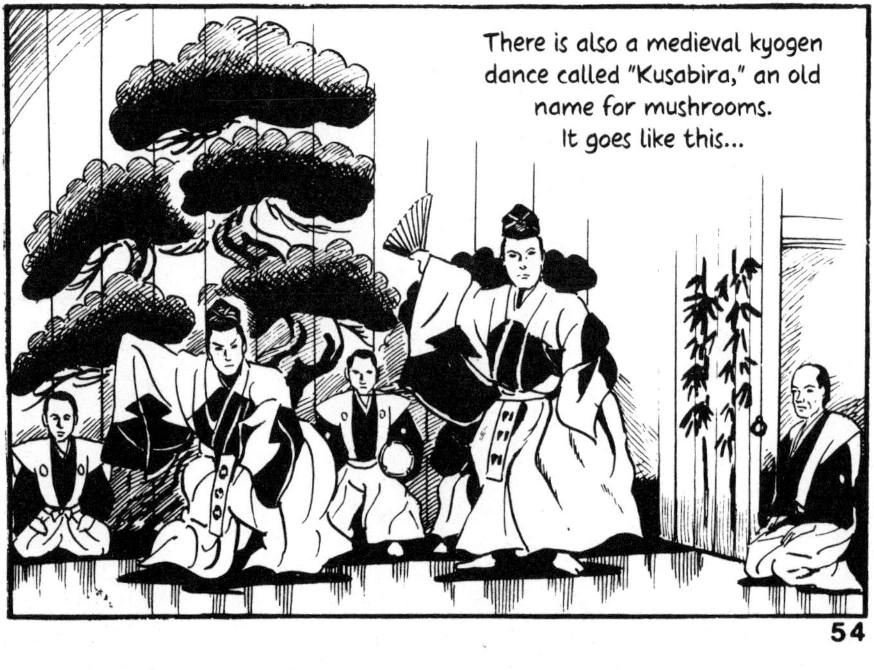
There is also a medieval kyogen dance called "Kusabira," an old name for mushrooms. It goes like this...

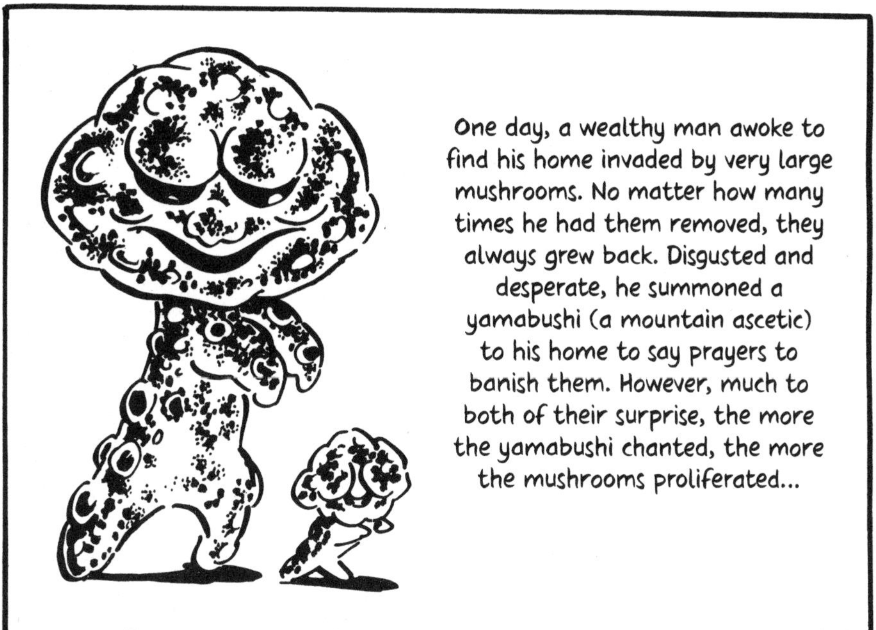
One day, a wealthy man awoke to find his home invaded by very large mushrooms. No matter how many times he had them removed, they always grew back. Disgusted and desperate, he summoned a yamabushi (a mountain ascetic) to his home to say prayers to banish them. However, much to both of their surprise, the more the yamabushi chanted, the more the mushrooms proliferated...

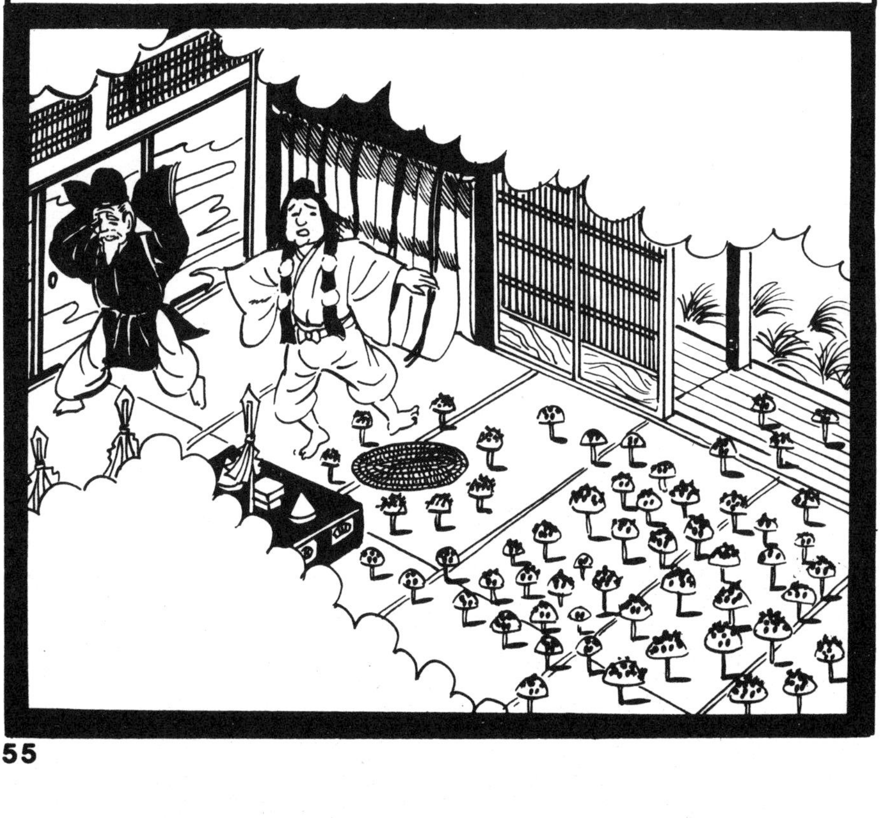

For this performance, a group of children dress up as mushrooms by donning straw hats. After entering the stage one by one, they dance around the yamabushi, gradually closing in on him. Eventually the wealthy man realizes that he has no choice but to abandon his home to the invading mushrooms. The play ends with him and the yamabushi rushing off stage, chased by the child mushrooms and a giant demon mushroom.

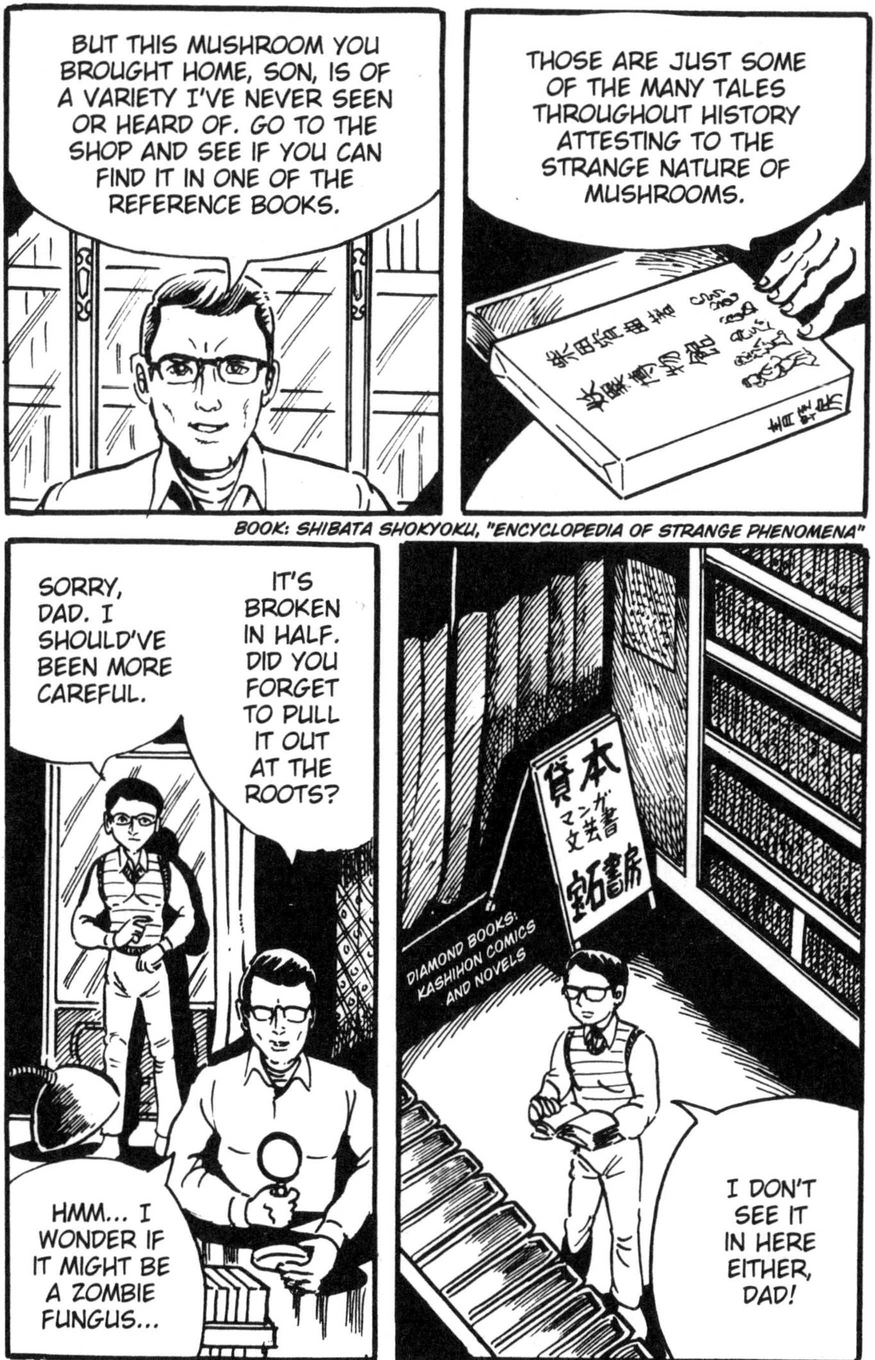
THOSE ARE JUST SOME OF THE MANY TALES THROUGHOUT HISTORY ATTESTING TO THE STRANGE NATURE OF MUSHROOMS.
BUT THIS MUSHROOM YOU BROUGHT HOME, SON, IS OF A VARIETY I'VE NEVER SEEN OR HEARD OF. GO TO THE SHOP AND SEE IF YOU CAN FIND IT IN ONE OF THE REFERENCE BOOKS.
BOOK: SHIBATA SHOKYOKU, "ENCYCLOPEDIA OF STRANGE PHENOMENA"
貸本
マンガ
文芸書
DIAMOND BOOKS: KASHIHON COMICS AND NOVELS
I DON'T SEE IT IN HERE EITHER, DAD!
IT'S BROKEN IN HALF. DID YOU FORGET TO PULL IT OUT AT THE ROOTS?
SORRY, DAD. I SHOULD'VE BEEN MORE CAREFUL.
HMM... I WONDER IF IT MIGHT BE A ZOMBIE FUNGUS...

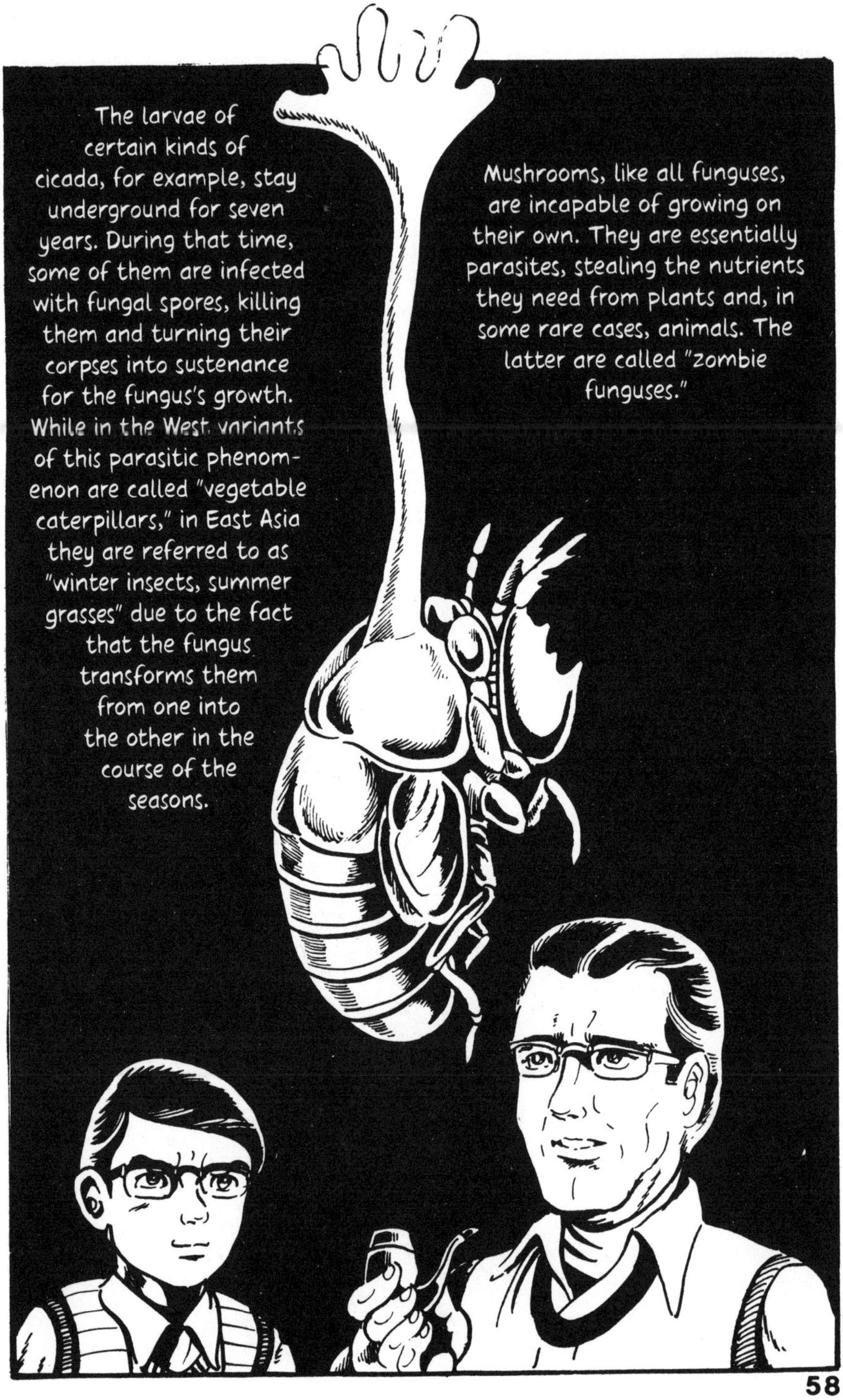
Mushrooms, like all funguses, are incapable of growing on their own. They are essentially parasites, stealing the nutrients they need from plants and, in some rare cases, animals. The latter are called "zombie funguses."
The larvae of certain kinds of cicada, for example, stay underground for seven years. During that time, some of them are infected with fungal spores, killing them and turning their corpses into sustenance for the fungus's growth. While in the West variants of this parasitic phenomenon are called "vegetable caterpillars," in East Asia they are referred to as "winter insects, summer grasses" due to the fact that the fungus transforms them from one into the other in the course of the seasons.

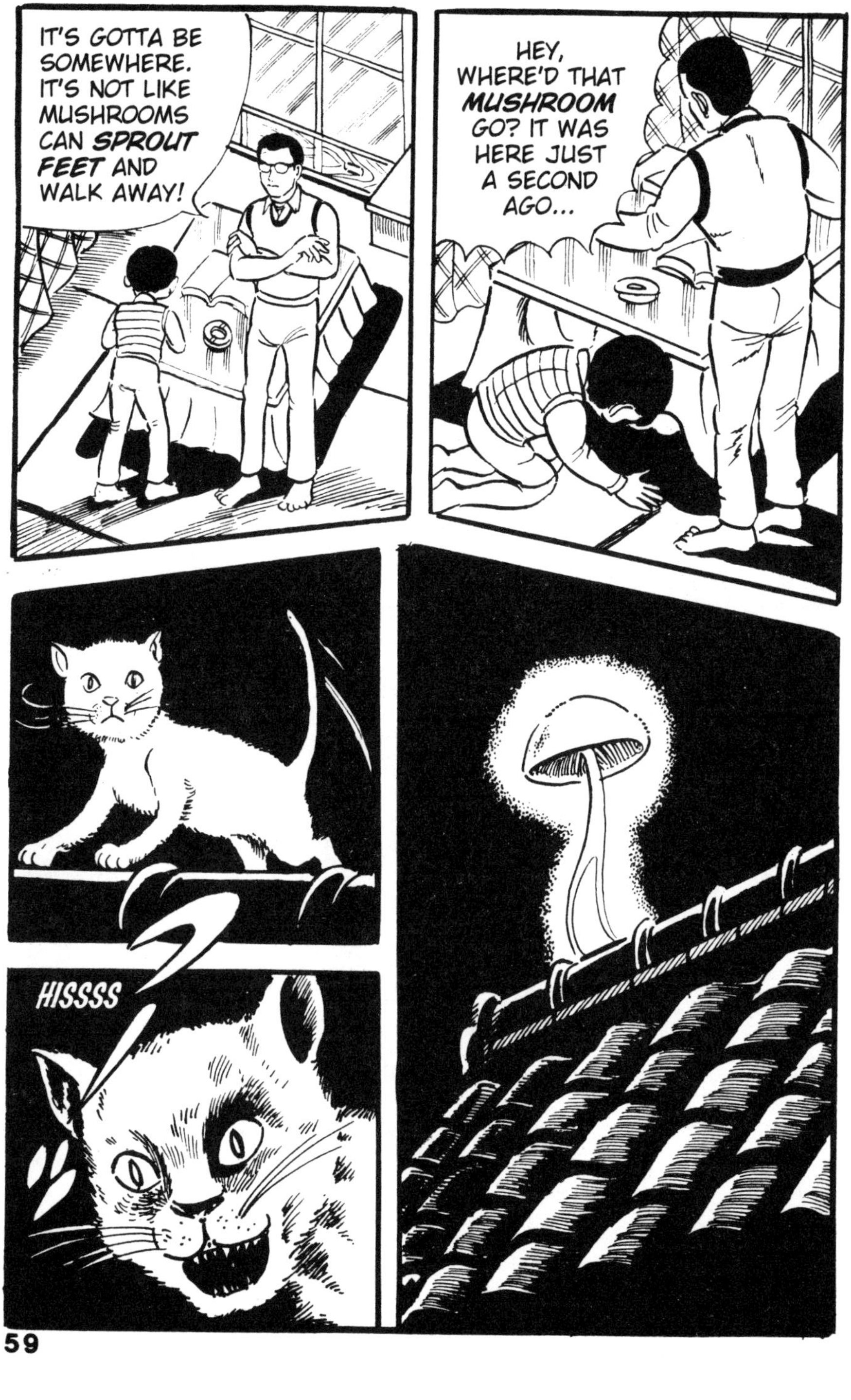
HEY, WHERE'D THAT MUSHROOM GO? IT WAS HERE JUST A SECOND AGO...
IT'S GOTTA BE SOMEWHERE. IT'S NOT LIKE MUSHROOMS CAN SPROUT FEET AND WALK AWAY!
HISSSS

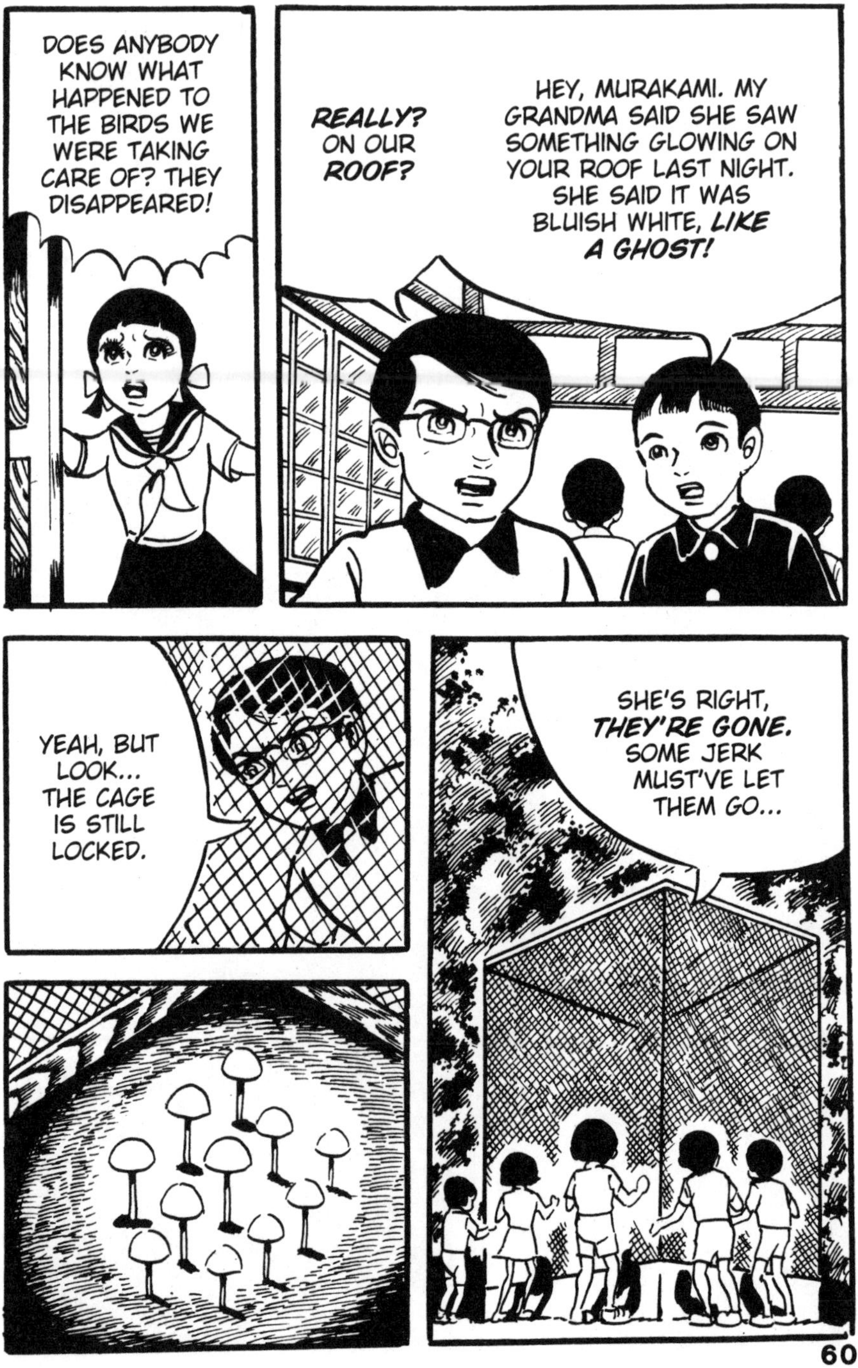
HEY, MURAKAMI. MY GRANDMA SAID SHE SAW SOMETHING GLOWING ON YOUR ROOF LAST NIGHT. SHE SAID IT WAS BLUISH WHITE, LIKE A GHOST!
REALLY? ON OUR ROOF?
DOES ANYBODY KNOW WHAT HAPPENED TO THE BIRDS WE WERE TAKING CARE OF? THEY DISAPPEARED!
SHE'S RIGHT, THEY'RE GONE. SOME JERK MUST'VE LET THEM GO...
YEAH, BUT LOOK... THE CAGE IS STILL LOCKED.

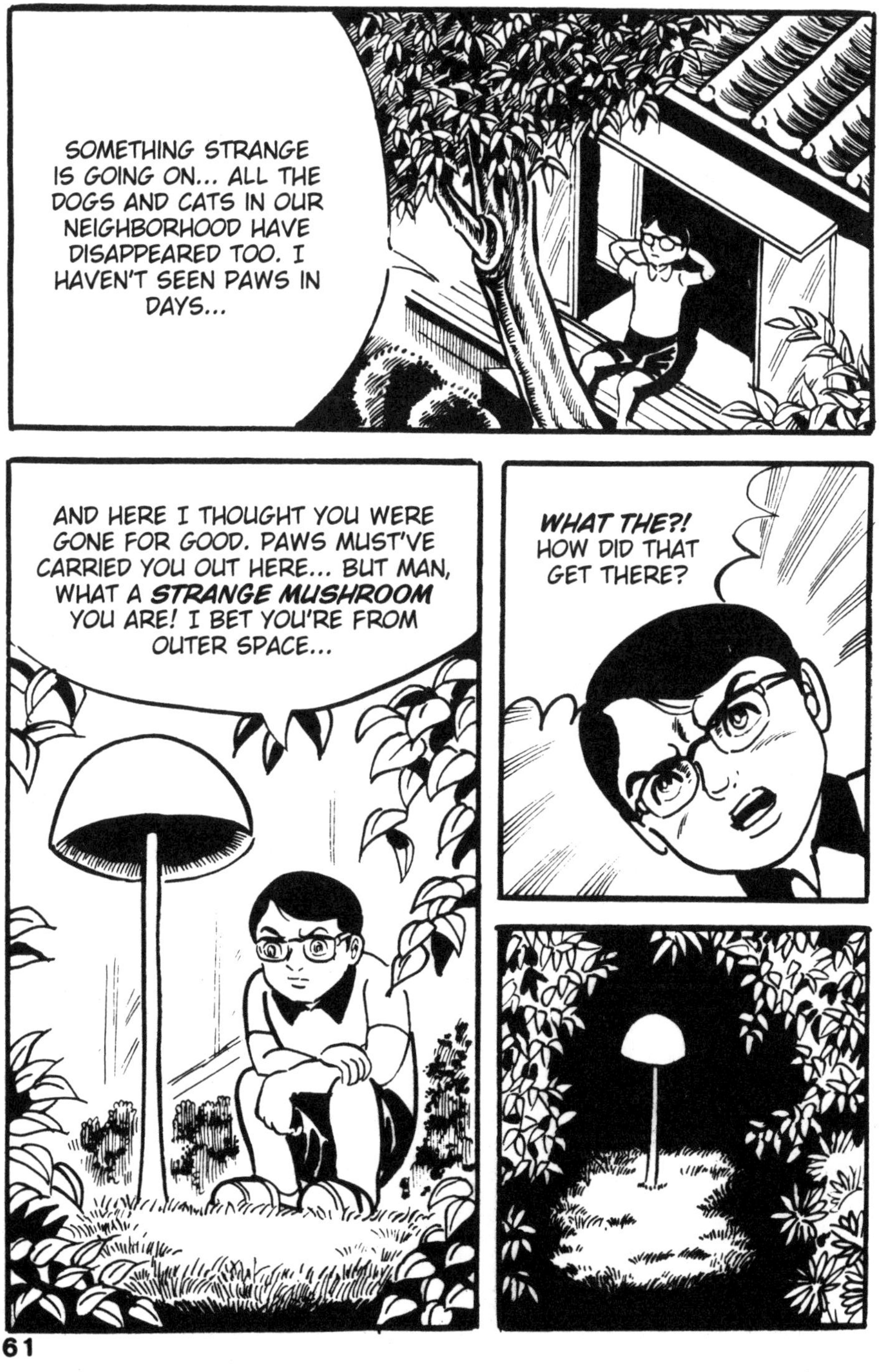
SOMETHING STRANGE IS GOING ON... ALL THE DOGS AND CATS IN OUR NEIGHBORHOOD HAVE DISAPPEARED TOO. I HAVEN'T SEEN PAWS IN DAYS...
WHAT THE?! HOW DID THAT GET THERE?
AND HERE I THOUGHT YOU WERE GONE FOR GOOD. PAWS MUST'VE CARRIED YOU OUT HERE... BUT MAN, WHAT A ***STRANGE MUSHROOM*** YOU ARE! I BET YOU'RE FROM OUTER SPACE...

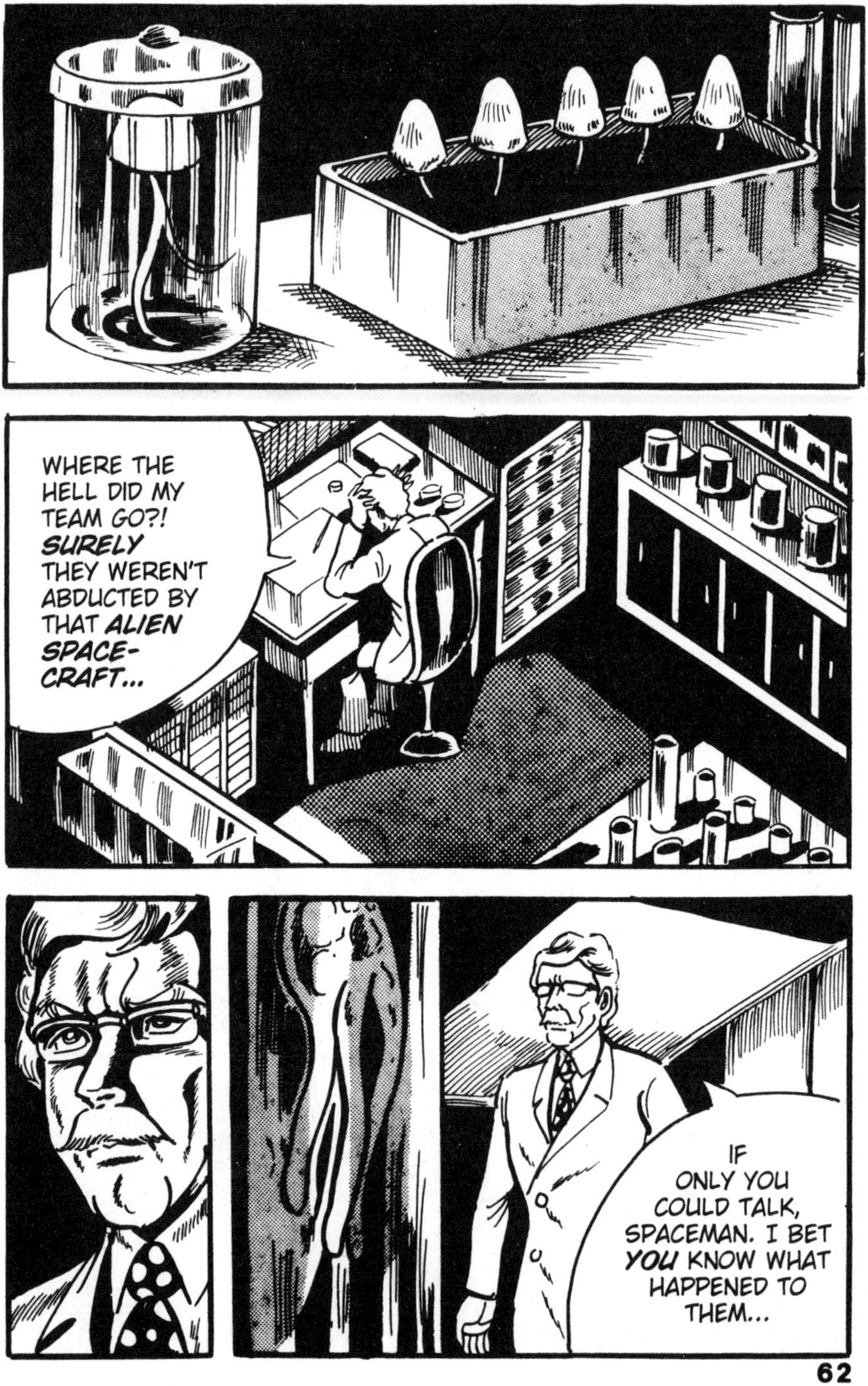
WHERE THE HELL DID MY TEAM GO?! **SURELY** THEY WEREN'T ABDUCTED BY THAT **ALIEN SPACE-CRAFT...**
IF ONLY YOU COULD TALK, SPACEMAN. I BET **YOU** KNOW WHAT HAPPENED TO THEM...

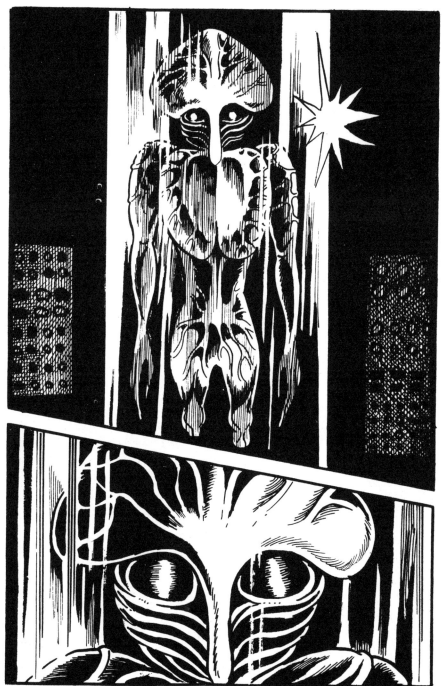

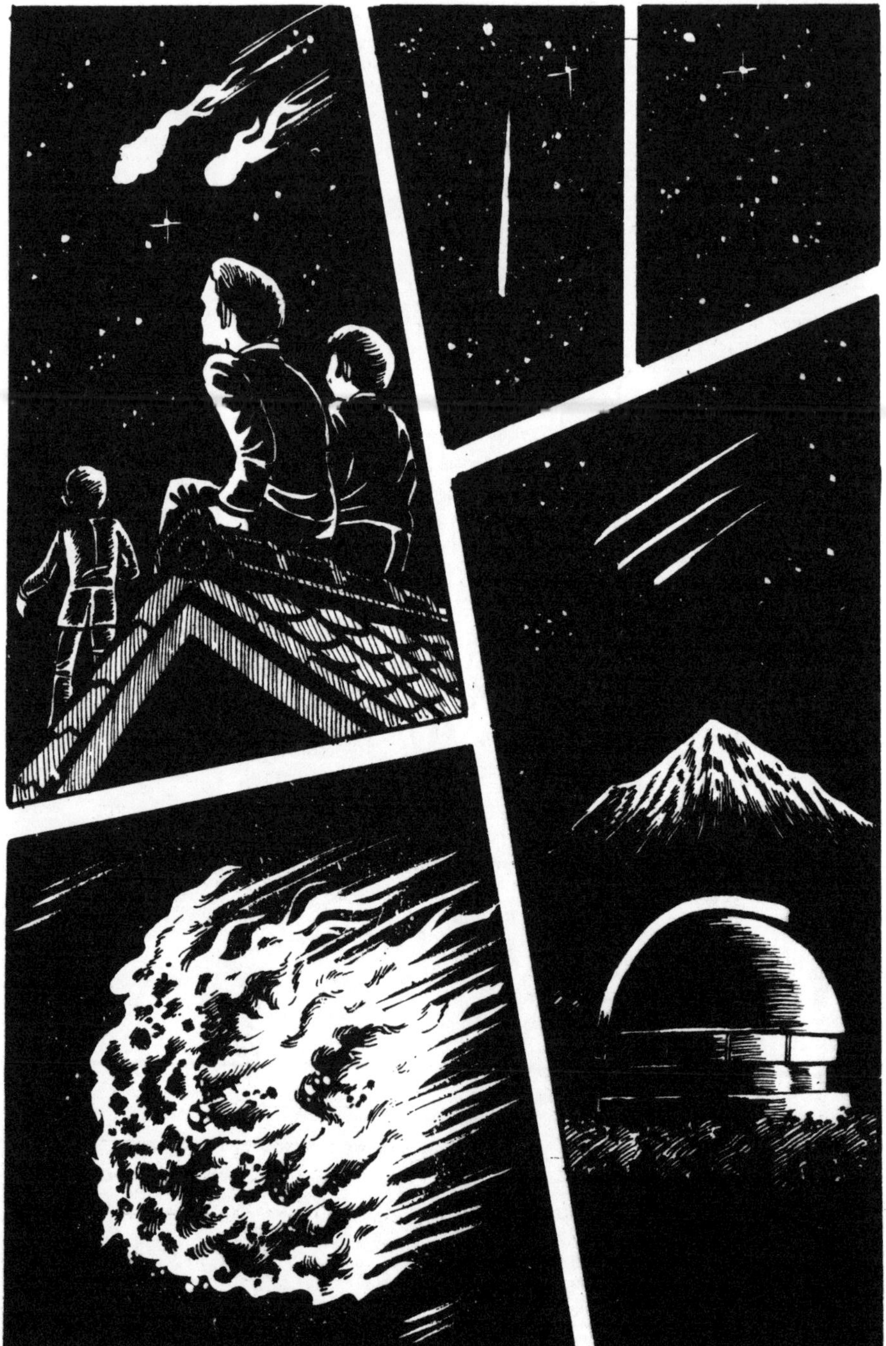

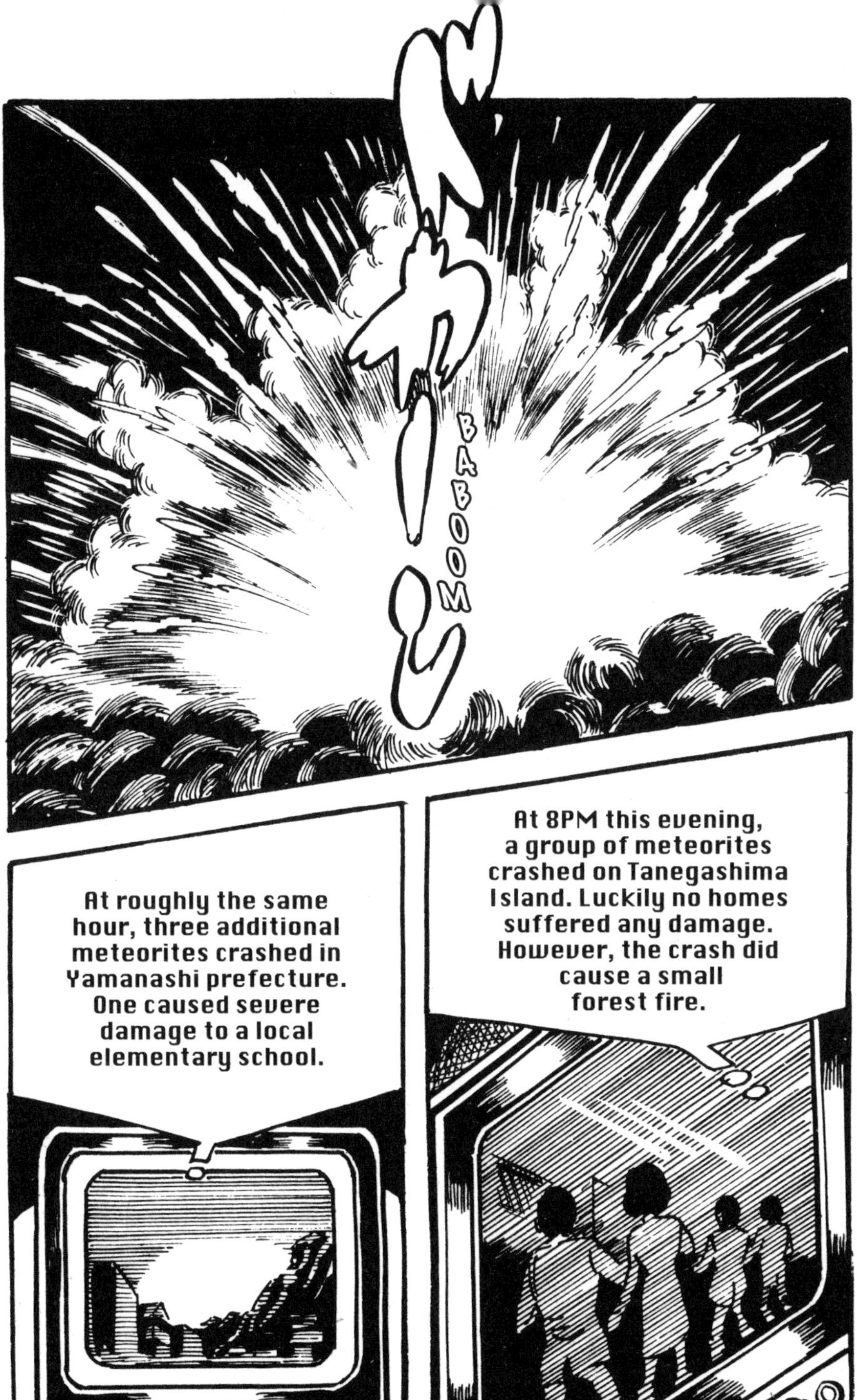
BABOOM
At 8PM this evening, a group of meteorites crashed on Tanegashima Island. Luckily no homes suffered any damage. However, the crash did cause a small forest fire.
At roughly the same hour, three additional meteorites crashed in Yamanashi prefecture. One caused severe damage to a local elementary school.

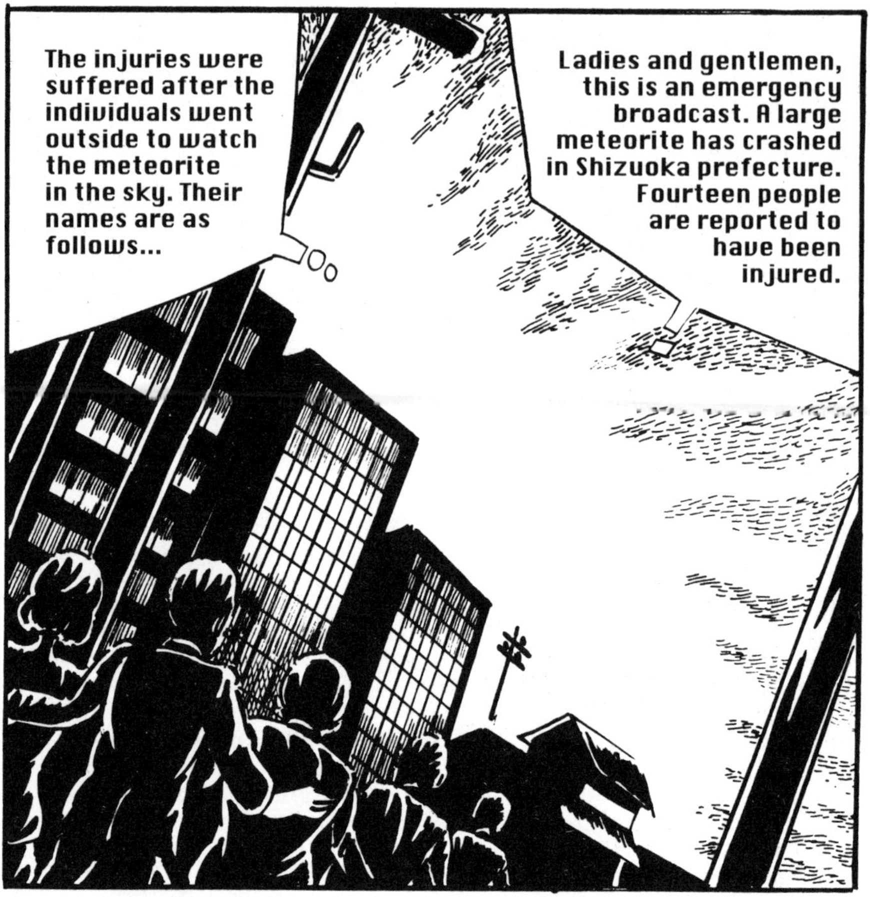
Ladies and gentlemen, this is an emergency broadcast. A large meteorite has crashed in Shizuoka prefecture. Fourteen people are reported to have been injured.
The injuries were suffered after the individuals went outside to watch the meteorite in the sky. Their names are as follows...

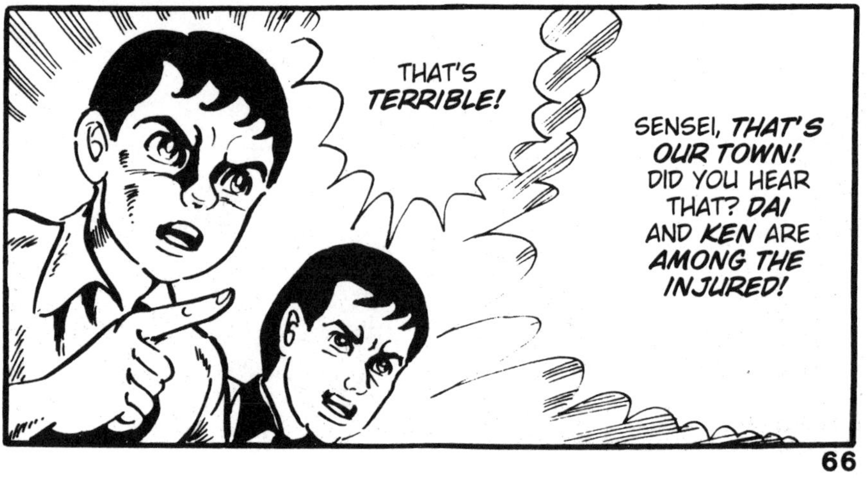
SENSEI, THAT'S OUR TOWN! DID YOU HEAR THAT? DAI AND KEN ARE AMONG THE INJURED!
THAT'S TERRIBLE!

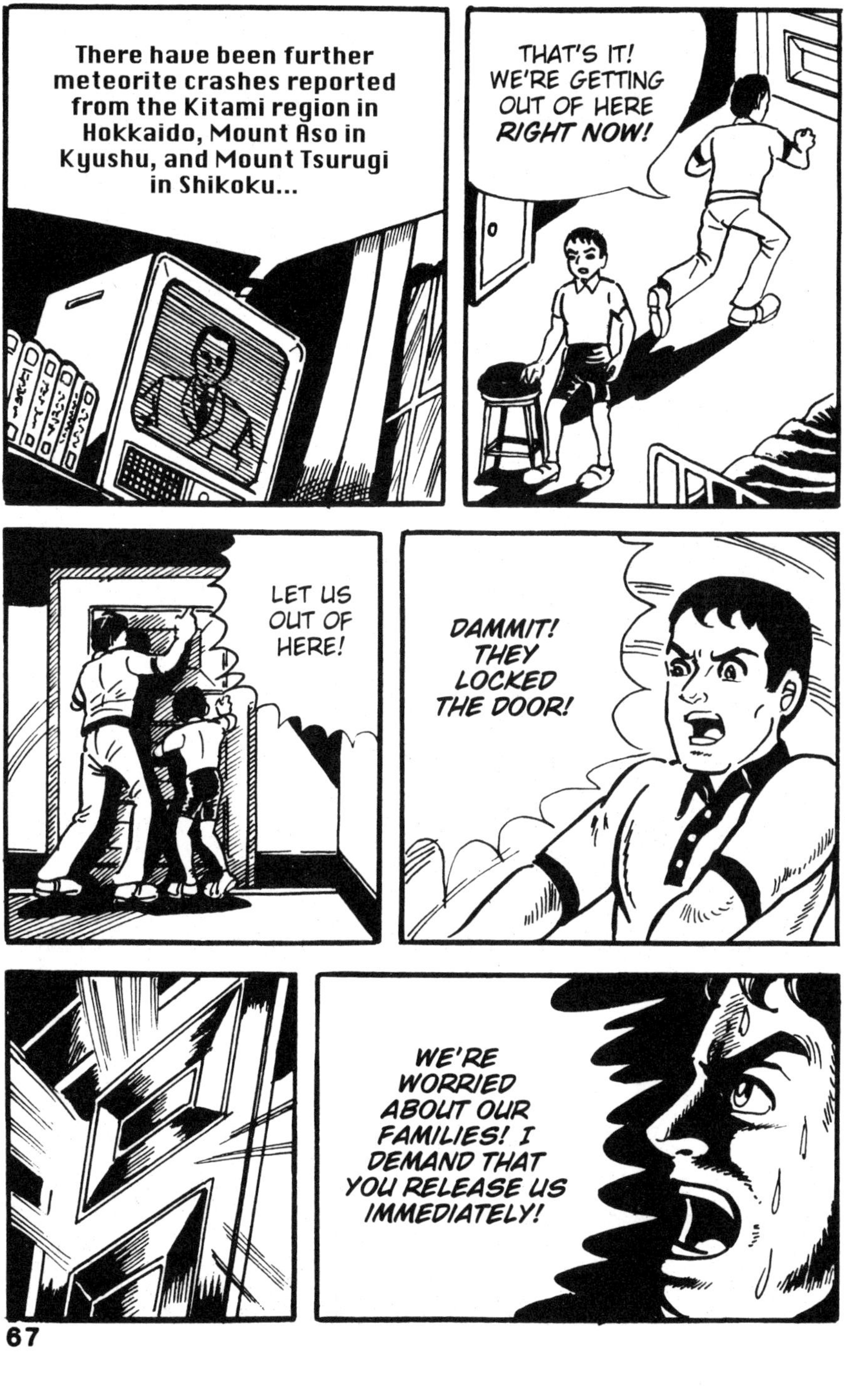
There have been further meteorite crashes reported from the Kitami region in Hokkaido, Mount Aso in Kyushu, and Mount Tsurugi in Shikoku...
THAT'S IT! WE'RE GETTING OUT OF HERE RIGHT NOW!
LET US OUT OF HERE!
DAMMIT! THEY LOCKED THE DOOR!
WE'RE WORRIED ABOUT OUR FAMILIES! I DEMAND THAT YOU RELEASE US IMMEDIATELY!

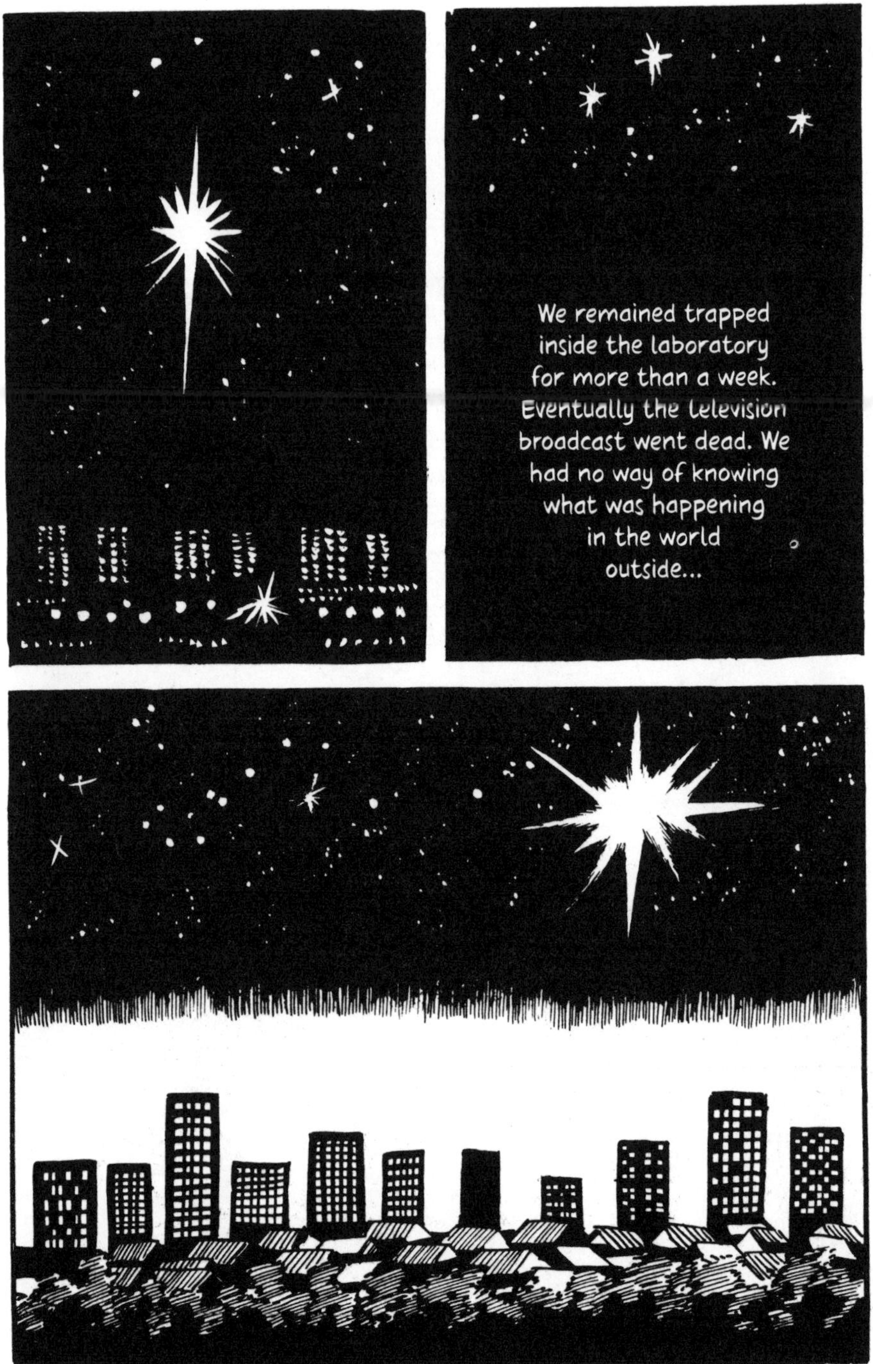
We remained trapped inside the laboratory for more than a week. Eventually the television broadcast went dead. We had no way of knowing what was happening in the world outside...

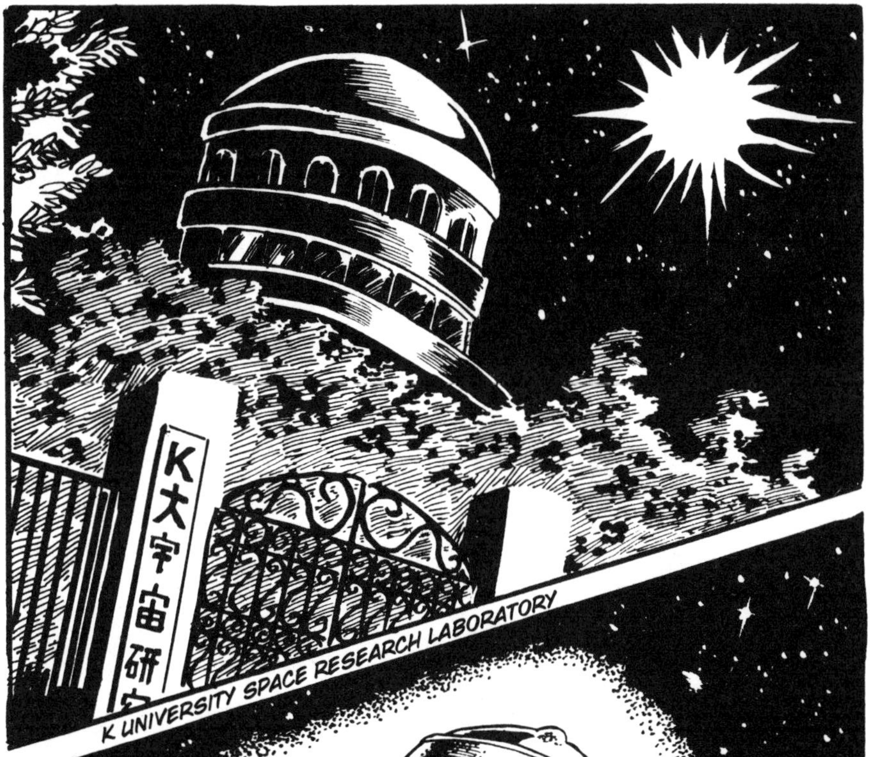
K大宇宙研究
K UNIVERSITY SPACE RESEARCH LABORATORY
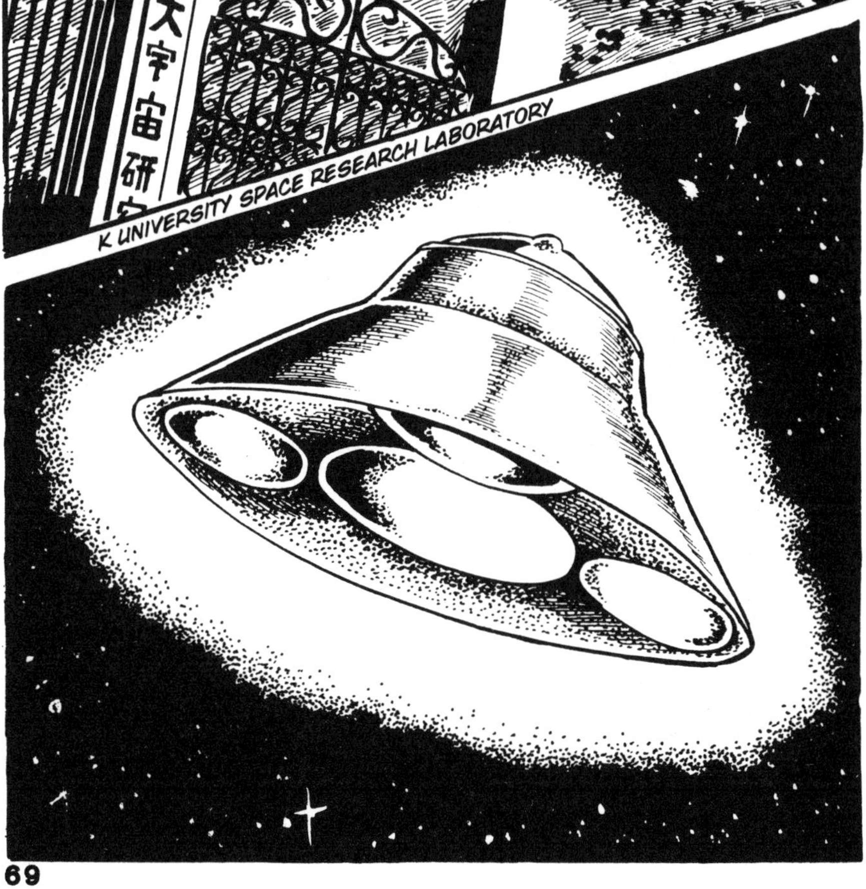

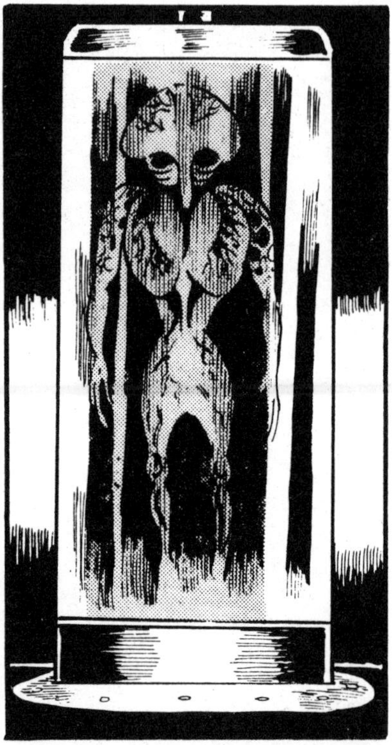
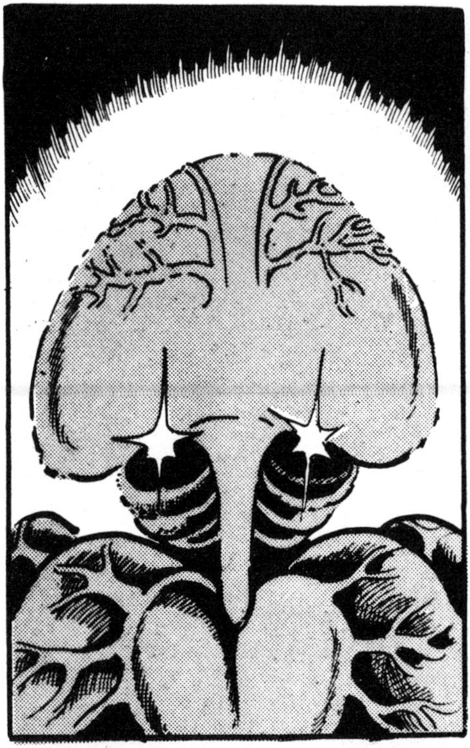
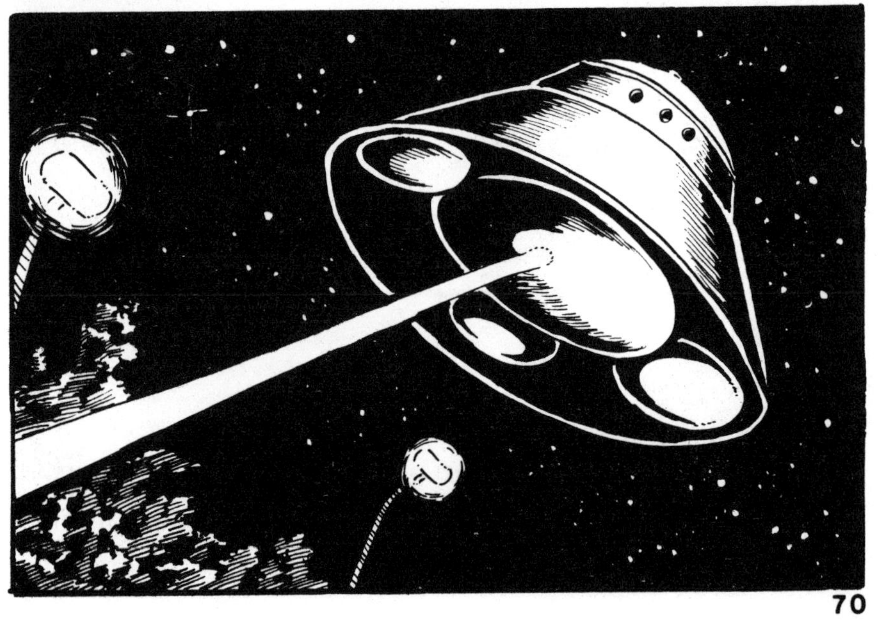

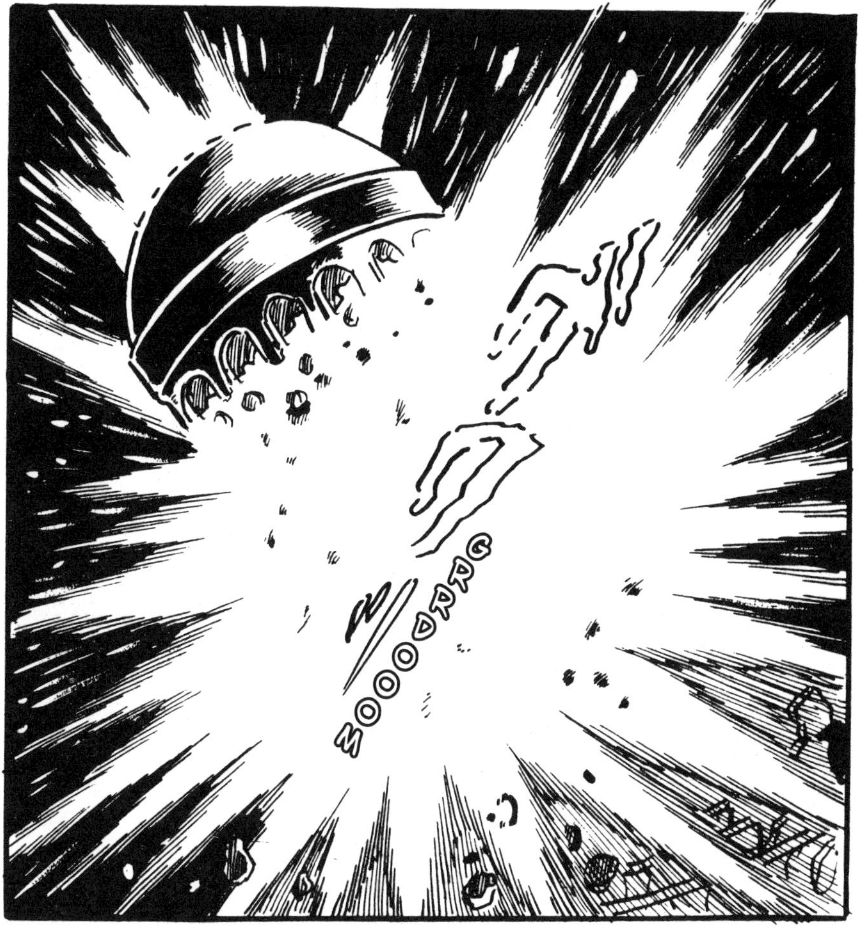
MOOODRRG

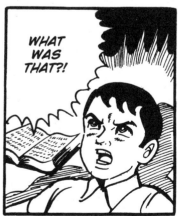

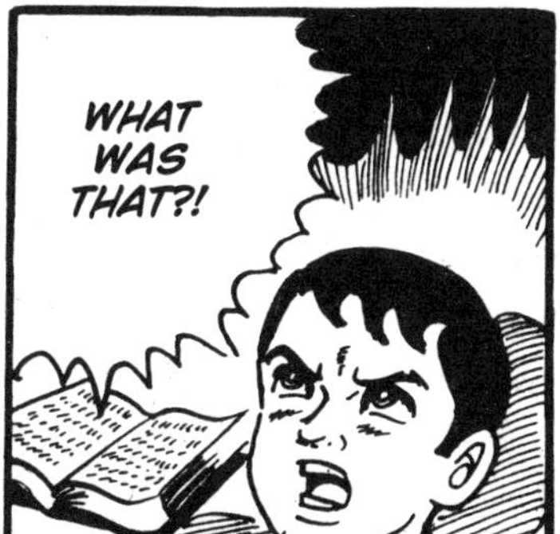
WHAT WAS THAT?!

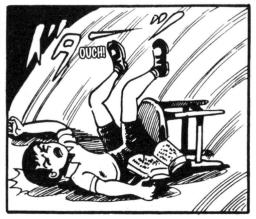

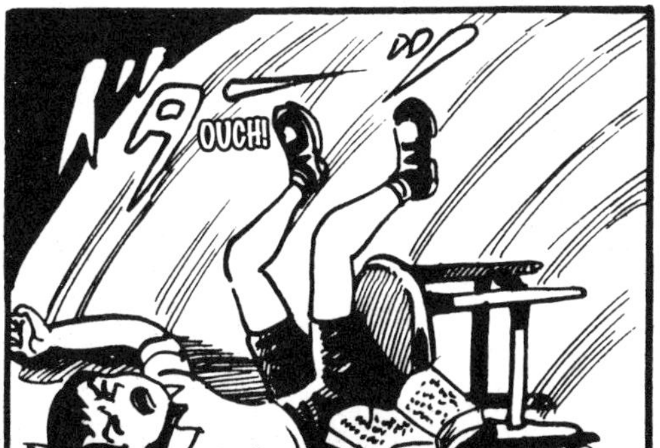
OUCH!

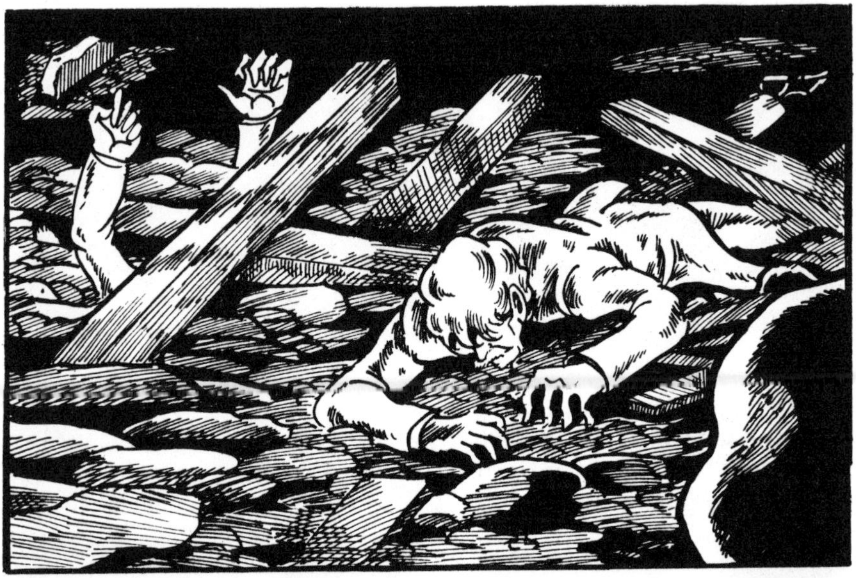
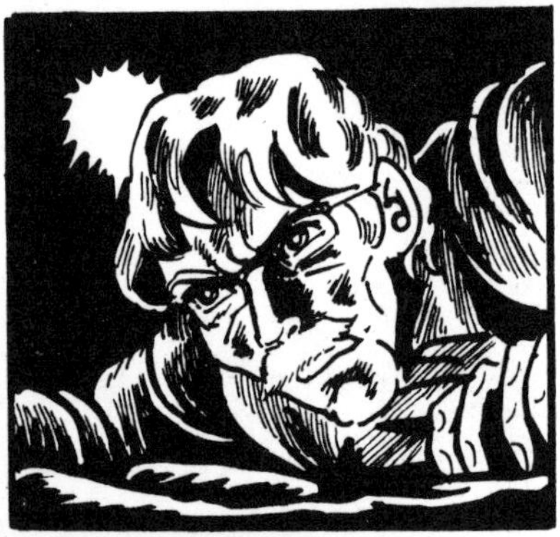
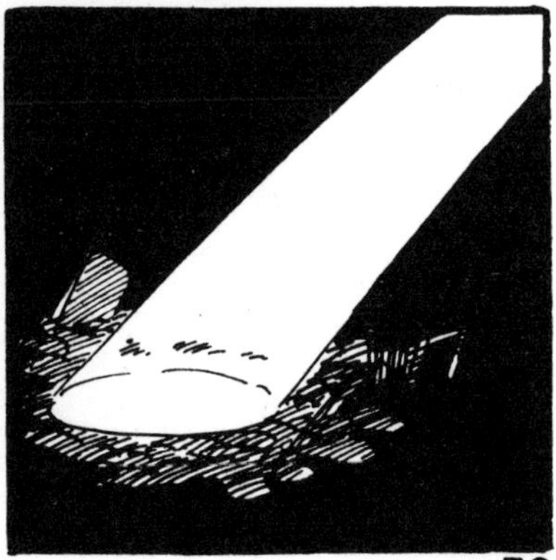
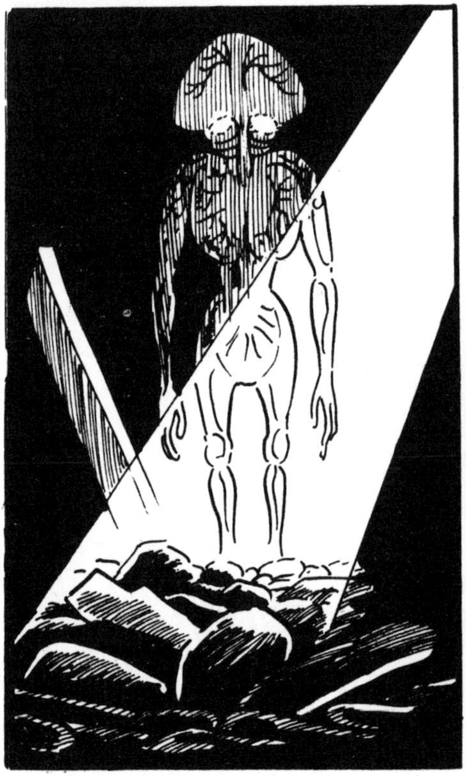

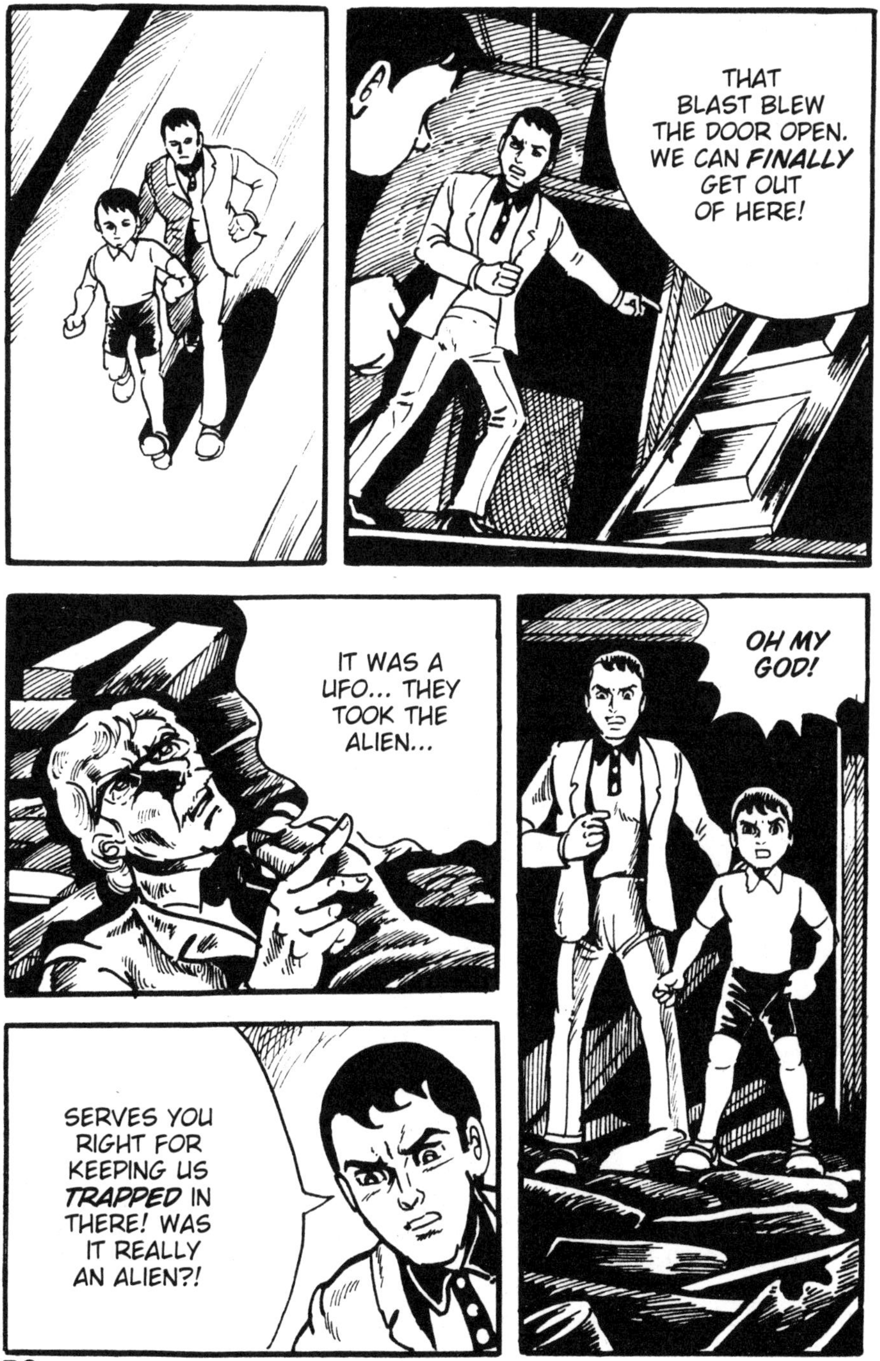
THAT BLAST BLEW THE DOOR OPEN. WE CAN *FINALLY* GET OUT OF HERE!
OH MY GOD!
IT WAS A UFO... THEY TOOK THE ALIEN...
SERVES YOU RIGHT FOR KEEPING US *TRAPPED* IN THERE! WAS IT REALLY AN ALIEN?!

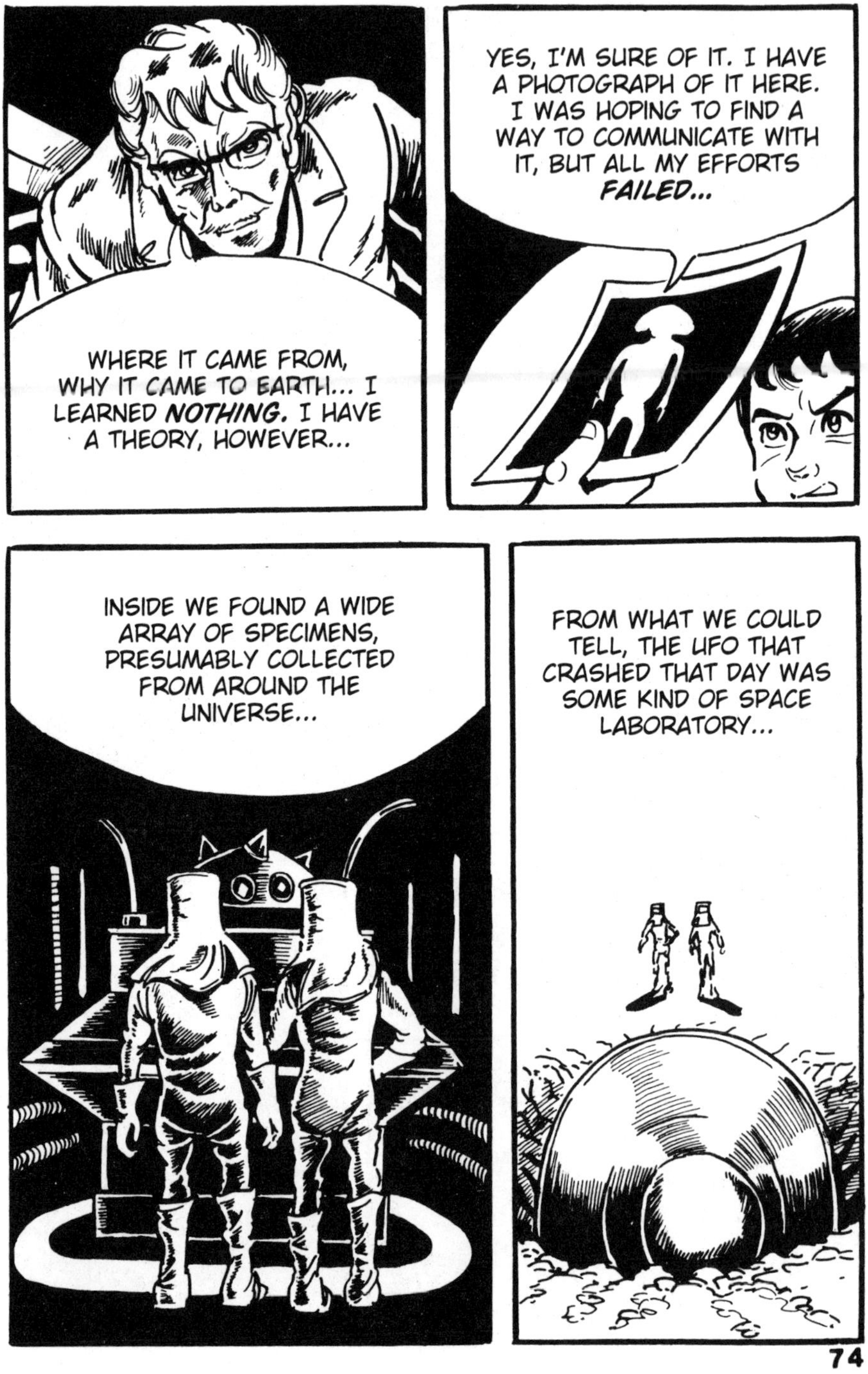
YES, I'M SURE OF IT. I HAVE A PHOTOGRAPH OF IT HERE. I WAS HOPING TO FIND A WAY TO COMMUNICATE WITH IT, BUT ALL MY EFFORTS FAILED...
WHERE IT CAME FROM, WHY IT CAME TO EARTH... I LEARNED NOTHING. I HAVE A THEORY, HOWEVER...
FROM WHAT WE COULD TELL, THE UFO THAT CRASHED THAT DAY WAS SOME KIND OF SPACE LABORATORY...
INSIDE WE FOUND A WIDE ARRAY OF SPECIMENS, PRESUMABLY COLLECTED FROM AROUND THE UNIVERSE...

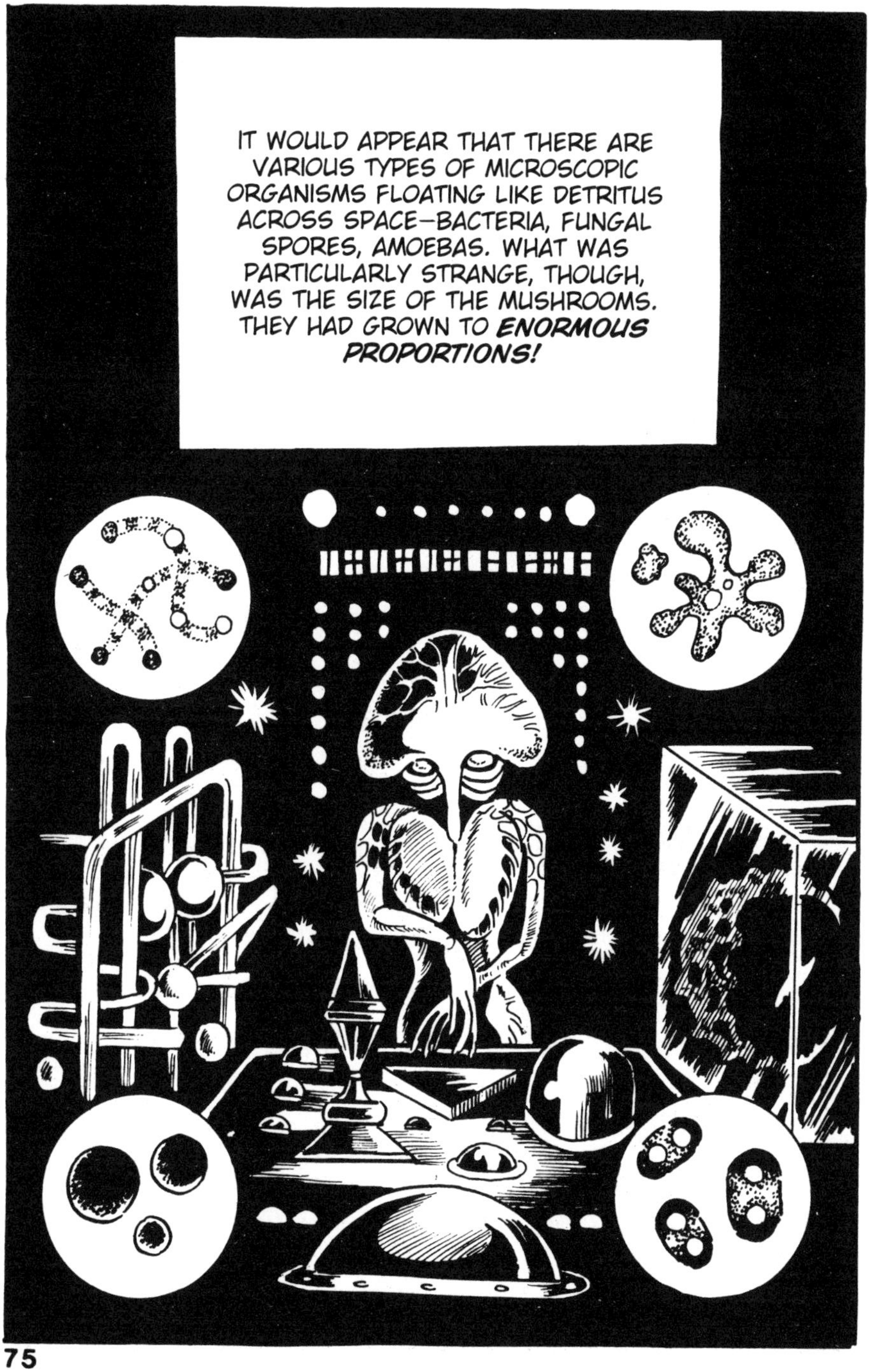
IT WOULD APPEAR THAT THERE ARE VARIOUS TYPES OF MICROSCOPIC ORGANISMS FLOATING LIKE DETRITUS ACROSS SPACE—BACTERIA, FUNGAL SPORES, AMOEBAS. WHAT WAS PARTICULARLY STRANGE, THOUGH, WAS THE SIZE OF THE MUSHROOMS. THEY HAD GROWN TO ***ENORMOUS PROPORTIONS!***

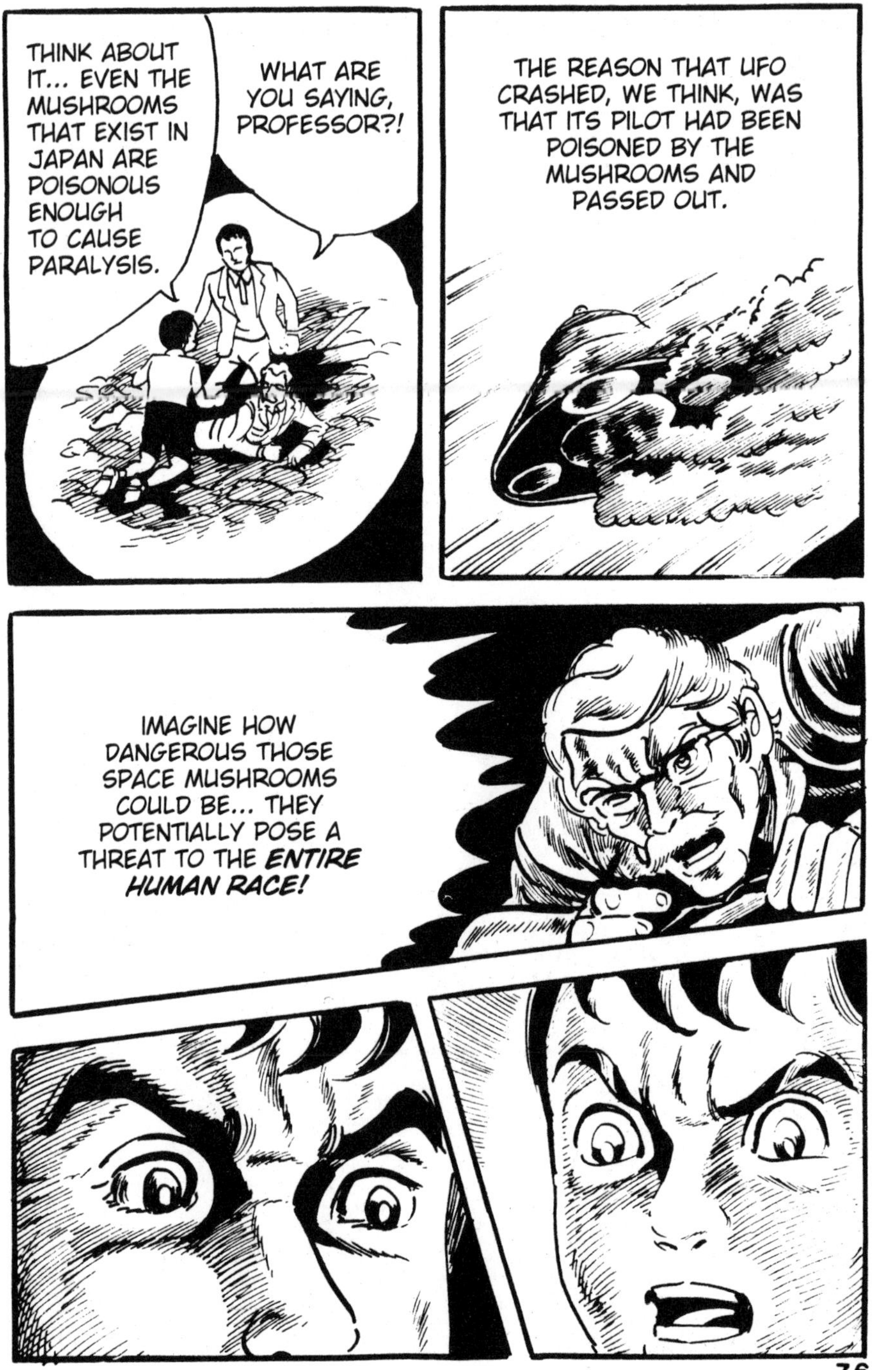
THINK ABOUT IT... EVEN THE MUSHROOMS THAT EXIST IN JAPAN ARE POISONOUS ENOUGH TO CAUSE PARALYSIS.
WHAT ARE YOU SAYING, PROFESSOR?!
THE REASON THAT UFO CRASHED, WE THINK, WAS THAT ITS PILOT HAD BEEN POISONED BY THE MUSHROOMS AND PASSED OUT.
IMAGINE HOW DANGEROUS THOSE SPACE MUSHROOMS COULD BE... THEY POTENTIALLY POSE A THREAT TO THE *ENTIRE HUMAN RACE!*

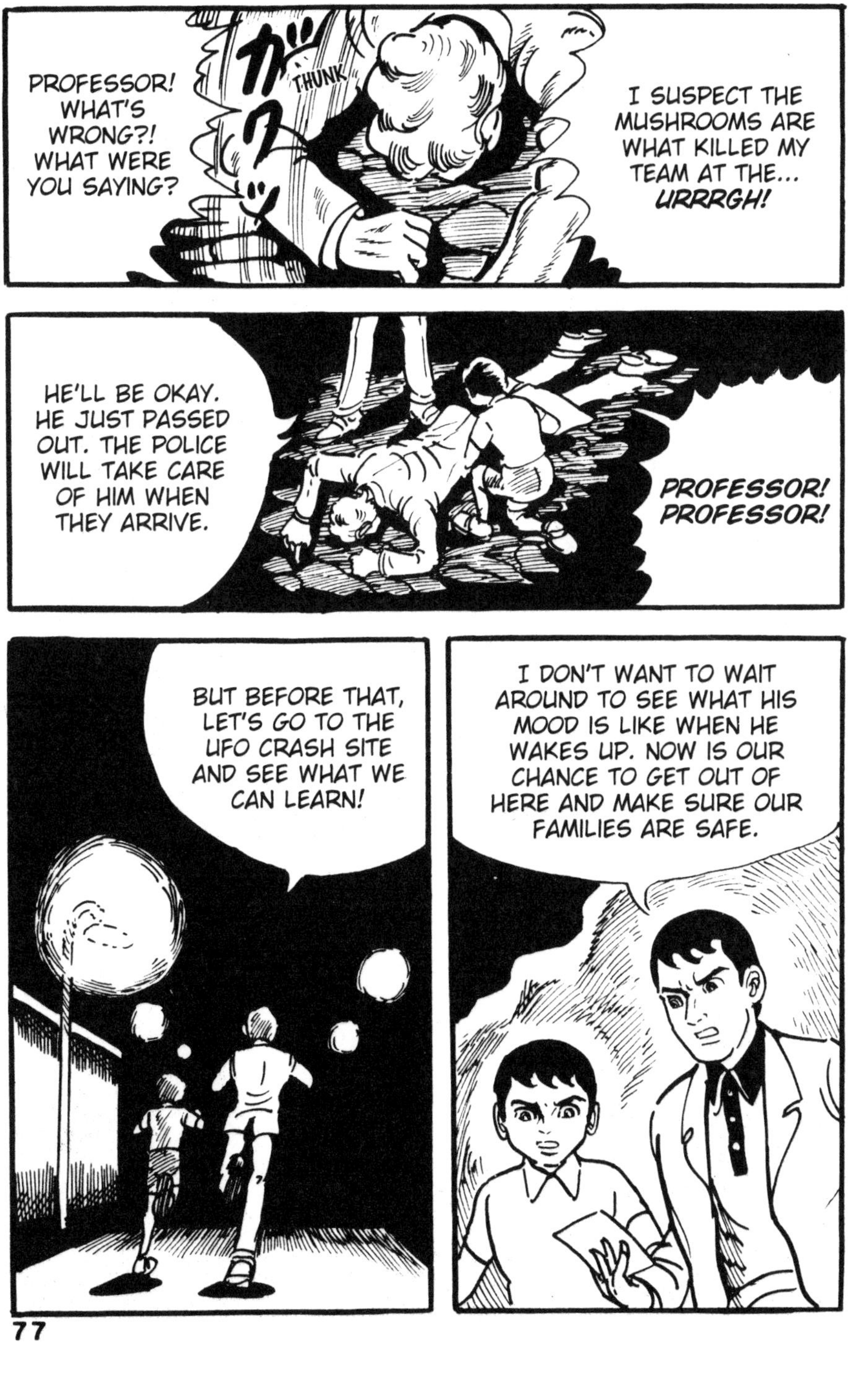
I SUSPECT THE MUSHROOMS ARE WHAT KILLED MY TEAM AT THE... *URRRGH!*
THUNK
PROFESSOR! WHAT'S WRONG?! WHAT WERE YOU SAYING?
PROFESSOR! PROFESSOR!
HE'LL BE OKAY. HE JUST PASSED OUT. THE POLICE WILL TAKE CARE OF HIM WHEN THEY ARRIVE.
I DON'T WANT TO WAIT AROUND TO SEE WHAT HIS MOOD IS LIKE WHEN HE WAKES UP. NOW IS OUR CHANCE TO GET OUT OF HERE AND MAKE SURE OUR FAMILIES ARE SAFE.
BUT BEFORE THAT, LET'S GO TO THE UFO CRASH SITE AND SEE WHAT WE CAN LEARN!

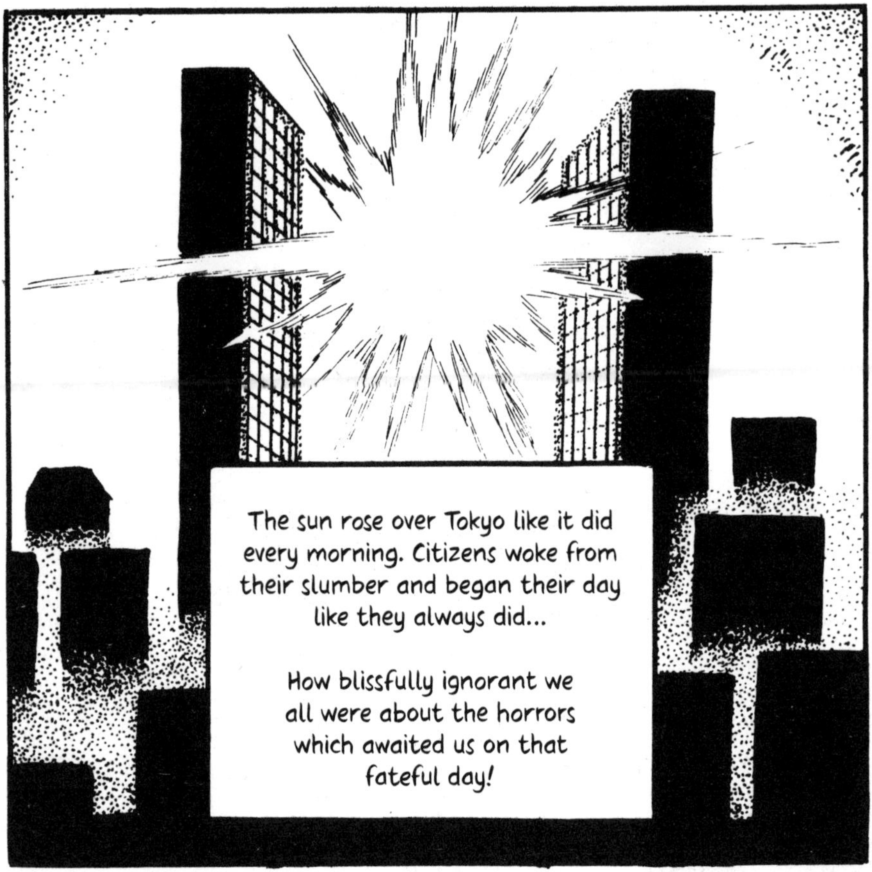
The sun rose over Tokyo like it did every morning. Citizens woke from their slumber and began their day like they always did...
How blissfully ignorant we all were about the horrors which awaited us on that fateful day!
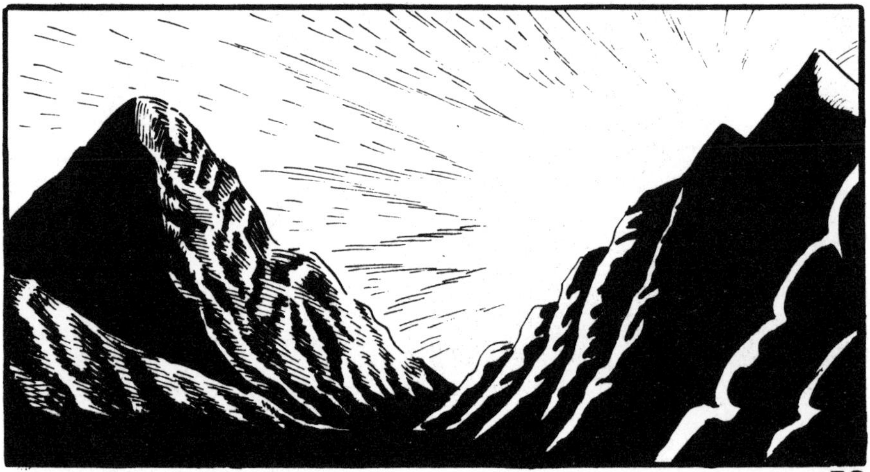

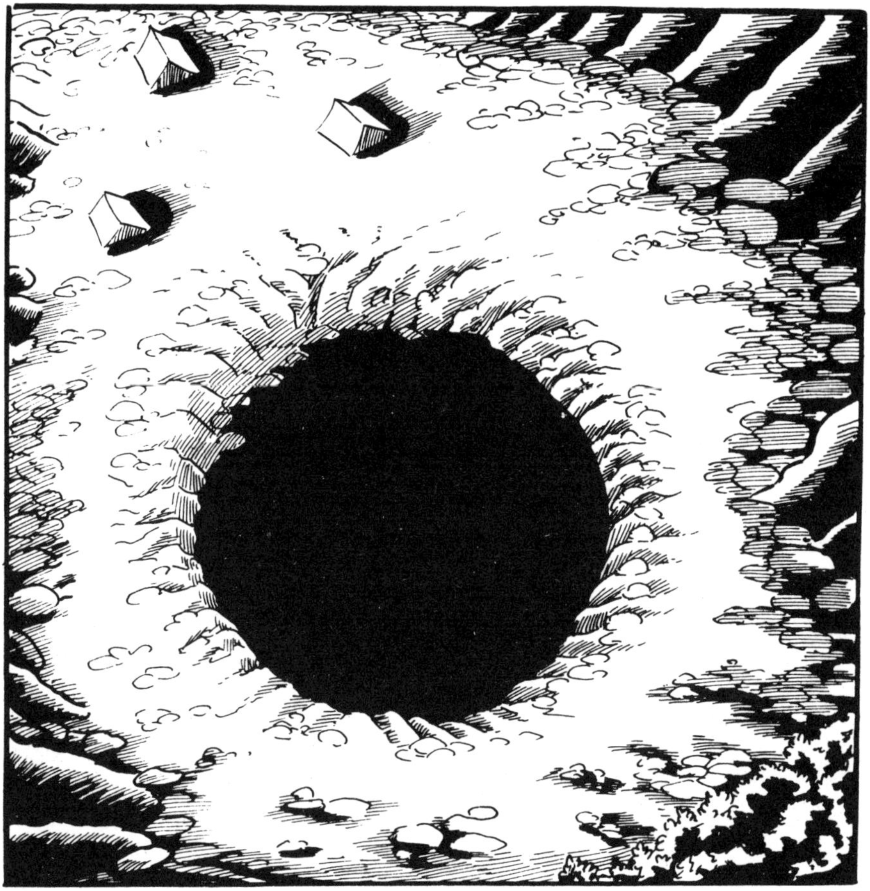

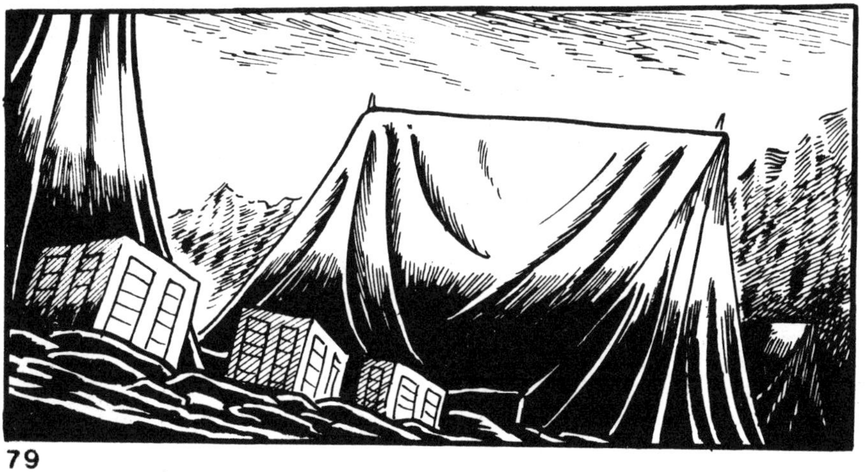

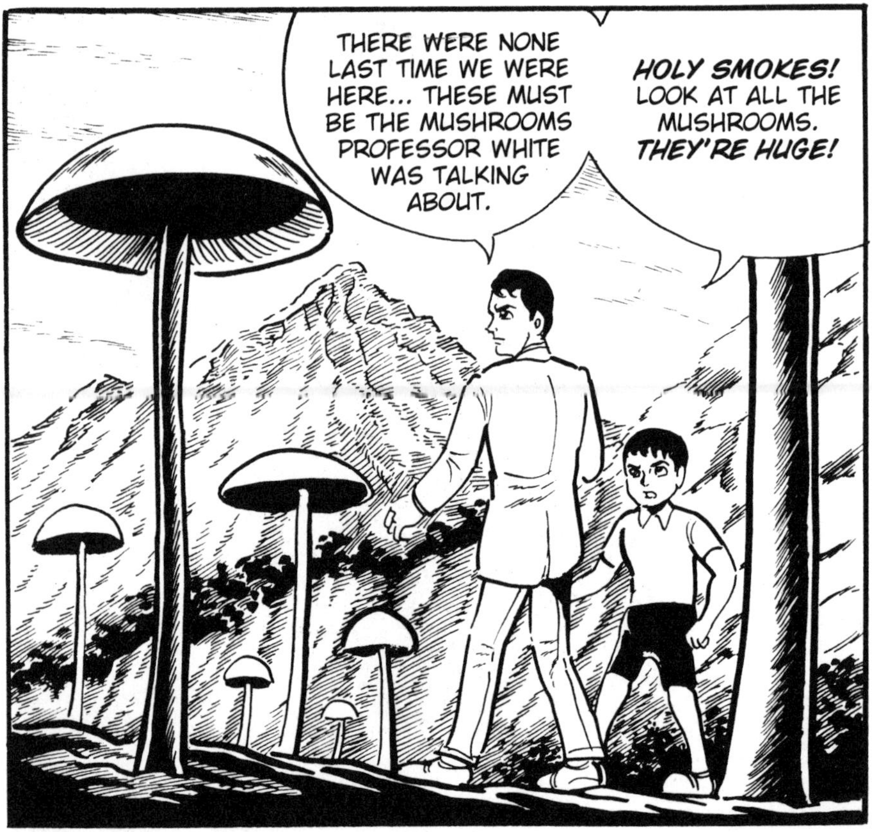
HOLY SMOKES! LOOK AT ALL THE MUSHROOMS. THEY'RE HUGE!
THERE WERE NONE LAST TIME WE WERE HERE... THESE MUST BE THE MUSHROOMS PROFESSOR WHITE WAS TALKING ABOUT.

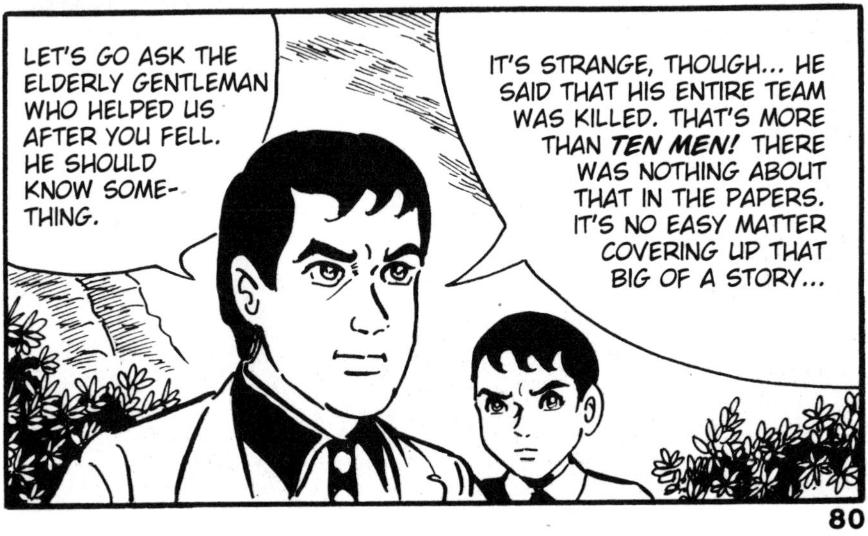
IT'S STRANGE, THOUGH... HE SAID THAT HIS ENTIRE TEAM WAS KILLED. THAT'S MORE THAN TEN MEN! THERE WAS NOTHING ABOUT THAT IN THE PAPERS. IT'S NO EASY MATTER COVERING UP THAT BIG OF A STORY...
LET'S GO ASK THE ELDERLY GENTLEMAN WHO HELPED US AFTER YOU FELL. HE SHOULD KNOW SOME-THING.

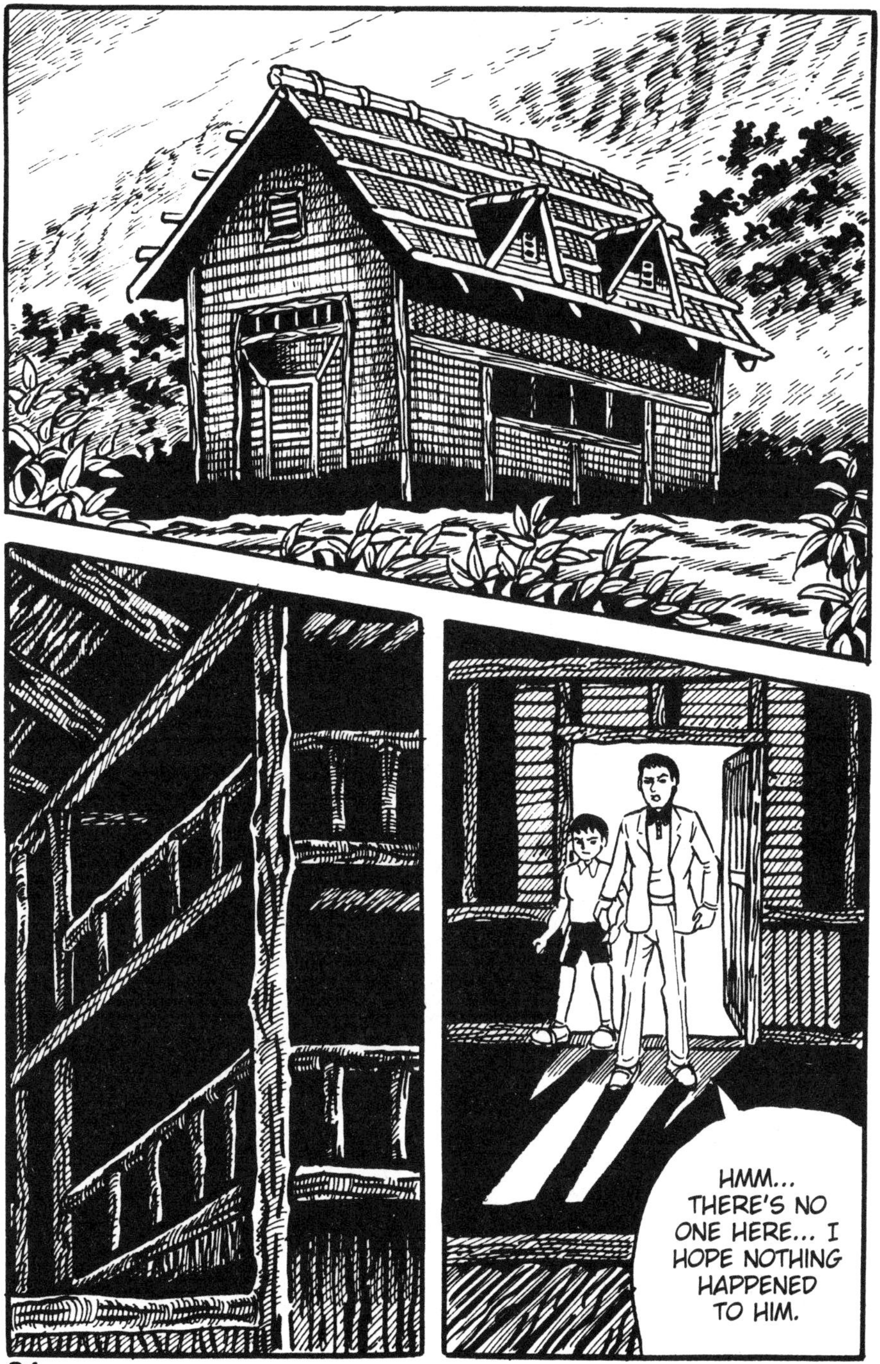
HMM... THERE'S NO ONE HERE... I HOPE NOTHING HAPPENED TO HIM.

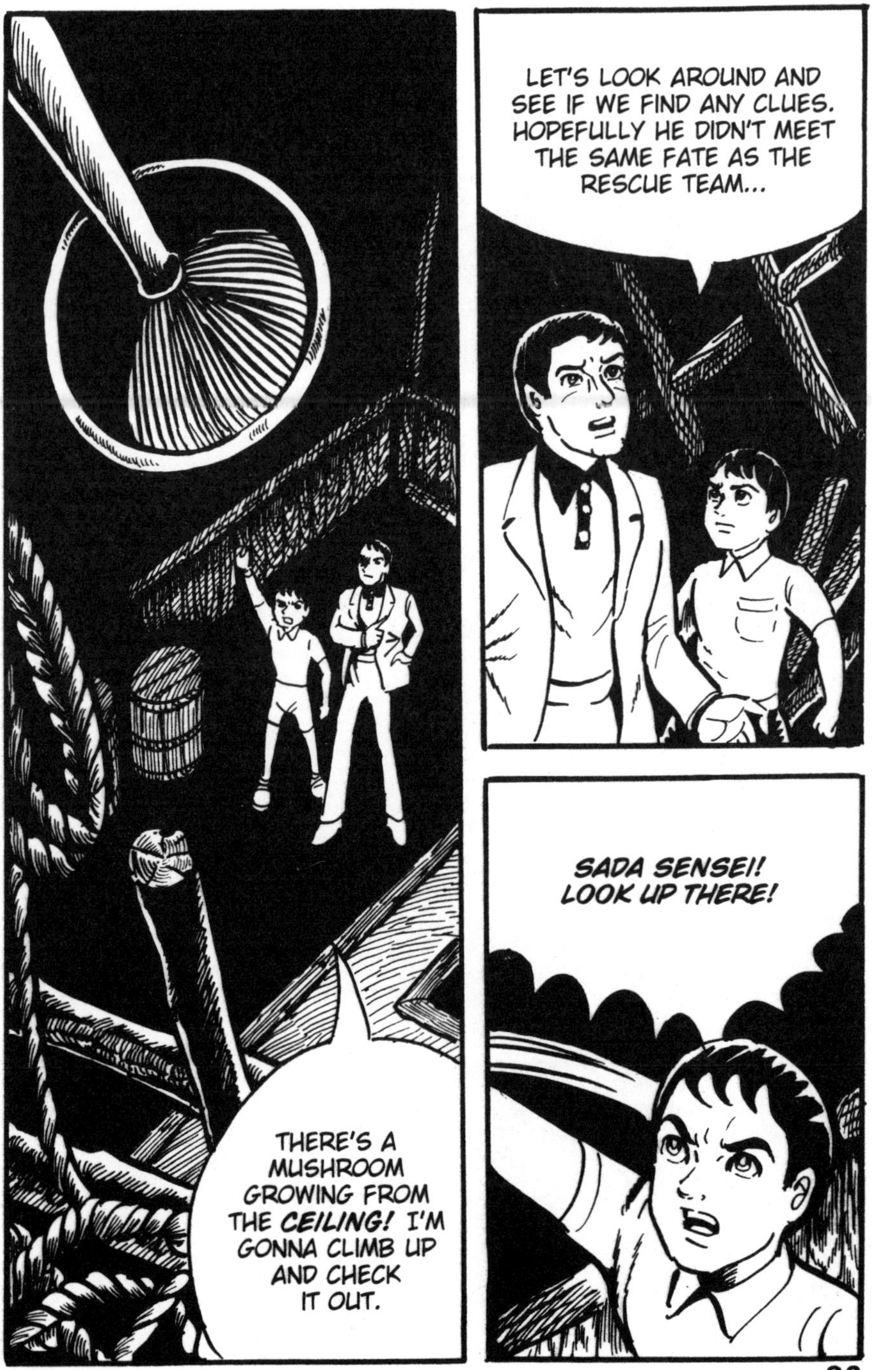
LET'S LOOK AROUND AND SEE IF WE FIND ANY CLUES. HOPEFULLY HE DIDN'T MEET THE SAME FATE AS THE RESCUE TEAM...
SADA SENSEI! LOOK UP THERE!
THERE'S A MUSHROOM GROWING FROM THE CEILING! I'M GONNA CLIMB UP AND CHECK IT OUT.

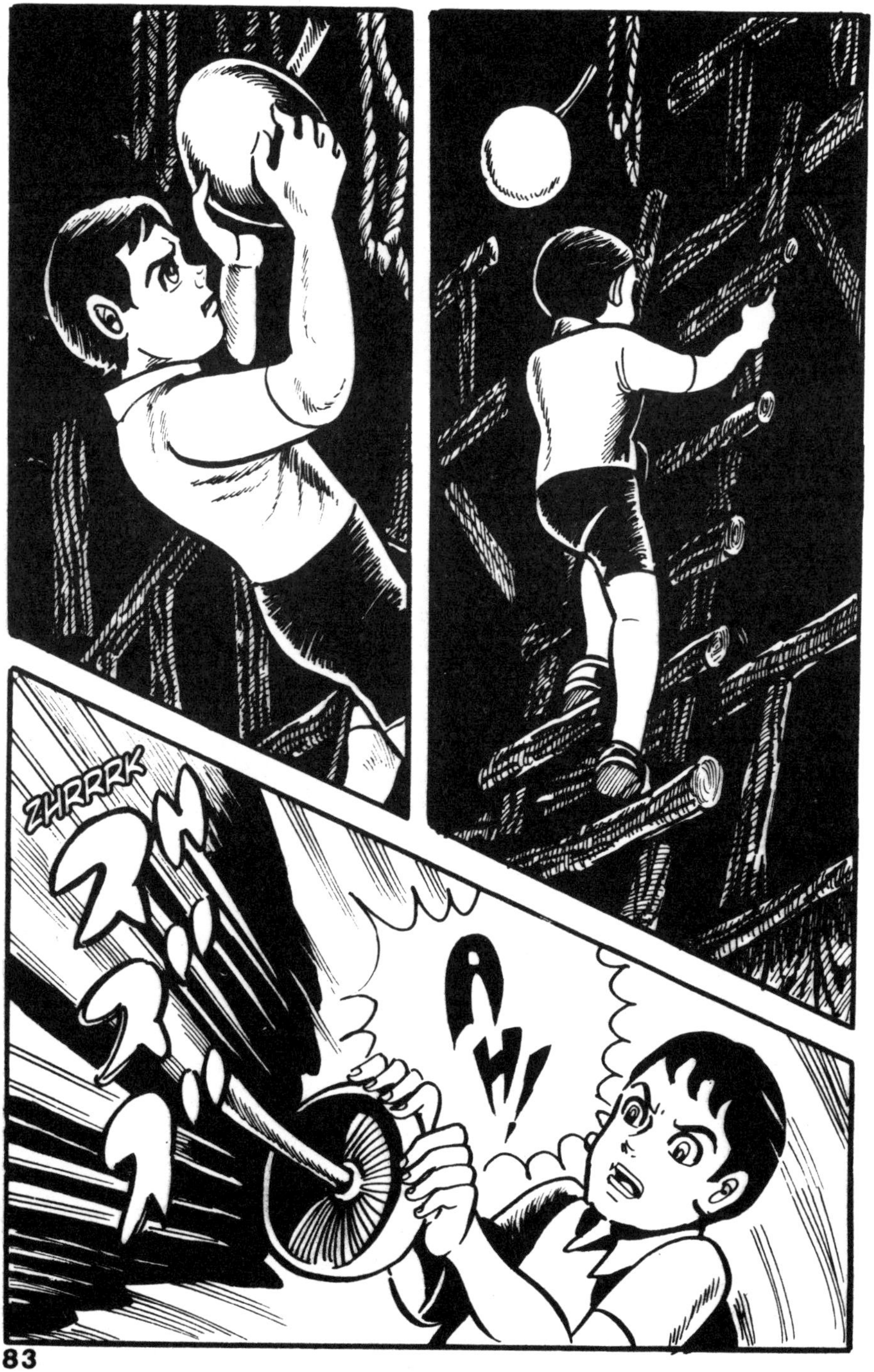
ZHRRRK
AH!

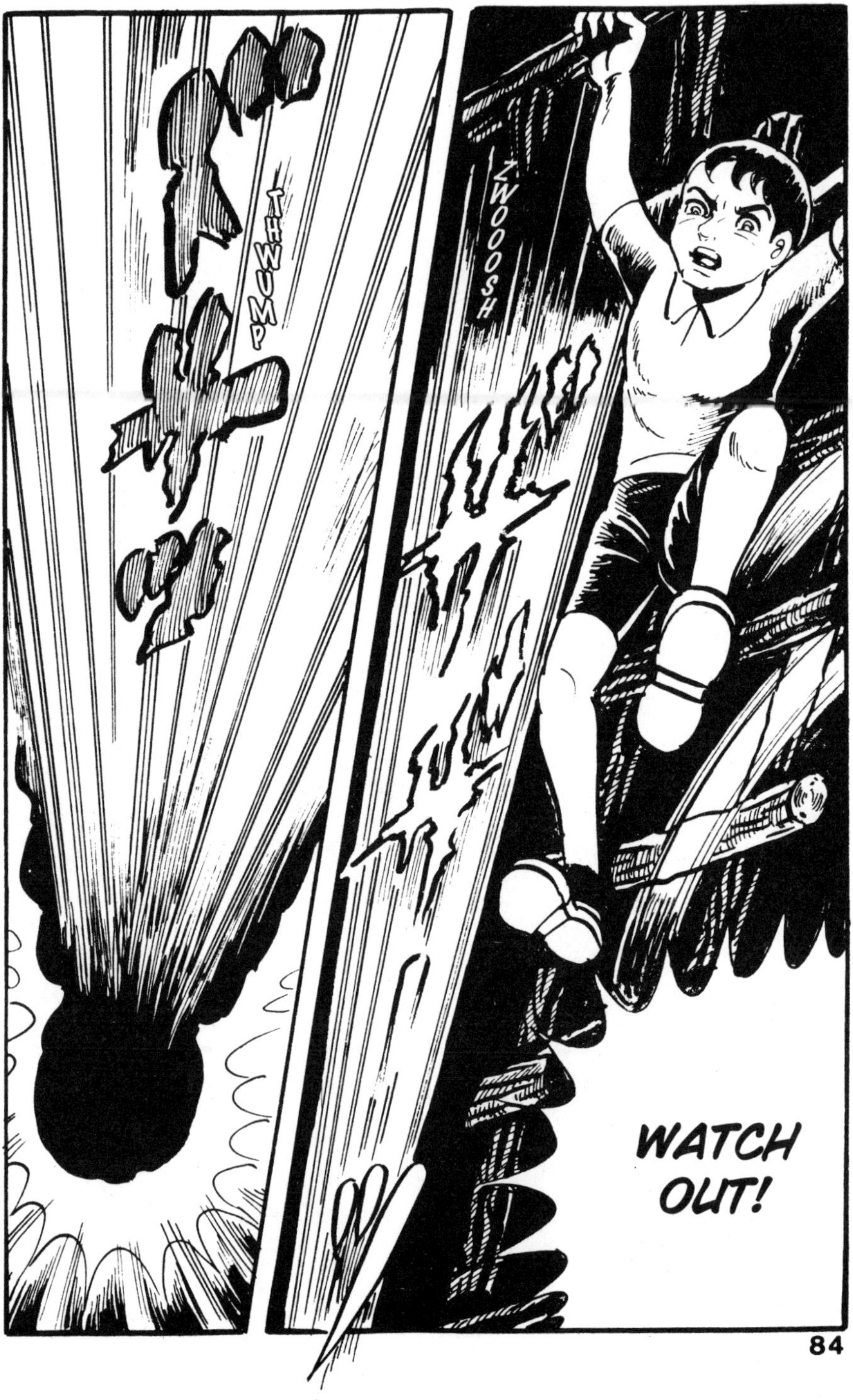
ZWOOOSH
WATCH OUT!
THWUMP

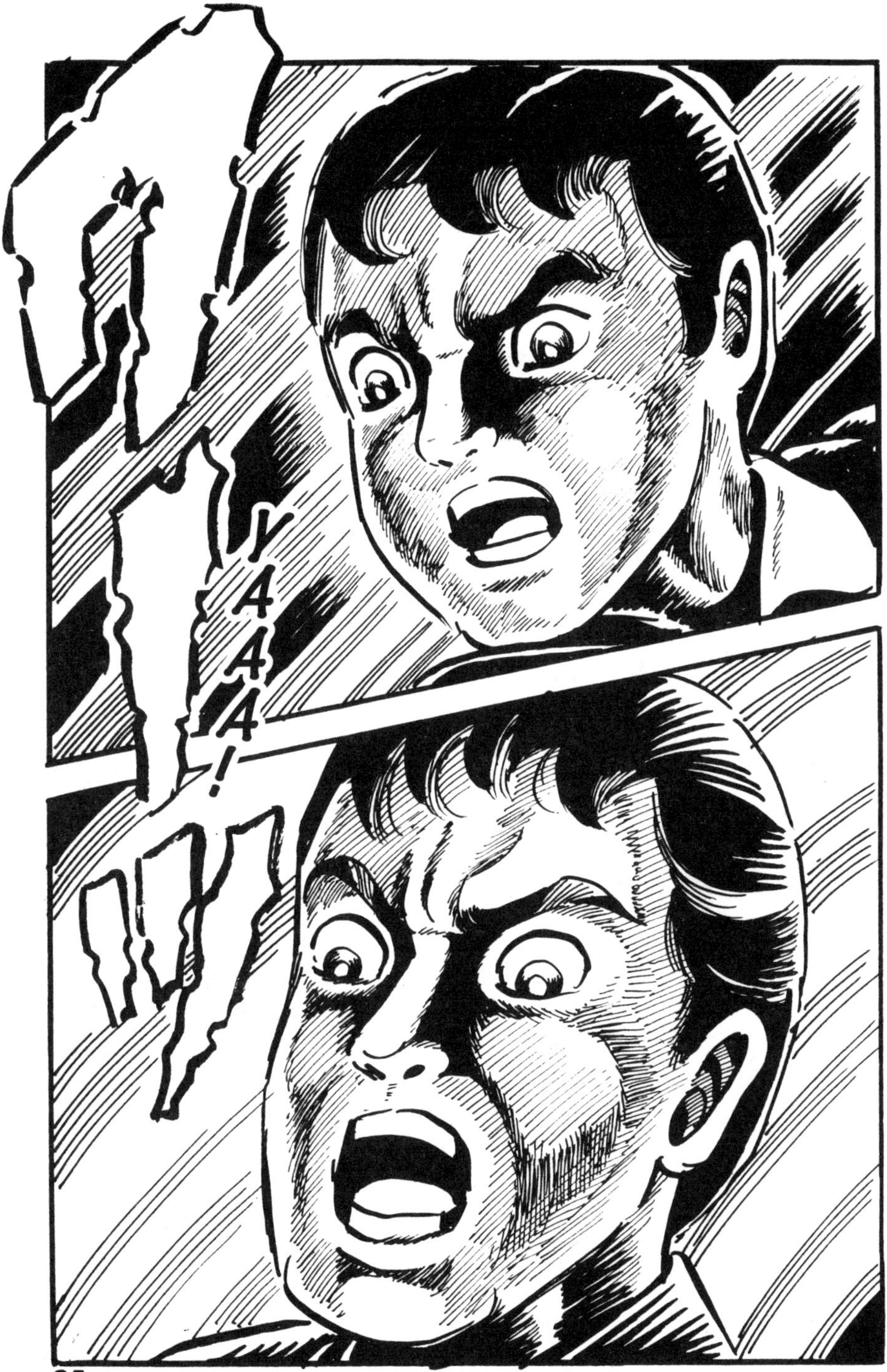
YAAAA!!

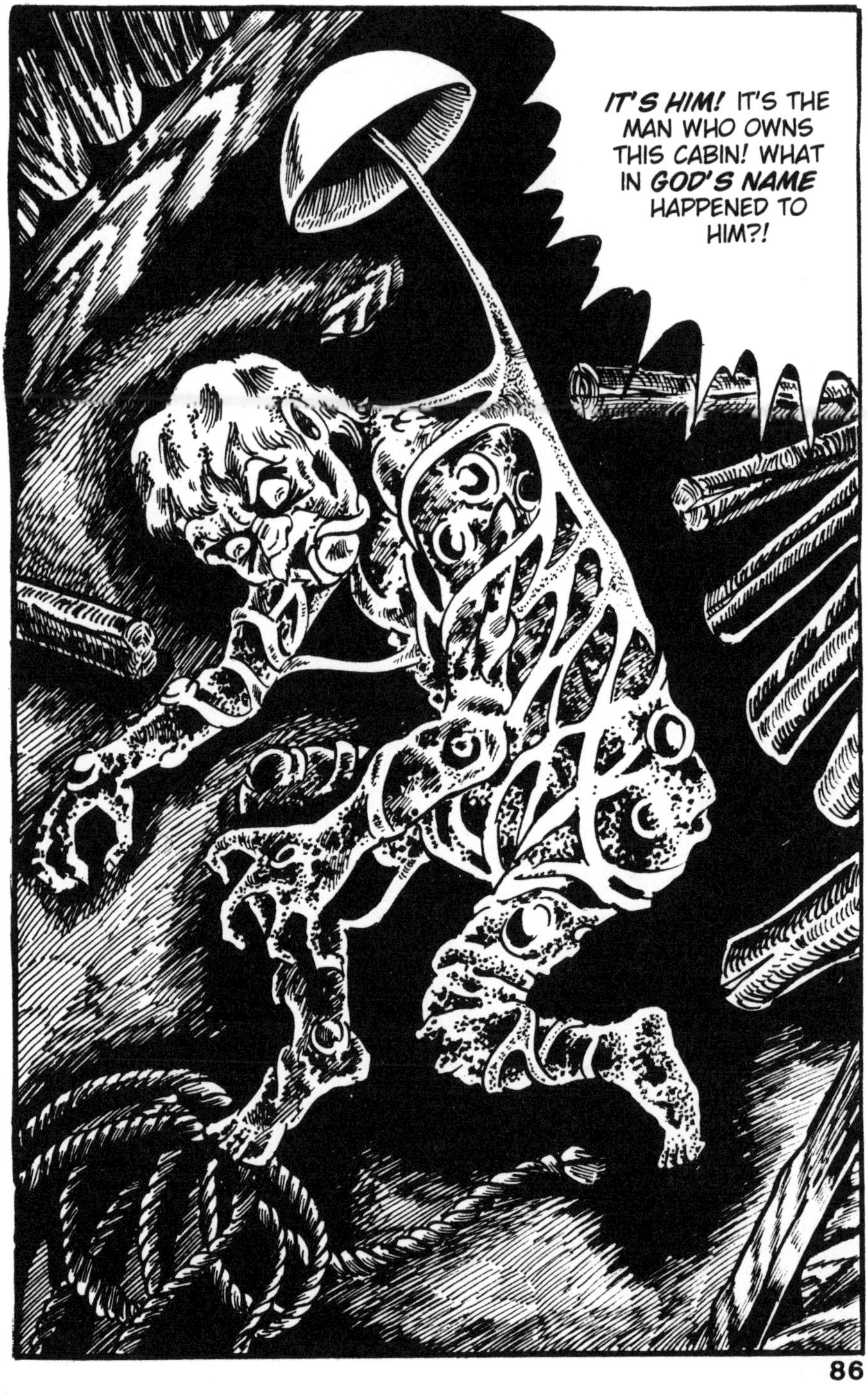
IT'S HIM! IT'S THE MAN WHO OWNS THIS CABIN! WHAT IN ***GOD'S NAME*** HAPPENED TO HIM?!

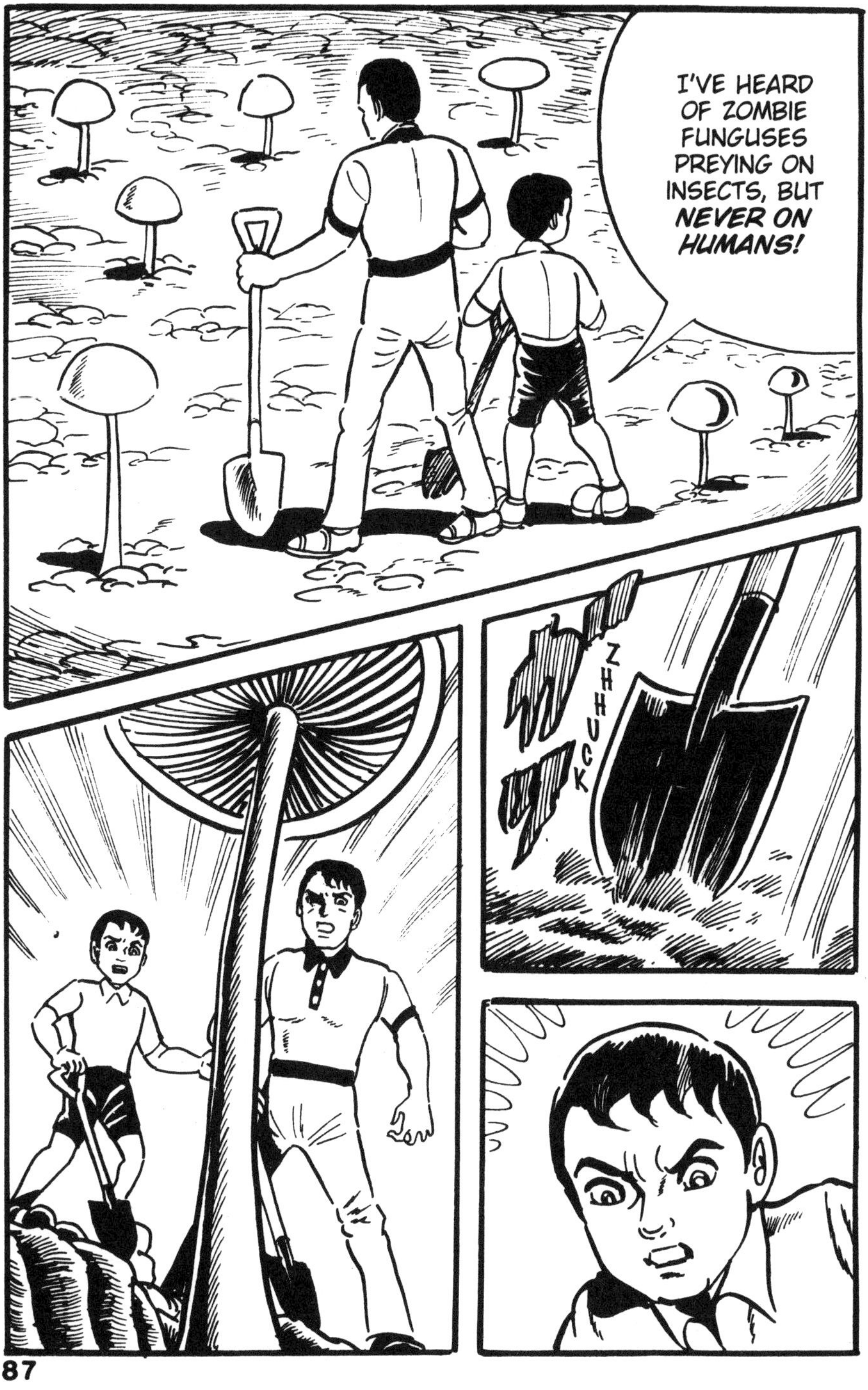
I'VE HEARD OF ZOMBIE FUNGUSES PREYING ON INSECTS, BUT ***NEVER ON HUMANS!***
ZHHUCK

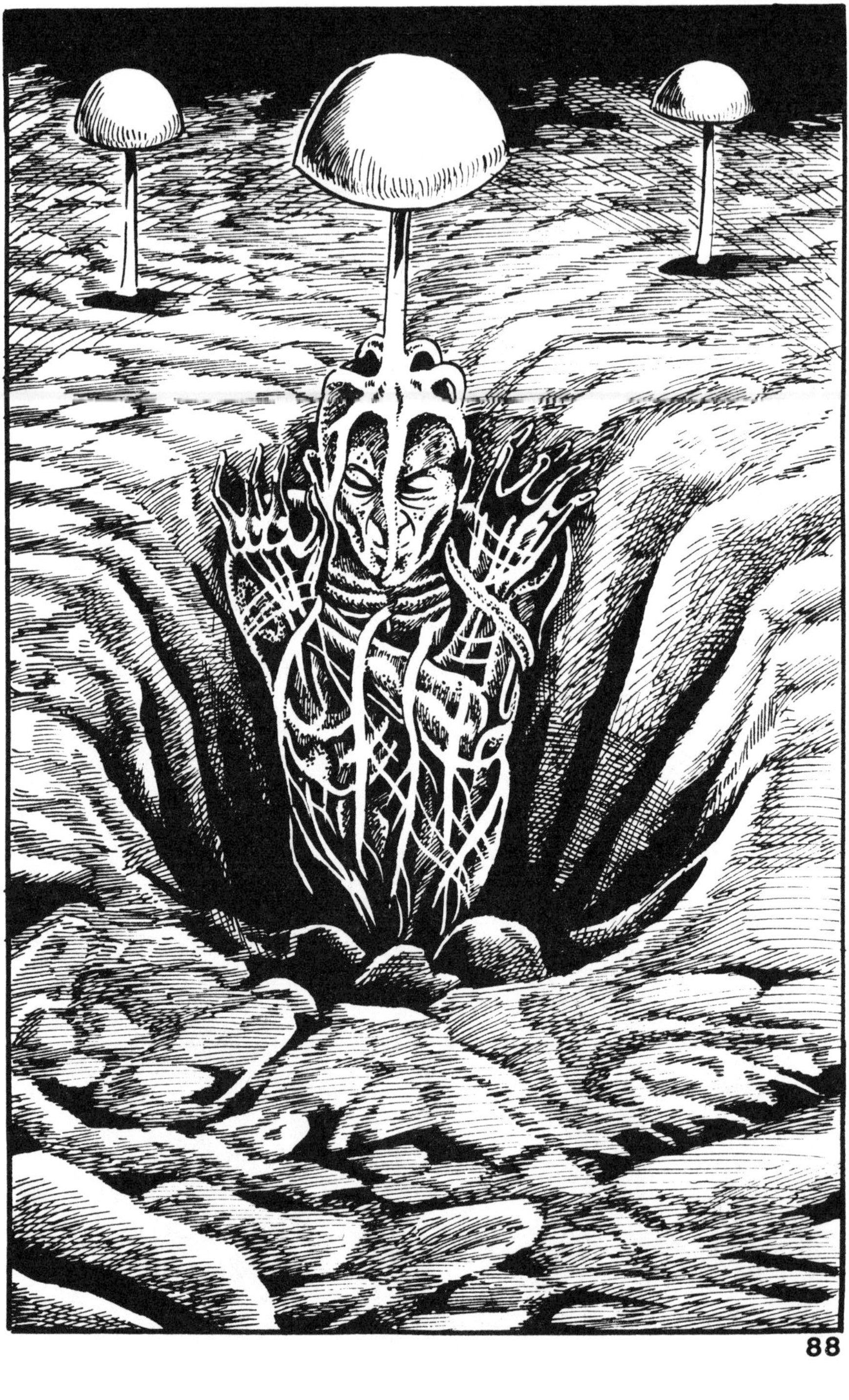

LOOK OVER HERE, SENSEI. THERE'S MUSHROOMS GROWING OUT OF A TOAD, A RABBIT, AND *EVEN A SNAKE!*

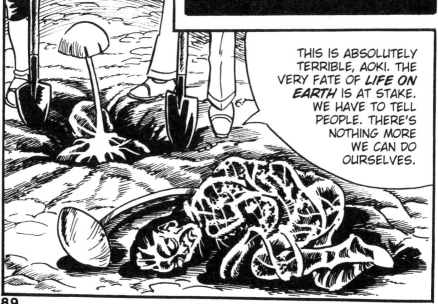

THIS IS ABSOLUTELY TERRIBLE, AOKI. THE VERY FATE OF *LIFE ON EARTH* IS AT STAKE. WE HAVE TO TELL PEOPLE. THERE'S NOTHING MORE WE CAN DO OURSELVES.

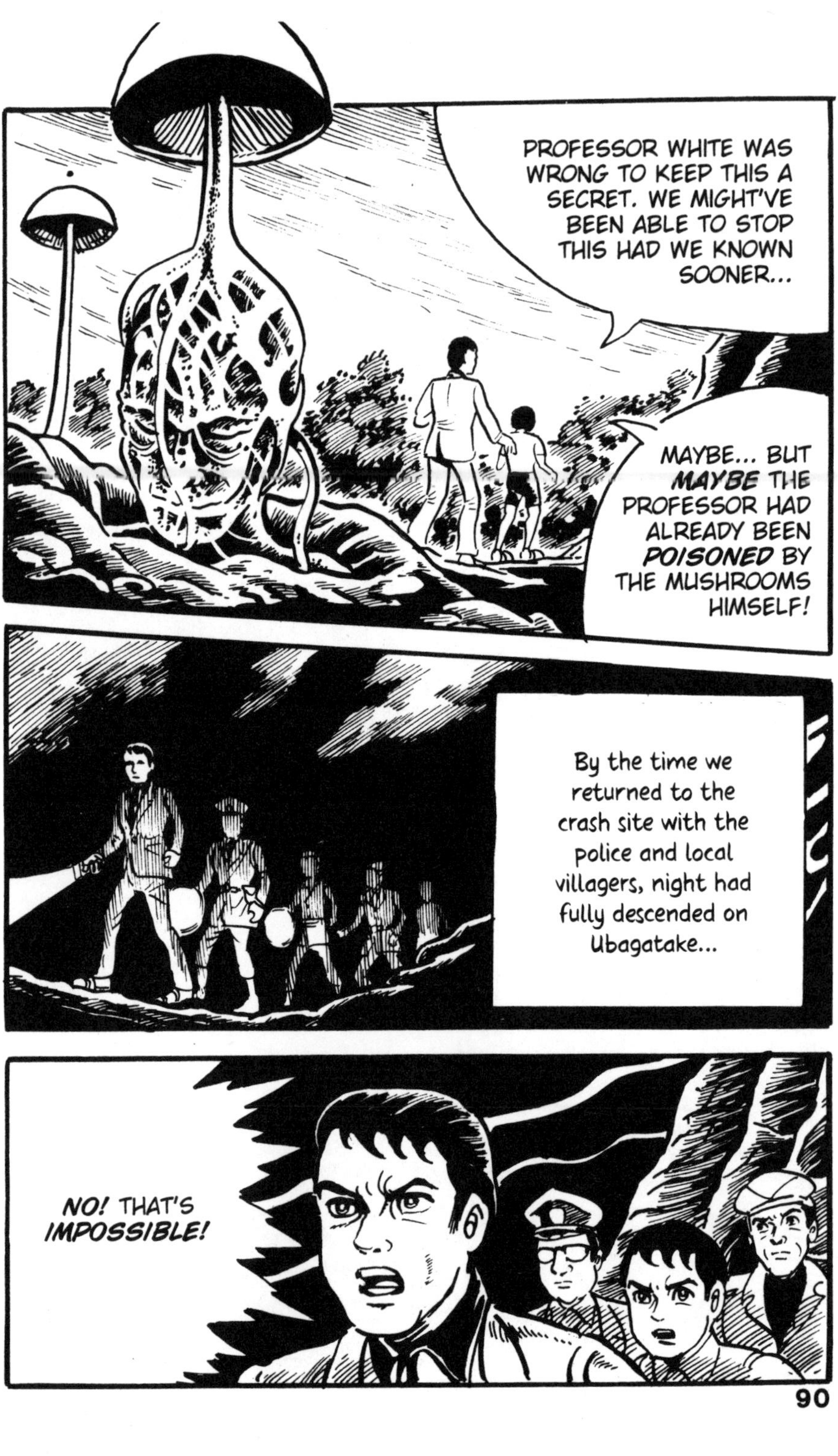
PROFESSOR WHITE WAS WRONG TO KEEP THIS A SECRET. WE MIGHT'VE BEEN ABLE TO STOP THIS HAD WE KNOWN SOONER...
MAYBE... BUT MAYBE THE PROFESSOR HAD ALREADY BEEN POISONED BY THE MUSHROOMS HIMSELF!
By the time we returned to the crash site with the police and local villagers, night had fully descended on Ubagatake...
NO! THAT'S IMPOSSIBLE!

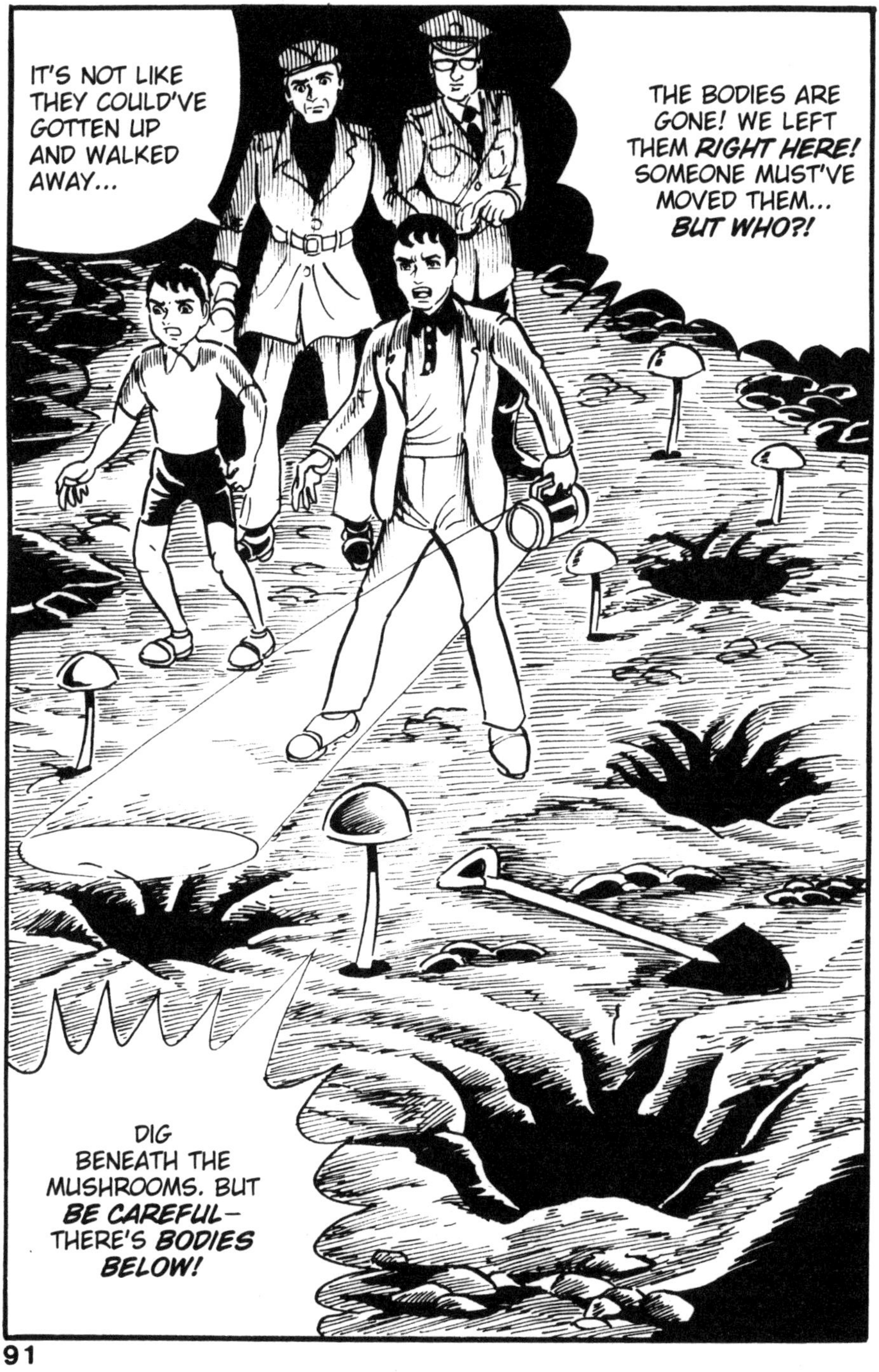
THE BODIES ARE GONE! WE LEFT THEM ***RIGHT HERE!*** SOMEONE MUST'VE MOVED THEM... ***BUT WHO?!***
IT'S NOT LIKE THEY COULD'VE GOTTEN UP AND WALKED AWAY...
DIG BENEATH THE MUSHROOMS. BUT ***BE CAREFUL***— THERE'S ***BODIES BELOW!***

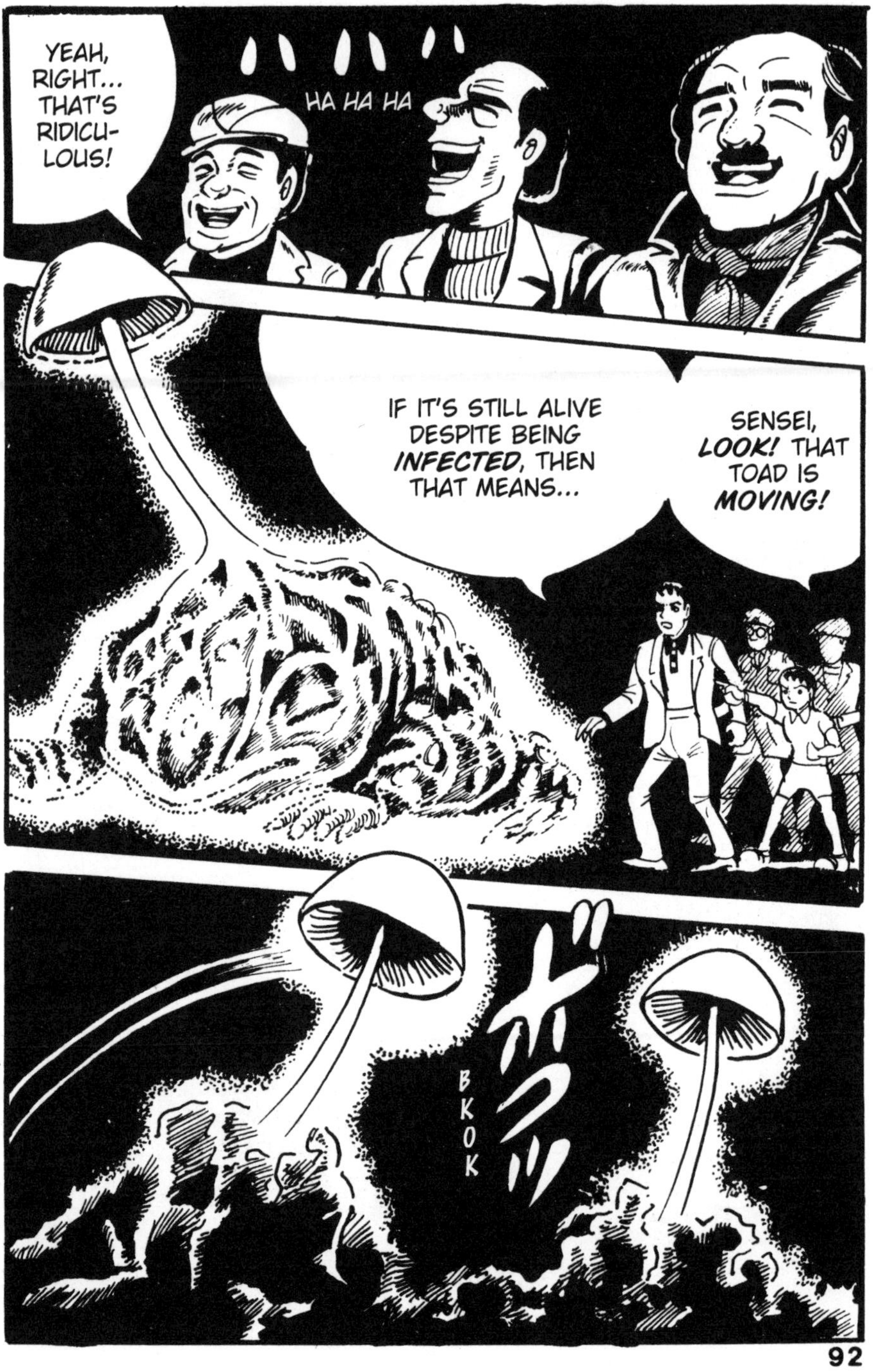
HA HA HA
YEAH, RIGHT... THAT'S RIDICU-LOUS!
SENSEI, LOOK! THAT TOAD IS MOVING!
IF IT'S STILL ALIVE DESPITE BEING INFECTED, THEN THAT MEANS...
BKOK

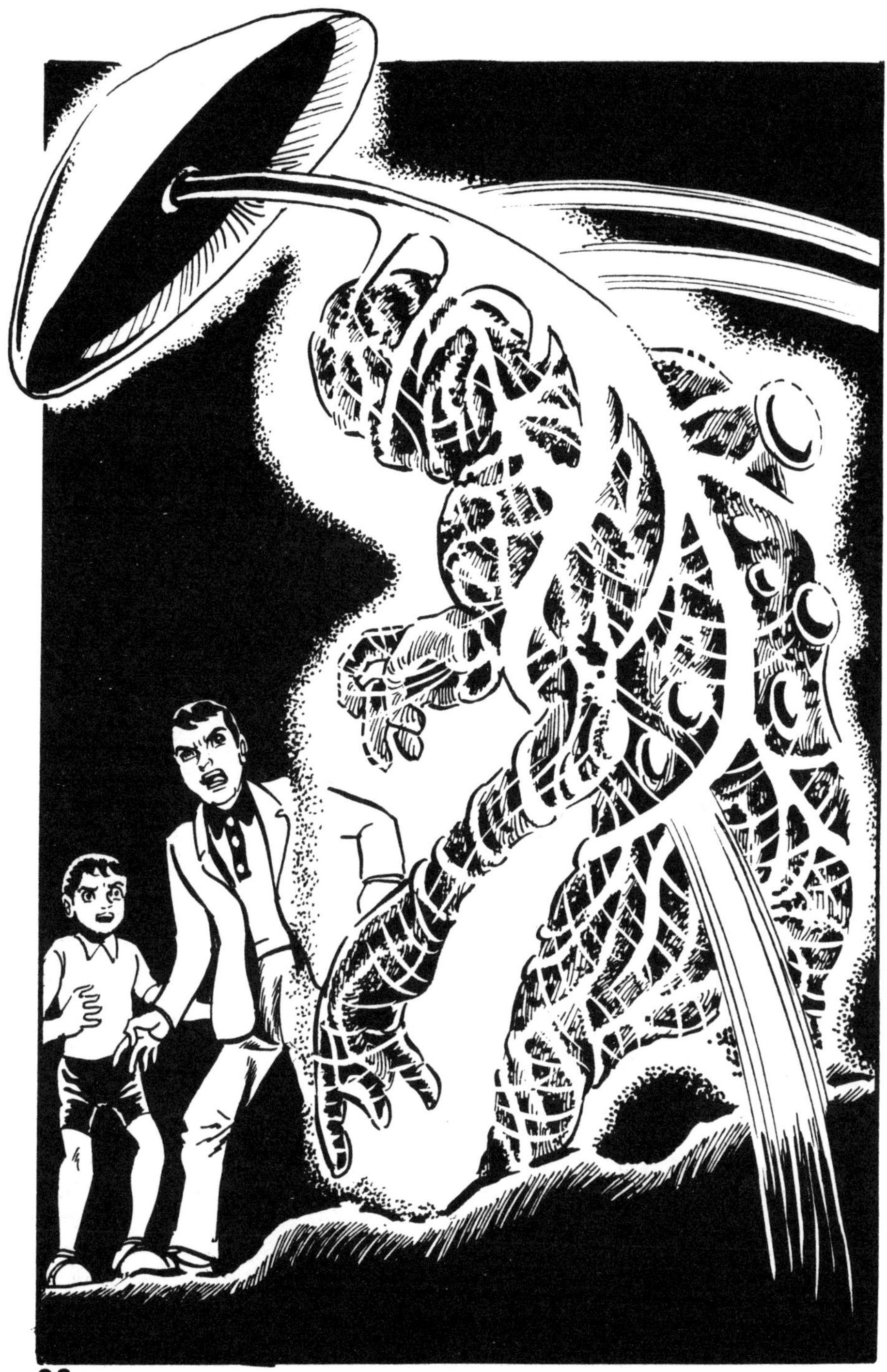

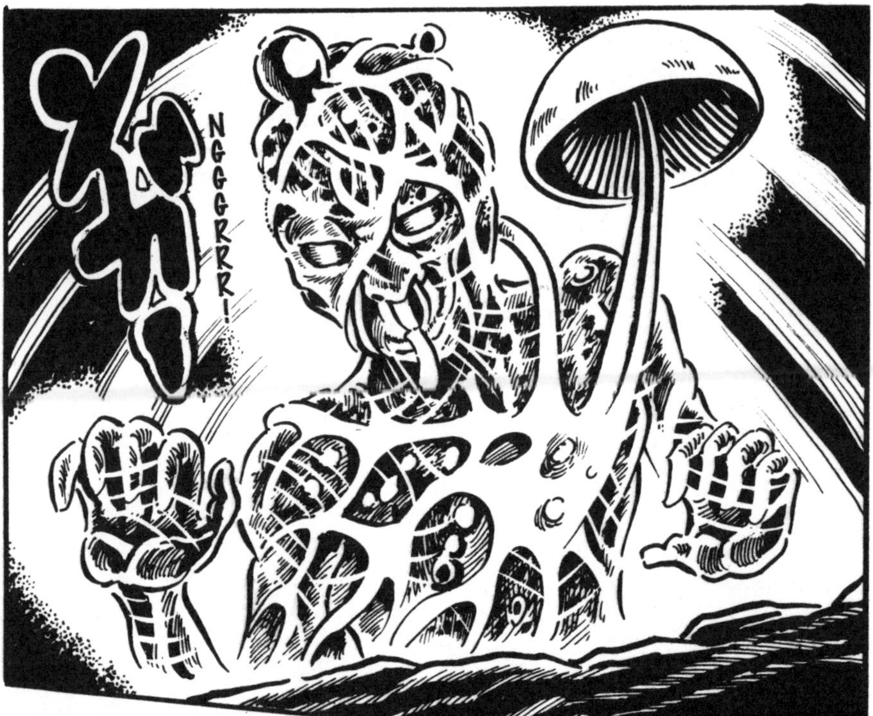
NGGGRRR!
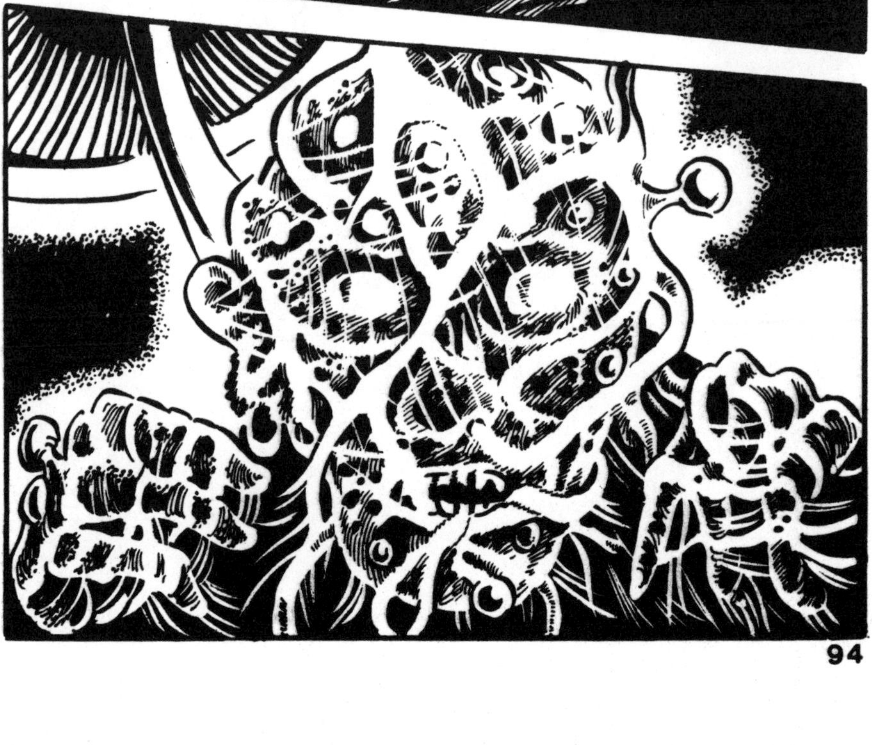

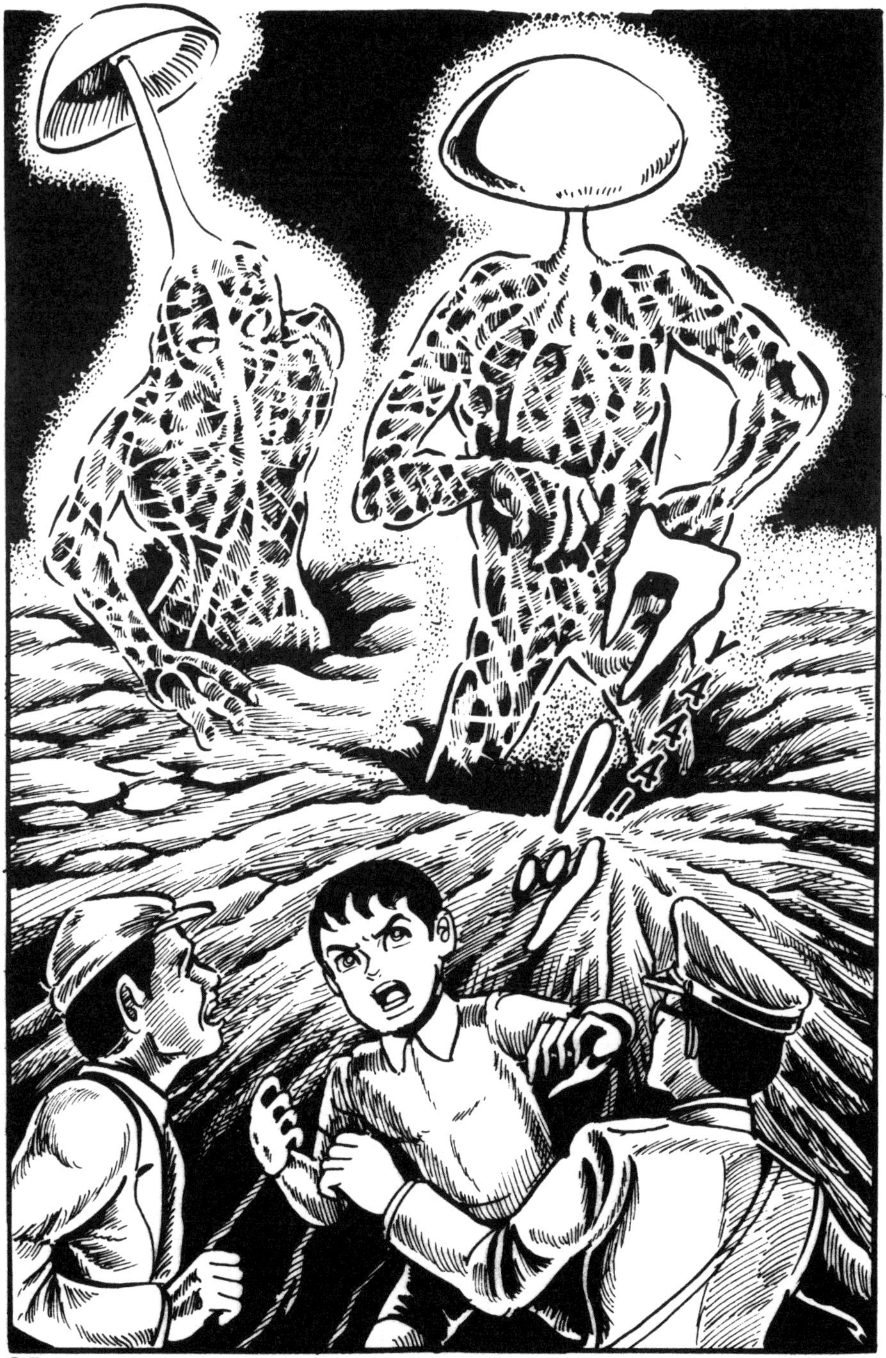
YAAAA!!

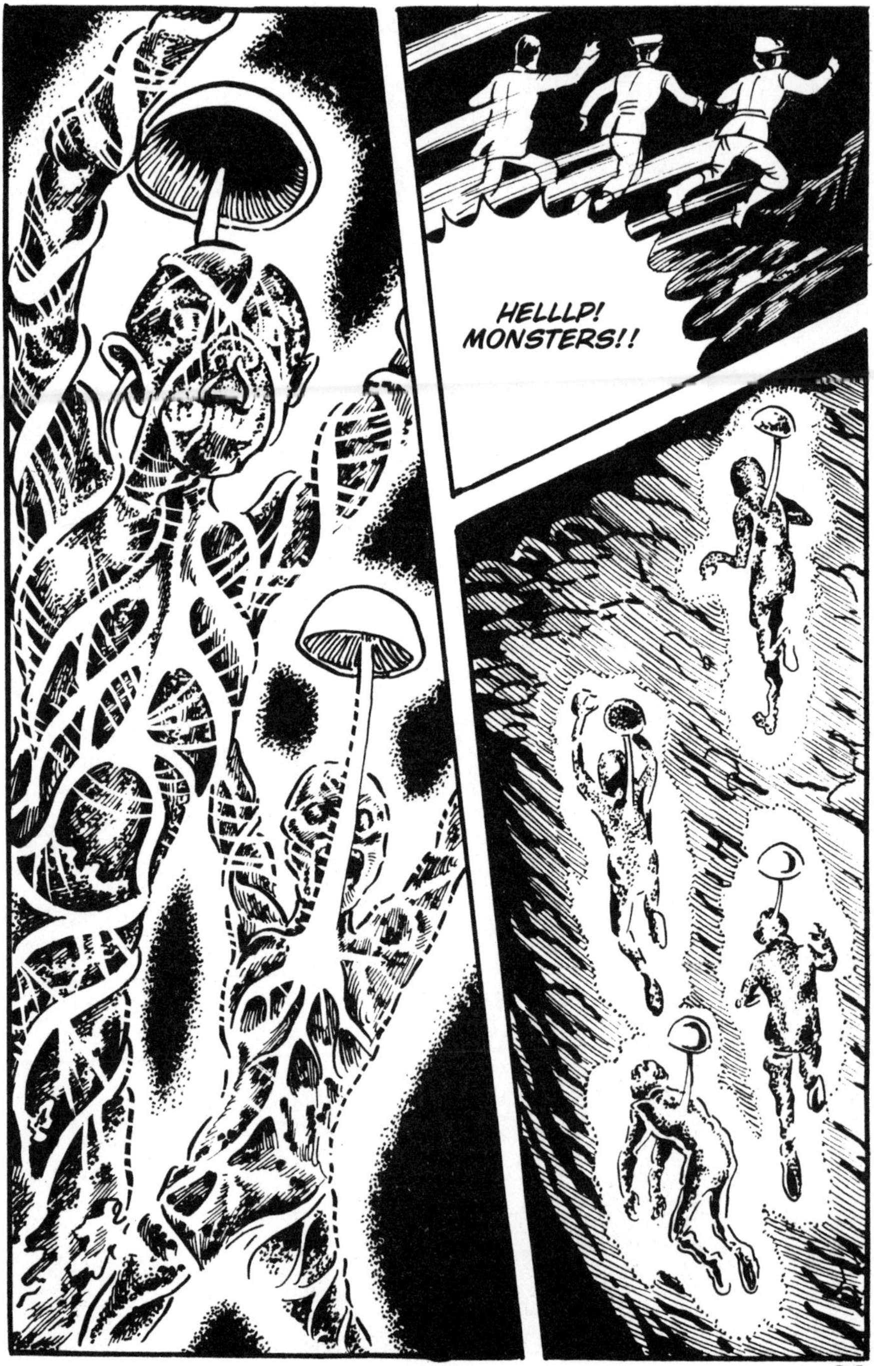
HELLLP! MONSTERS!!

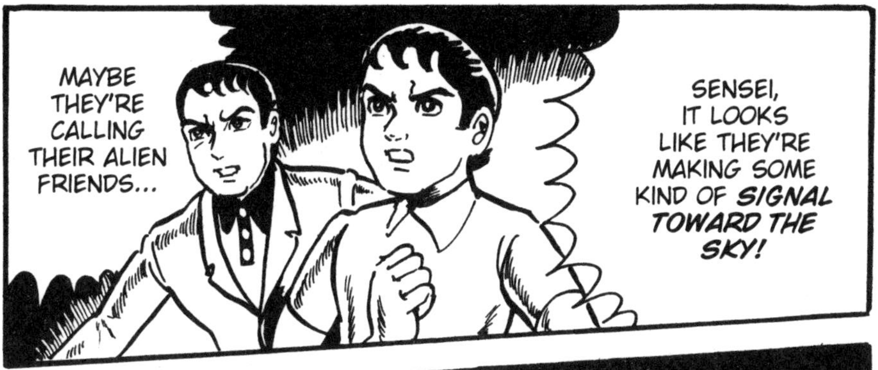
SENSEI, IT LOOKS LIKE THEY'RE MAKING SOME KIND OF ***SIGNAL TOWARD THE SKY!***
MAYBE THEY'RE CALLING THEIR ALIEN FRIENDS...

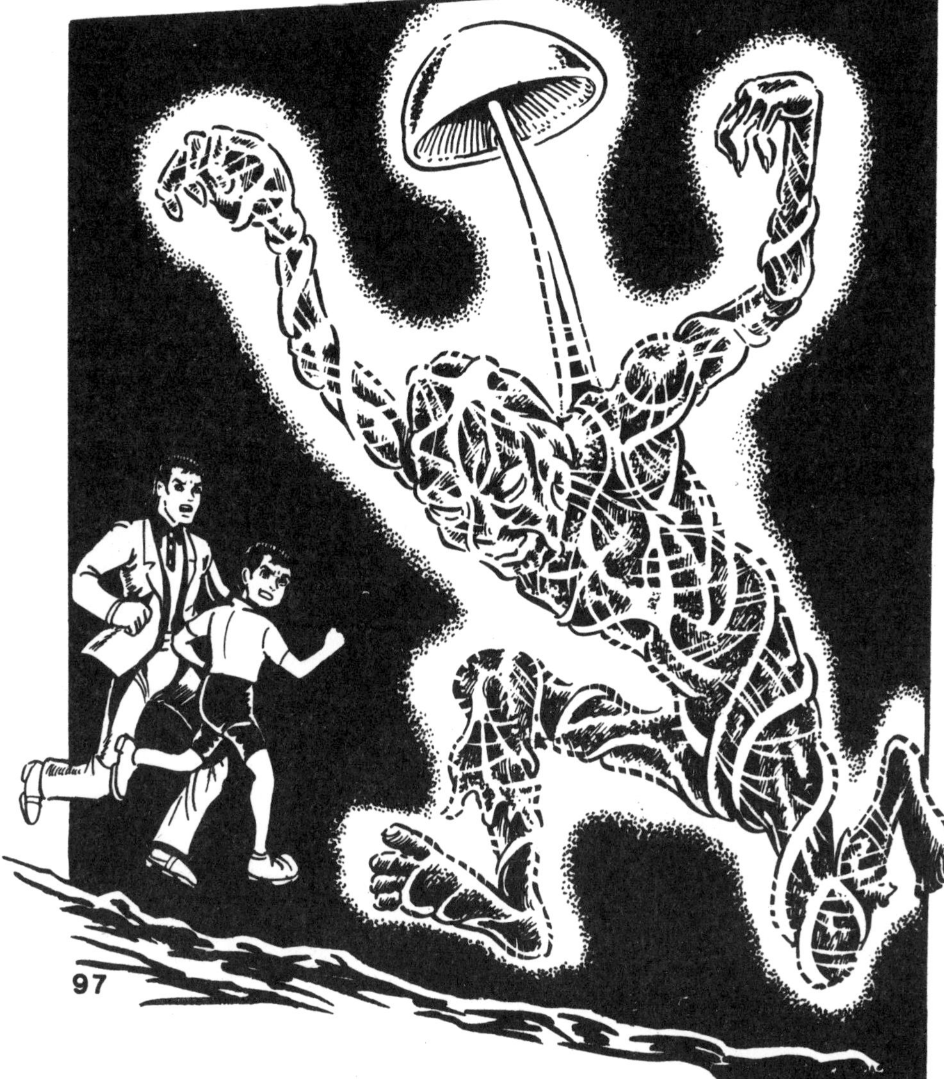

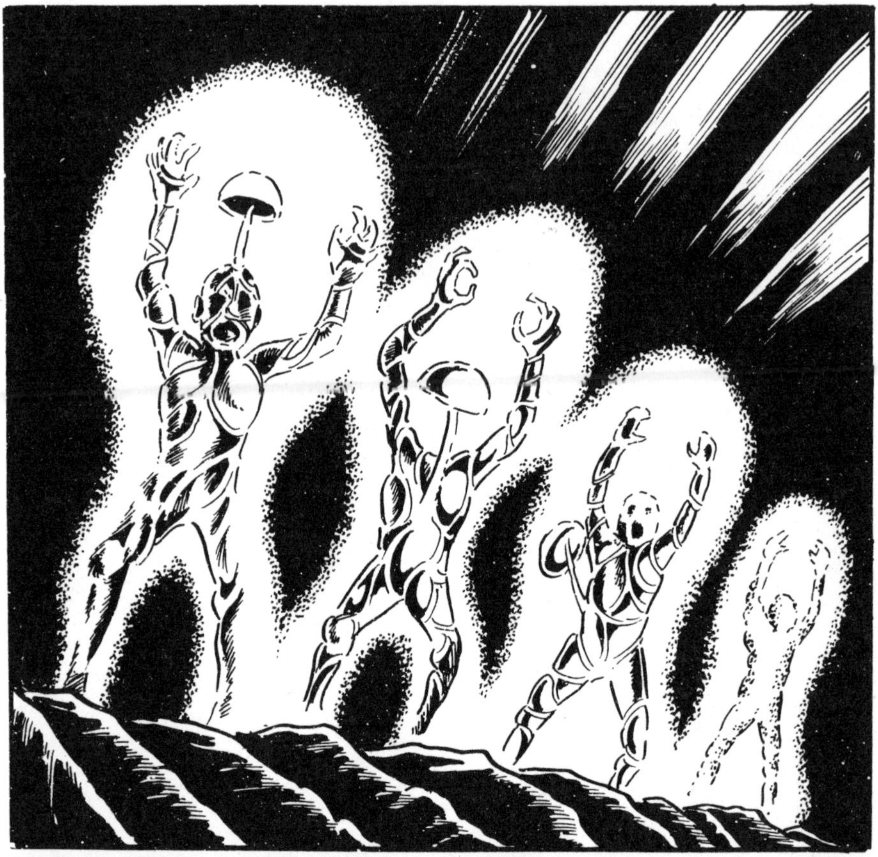
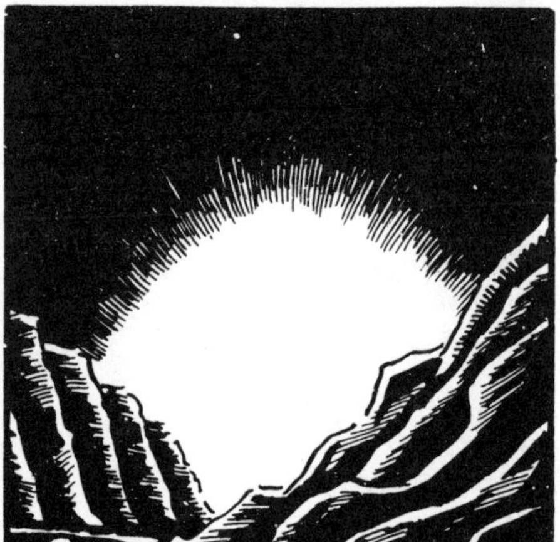
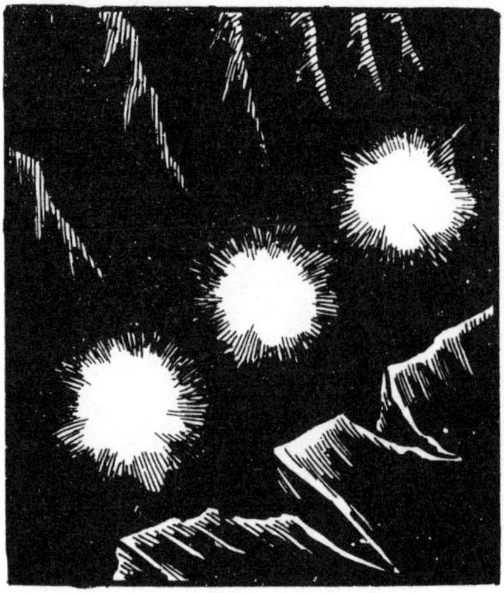

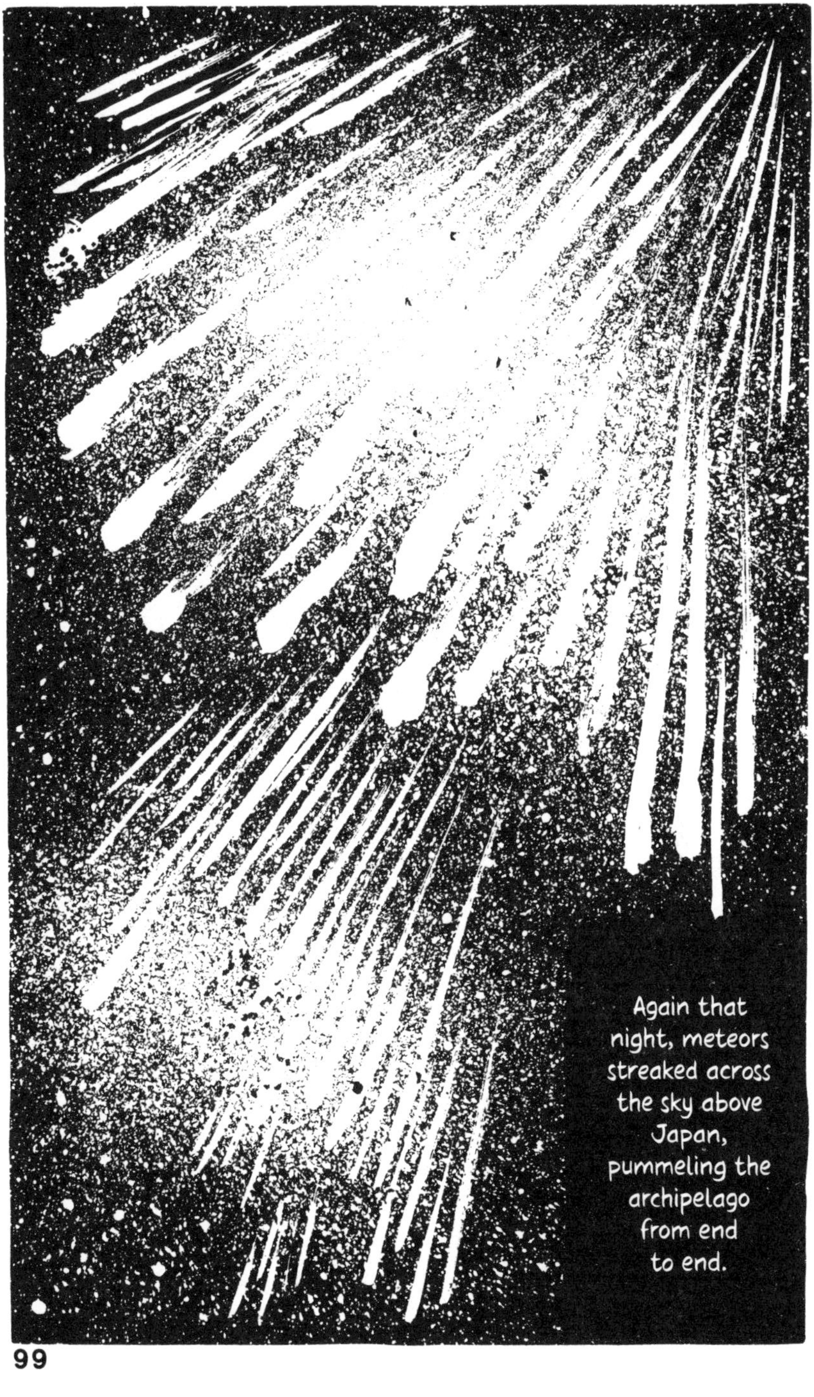
Again that night, meteors streaked across the sky above Japan, pummeling the archipelago from end to end.

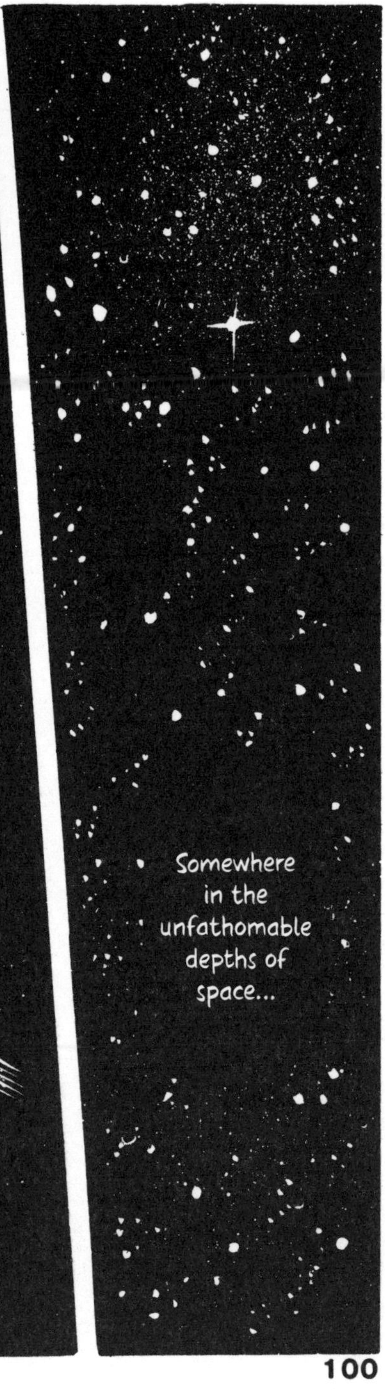
Somewhere in the unfathomable depths of space...
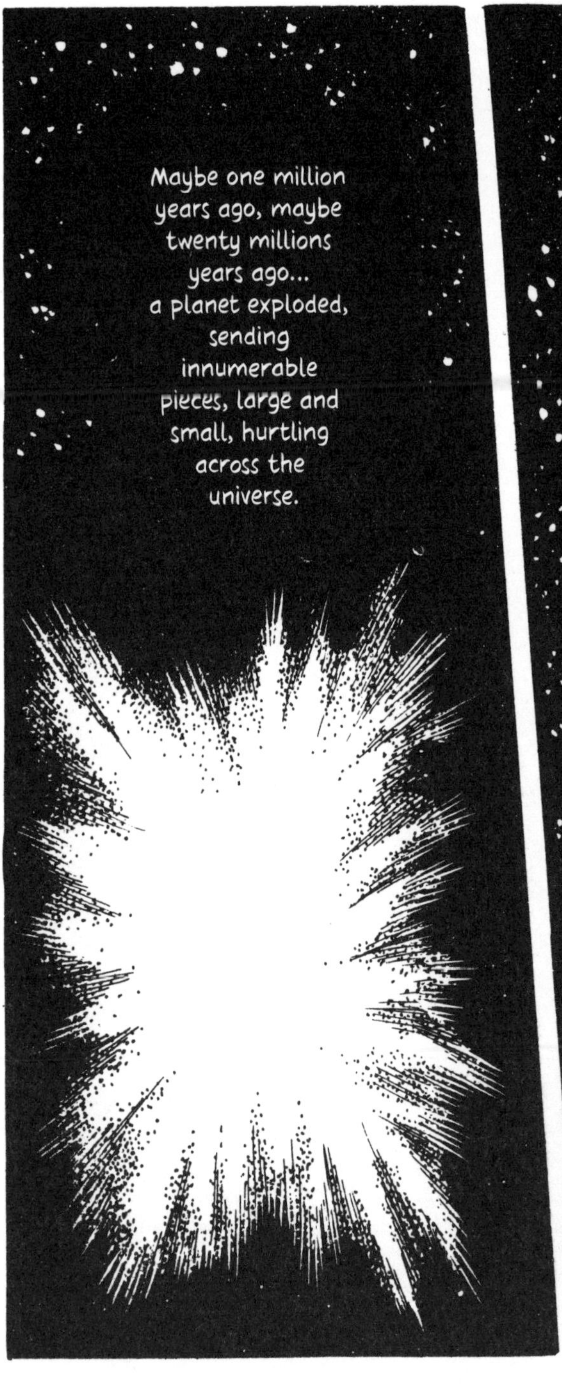
Maybe one million years ago, maybe twenty millions years ago... a planet exploded, sending innumerable pieces, large and small, hurtling across the universe.

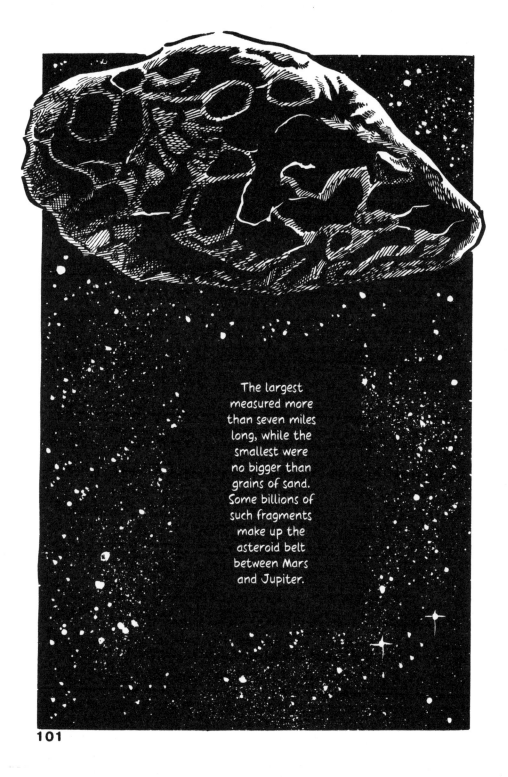

The largest
measured more
than seven miles
long, while the
smallest were
no bigger than
grains of sand.
Some billions of
such fragments
make up the
asteroid belt
between Mars
and Jupiter.

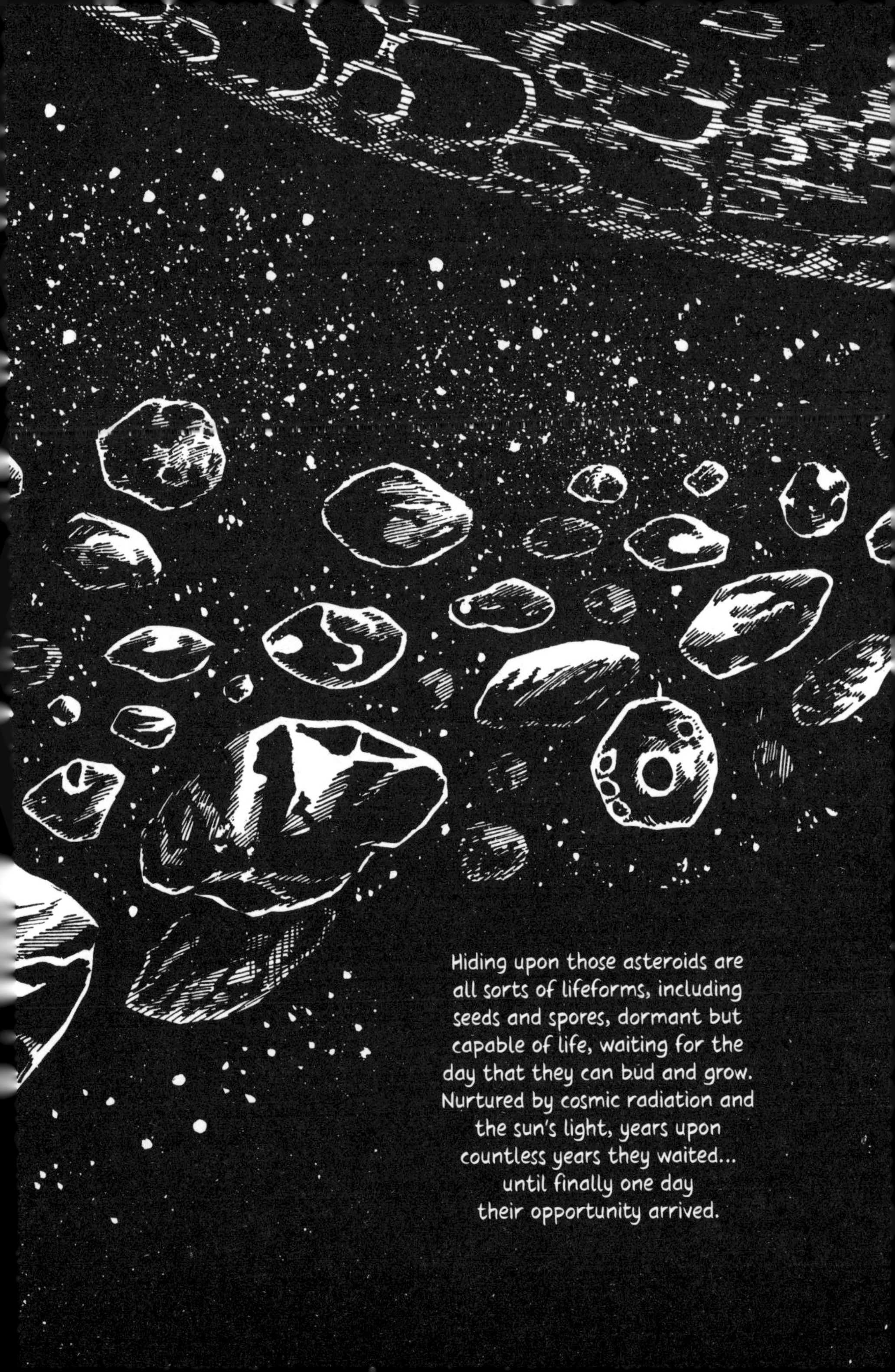
Hiding upon those asteroids are all sorts of lifeforms, including seeds and spores, dormant but capable of life, waiting for the day that they can bud and grow. Nurtured by cosmic radiation and the sun's light, years upon countless years they waited... until finally one day their opportunity arrived.

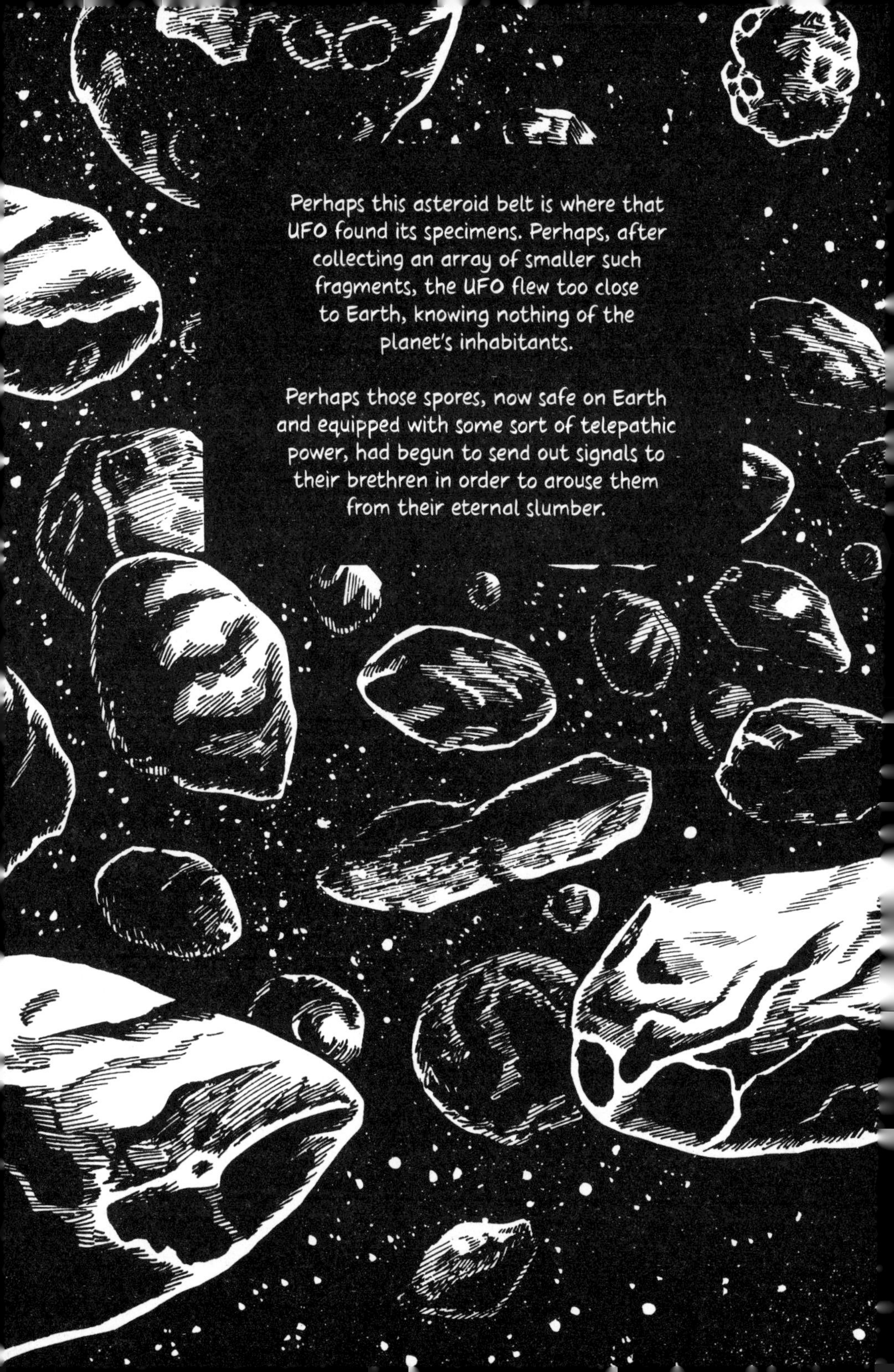
Perhaps this asteroid belt is where that UFO found its specimens. Perhaps, after collecting an array of smaller such fragments, the UFO flew too close to Earth, knowing nothing of the planet's inhabitants.
Perhaps those spores, now safe on Earth and equipped with some sort of telepathic power, had begun to send out signals to their brethren in order to arouse them from their eternal slumber.

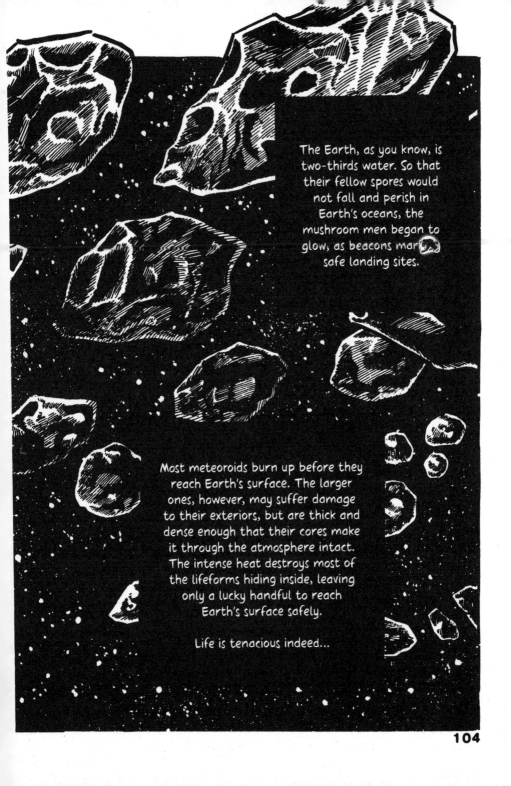

The Earth, as you know, is two-thirds water. So that their fellow spores would not fall and perish in Earth's oceans, the mushroom men began to glow, as beacons marking safe landing sites.

Most meteoroids burn up before they reach Earth's surface. The larger ones, however, may suffer damage to their exteriors, but are thick and dense enough that their cores make it through the atmosphere intact. The intense heat destroys most of the lifeforms hiding inside, leaving only a lucky handful to reach Earth's surface safely.

Life is tenacious indeed...

104

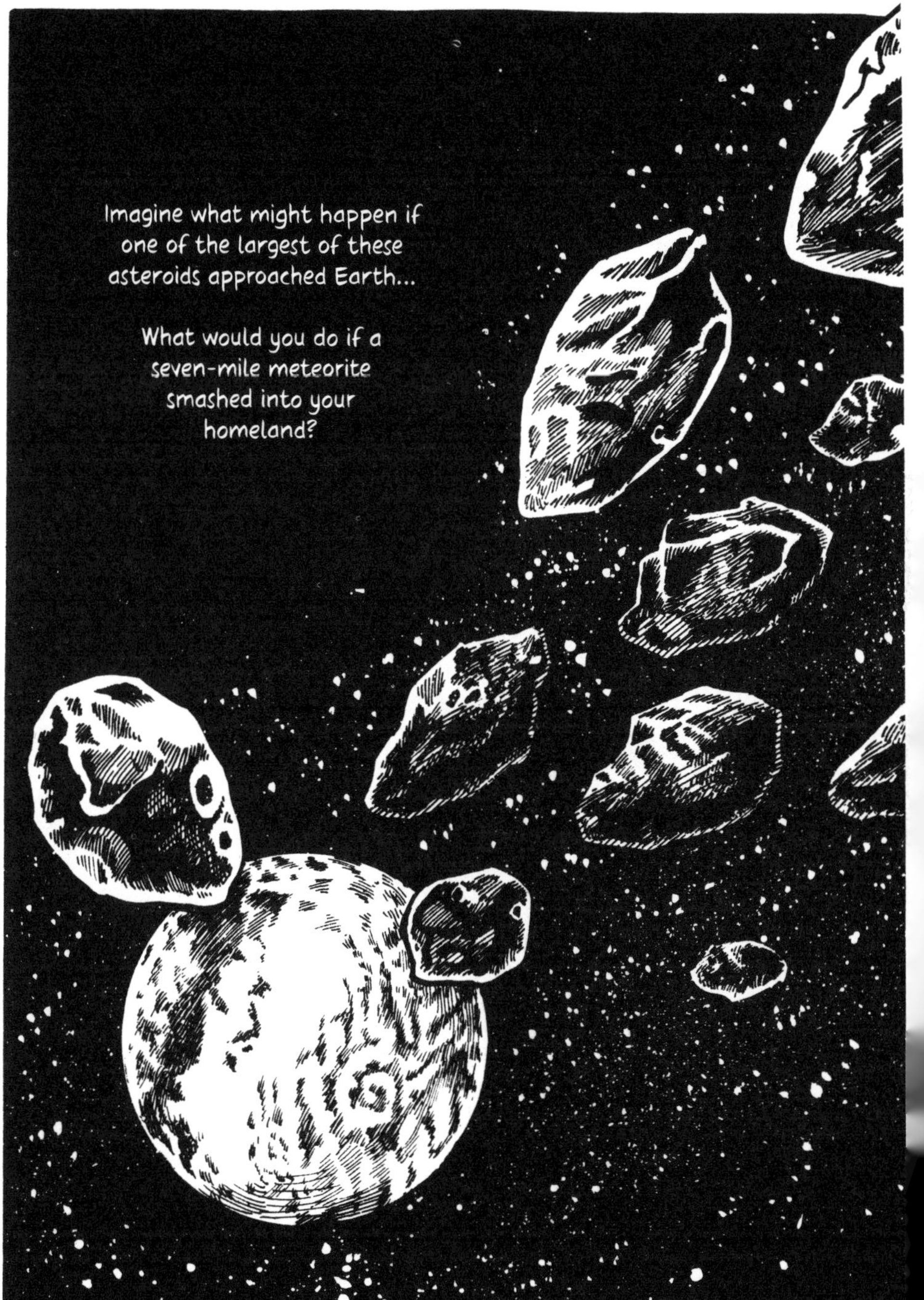
Imagine what might happen if one of the largest of these asteroids approached Earth...
What would you do if a seven-mile meteorite smashed into your homeland?

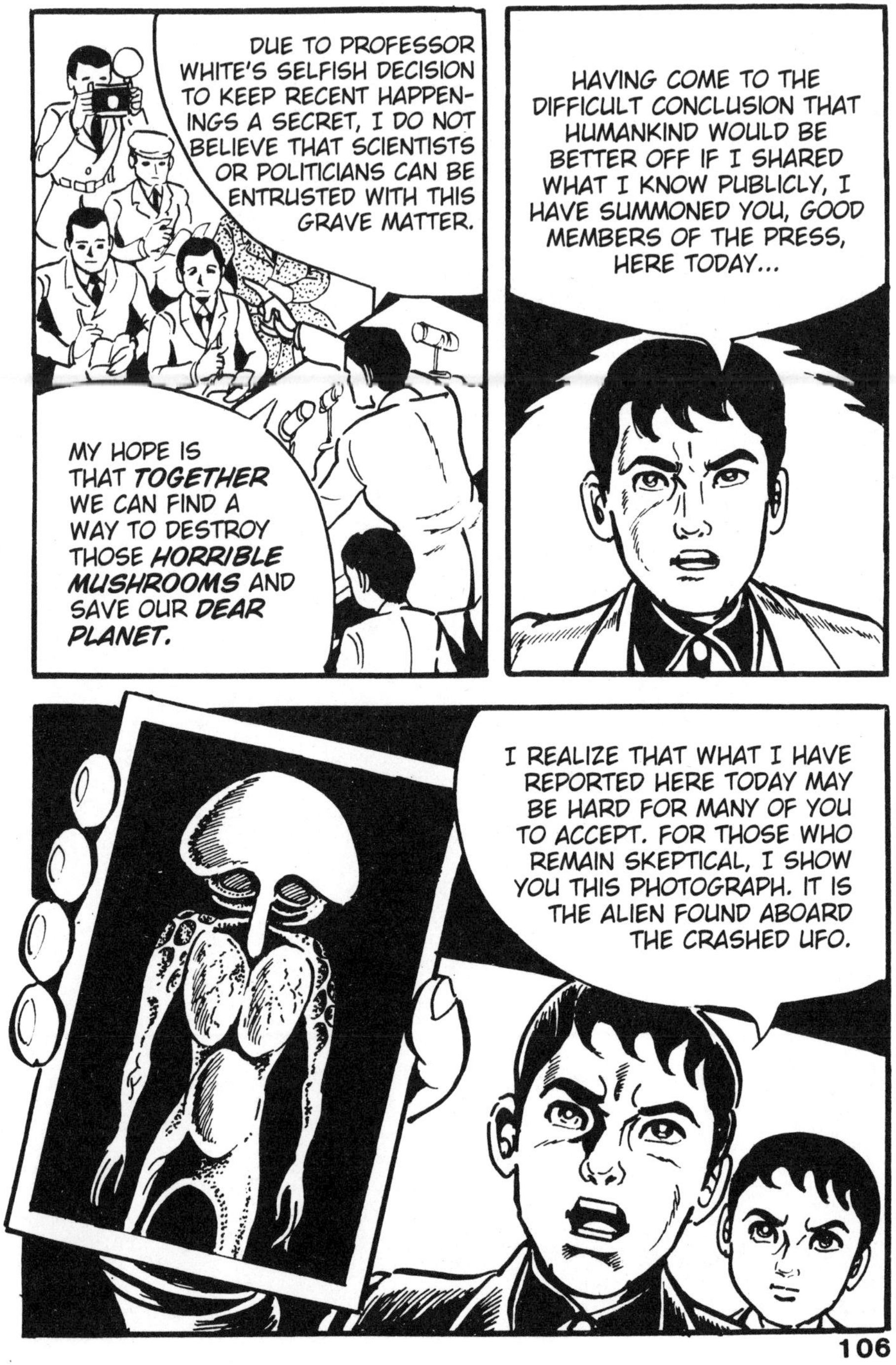
HAVING COME TO THE DIFFICULT CONCLUSION THAT HUMANKIND WOULD BE BETTER OFF IF I SHARED WHAT I KNOW PUBLICLY, I HAVE SUMMONED YOU, GOOD MEMBERS OF THE PRESS, HERE TODAY...
DUE TO PROFESSOR WHITE'S SELFISH DECISION TO KEEP RECENT HAPPENINGS A SECRET, I DO NOT BELIEVE THAT SCIENTISTS OR POLITICIANS CAN BE ENTRUSTED WITH THIS GRAVE MATTER.
MY HOPE IS THAT ***TOGETHER*** WE CAN FIND A WAY TO DESTROY THOSE ***HORRIBLE MUSHROOMS*** AND SAVE OUR ***DEAR PLANET.***
I REALIZE THAT WHAT I HAVE REPORTED HERE TODAY MAY BE HARD FOR MANY OF YOU TO ACCEPT. FOR THOSE WHO REMAIN SKEPTICAL, I SHOW YOU THIS PHOTOGRAPH. IT IS THE ALIEN FOUND ABOARD THE CRASHED UFO.

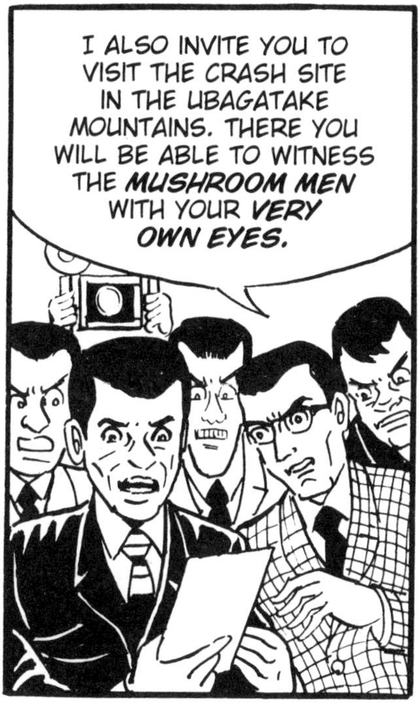
I ALSO INVITE YOU TO VISIT THE CRASH SITE IN THE UBAGATAKE MOUNTAINS. THERE YOU WILL BE ABLE TO WITNESS THE MUSHROOM MEN WITH YOUR VERY OWN EYES.

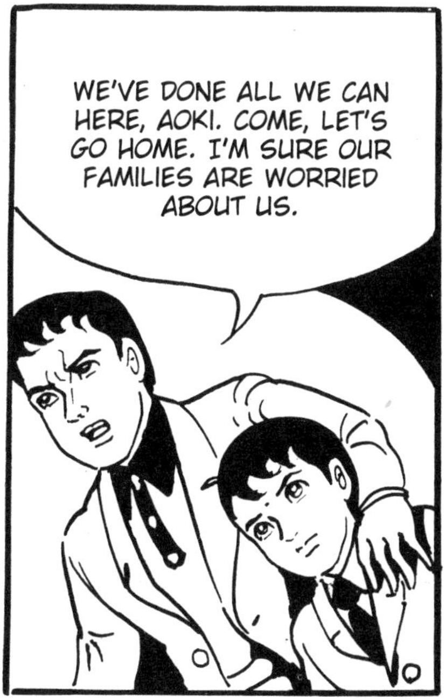
WE'VE DONE ALL WE CAN HERE, AOKI. COME, LET'S GO HOME. I'M SURE OUR FAMILIES ARE WORRIED ABOUT US.

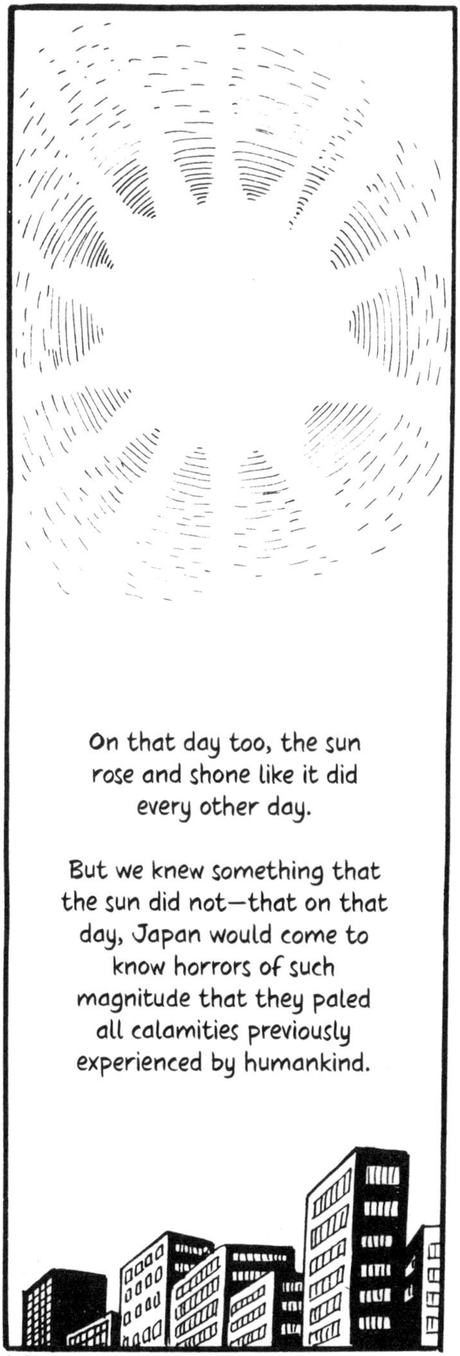
On that day too, the sun rose and shone like it did every other day.
But we knew something that the sun did not—that on that day, Japan would come to know horrors of such magnitude that they paled all calamities previously experienced by humankind.

Bizarre Mushroom Tales, No. 5

Once upon a time, there was a large chesnut tree deep in the mountains, on which sprouted a curious mushroom. As the mushroom grew, it developed eyes, and with those eyes spotted a bird that came to feast on the chestnut tree's fruit. Thinking that the bird looked tasty, the mushroom developed a mouth and hands and feet, then captured the bird and devoured it.

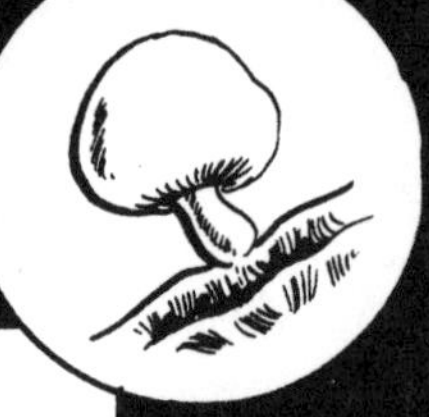

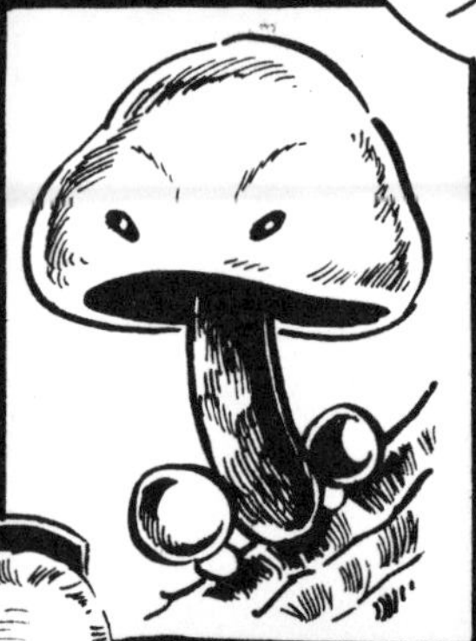

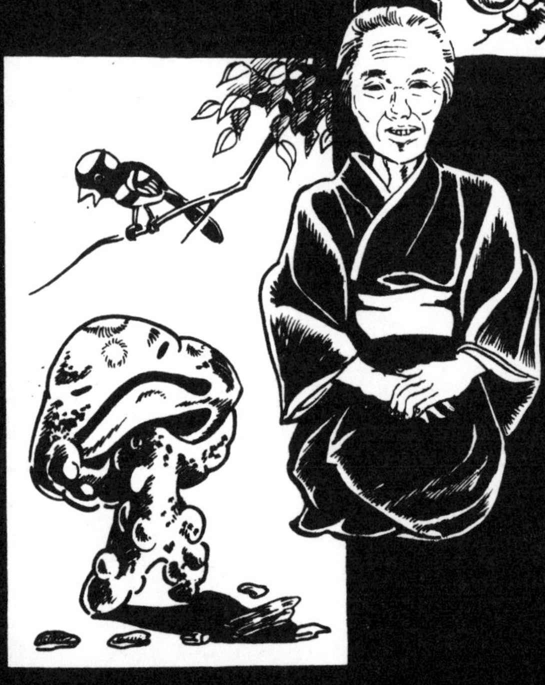

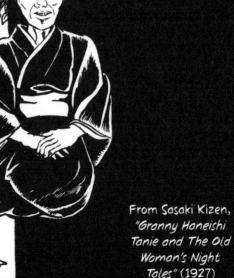

From Sasaki Kizen, *"Granny Haneishi Tanie and The Old Woman's Night Tales"* (1927)

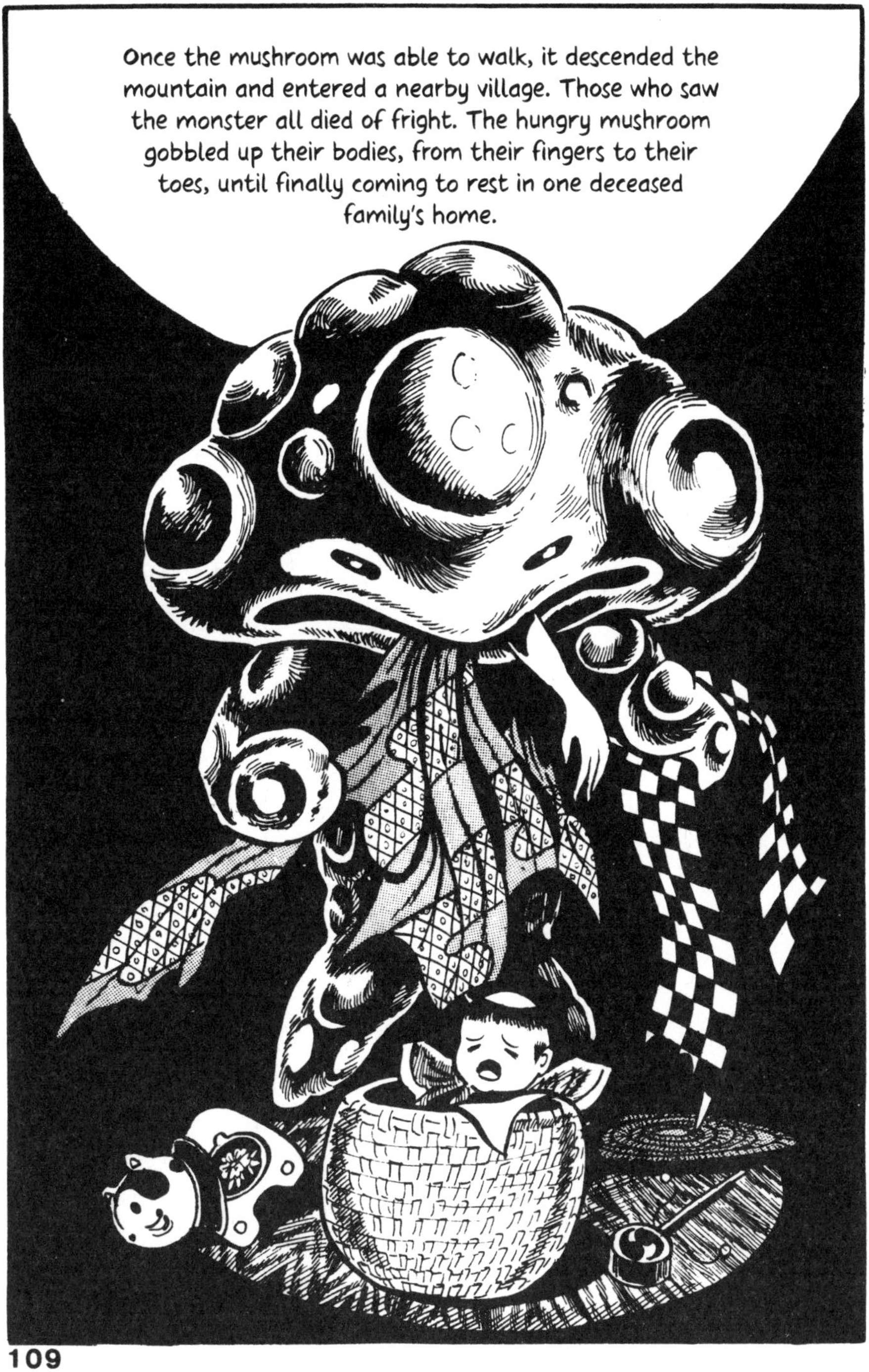
Once the mushroom was able to walk, it descended the mountain and entered a nearby village. Those who saw the monster all died of fright. The hungry mushroom gobbled up their bodies, from their fingers to their toes, until finally coming to rest in one deceased family's home.

Then one day, an itinerant mask-seller arrived in the village, ignorant of the tragedy that had befallen the place. Seeing no one around, he figured the village was abandoned, so decided to spend the night in one of the empty houses.

After lighting a fire in the hearth, he lined up his masks and counted his money. Suddenly, from behind, he heard a loud sound, like a giant trodding upon the floor.

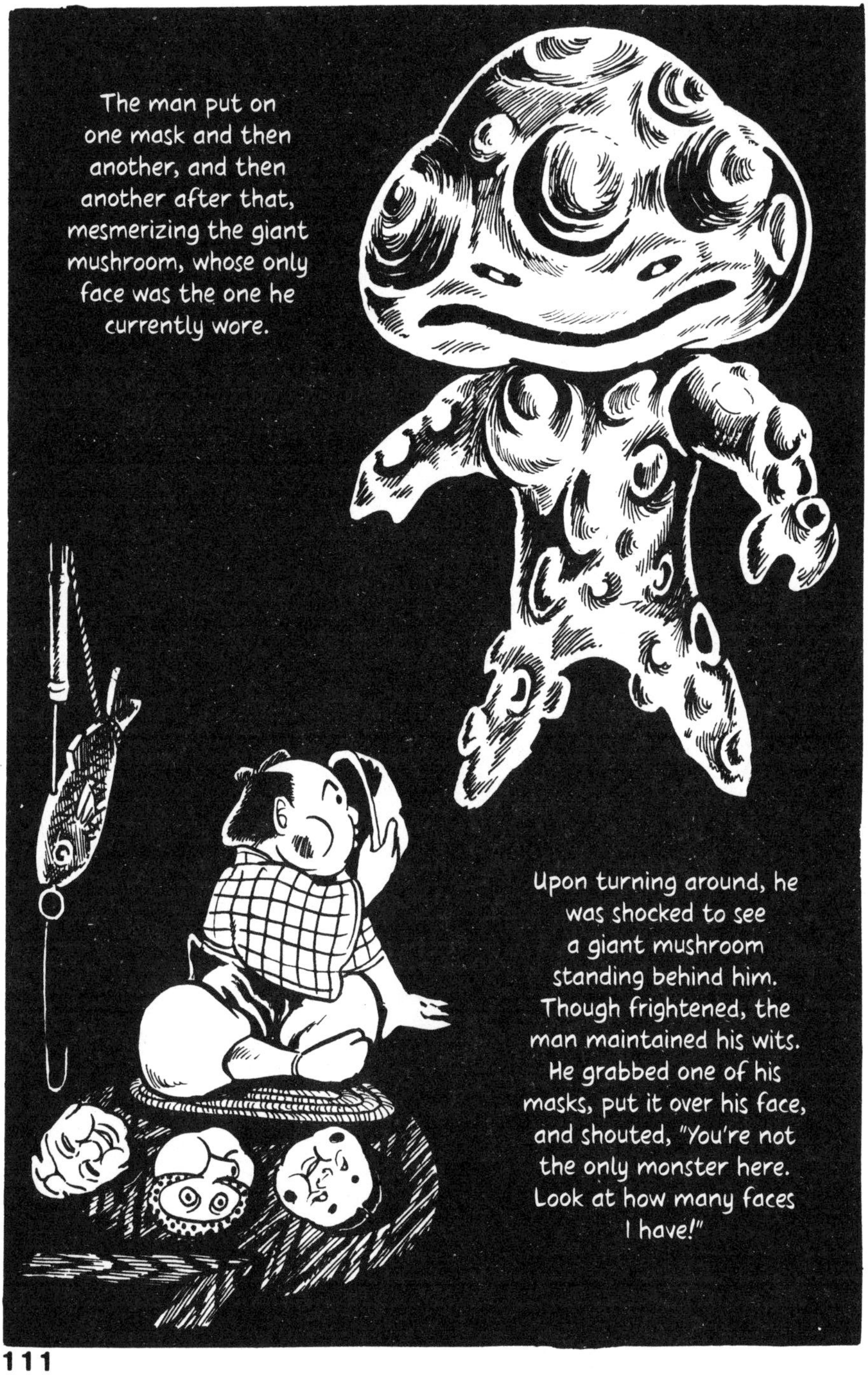
The man put on one mask and then another, and then another after that, mesmerizing the giant mushroom, whose only face was the one he currently wore.
Upon turning around, he was shocked to see a giant mushroom standing behind him. Though frightened, the man maintained his wits. He grabbed one of his masks, put it over his face, and shouted, "You're not the only monster here. Look at how many faces I have!"

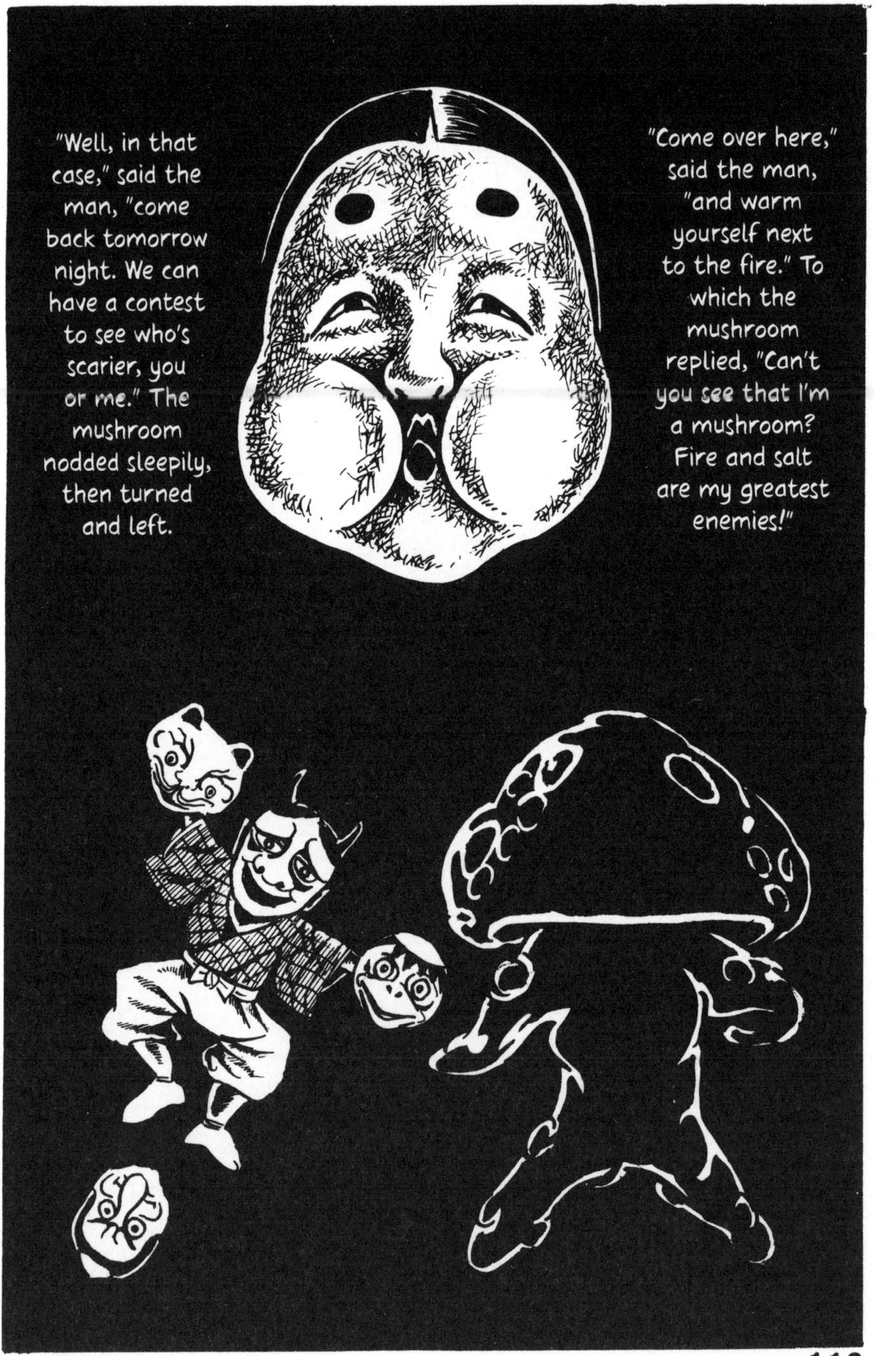
"Come over here," said the man, "and warm yourself next to the fire." To which the mushroom replied, "Can't you see that I'm a mushroom? Fire and salt are my greatest enemies!"
"Well, in that case," said the man, "come back tomorrow night. We can have a contest to see who's scarier, you or me." The mushroom nodded sleepily, then turned and left.

Early the next morning, the man ran from house to house looking for villagers, finding them hiding frightened in their homes. "Come out and help me," he told them. "Gather all the buckets you can find. Fill them with hot water. Mix in as much salt as you have. Now carry them to this house over here!"

Back at the empty house, the mushroom was sound asleep, snoring to the heavens. Before he could wake, the villagers began dousing him with hot salt water. As they did so, he frothed and moaned, expanding in size before melting into a puddle of mushroomy goo.
The end.

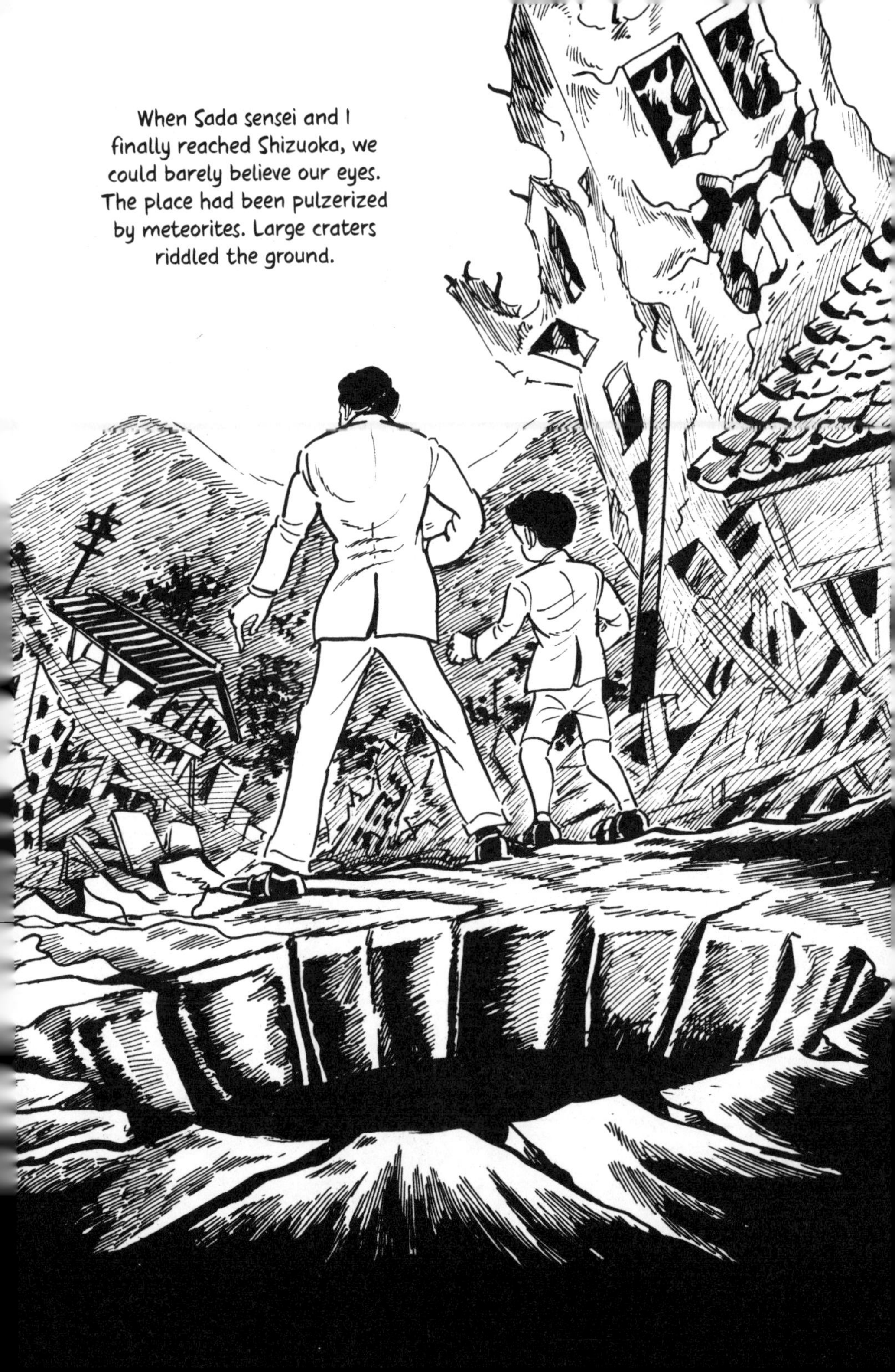
When Sada sensei and I finally reached Shizuoka, we could barely believe our eyes. The place had been pulzerized by meteorites. Large craters riddled the ground.

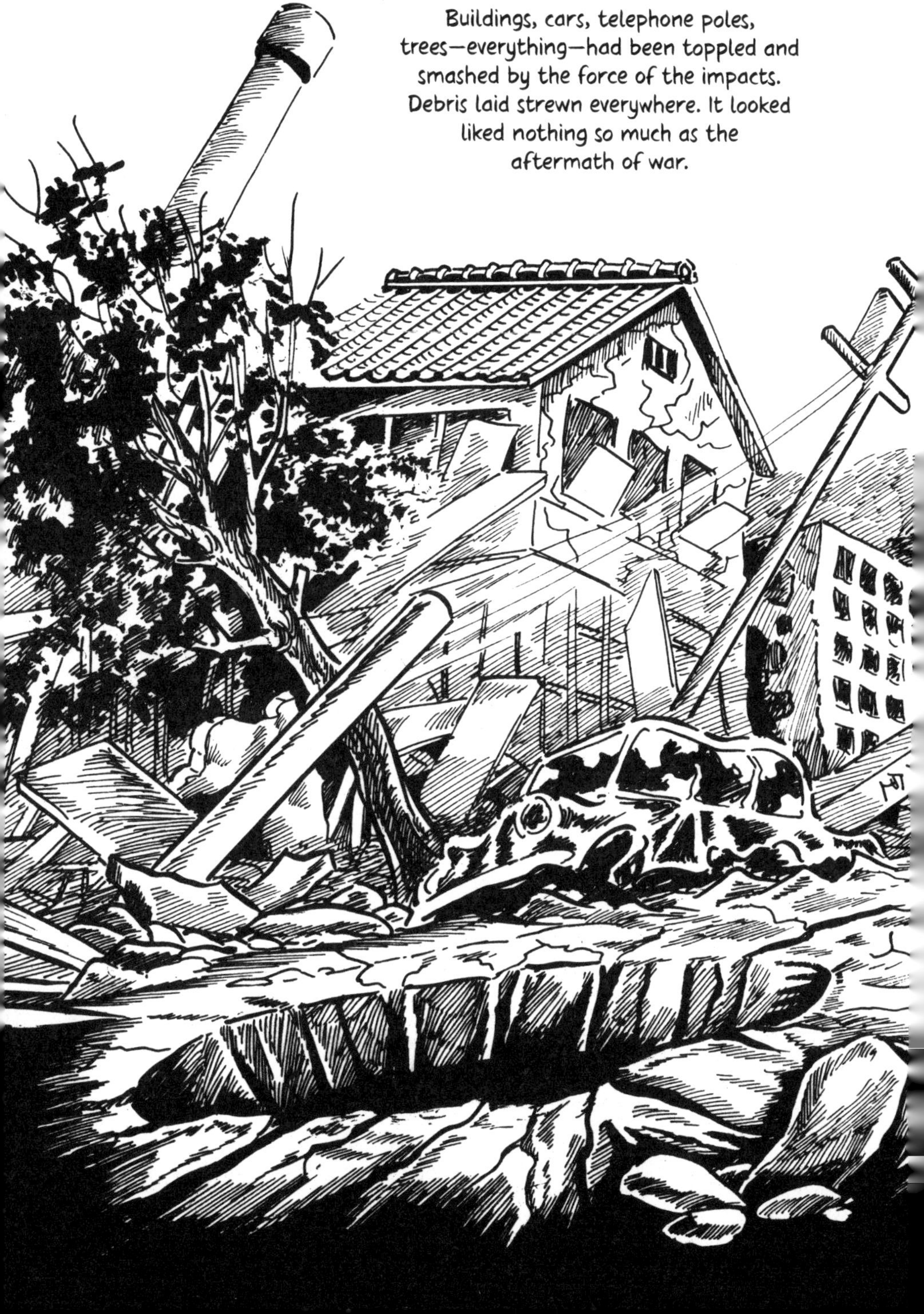
Buildings, cars, telephone poles, trees—everything—had been toppled and smashed by the force of the impacts. Debris laid strewn everywhere. It looked liked nothing so much as the aftermath of war.

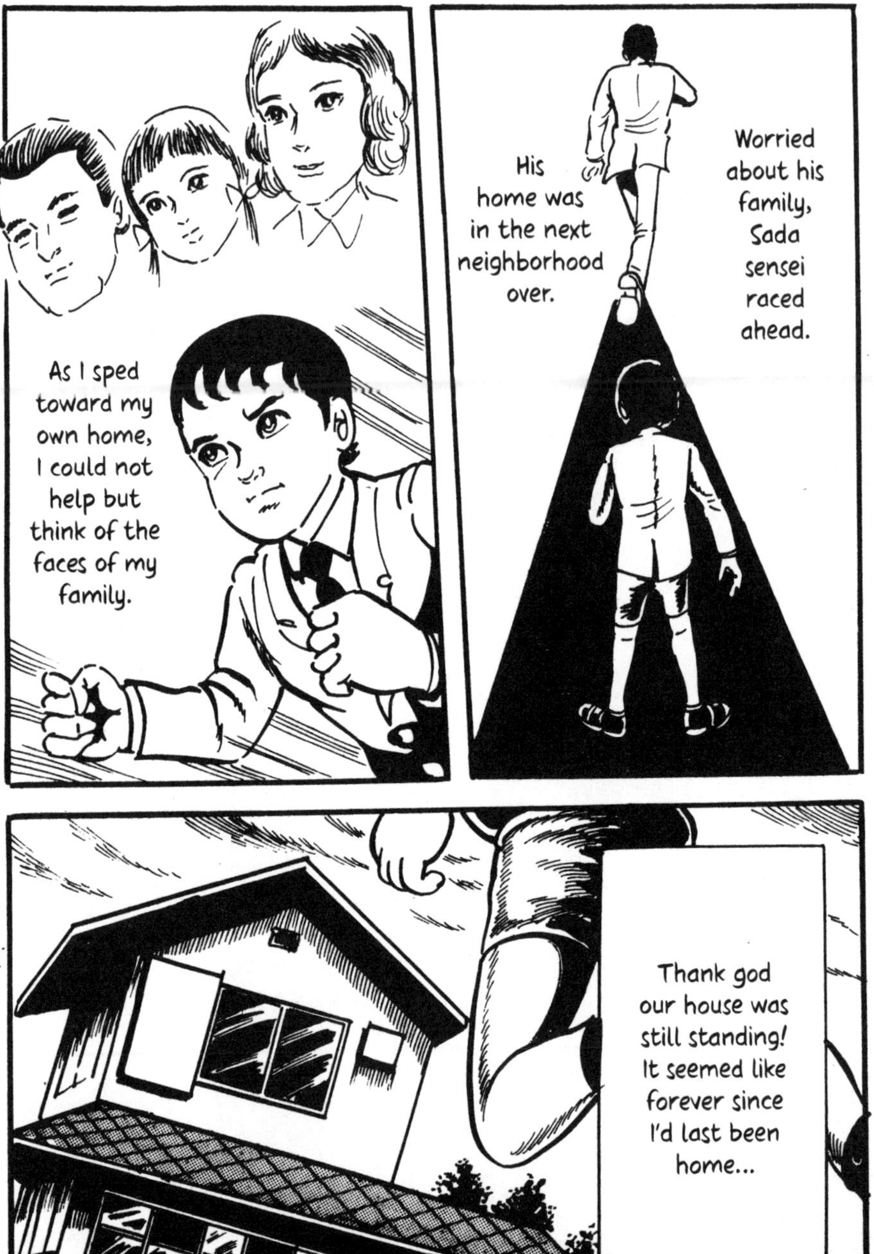
Worried about his family, Sada sensei raced ahead.
His home was in the next neighborhood over.
As I sped toward my own home, I could not help but think of the faces of my family.
Thank god our house was still standing! It seemed like forever since I'd last been home...

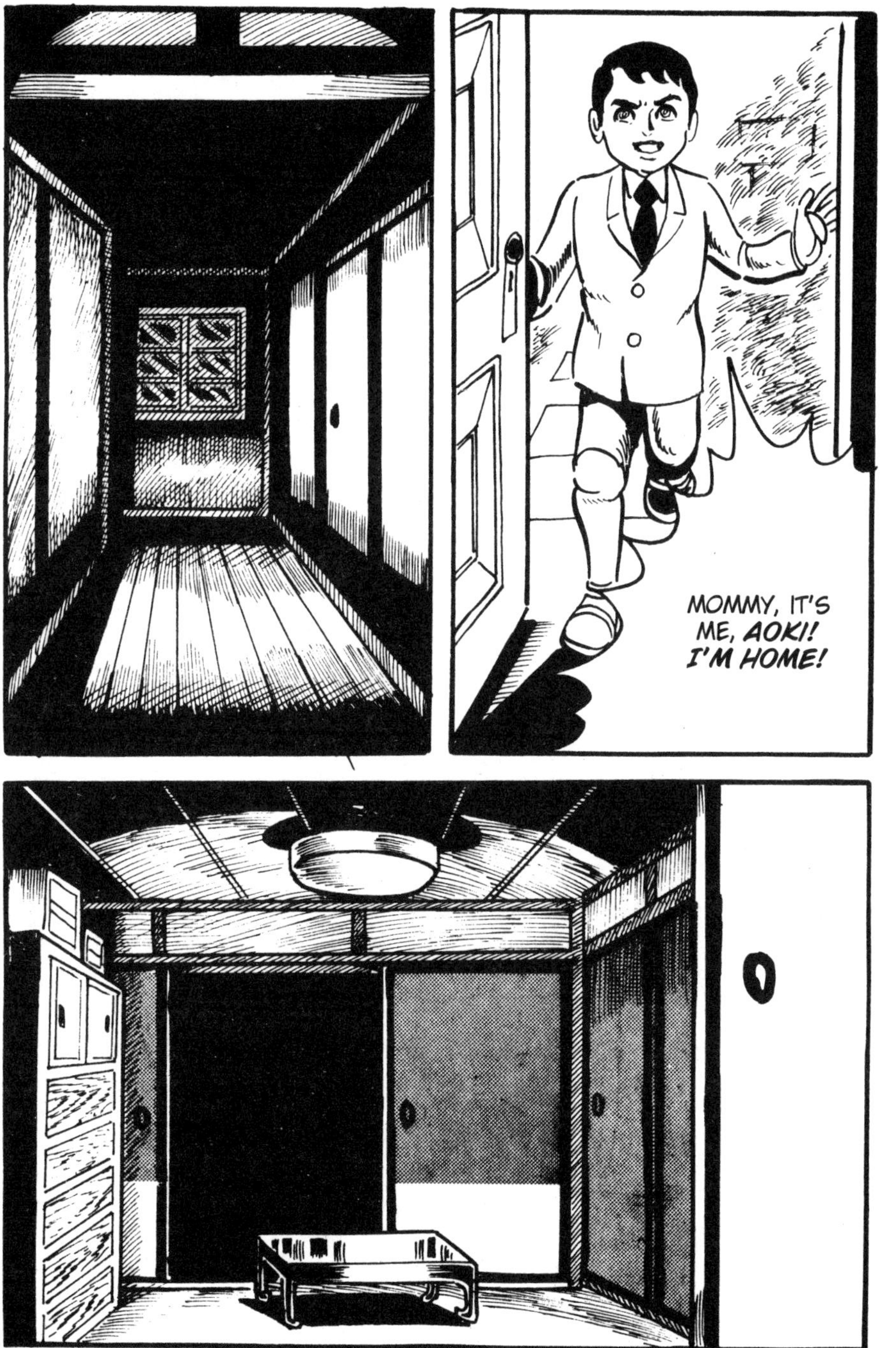
MOMMY, IT'S ME, AOKI! I'M HOME!

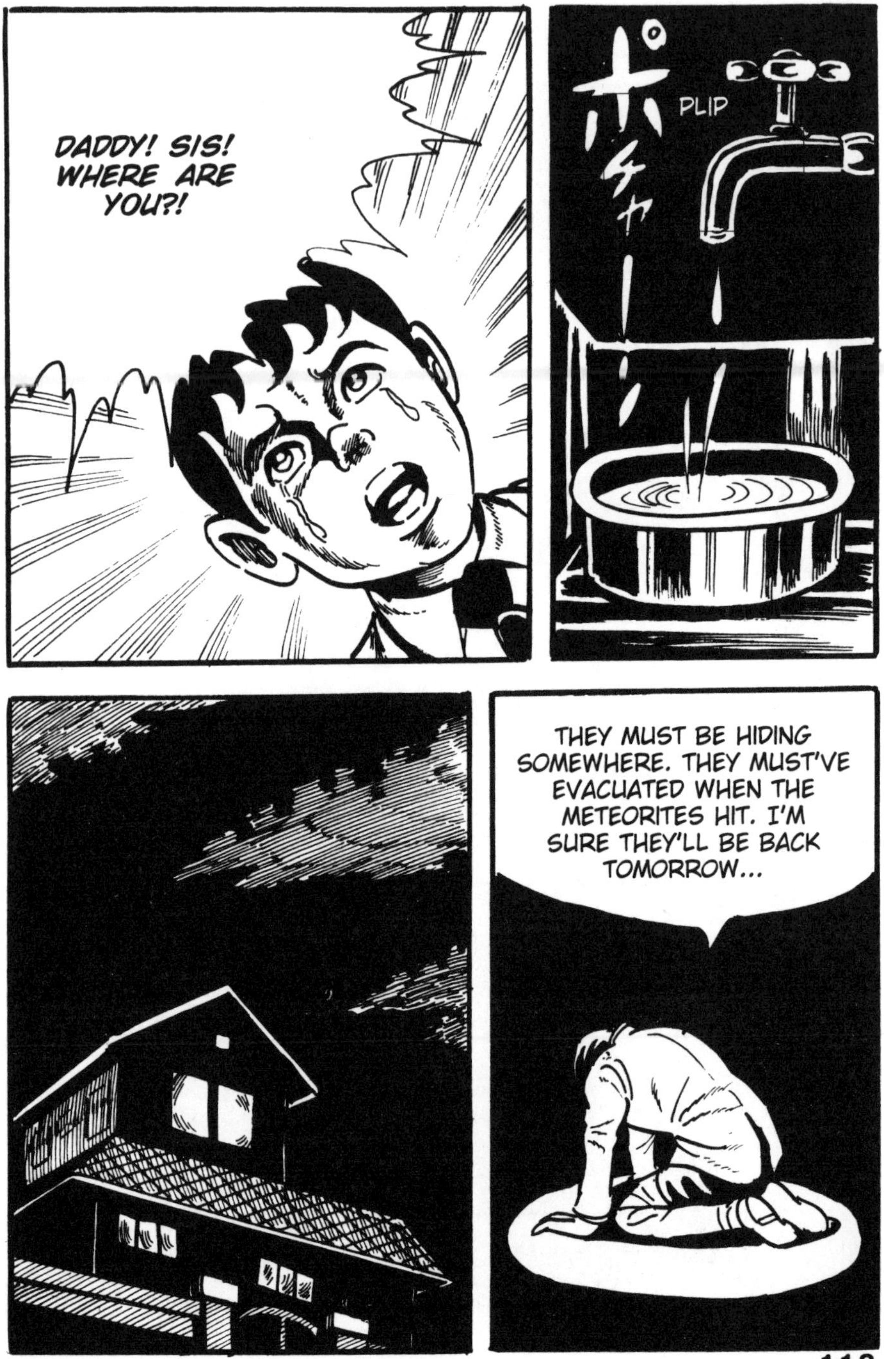
ポチャーン
PLIP
DADDY! SIS! WHERE ARE YOU?!
THEY MUST BE HIDING SOMEWHERE. THEY MUST'VE EVACUATED WHEN THE METEORITES HIT. I'M SURE THEY'LL BE BACK TOMORROW...

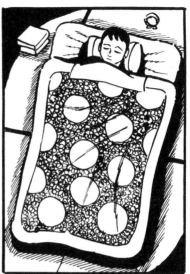

TUP
TUP

TUP

I COULD
SWEAR
I HEARD
FOOTSTEPS.
MY PARENTS
MUST BE
HOME.

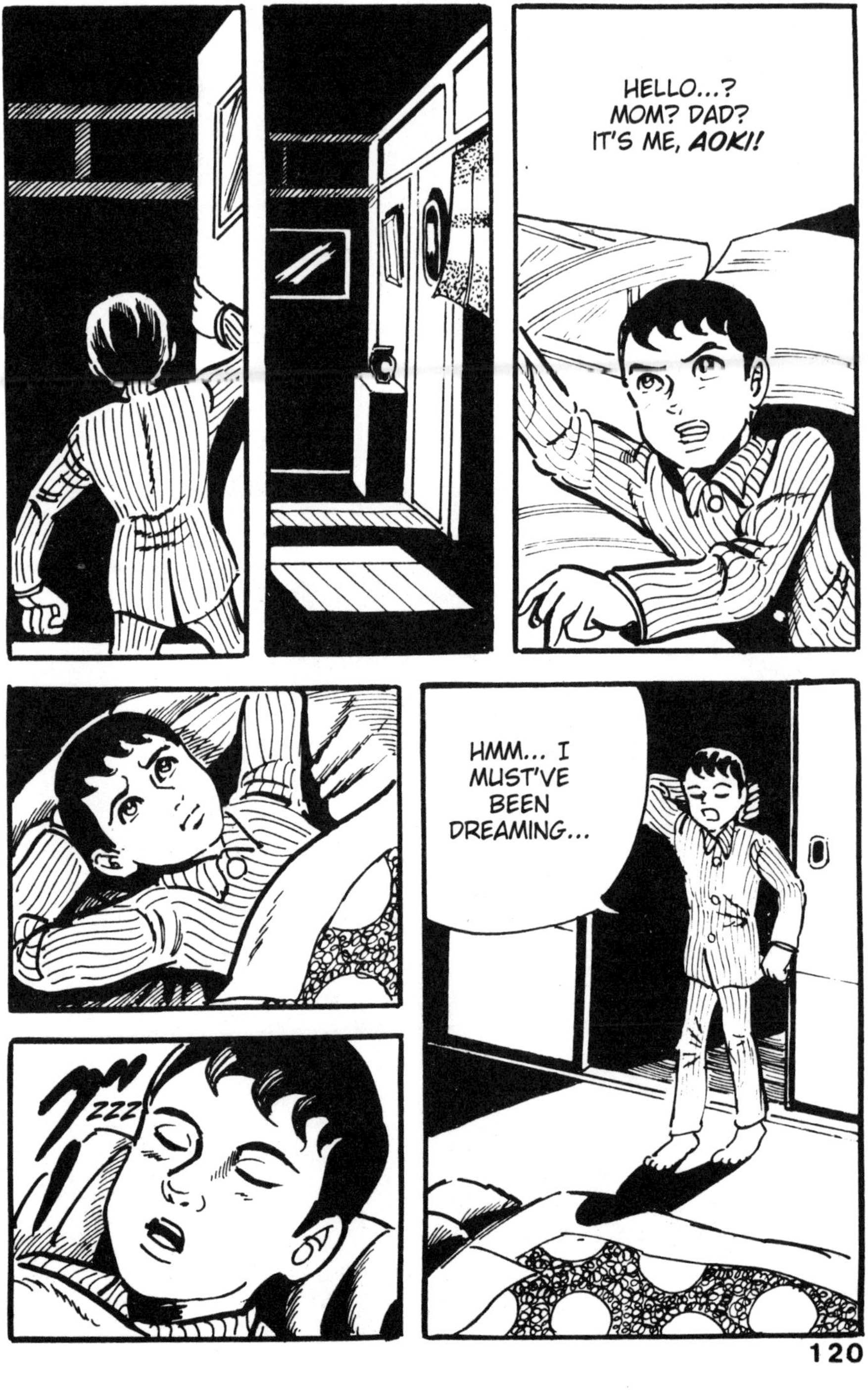
HELLO...? MOM? DAD? IT'S ME, *AOKI!*
HMM... I MUST'VE BEEN DREAMING...
ZZZ

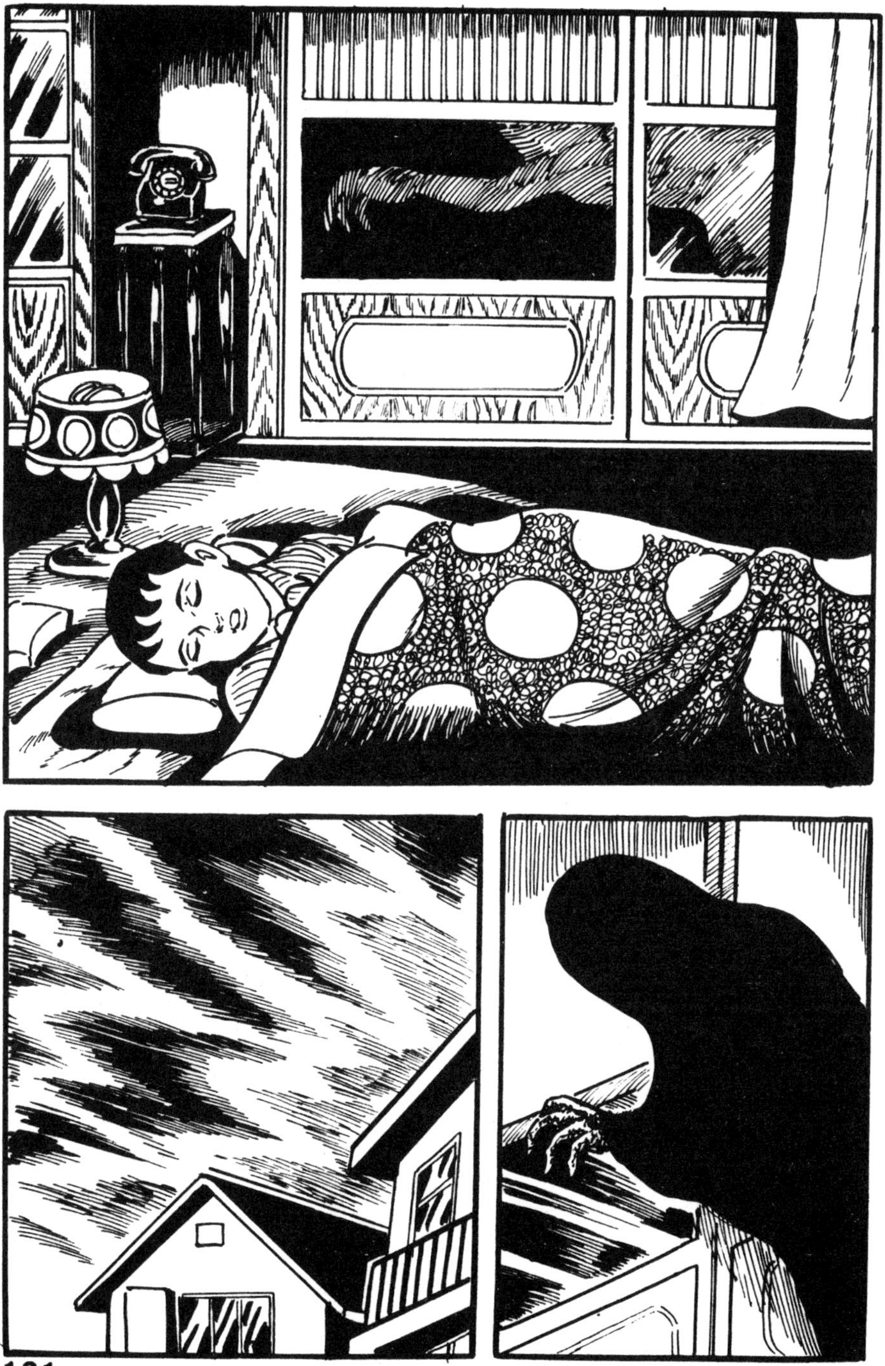

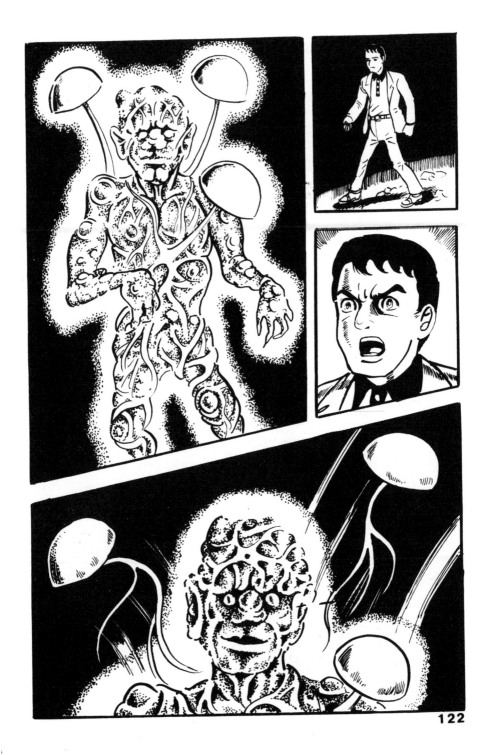

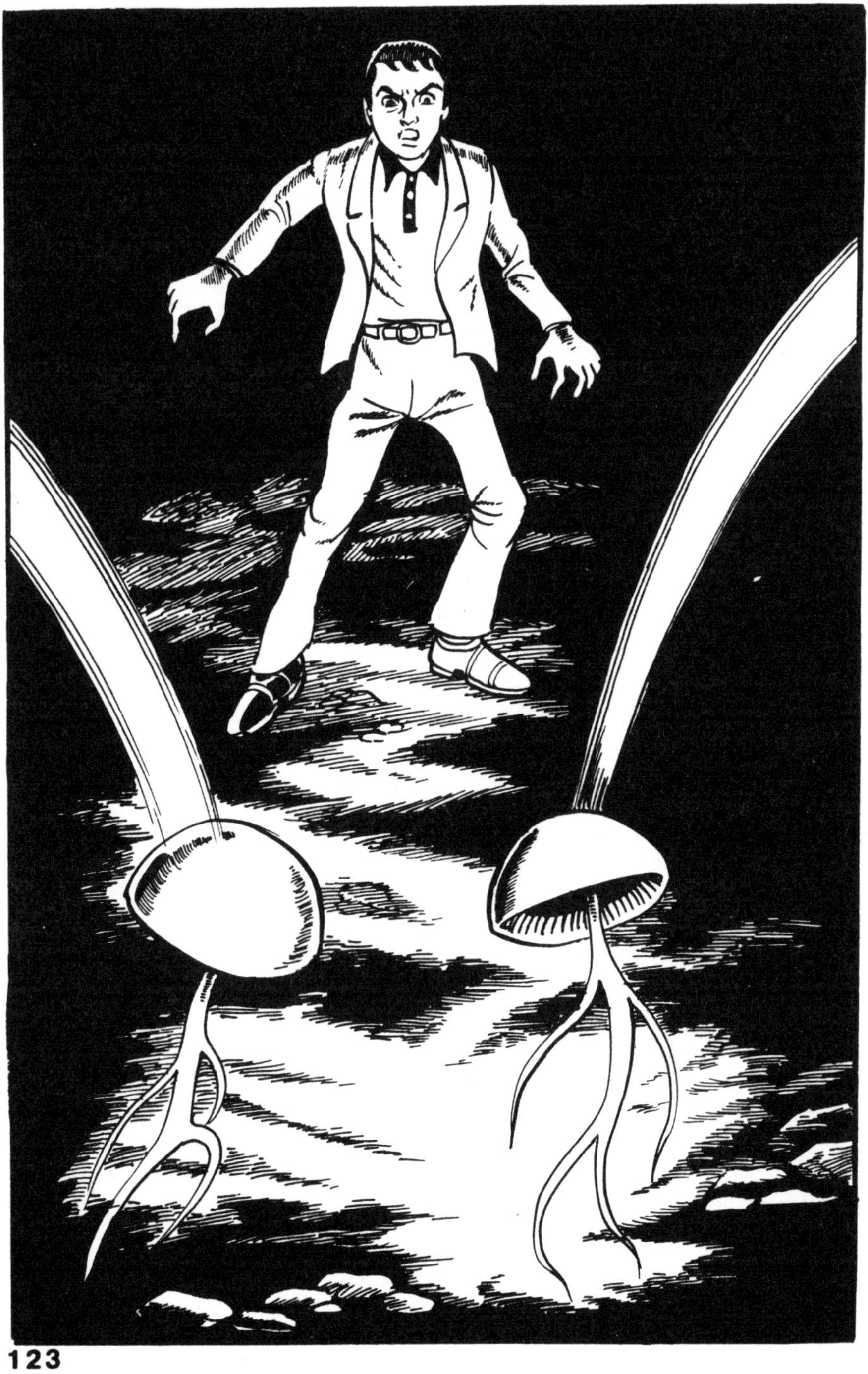

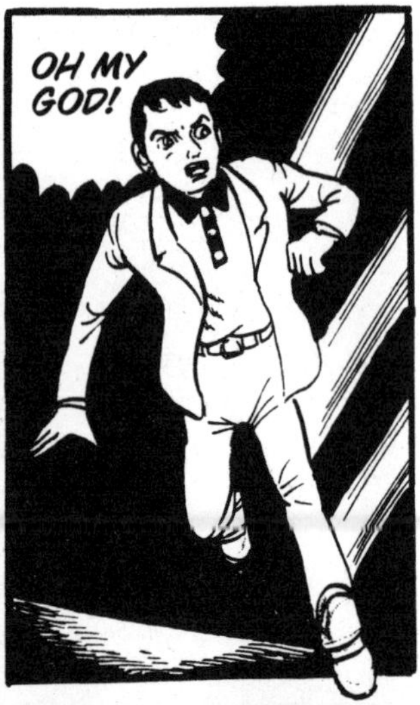
OH MY GOD!
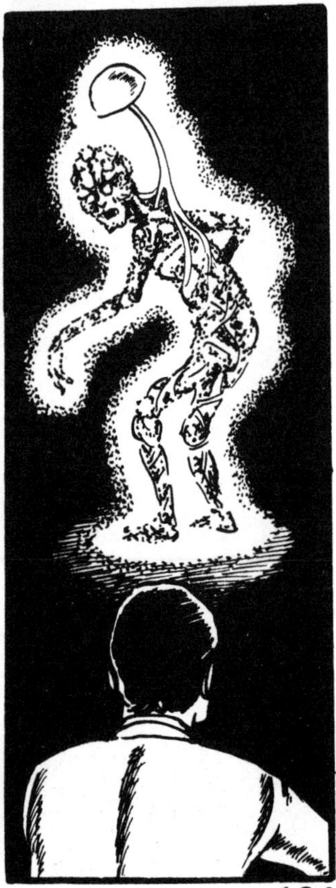
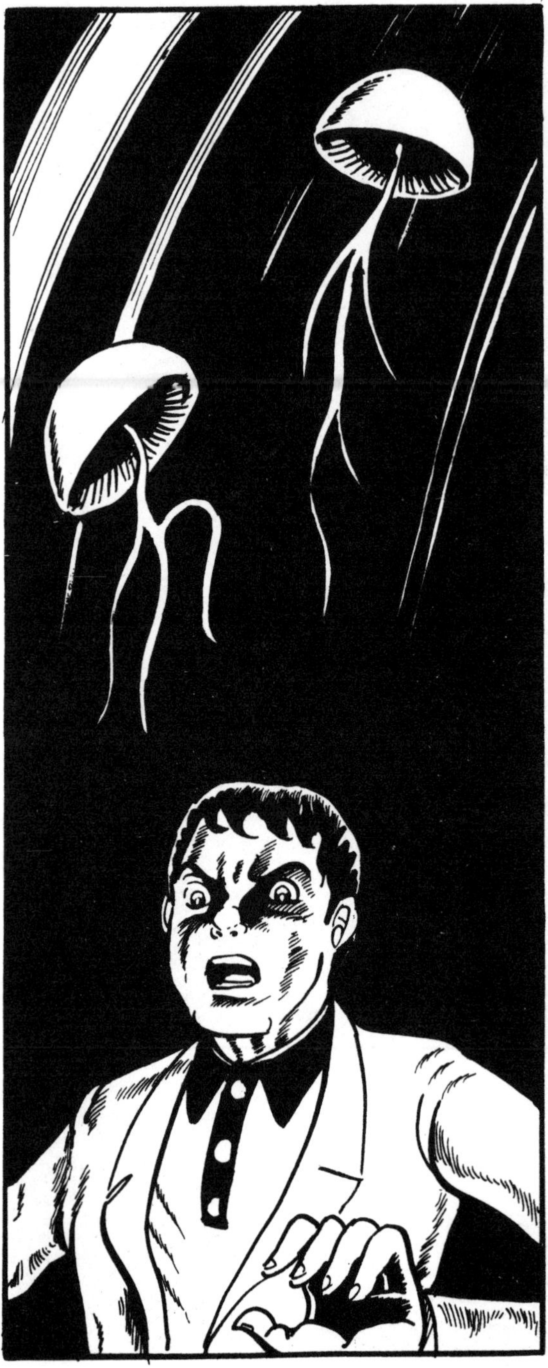

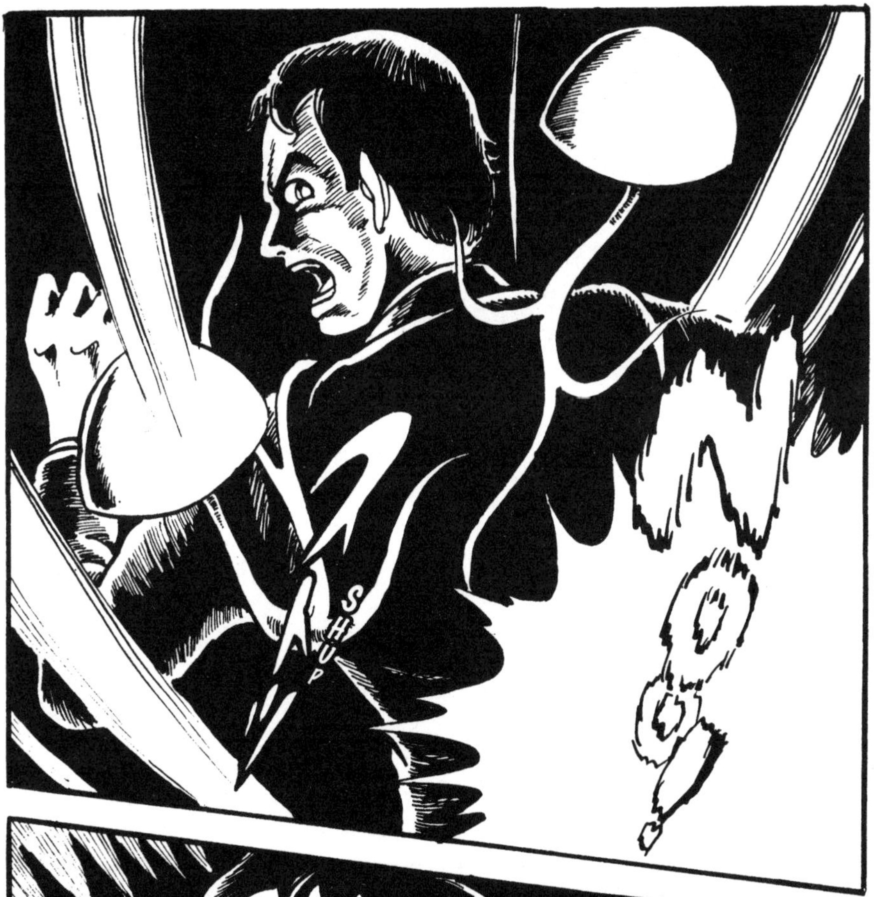
SHUP
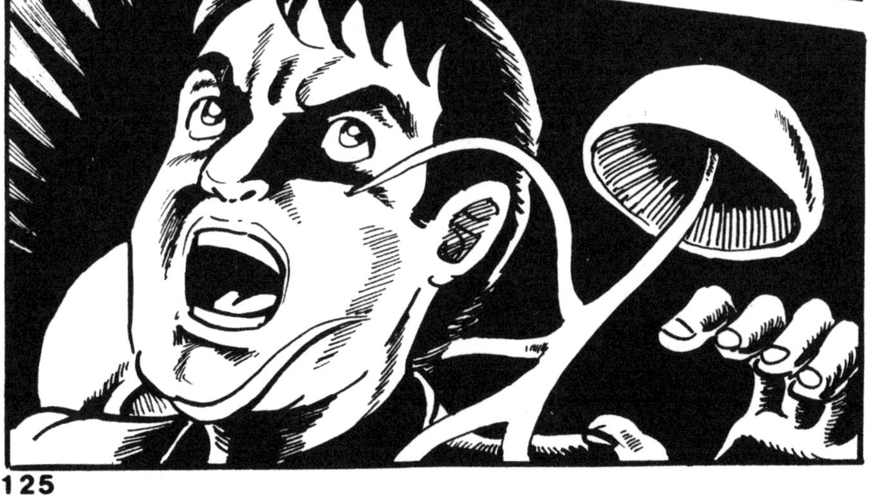

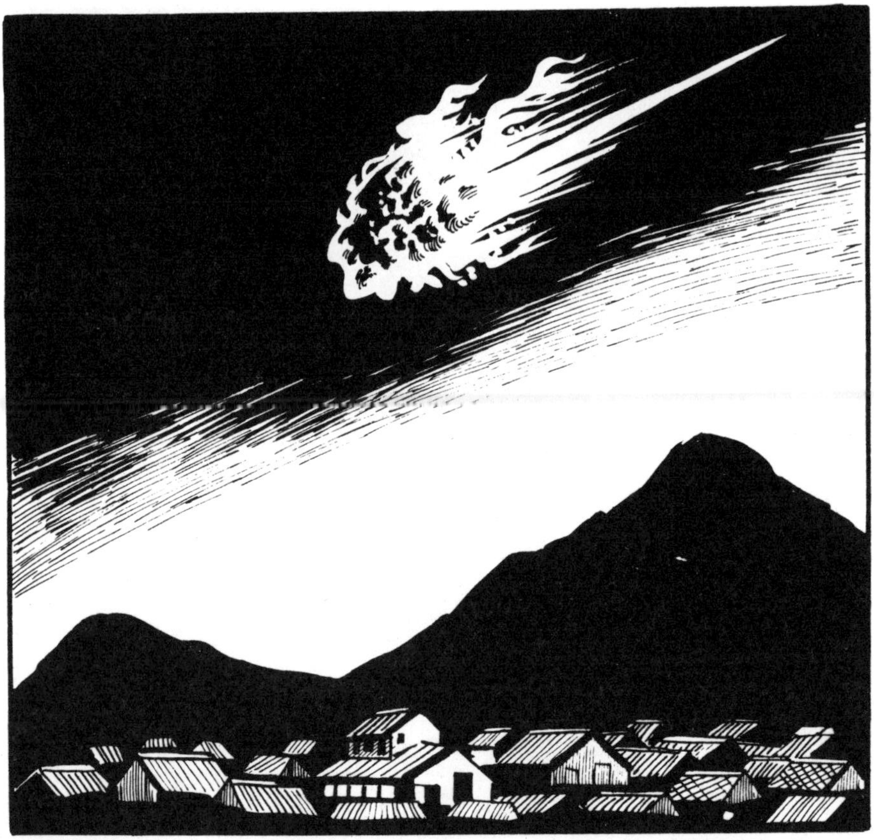
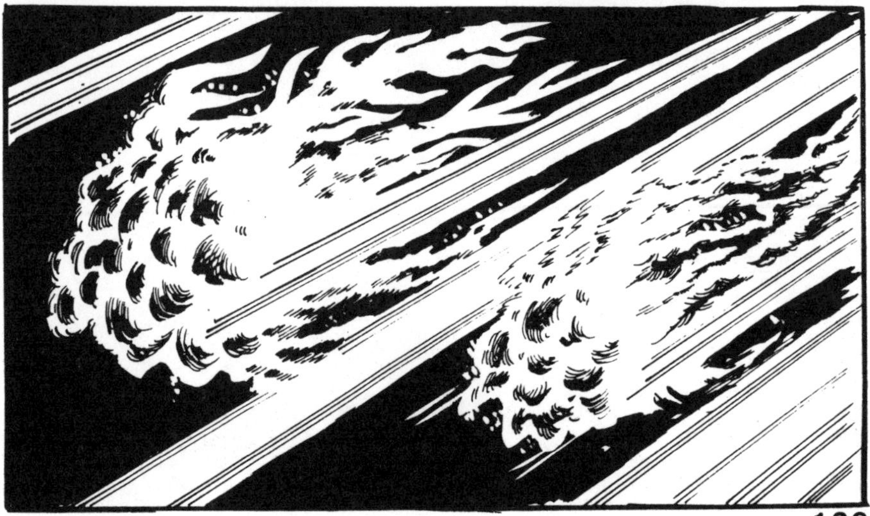

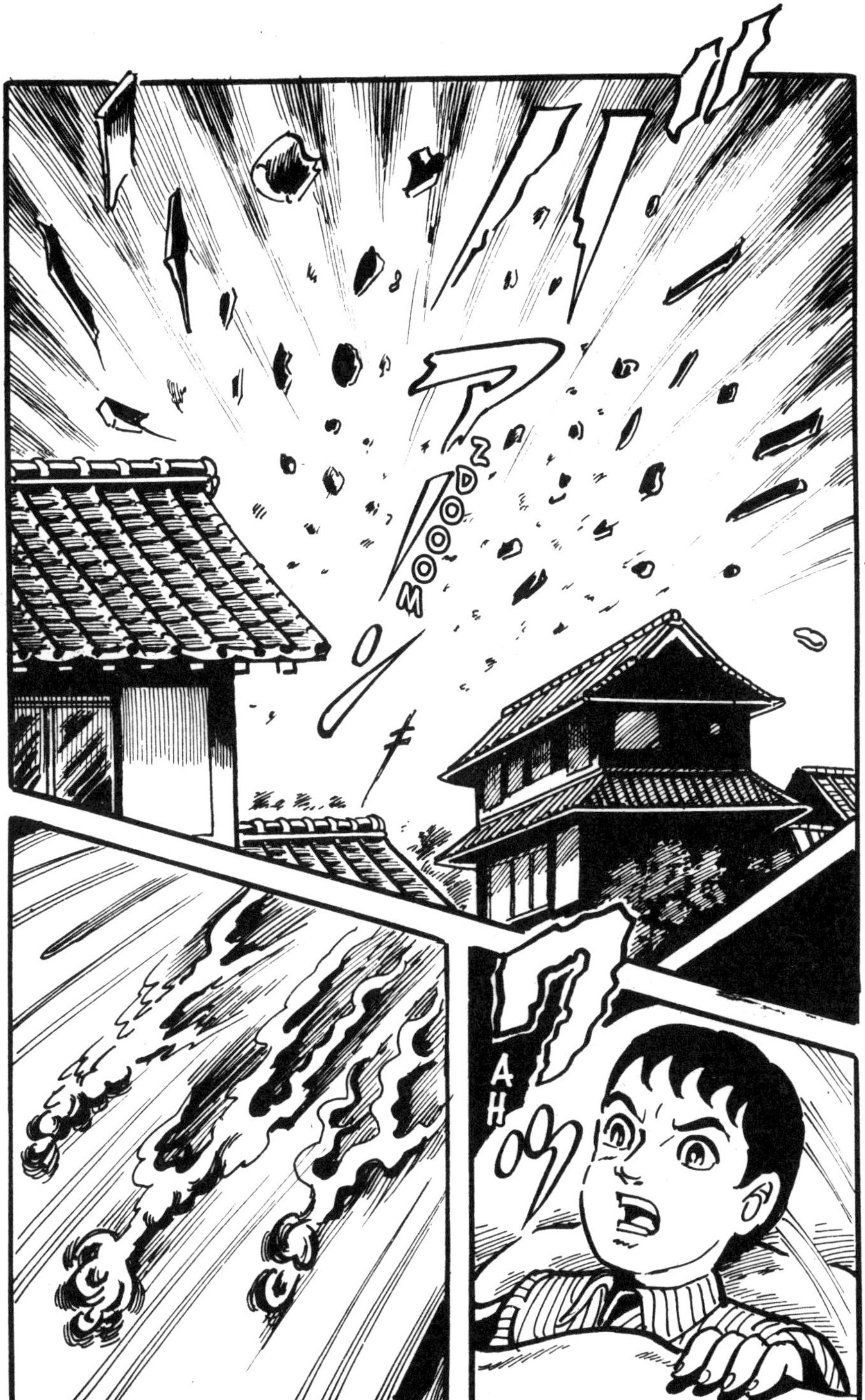
ZDOOOOM
AH

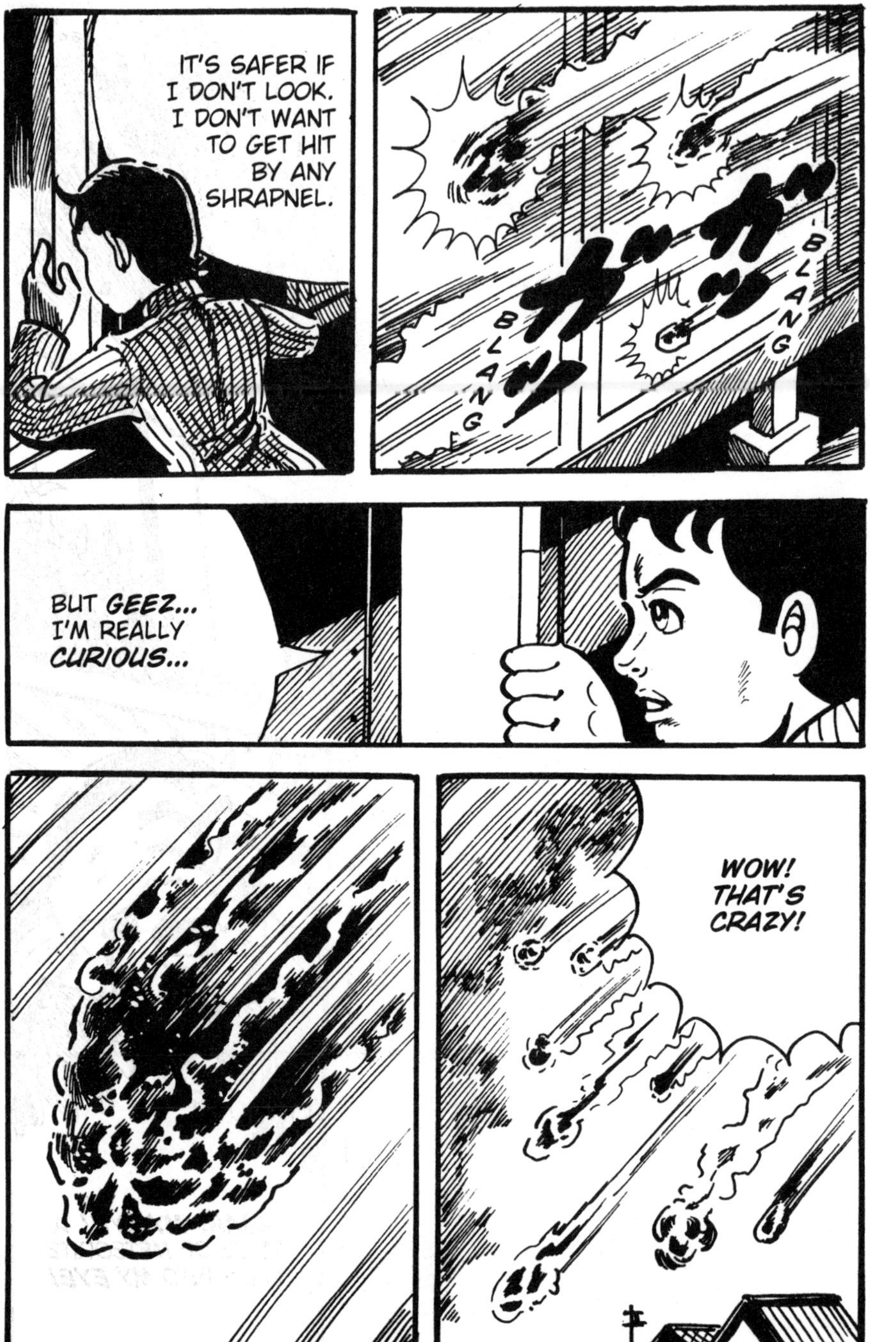
BLANG
BLANG
IT'S SAFER IF I DON'T LOOK. I DON'T WANT TO GET HIT BY ANY SHRAPNEL.
BUT GEEZ... I'M REALLY CURIOUS...
WOW! THAT'S CRAZY!

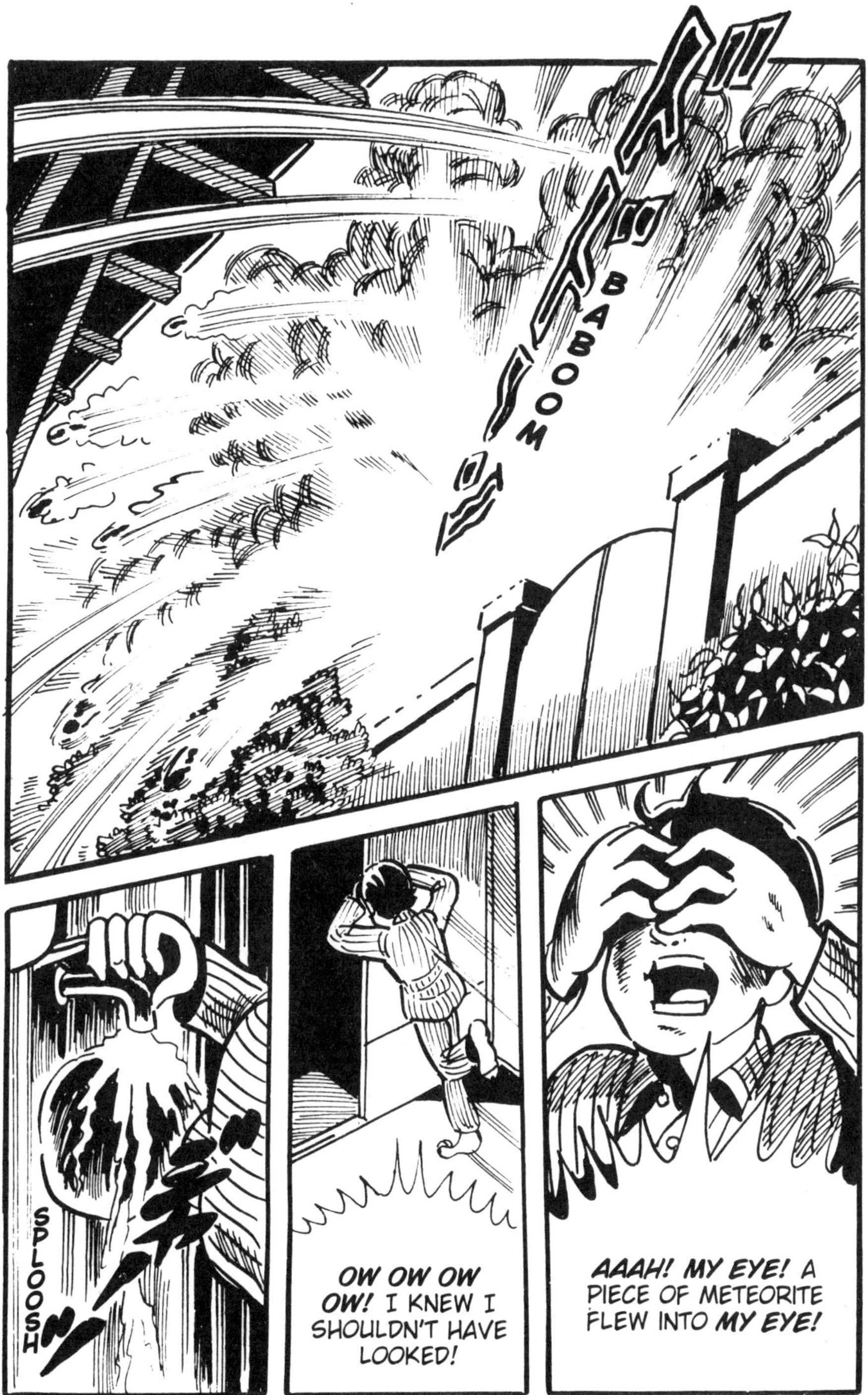
BABOOM
AAAH! MY EYE! A PIECE OF METEORITE FLEW INTO MY EYE!
OW OW OW OW! I KNEW I SHOULDN'T HAVE LOOKED!
SPLOOSH

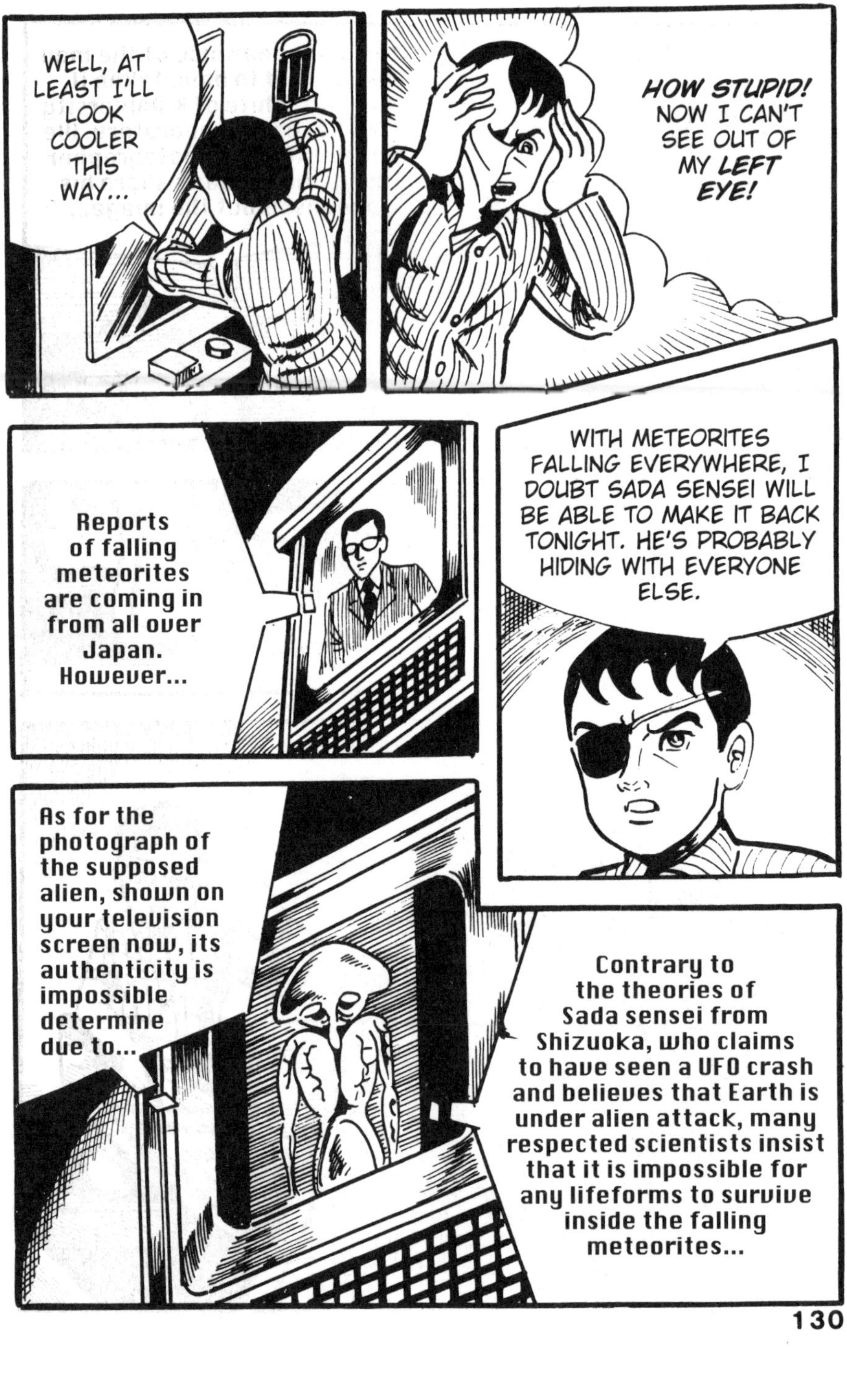
WELL, AT LEAST I'LL LOOK COOLER THIS WAY...
HOW STUPID! NOW I CAN'T SEE OUT OF MY LEFT EYE!
Reports of falling meteorites are coming in from all over Japan. However...
WITH METEORITES FALLING EVERYWHERE, I DOUBT SADA SENSEI WILL BE ABLE TO MAKE IT BACK TONIGHT. HE'S PROBABLY HIDING WITH EVERYONE ELSE.
As for the photograph of the supposed alien, shown on your television screen now, its authenticity is impossible determine due to...
Contrary to the theories of Sada sensei from Shizuoka, who claims to have seen a UFO crash and believes that Earth is under alien attack, many respected scientists insist that it is impossible for any lifeforms to survive inside the falling meteorites...

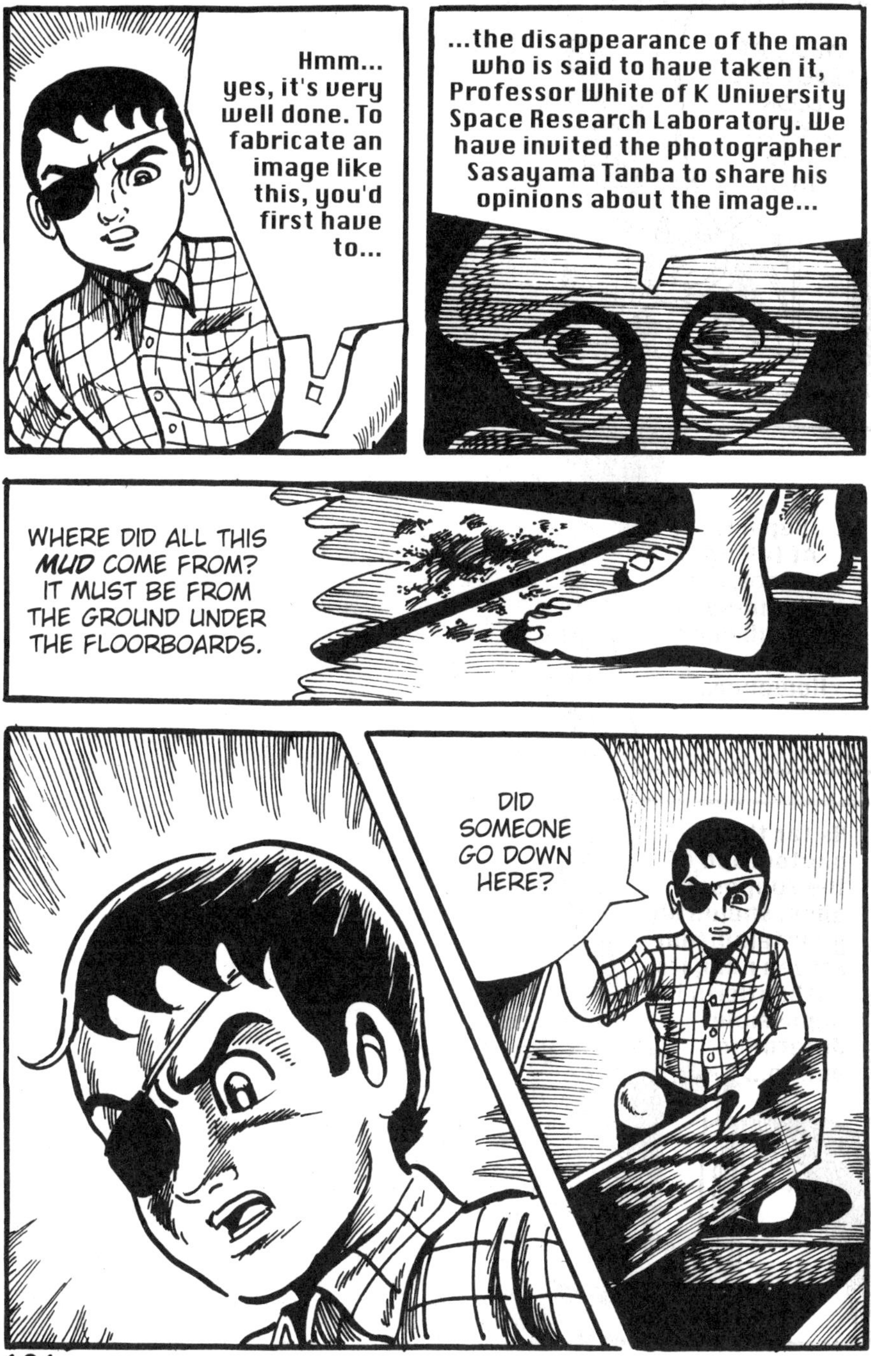
...the disappearance of the man who is said to have taken it, Professor White of K University Space Research Laboratory. We have invited the photographer Sasayama Tanba to share his opinions about the image...
Hmm... yes, it's very well done. To fabricate an image like this, you'd first have to...
WHERE DID ALL THIS MUD COME FROM? IT MUST BE FROM THE GROUND UNDER THE FLOORBOARDS.
DID SOMEONE GO DOWN HERE?

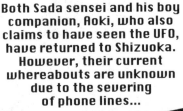

Both Sada sensei and his boy companion, Aoki, who also claims to have seen the UFO, have returned to Shizuoka. However, their current whereabouts are unknown due to the severing of phone lines...

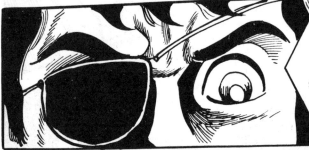

...caused by the falling meteorites. Many other regions are experiencing similar difficulties. Meanwhile, in the suburbs of Tokyo...

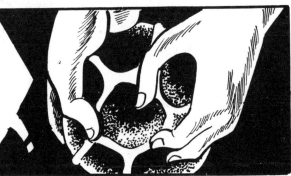

...false claims of UFO attacks have caused mass panic at the Takashimadaira Public Housing Complex. Reports of housewives raiding grocery stores have...

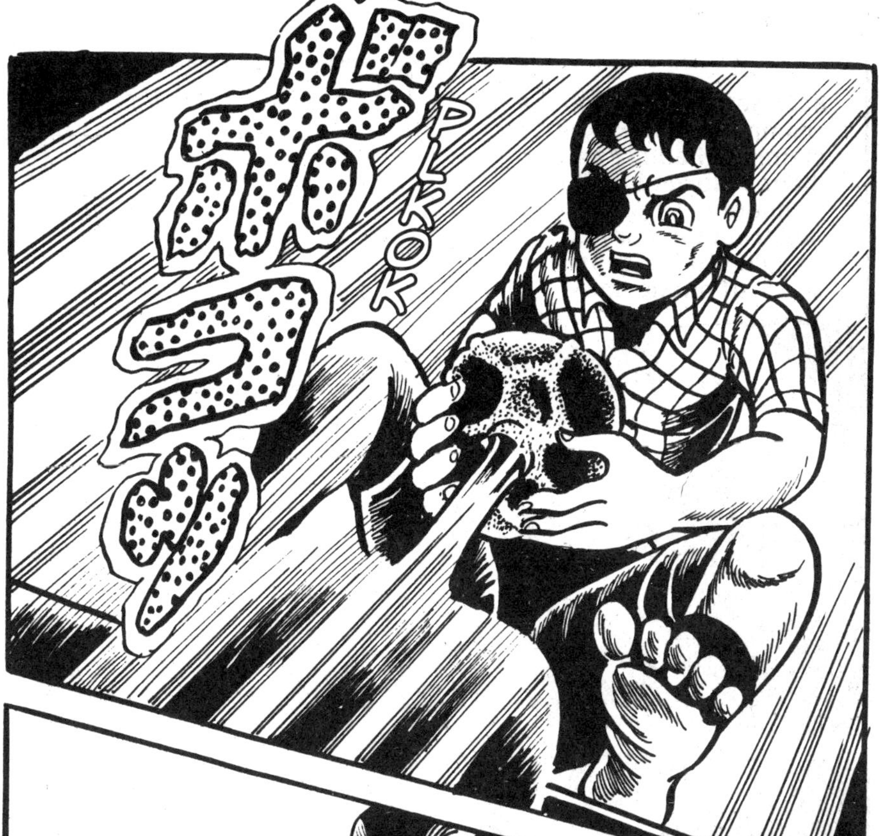
PIKOK

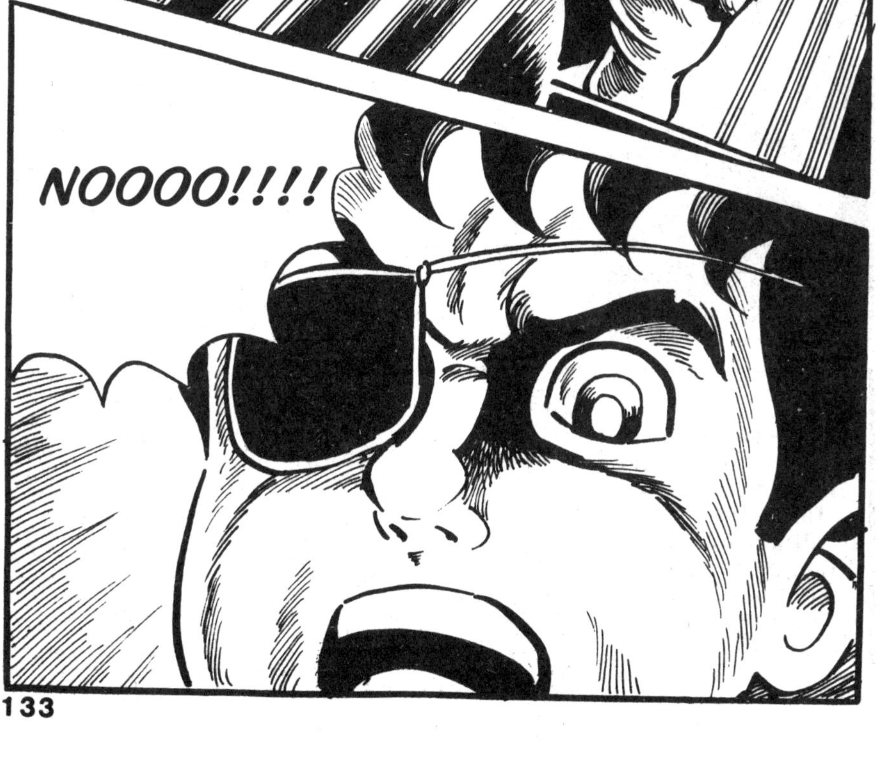
NOOOO!!!!

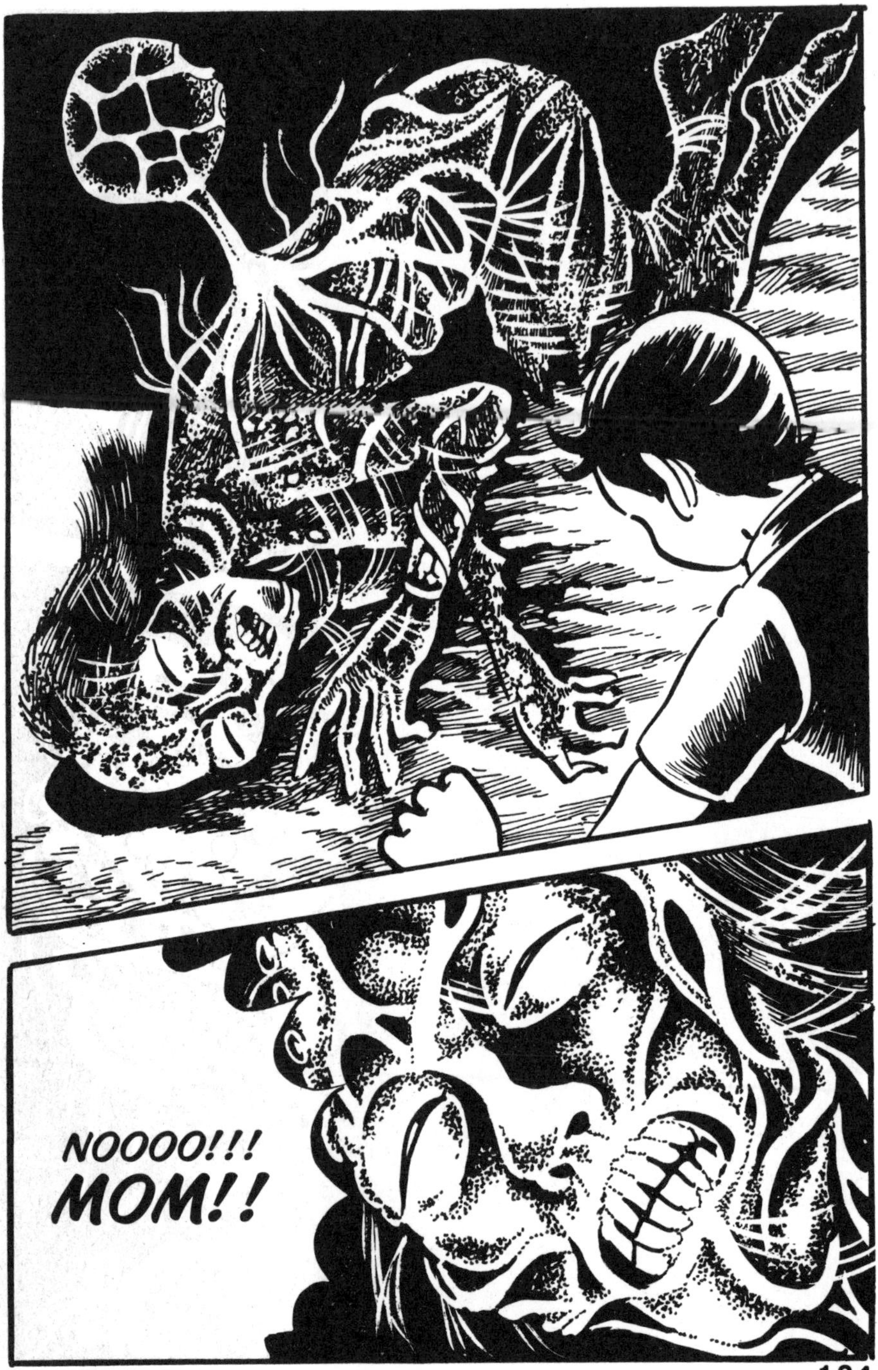
NOOOO!!!
MOM!!

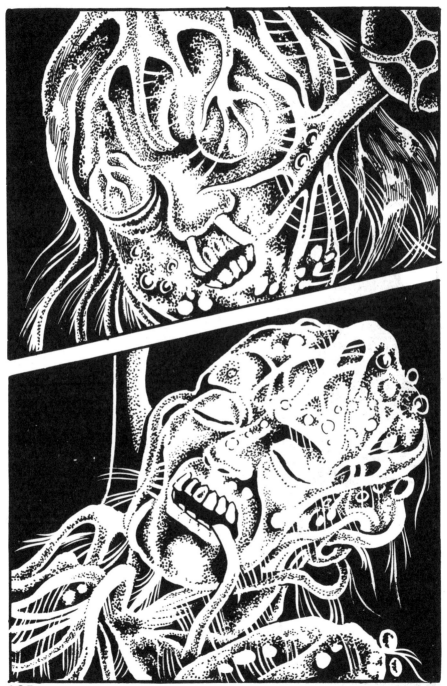

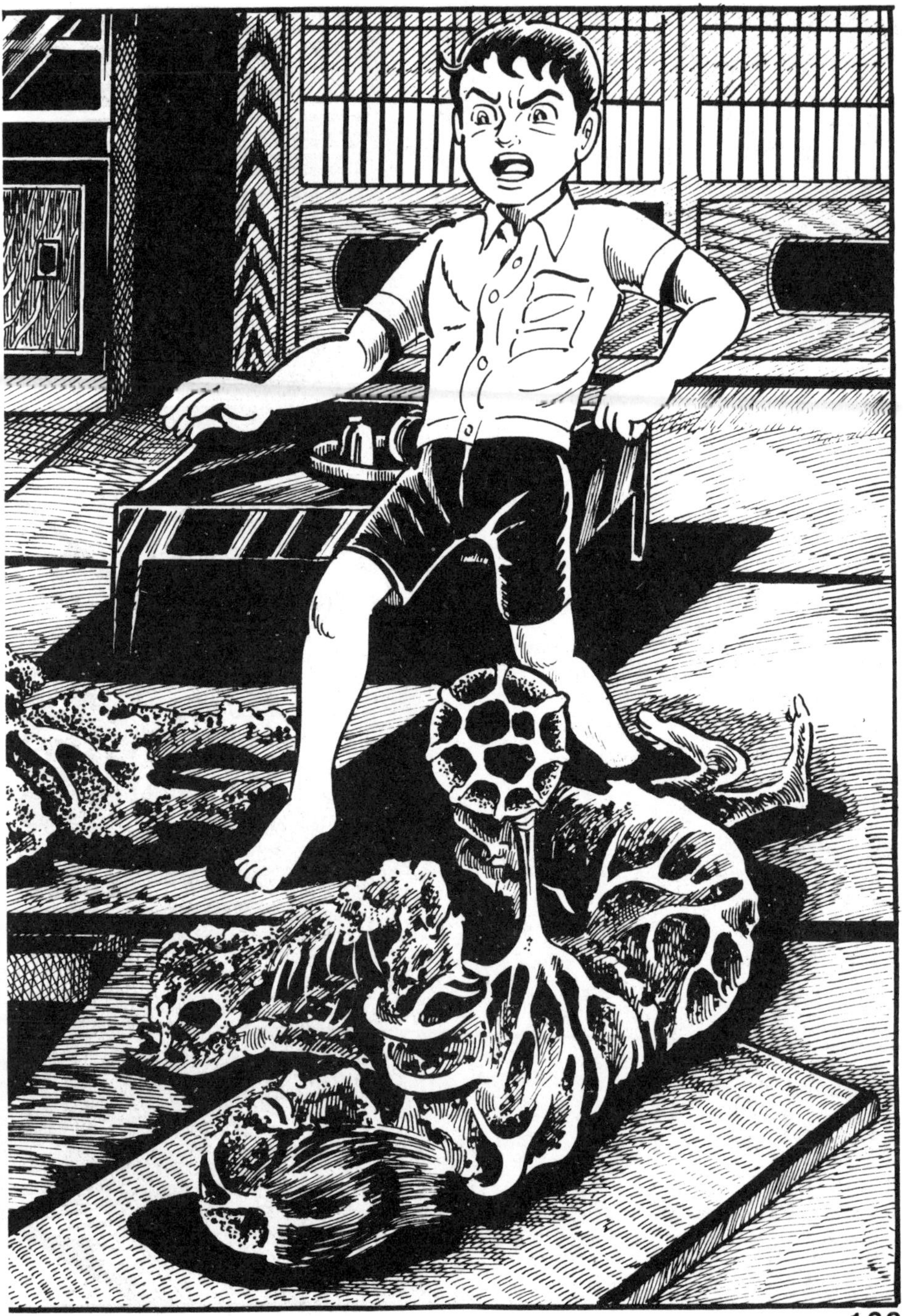

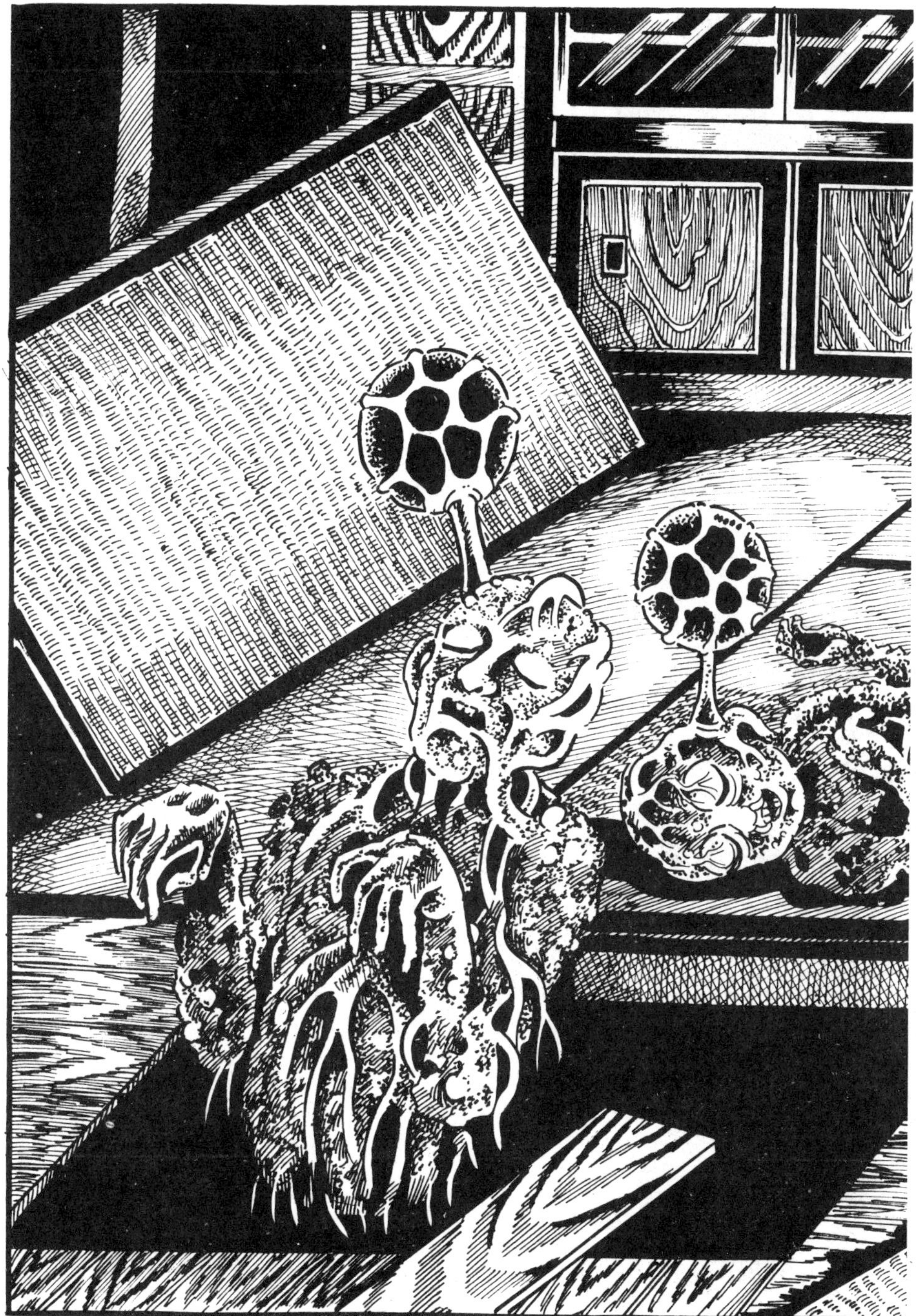

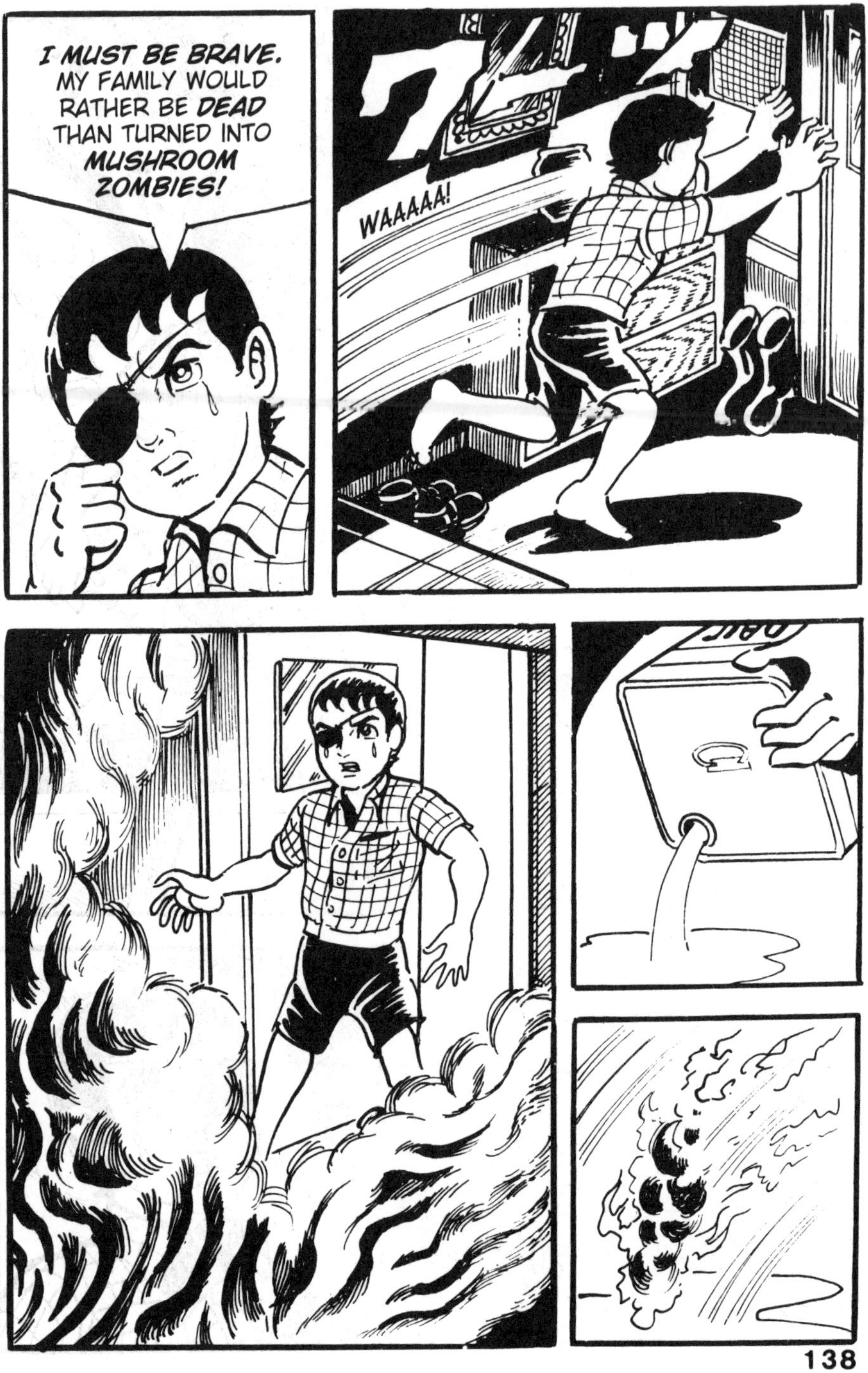
WAAAAA!
I MUST BE BRAVE. MY FAMILY WOULD RATHER BE DEAD THAN TURNED INTO MUSHROOM ZOMBIES!

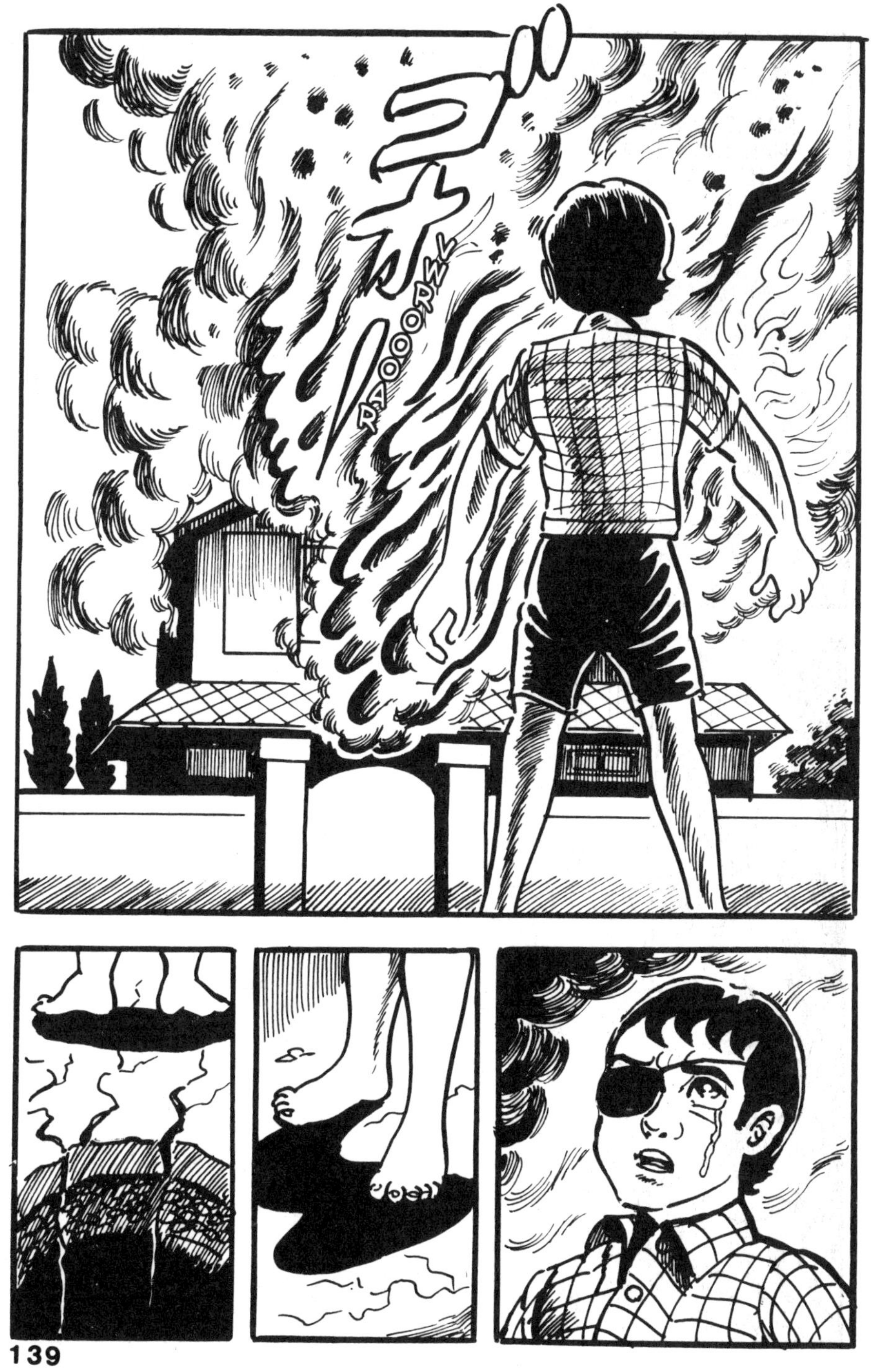
ゴオ
VWROOOAR

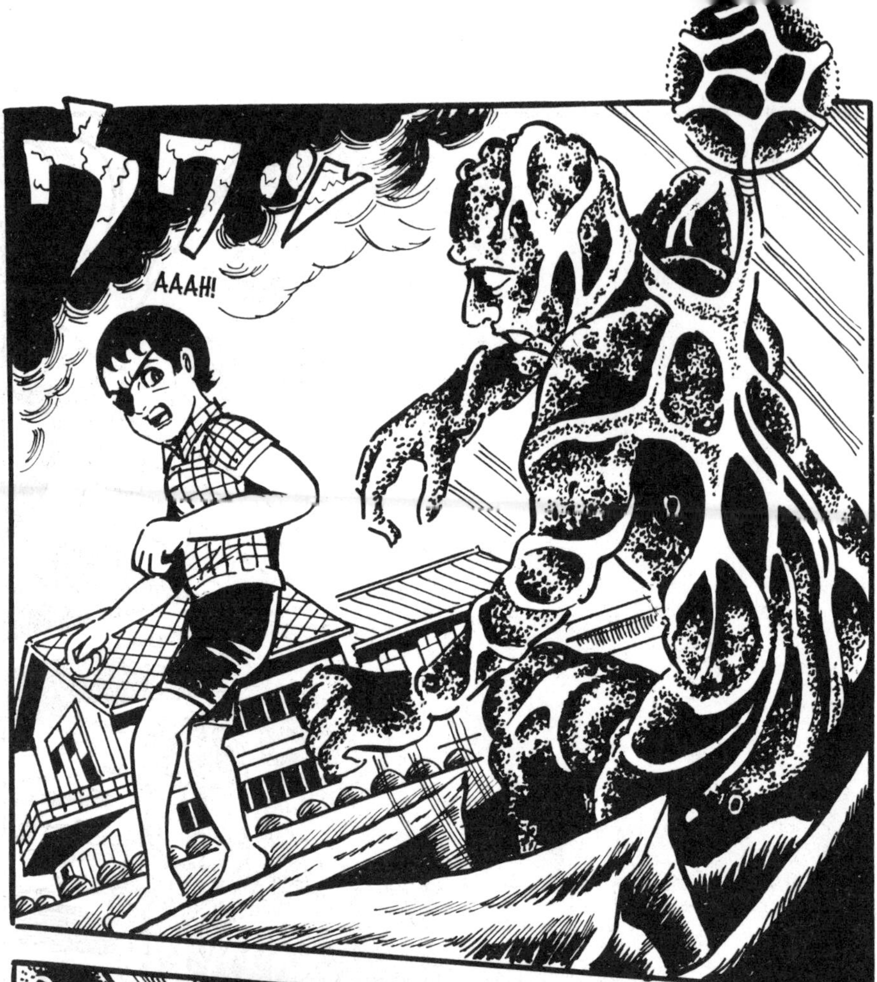
ウワッ
AAAH!
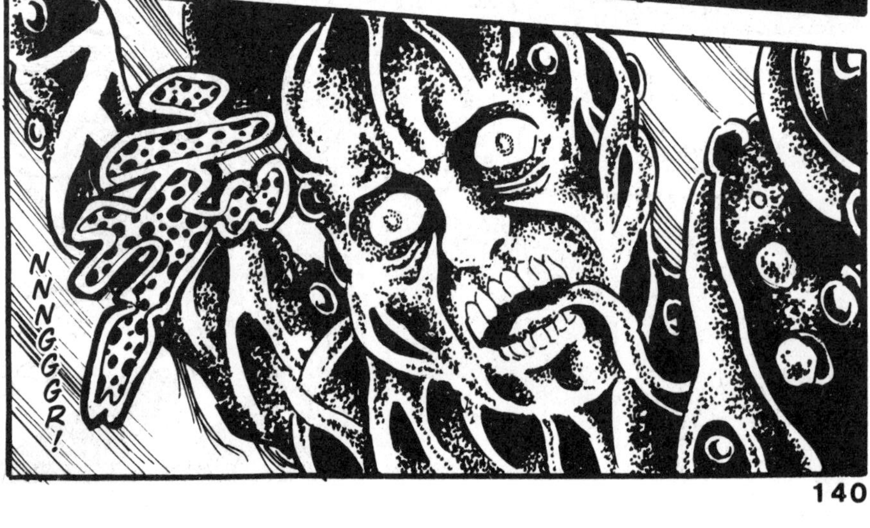
NNNGGGR!

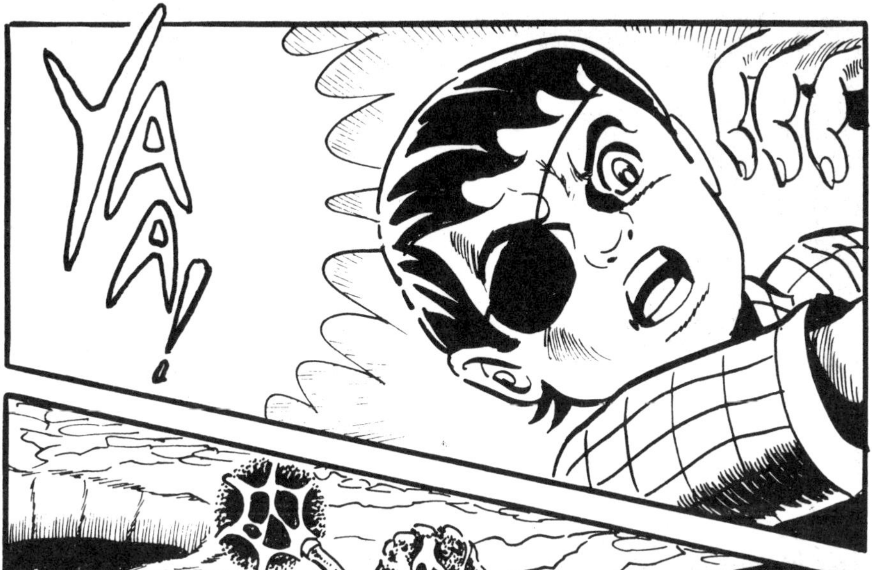
YAAA!
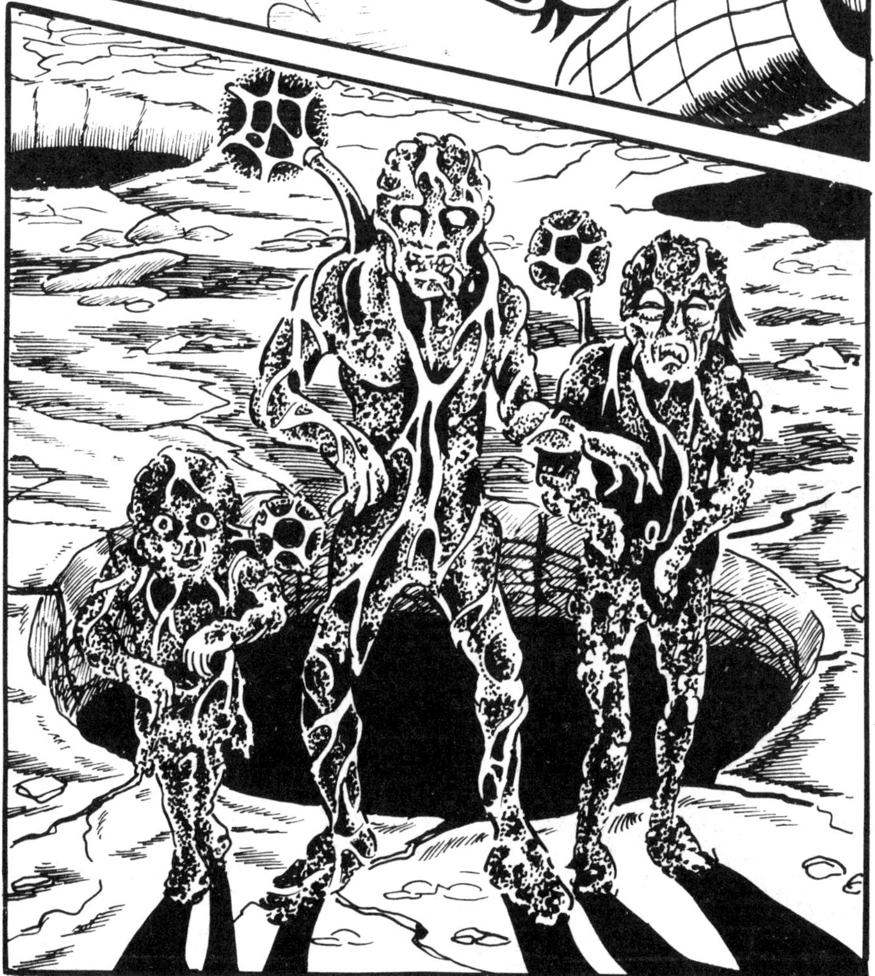

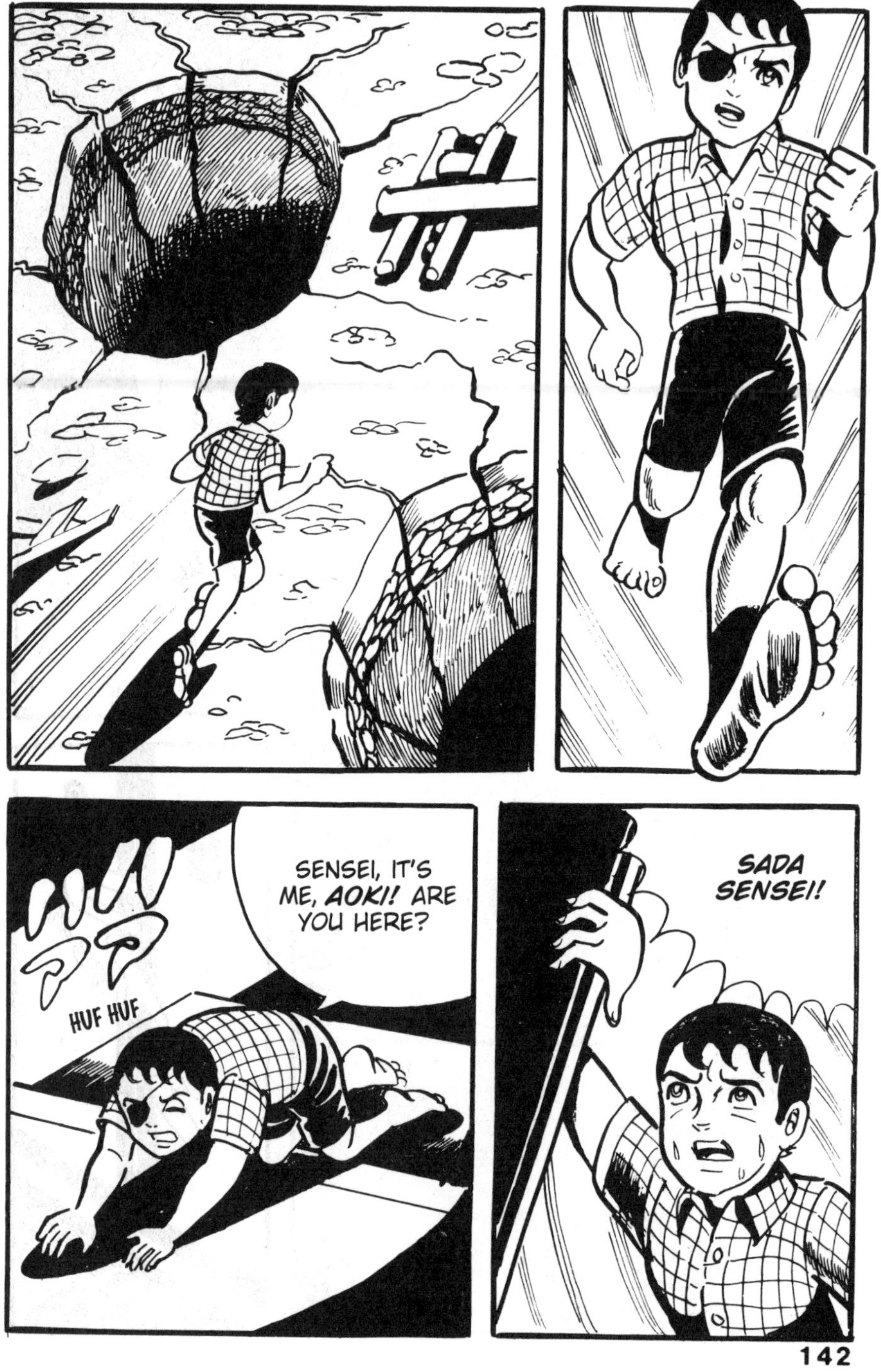
SADA SENSEI!
SENSEI, IT'S ME, AOKI! ARE YOU HERE?
HUF HUF

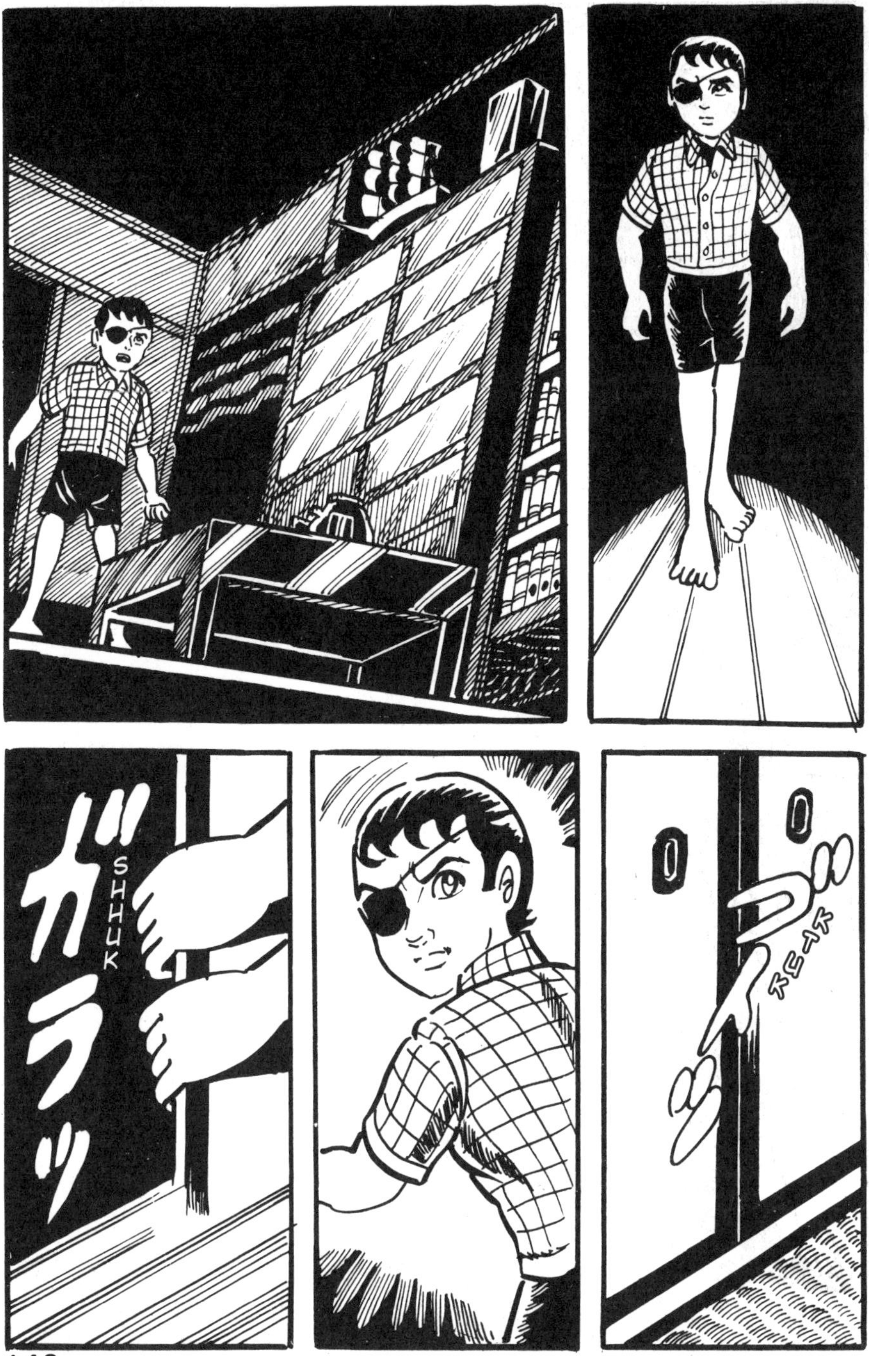
ガラッ
SHHUK

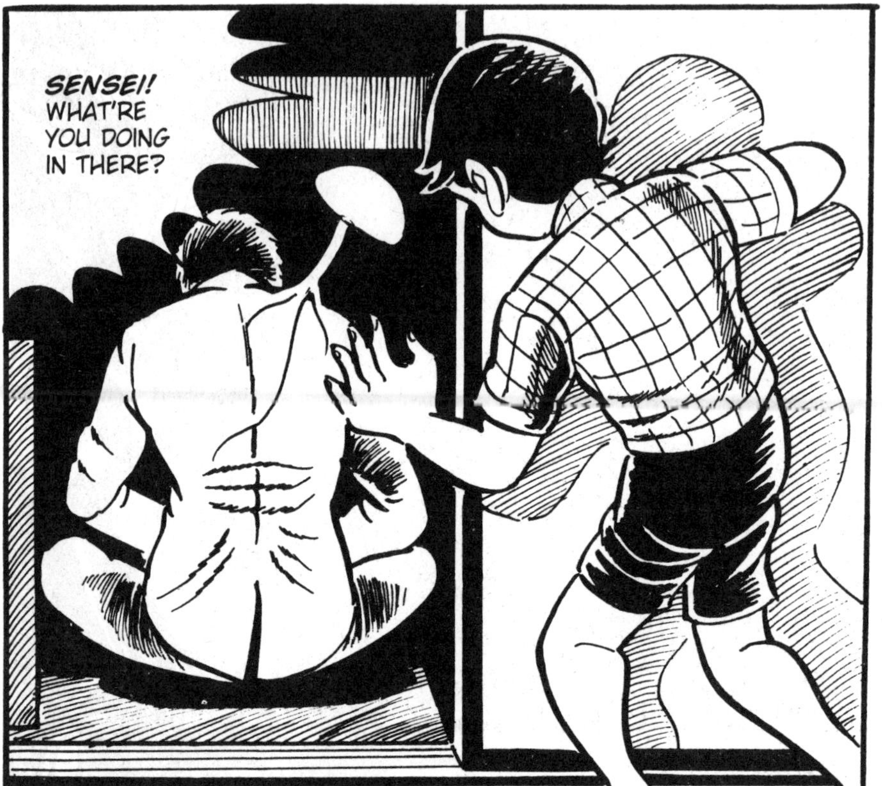
SENSEI! WHAT'RE YOU DOING IN THERE?

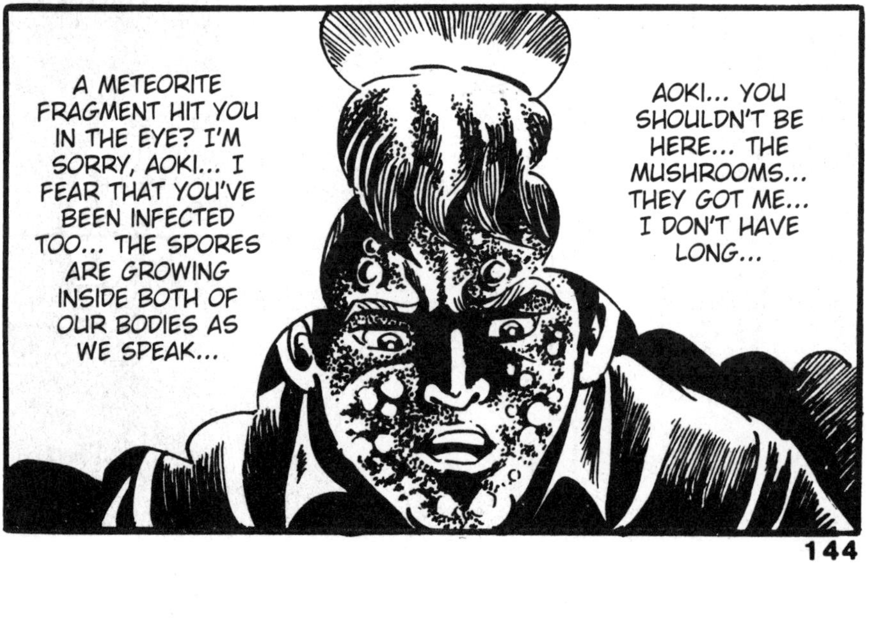
AOKI... YOU SHOULDN'T BE HERE... THE MUSHROOMS... THEY GOT ME... I DON'T HAVE LONG...
A METEORITE FRAGMENT HIT YOU IN THE EYE? I'M SORRY, AOKI... I FEAR THAT YOU'VE BEEN INFECTED TOO... THE SPORES ARE GROWING INSIDE BOTH OF OUR BODIES AS WE SPEAK...

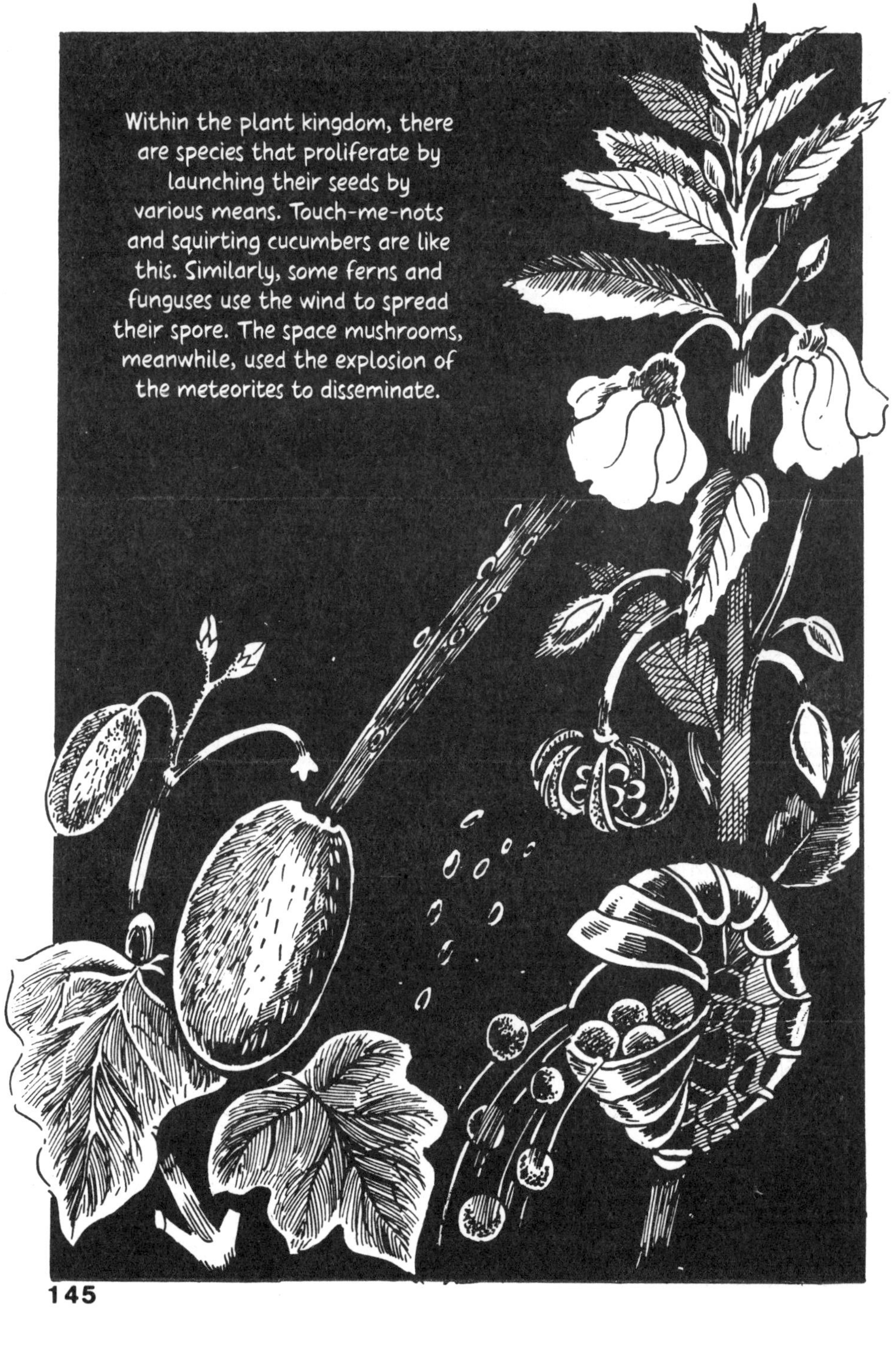
Within the plant kingdom, there are species that proliferate by launching their seeds by various means. Touch-me-nots and squirting cucumbers are like this. Similarly, some ferns and funguses use the wind to spread their spore. The space mushrooms, meanwhile, used the explosion of the meteorites to disseminate.

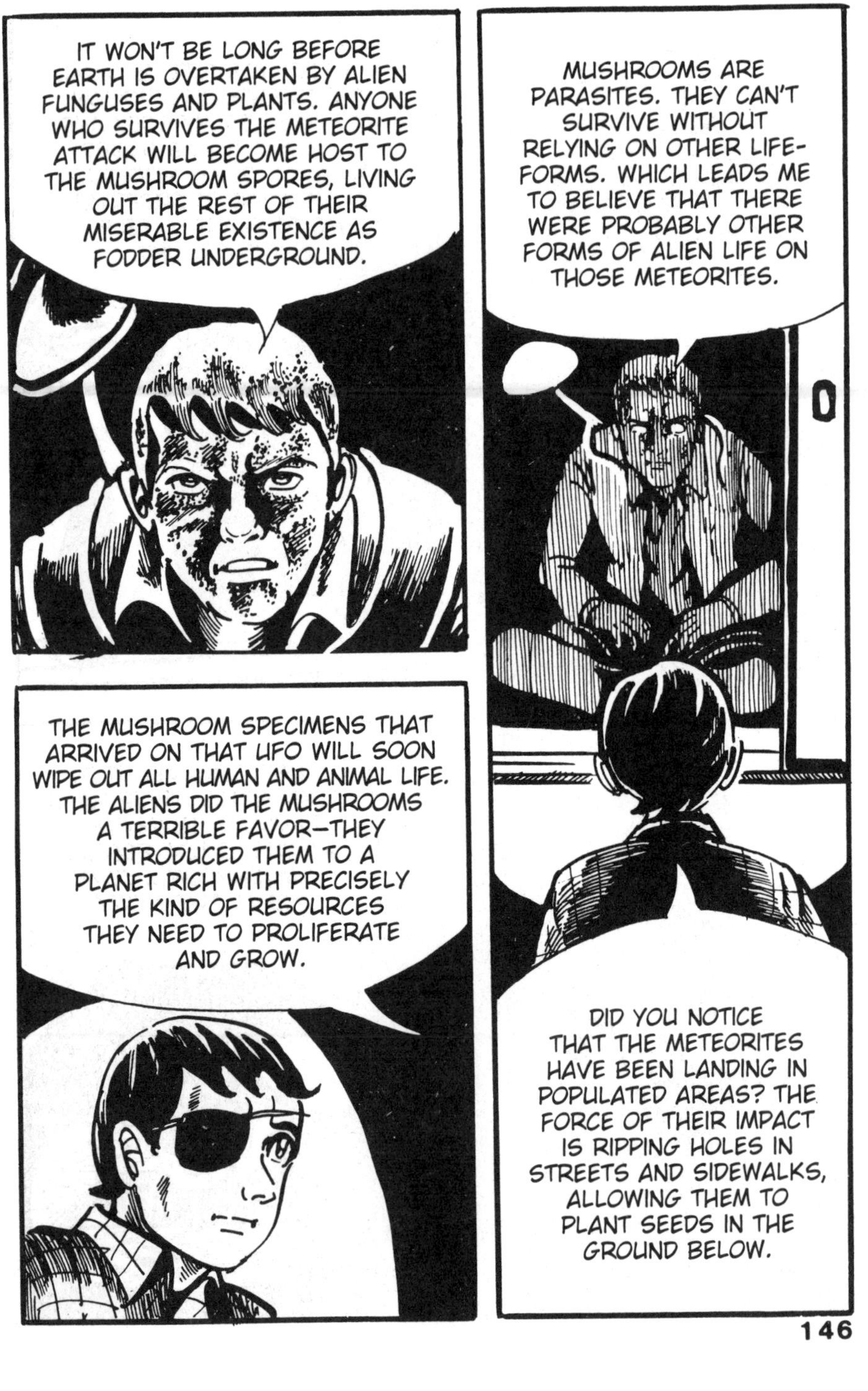
MUSHROOMS ARE PARASITES. THEY CAN'T SURVIVE WITHOUT RELYING ON OTHER LIFE-FORMS. WHICH LEADS ME TO BELIEVE THAT THERE WERE PROBABLY OTHER FORMS OF ALIEN LIFE ON THOSE METEORITES.
IT WON'T BE LONG BEFORE EARTH IS OVERTAKEN BY ALIEN FUNGUSES AND PLANTS. ANYONE WHO SURVIVES THE METEORITE ATTACK WILL BECOME HOST TO THE MUSHROOM SPORES, LIVING OUT THE REST OF THEIR MISERABLE EXISTENCE AS FODDER UNDERGROUND.
DID YOU NOTICE THAT THE METEORITES HAVE BEEN LANDING IN POPULATED AREAS? THE FORCE OF THEIR IMPACT IS RIPPING HOLES IN STREETS AND SIDEWALKS, ALLOWING THEM TO PLANT SEEDS IN THE GROUND BELOW.
THE MUSHROOM SPECIMENS THAT ARRIVED ON THAT UFO WILL SOON WIPE OUT ALL HUMAN AND ANIMAL LIFE. THE ALIENS DID THE MUSHROOMS A TERRIBLE FAVOR—THEY INTRODUCED THEM TO A PLANET RICH WITH PRECISELY THE KIND OF RESOURCES THEY NEED TO PROLIFERATE AND GROW.

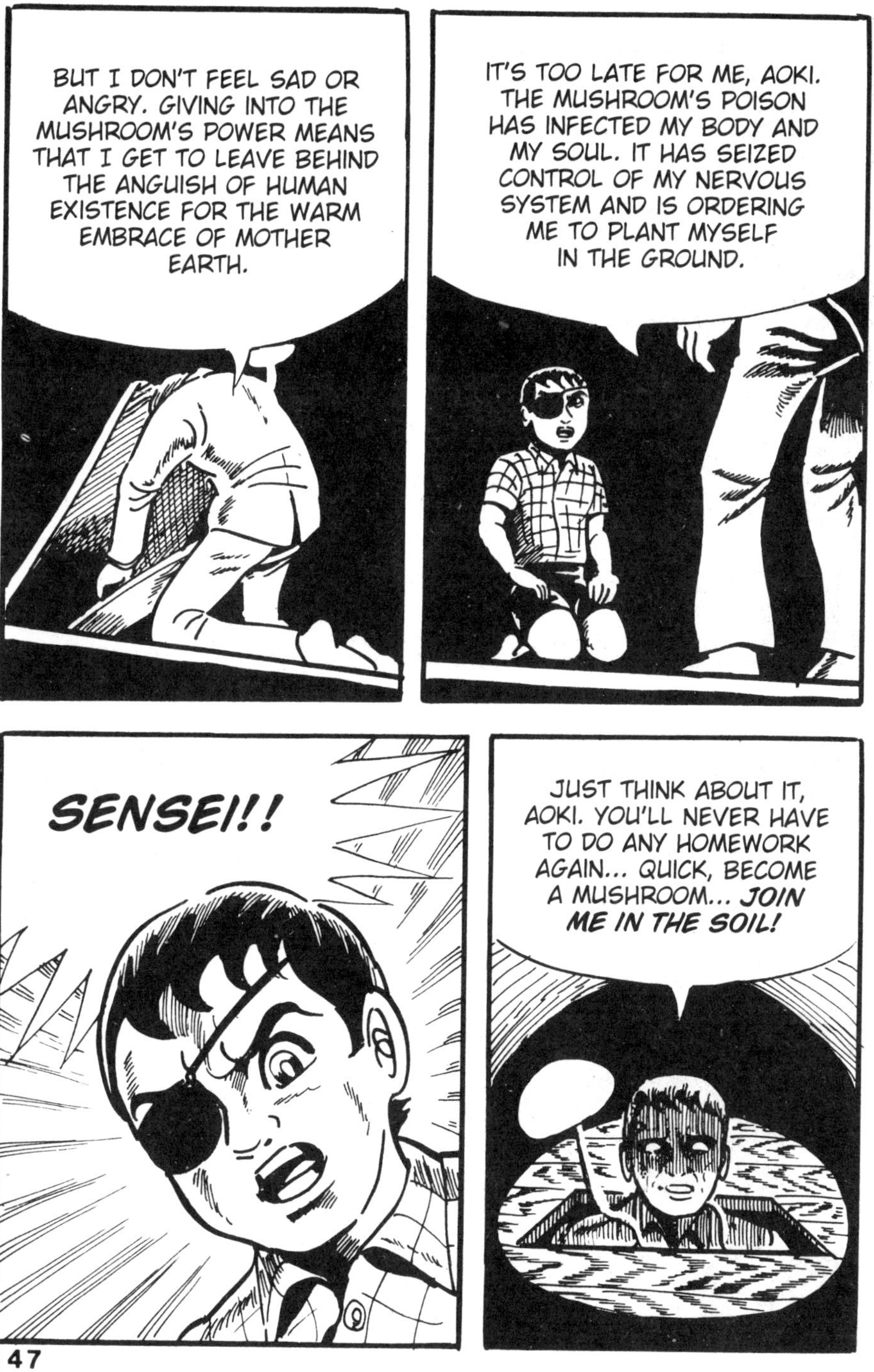
IT'S TOO LATE FOR ME, AOKI. THE MUSHROOM'S POISON HAS INFECTED MY BODY AND MY SOUL. IT HAS SEIZED CONTROL OF MY NERVOUS SYSTEM AND IS ORDERING ME TO PLANT MYSELF IN THE GROUND.
BUT I DON'T FEEL SAD OR ANGRY. GIVING INTO THE MUSHROOM'S POWER MEANS THAT I GET TO LEAVE BEHIND THE ANGUISH OF HUMAN EXISTENCE FOR THE WARM EMBRACE OF MOTHER EARTH.
JUST THINK ABOUT IT, AOKI. YOU'LL NEVER HAVE TO DO ANY HOMEWORK AGAIN... QUICK, BECOME A MUSHROOM... *JOIN ME IN THE SOIL!*
SENSEI!!

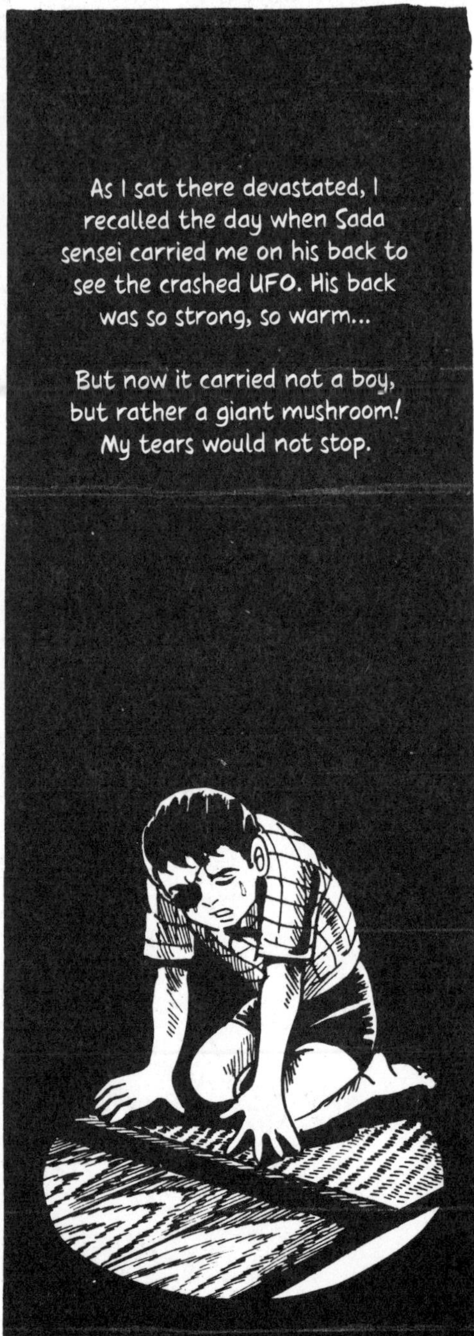
As I sat there devastated, I recalled the day when Sada sensei carried me on his back to see the crashed UFO. His back was so strong, so warm...
But now it carried not a boy, but rather a giant mushroom! My tears would not stop.

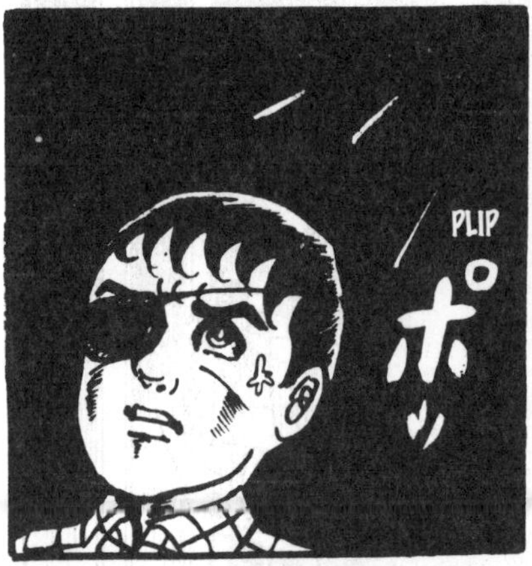
PLIP
ポッ

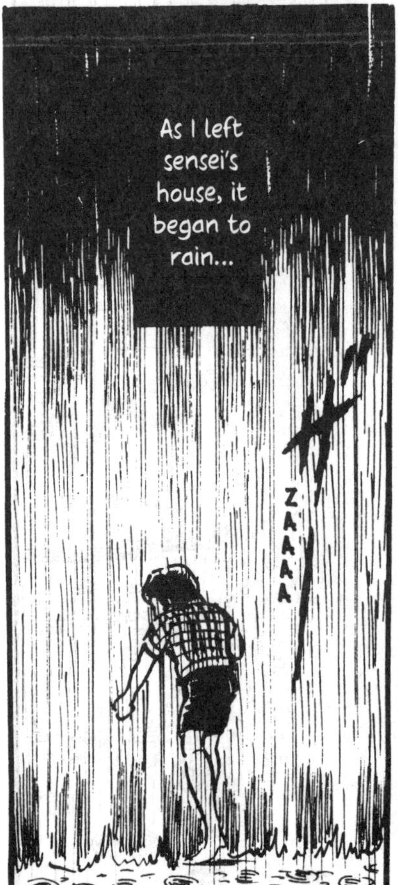
As I left sensei's house, it began to rain...
ZAAAA

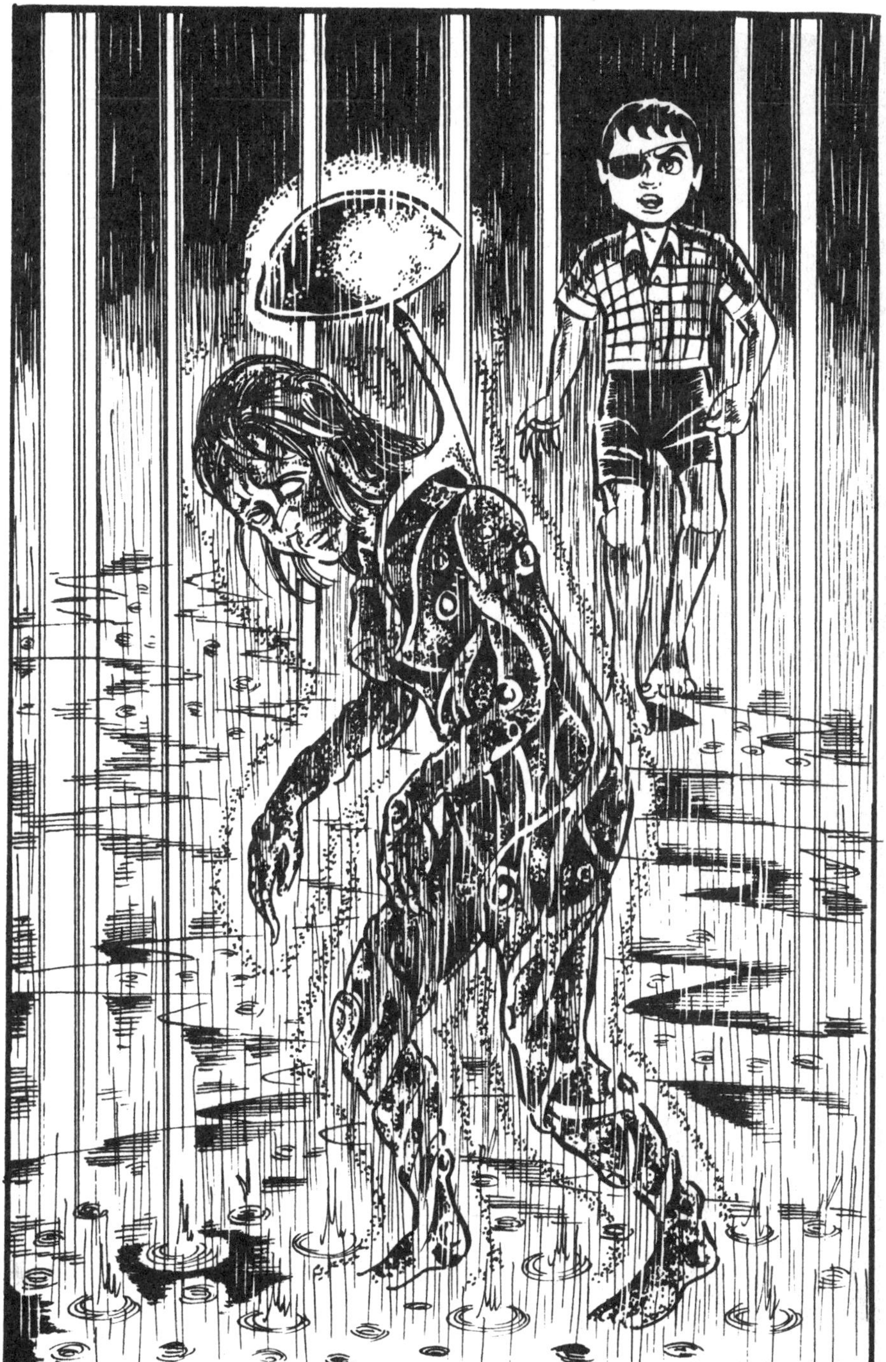

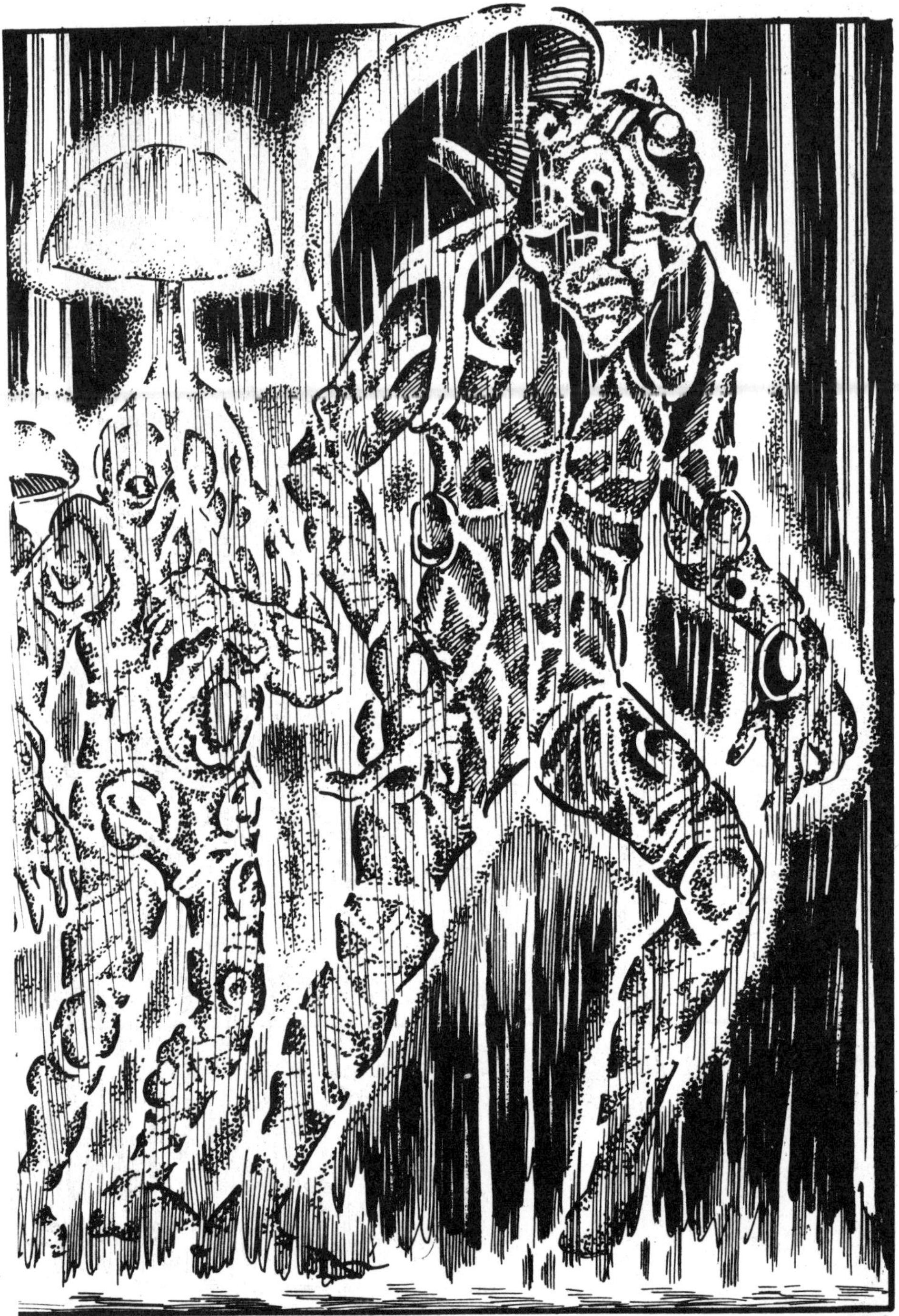

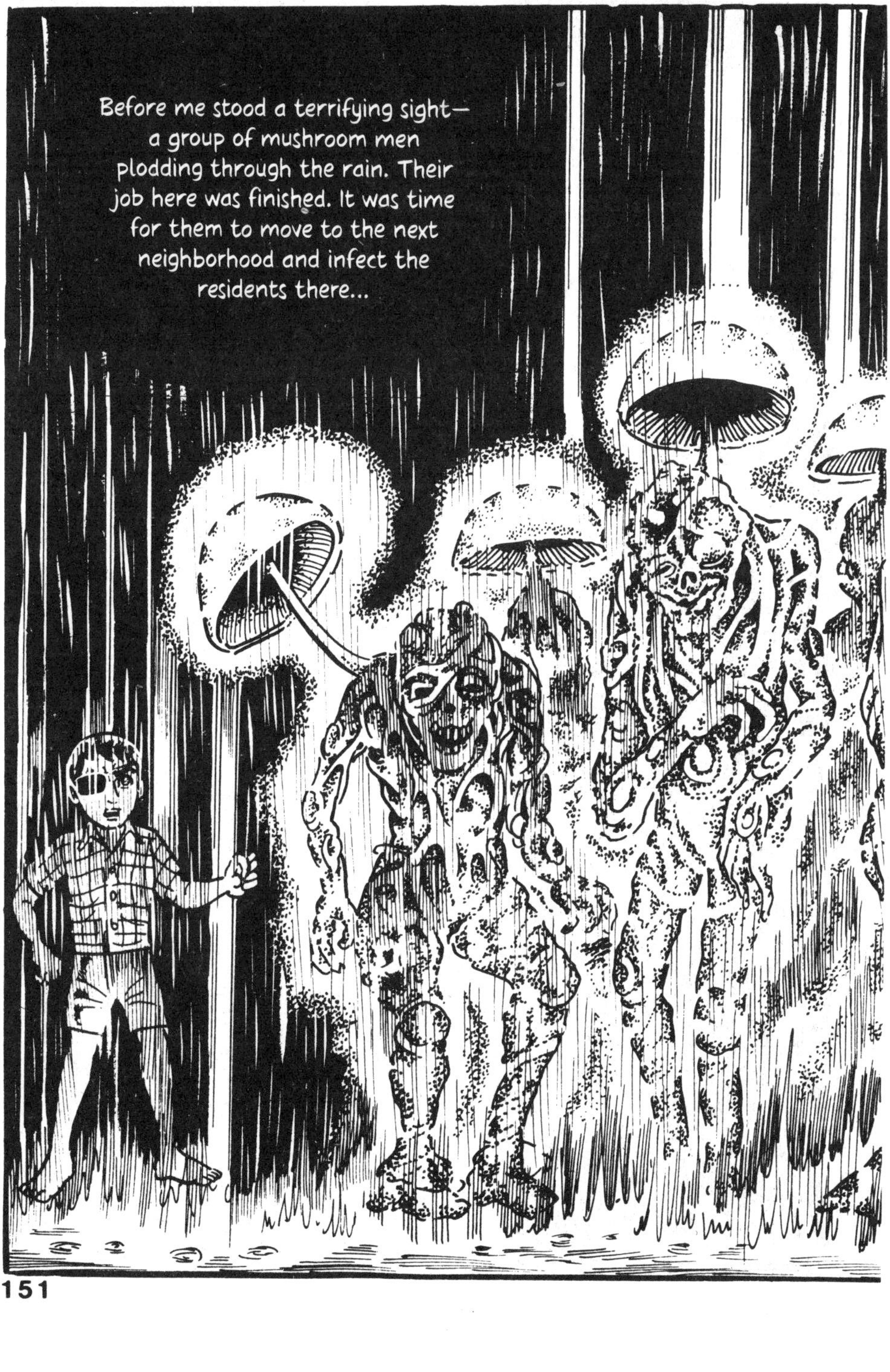
Before me stood a terrifying sight—a group of mushroom men plodding through the rain. Their job here was finished. It was time for them to move to the next neighborhood and infect the residents there...

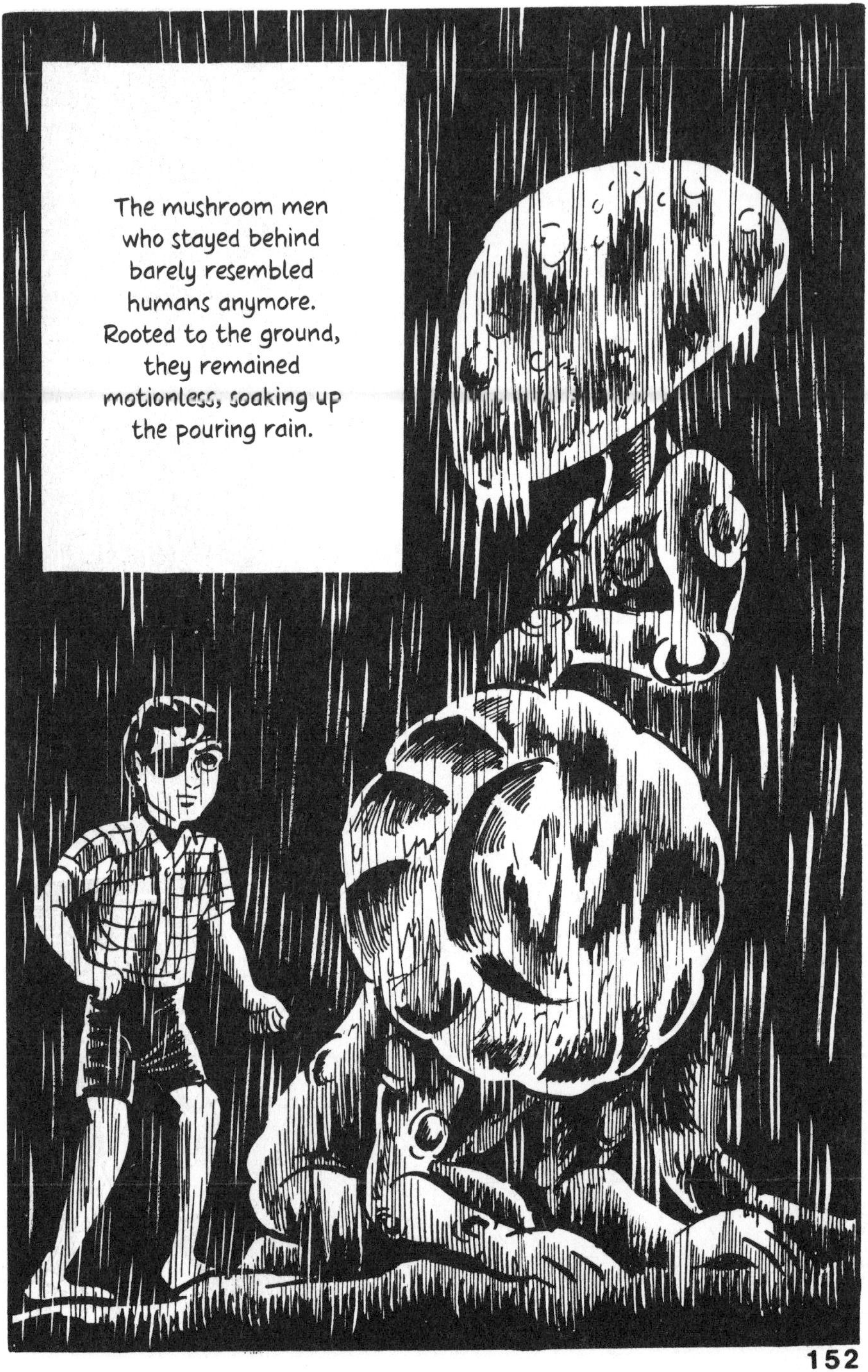
The mushroom men who stayed behind barely resembled humans anymore. Rooted to the ground, they remained motionless, soaking up the pouring rain.

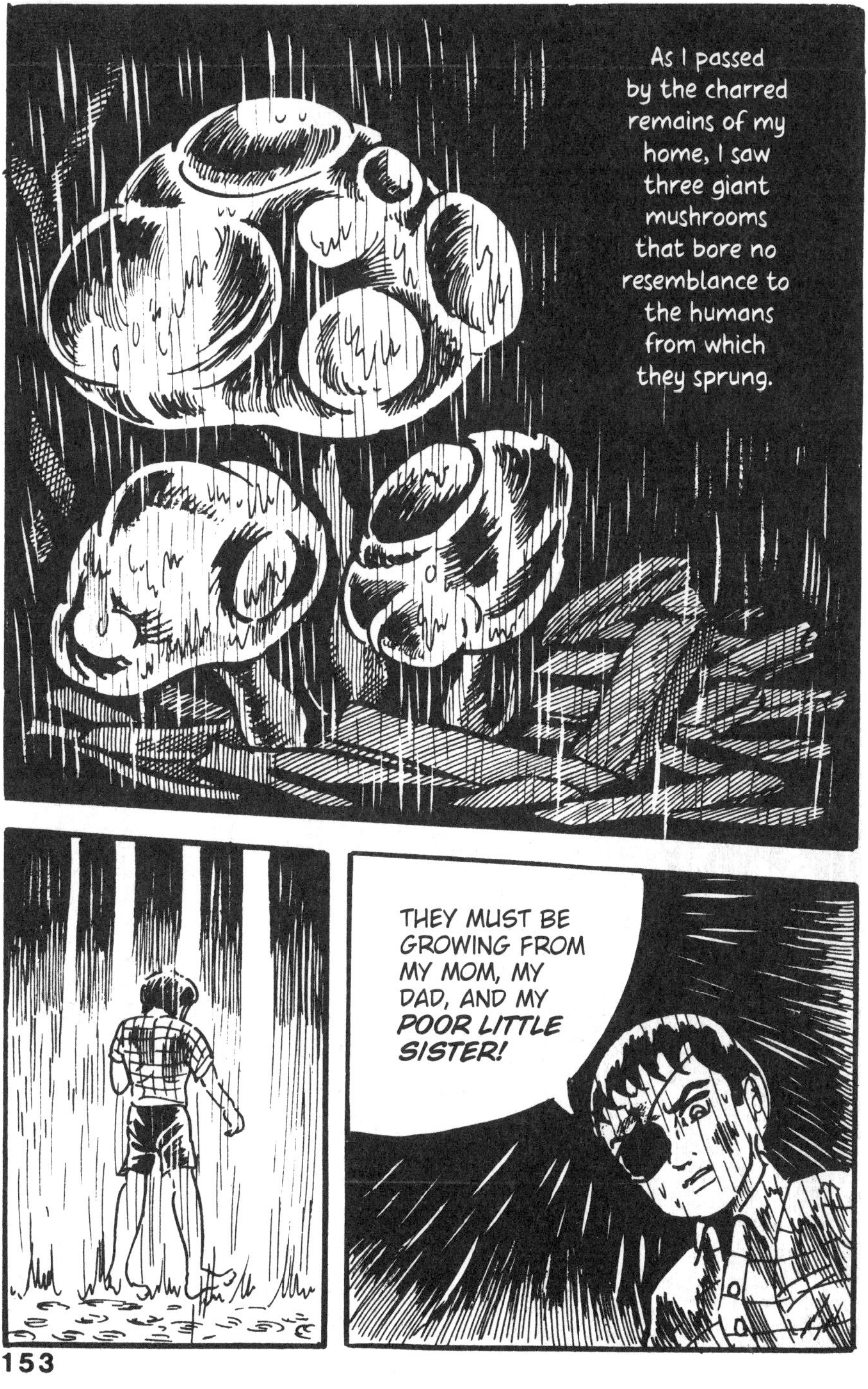
As I passed by the charred remains of my home, I saw three giant mushrooms that bore no resemblance to the humans from which they sprung.
THEY MUST BE GROWING FROM MY MOM, MY DAD, AND MY *POOR LITTLE SISTER!*

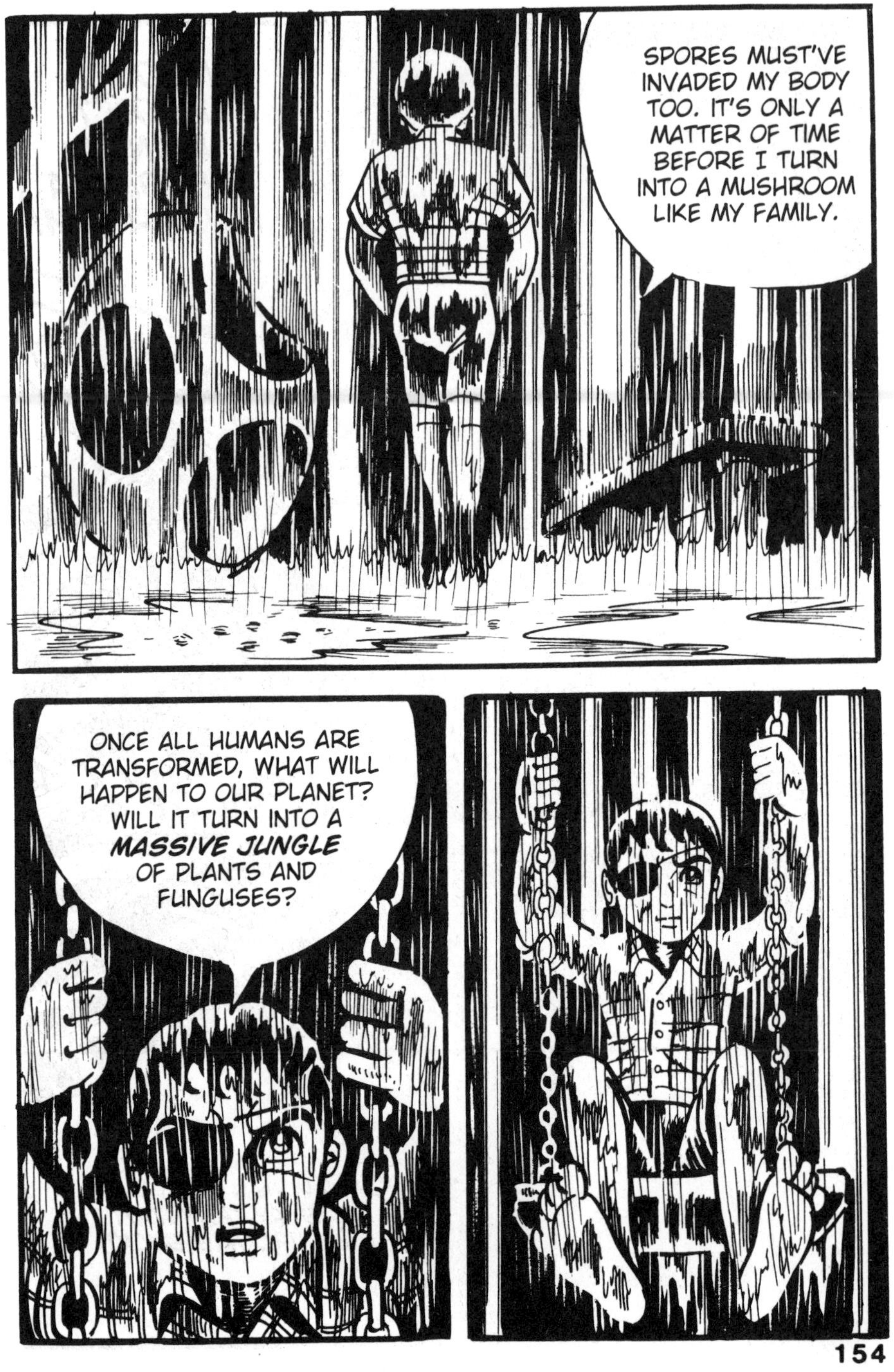
SPORES MUST'VE INVADED MY BODY TOO. IT'S ONLY A MATTER OF TIME BEFORE I TURN INTO A MUSHROOM LIKE MY FAMILY.
ONCE ALL HUMANS ARE TRANSFORMED, WHAT WILL HAPPEN TO OUR PLANET? WILL IT TURN INTO A ***MASSIVE JUNGLE*** OF PLANTS AND FUNGUSES?

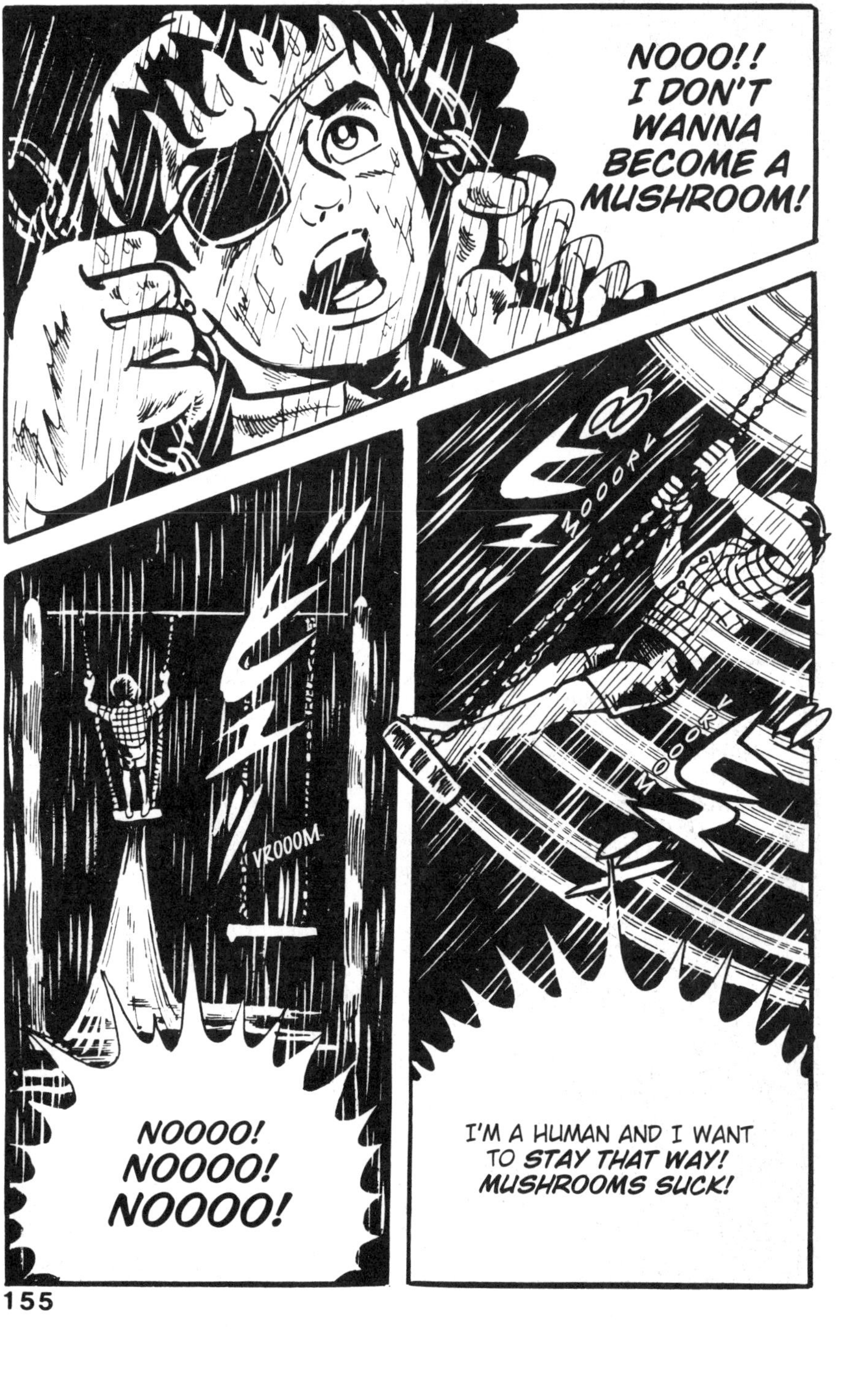
NOOO!! I DON'T WANNA BECOME A MUSHROOM!
VROOM
I'M A HUMAN AND I WANT TO STAY THAT WAY! MUSHROOMS SUCK!
VROOOM
NOOOO! NOOOO! NOOOO!

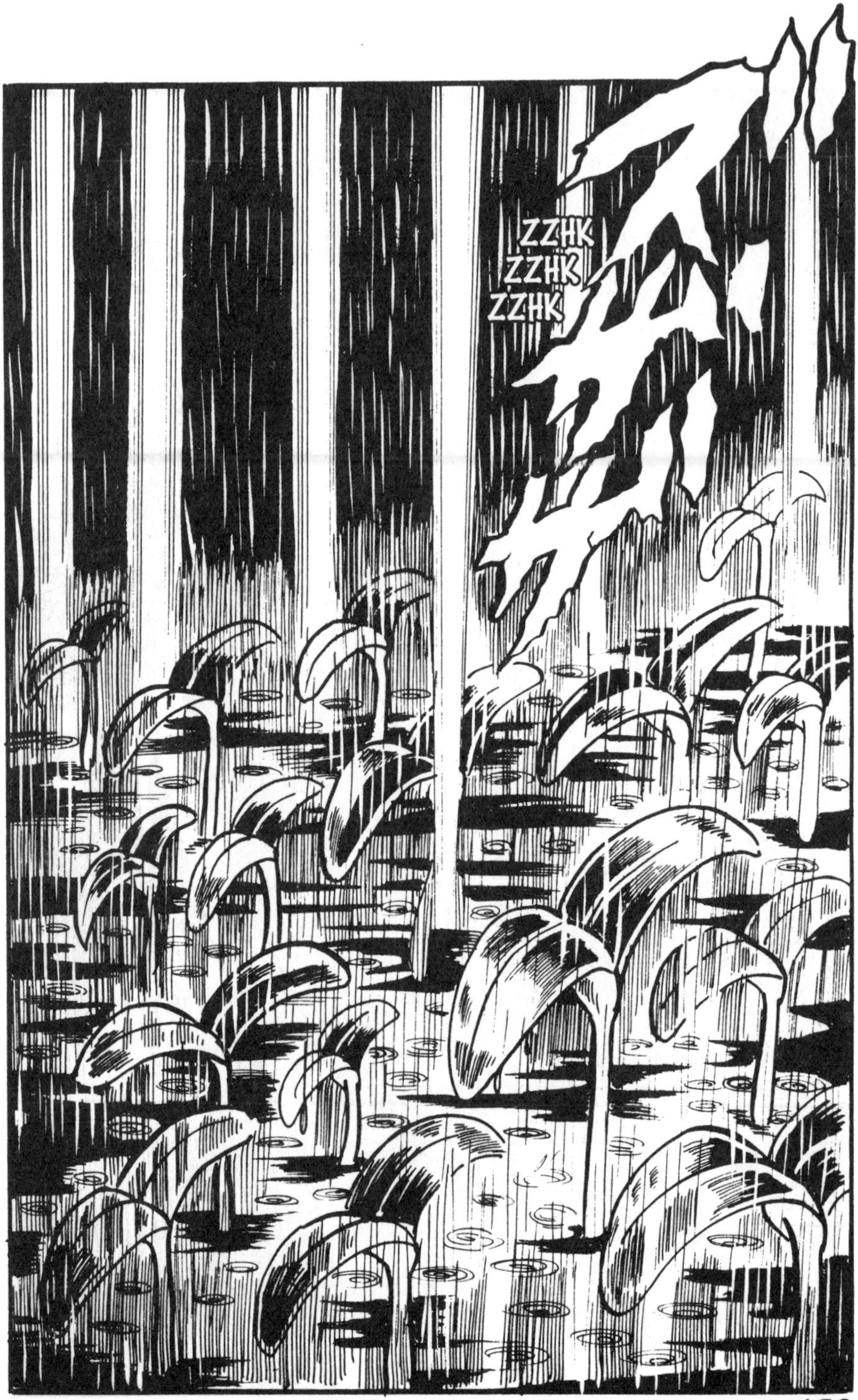
ZZHK
ZZHK
ZZHK

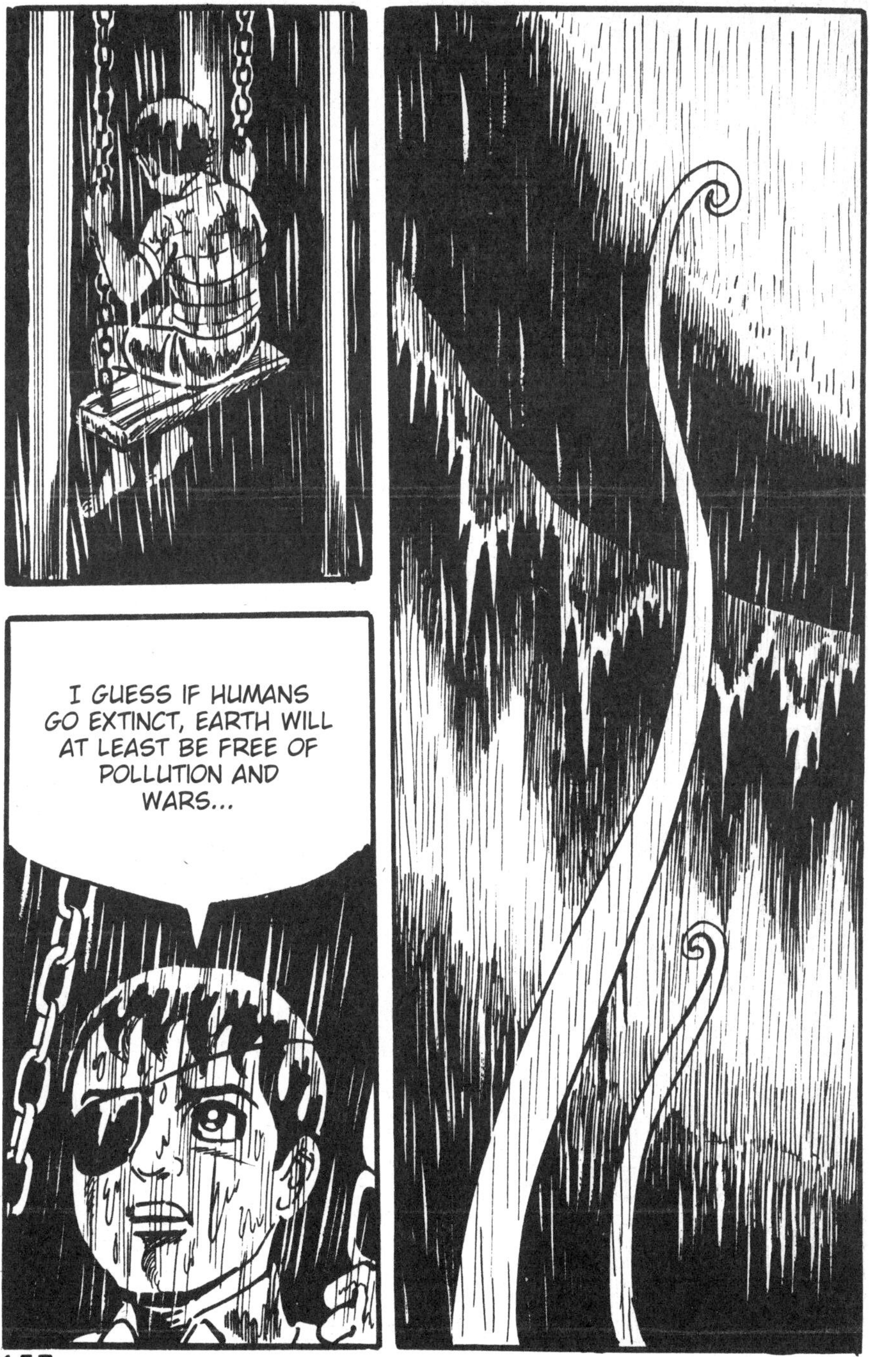
I GUESS IF HUMANS GO EXTINCT, EARTH WILL AT LEAST BE FREE OF POLLUTION AND WARS...

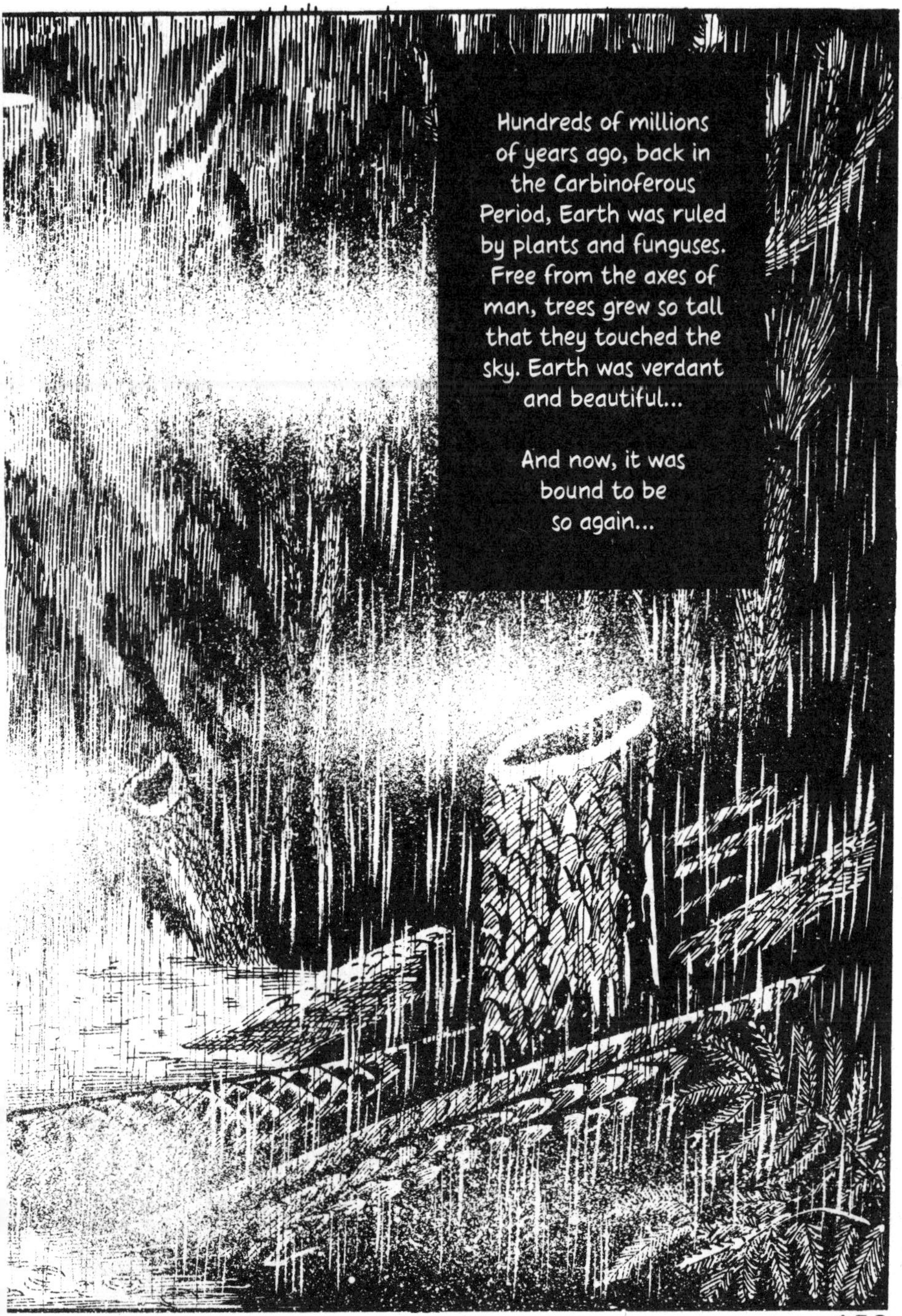
Hundreds of millions of years ago, back in the Carbinoferous Period, Earth was ruled by plants and funguses. Free from the axes of man, trees grew so tall that they touched the sky. Earth was verdant and beautiful...
And now, it was bound to be so again...

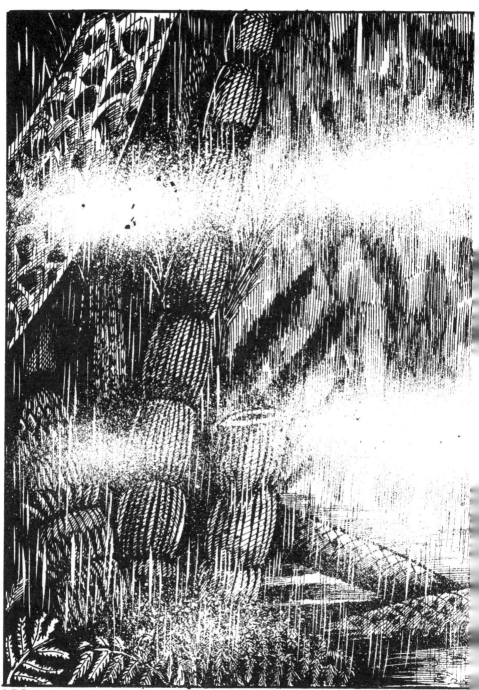

159

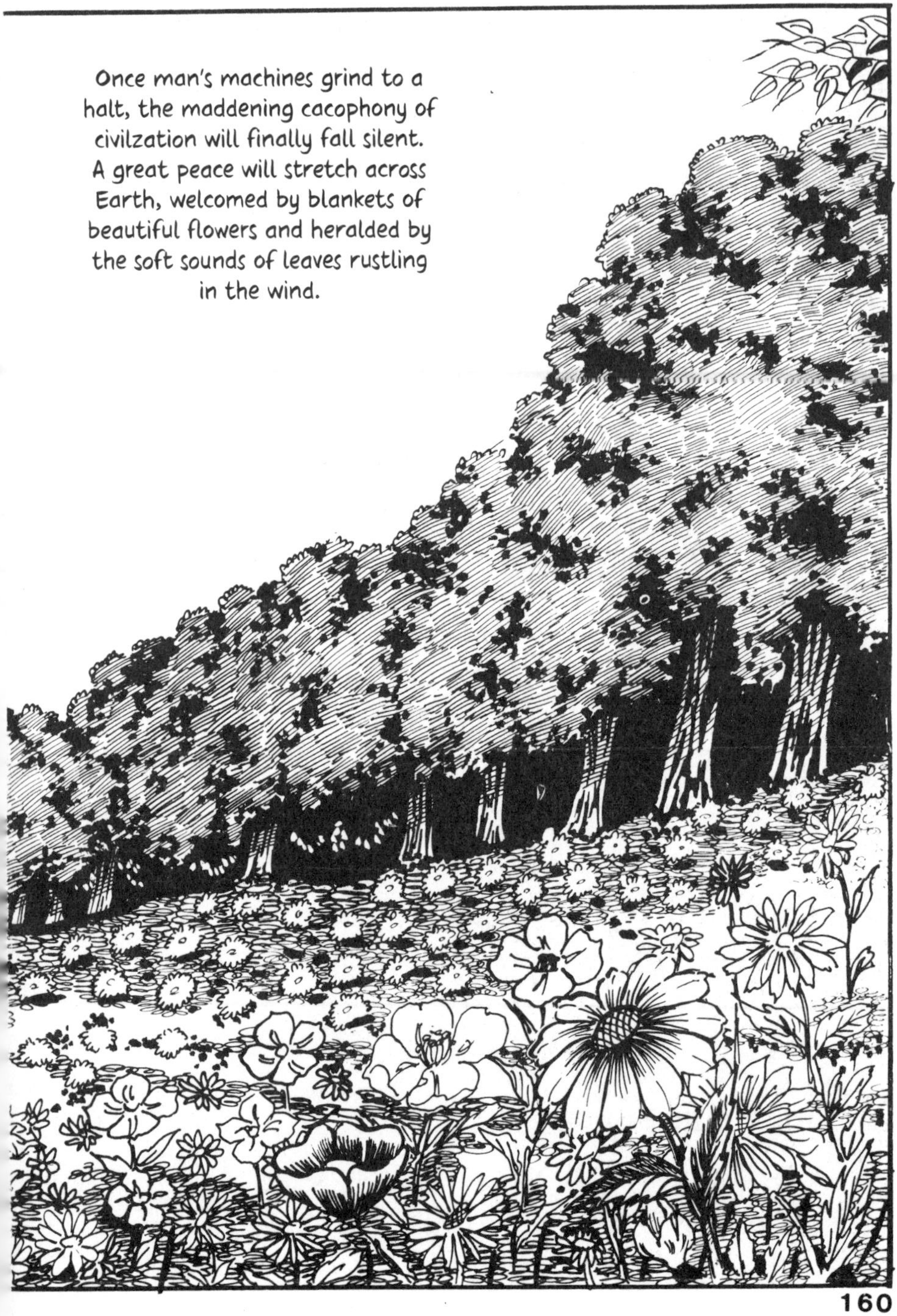
Once man's machines grind to a halt, the maddening cacophony of civilzation will finally fall silent. A great peace will stretch across Earth, welcomed by blankets of beautiful flowers and heralded by the soft sounds of leaves rustling in the wind.

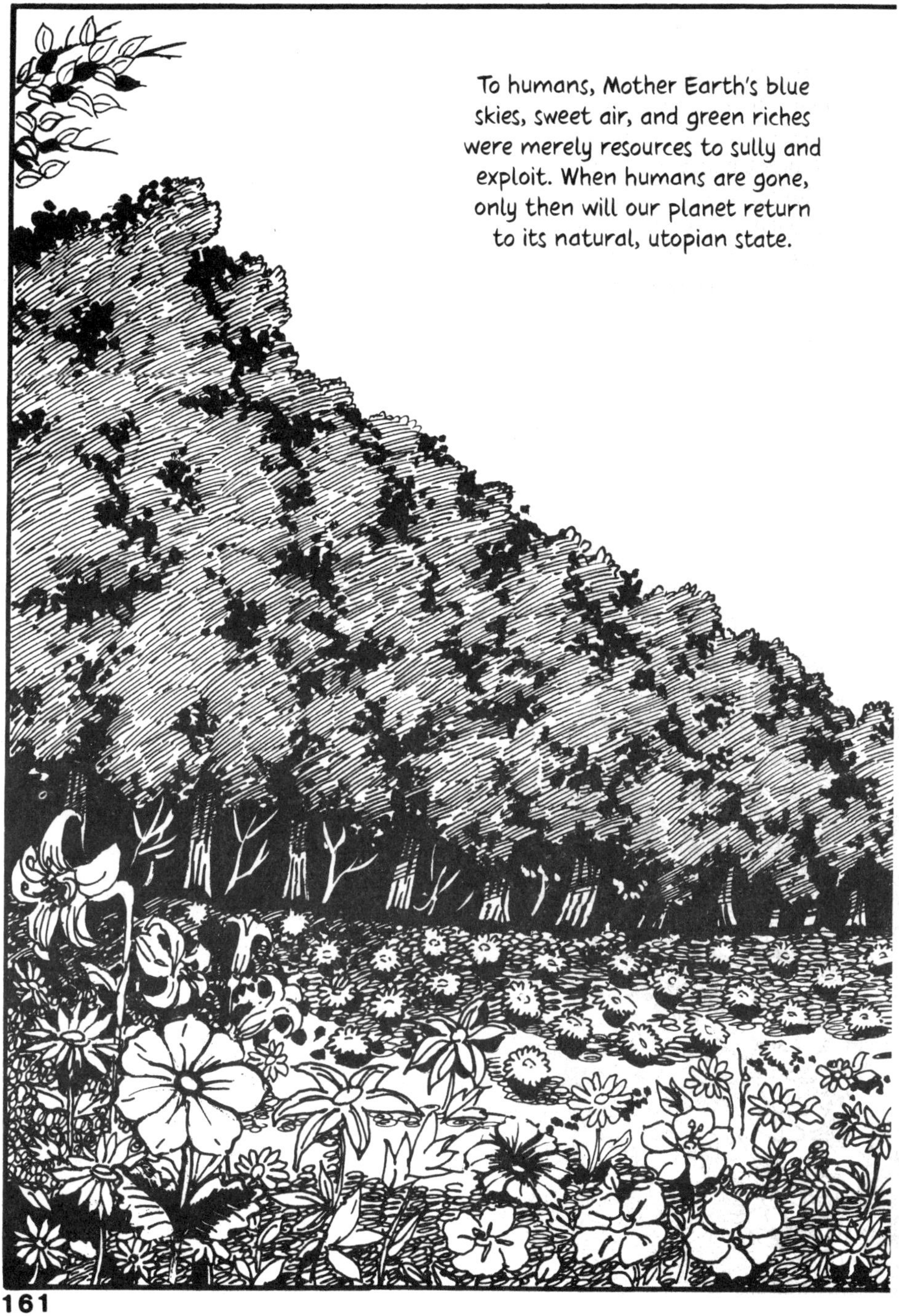
To humans, Mother Earth's blue skies, sweet air, and green riches were merely resources to sully and exploit. When humans are gone, only then will our planet return to its natural, utopian state.

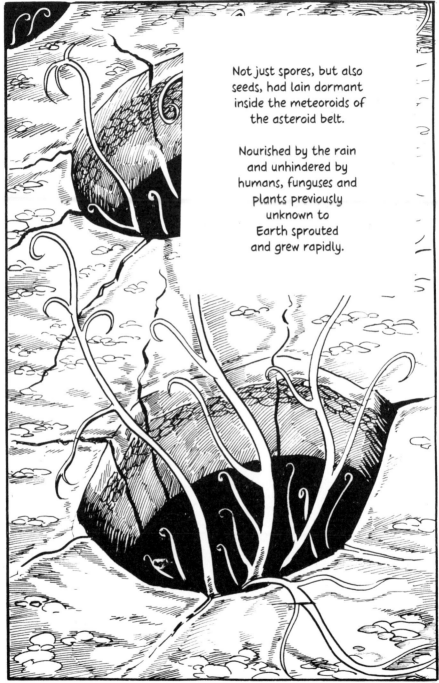

Not just spores, but also seeds, had lain dormant inside the meteoroids of the asteroid belt.

Nourished by the rain and unhindered by humans, funguses and plants previously unknown to Earth sprouted and grew rapidly.

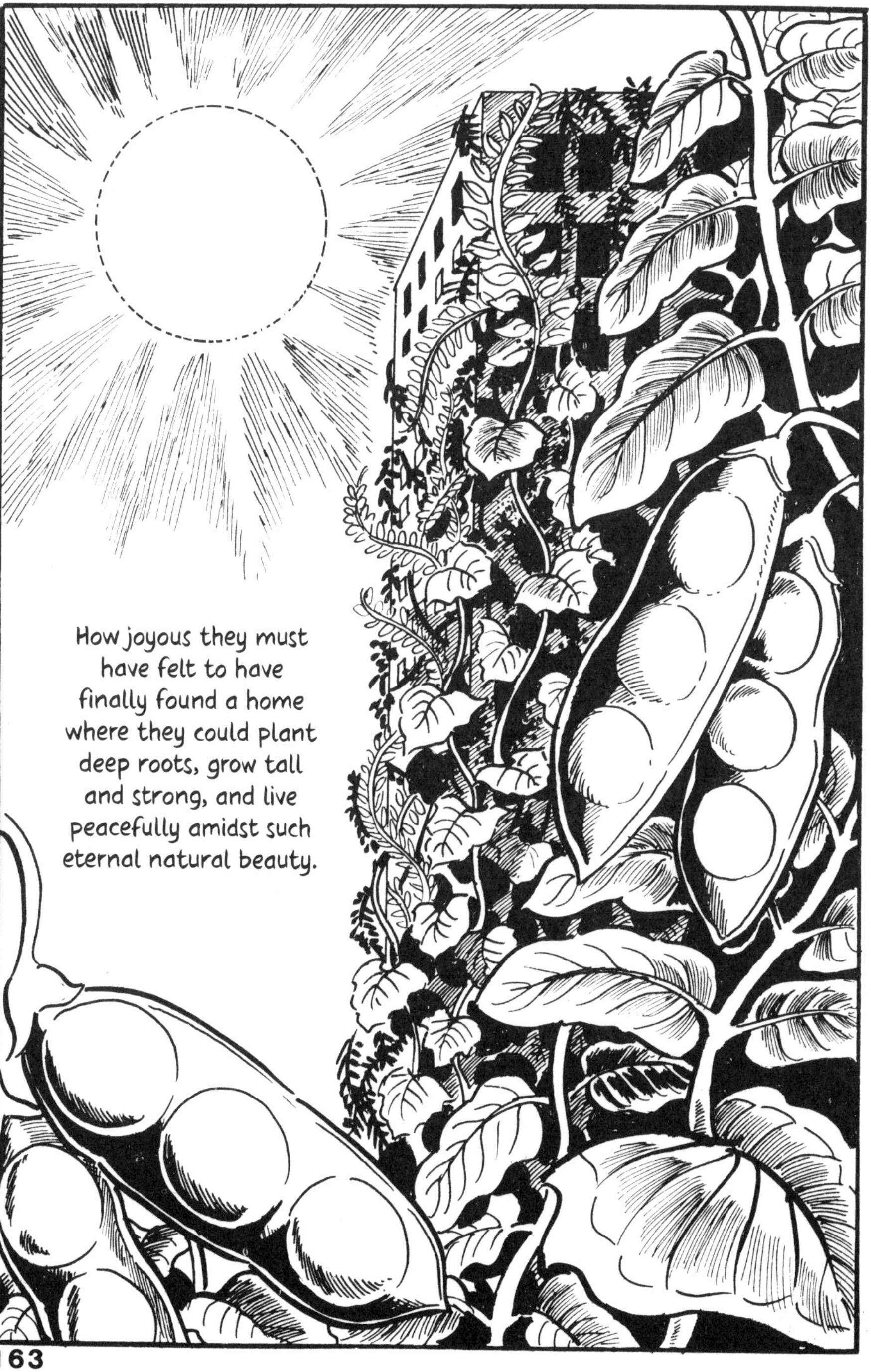
How joyous they must have felt to have finally found a home where they could plant deep roots, grow tall and strong, and live peacefully amidst such eternal natural beauty.

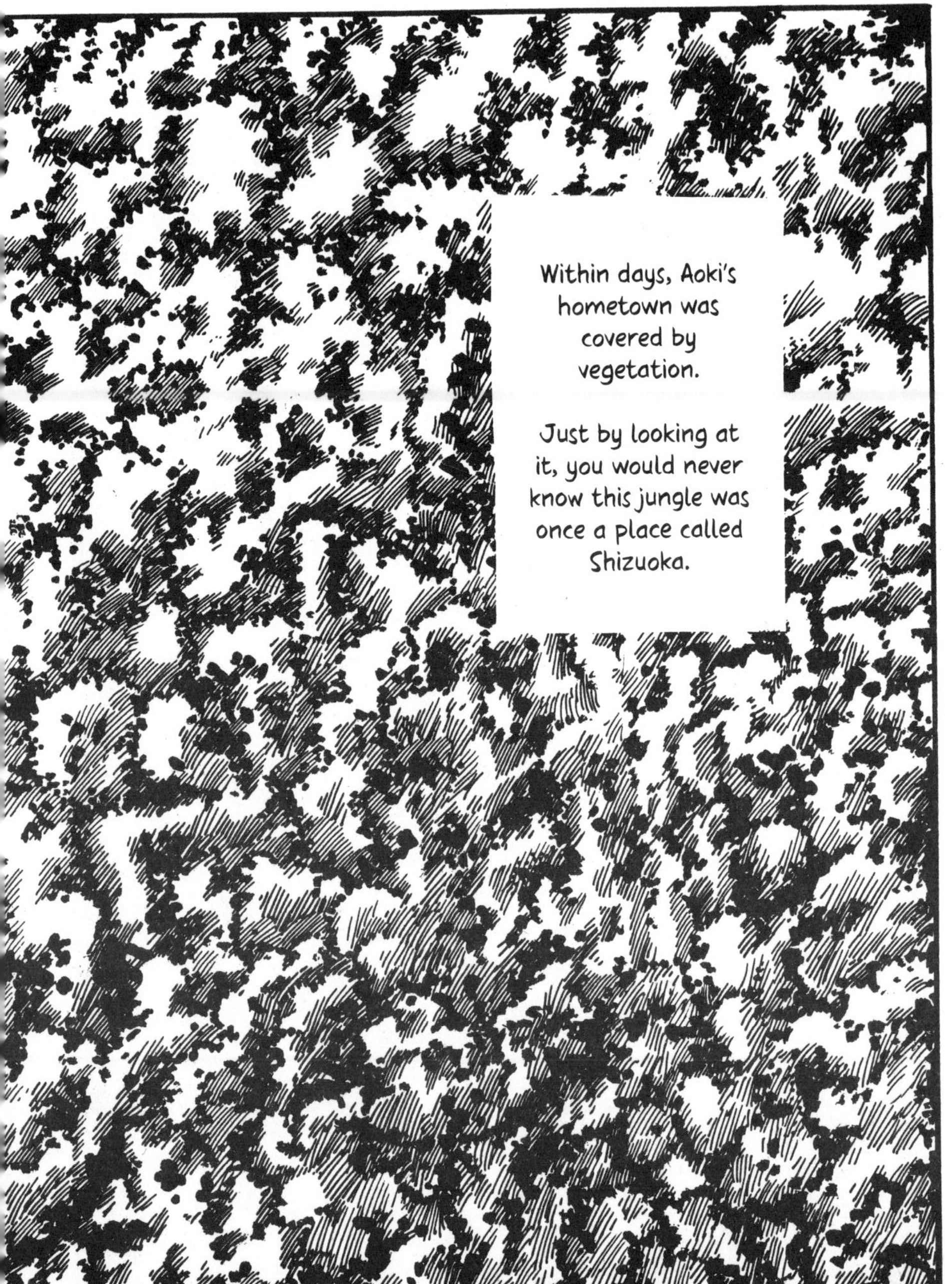
Within days, Aoki's hometown was covered by vegetation.
Just by looking at it, you would never know this jungle was once a place called Shizuoka.

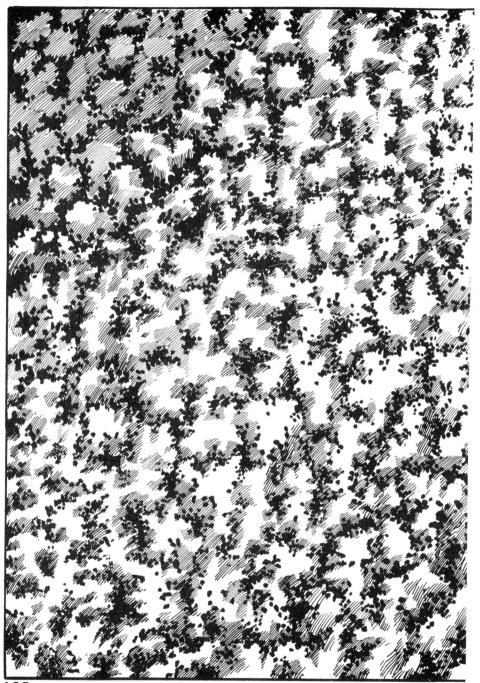

165

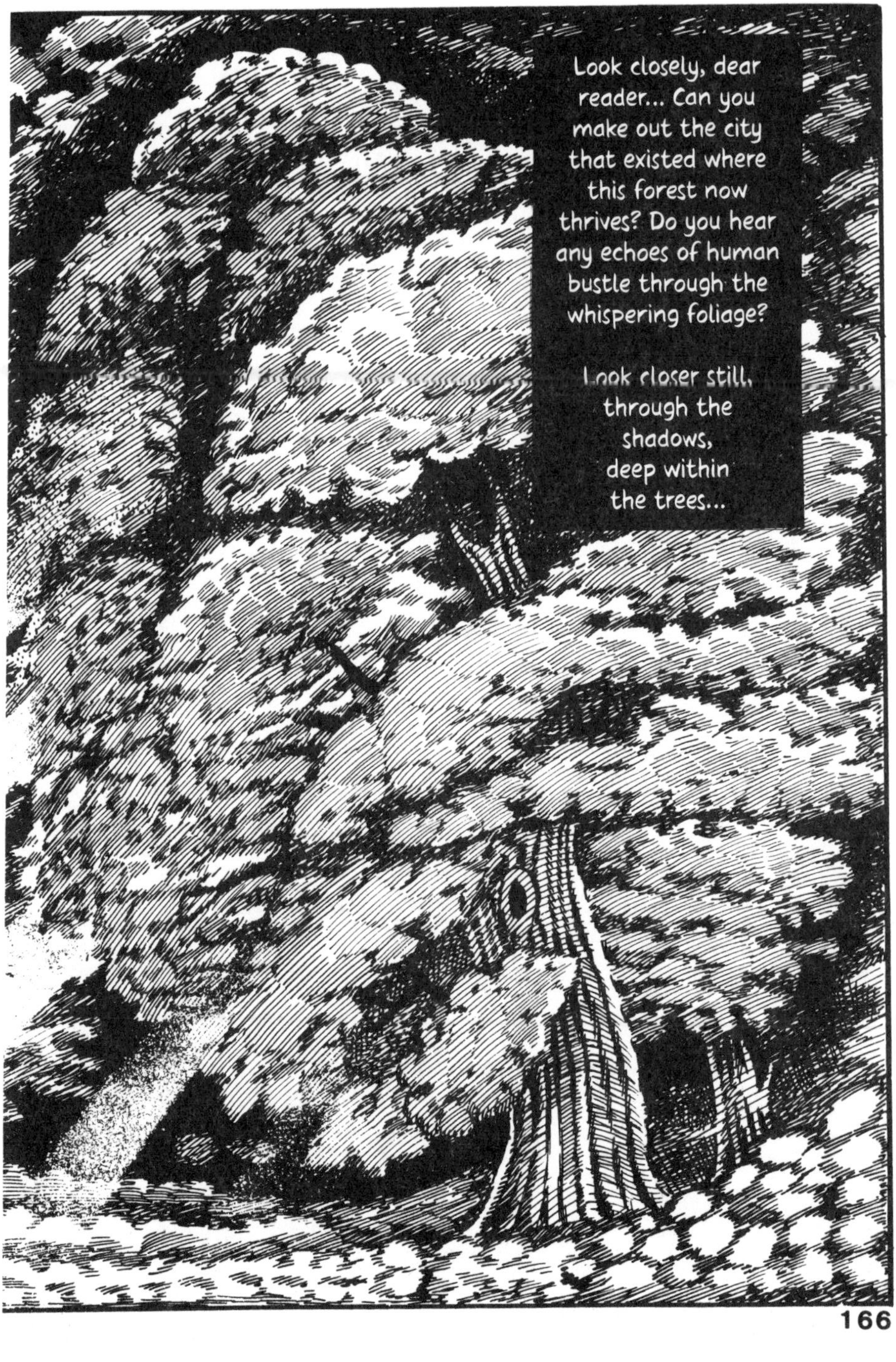
Look closely, dear reader... Can you make out the city that existed where this forest now thrives? Do you hear any echoes of human bustle through the whispering foliage?
Look closer still, through the shadows, deep within the trees...

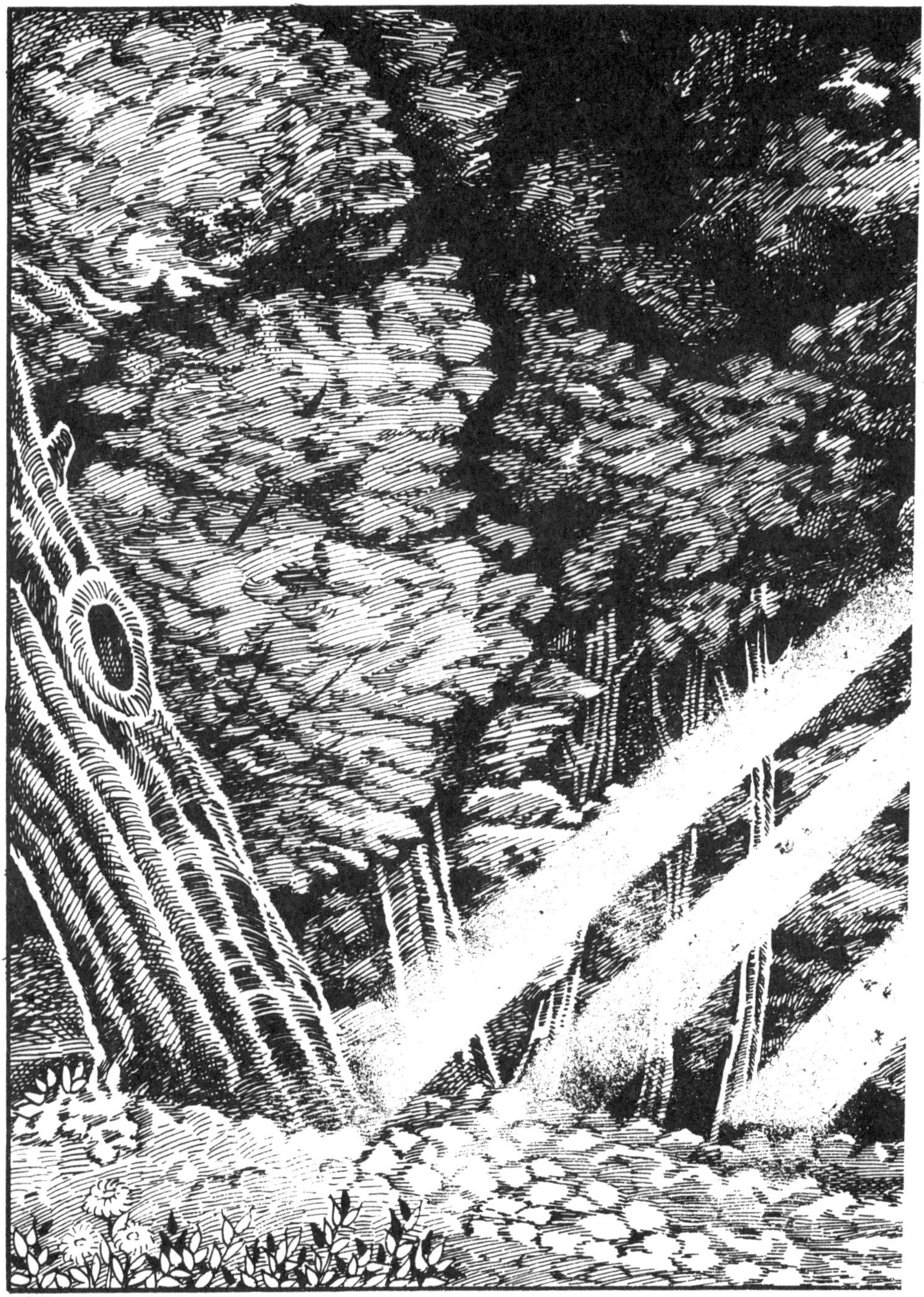

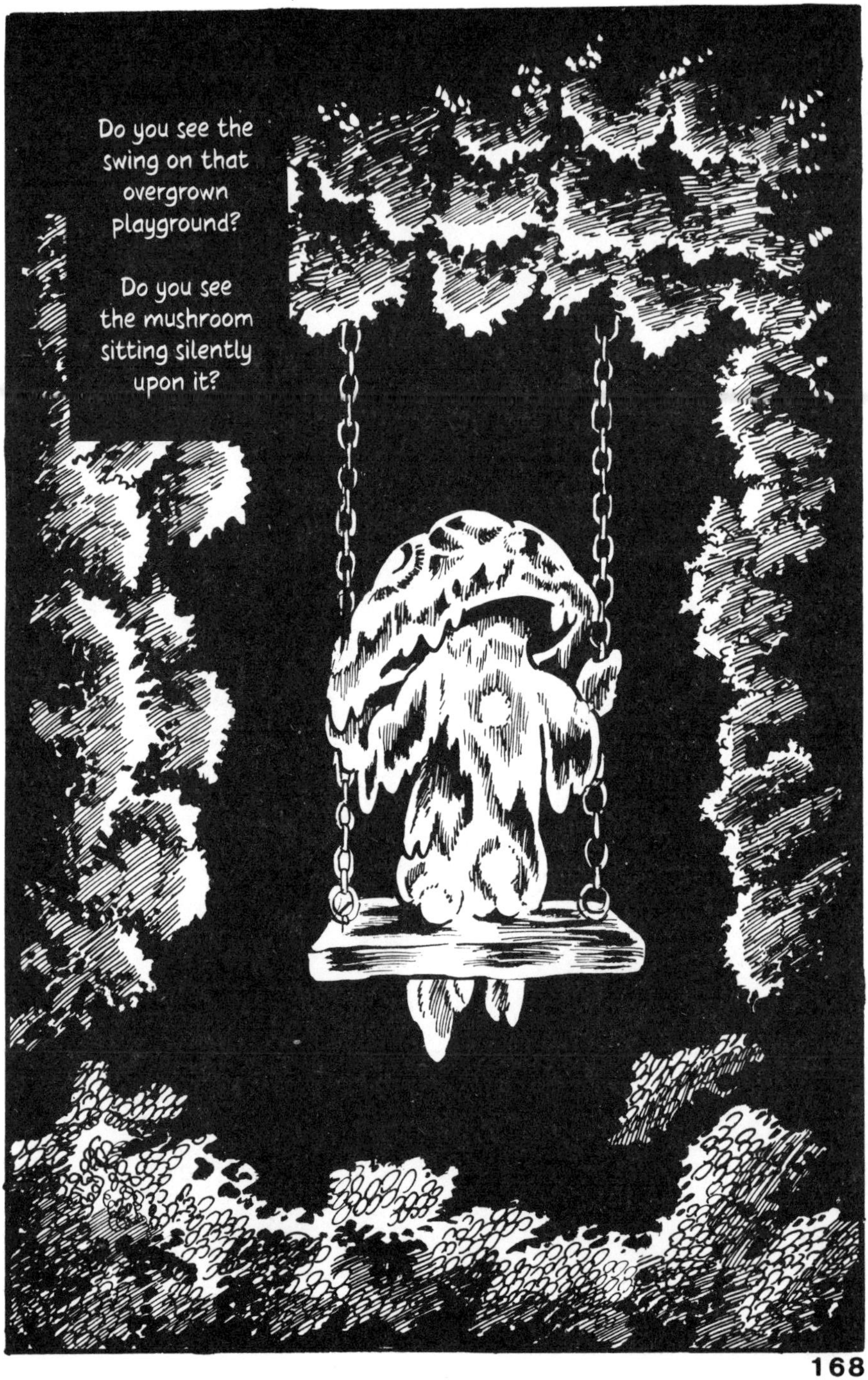
Do you see the swing on that overgrown playground?
Do you see the mushroom sitting silently upon it?

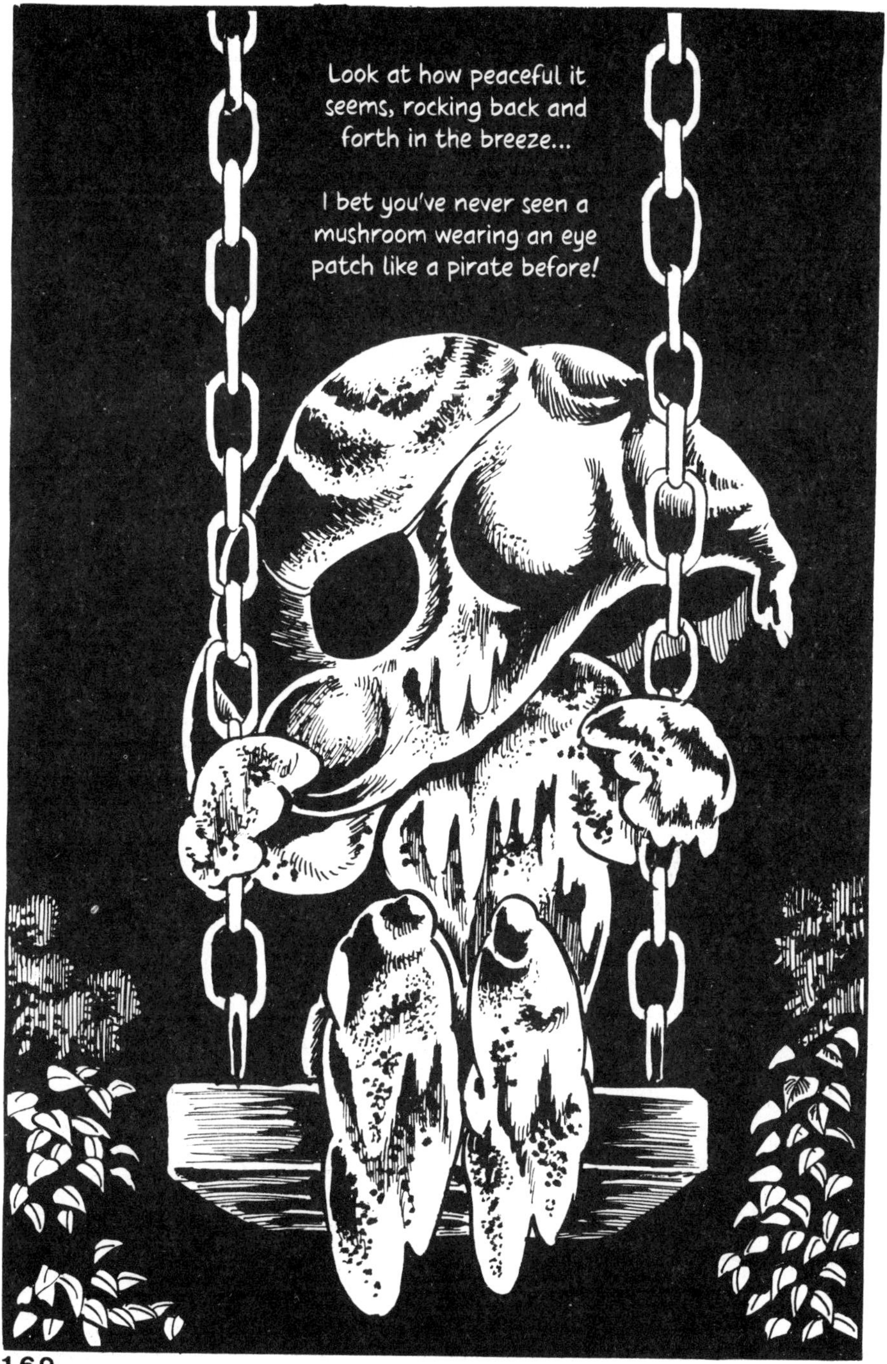
Look at how peaceful it seems, rocking back and forth in the breeze...
I bet you've never seen a mushroom wearing an eye patch like a pirate before!

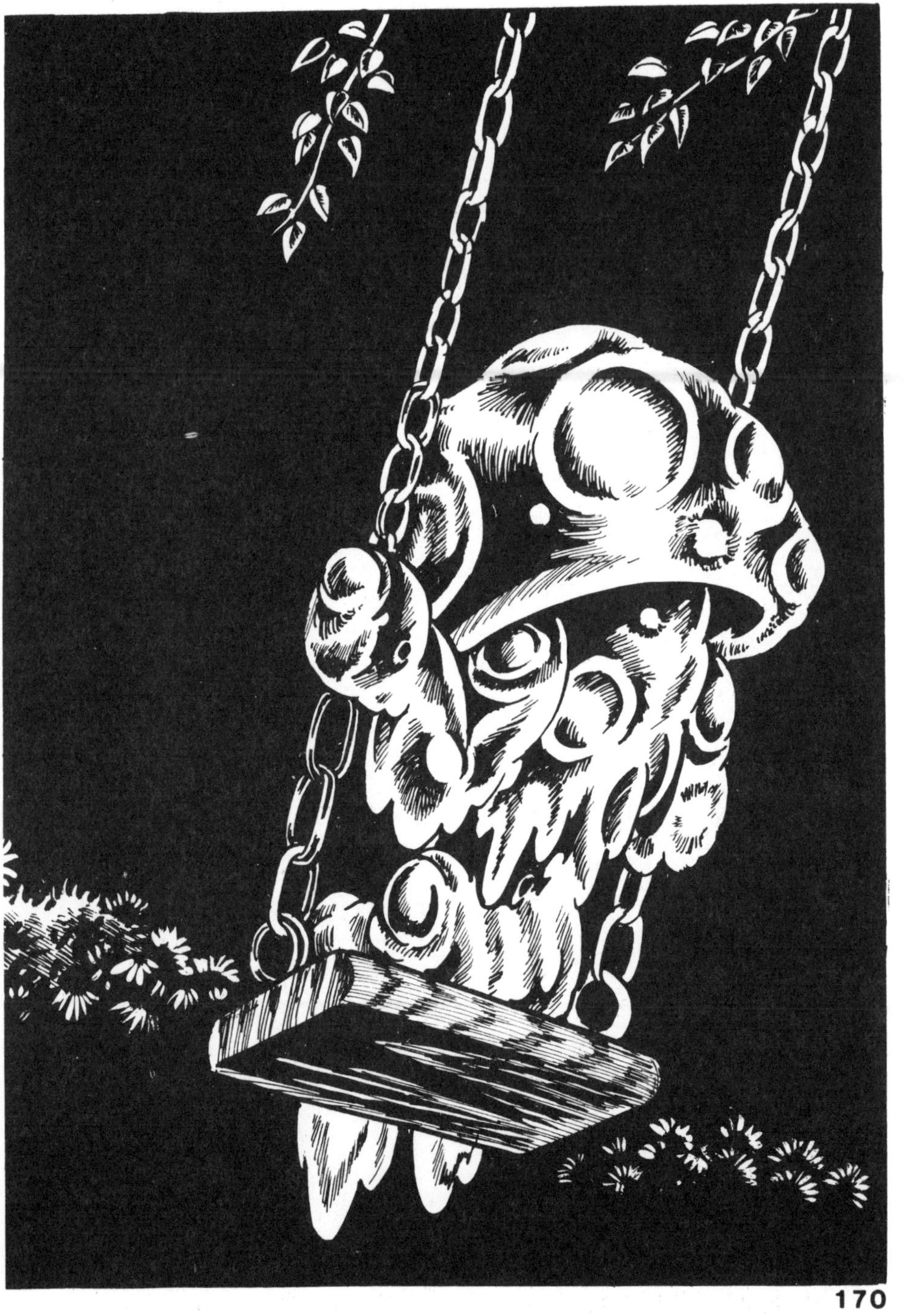

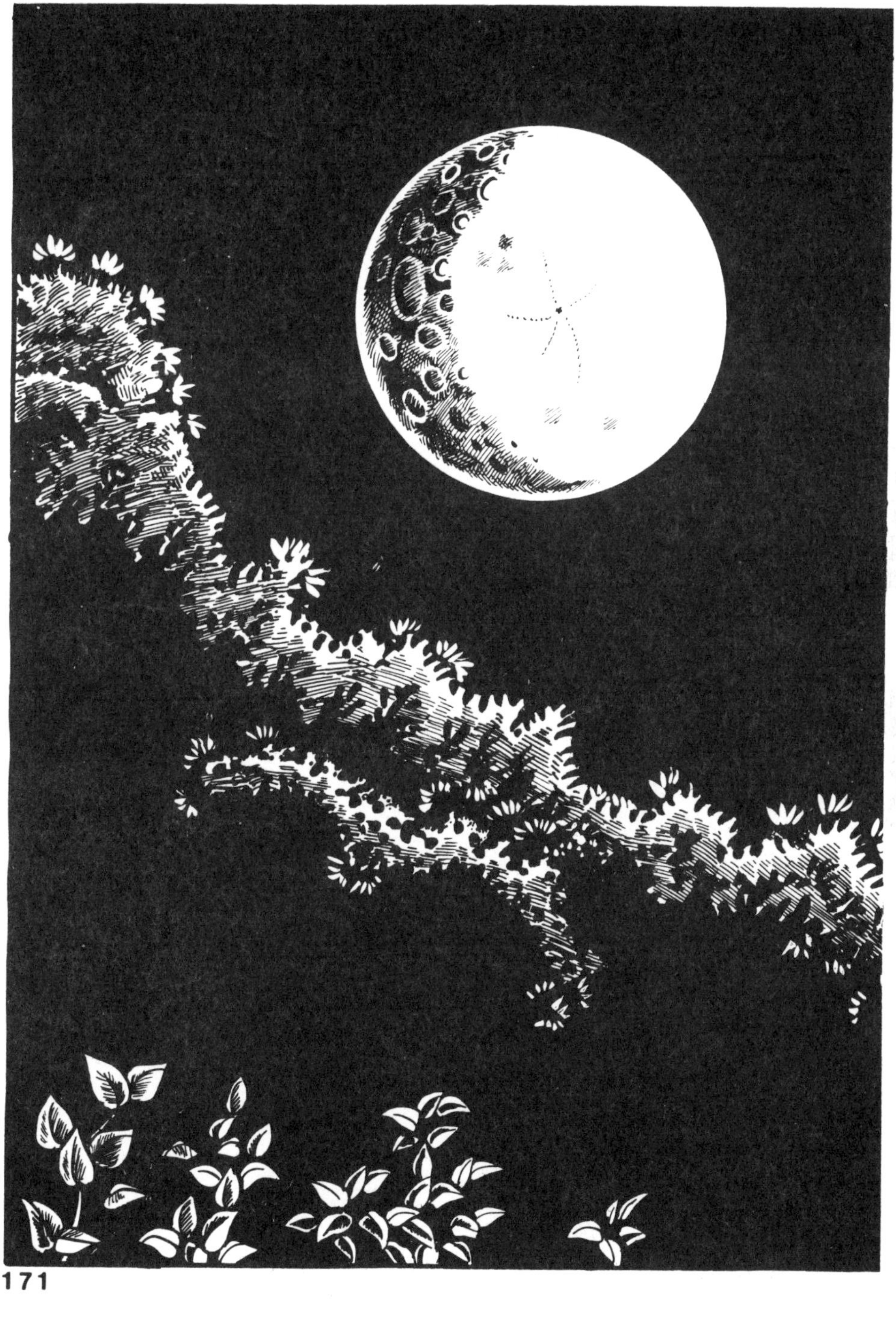

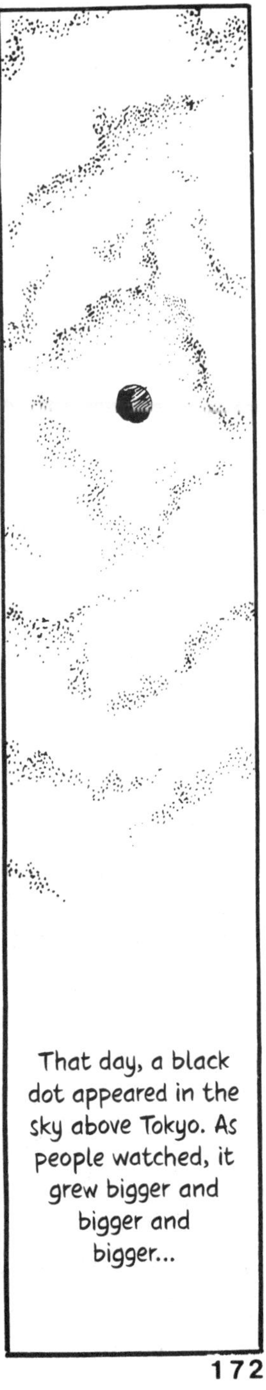
That day, a black dot appeared in the sky above Tokyo. As people watched, it grew bigger and bigger and bigger...
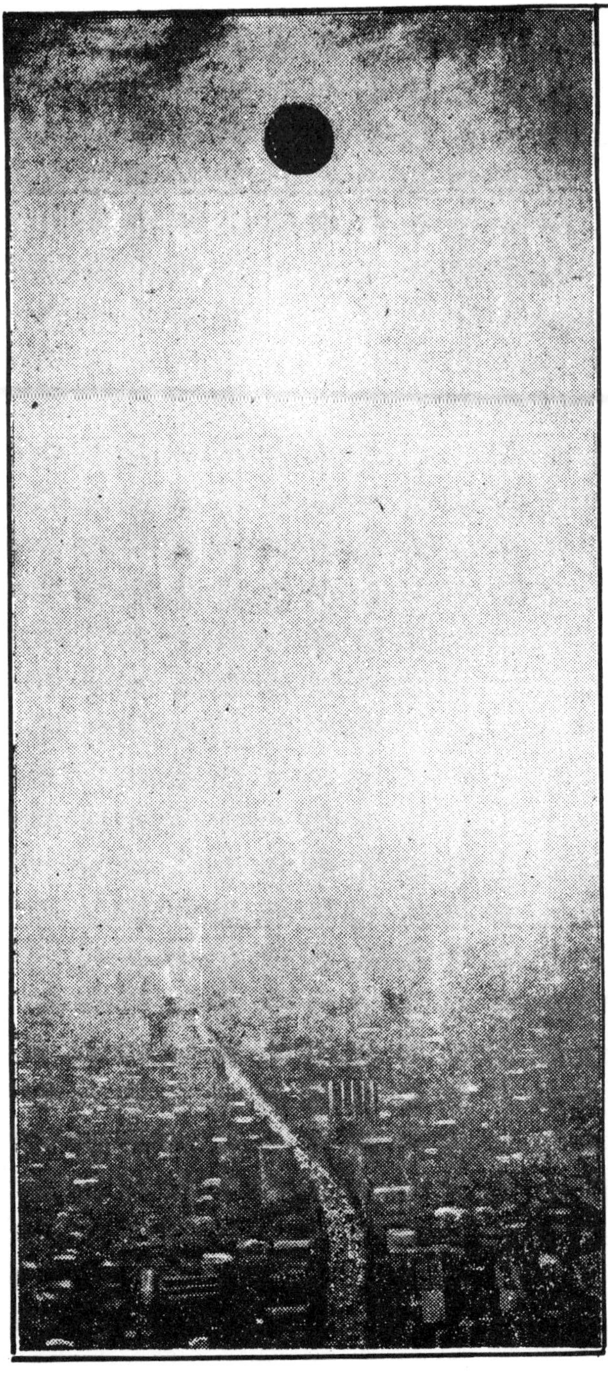

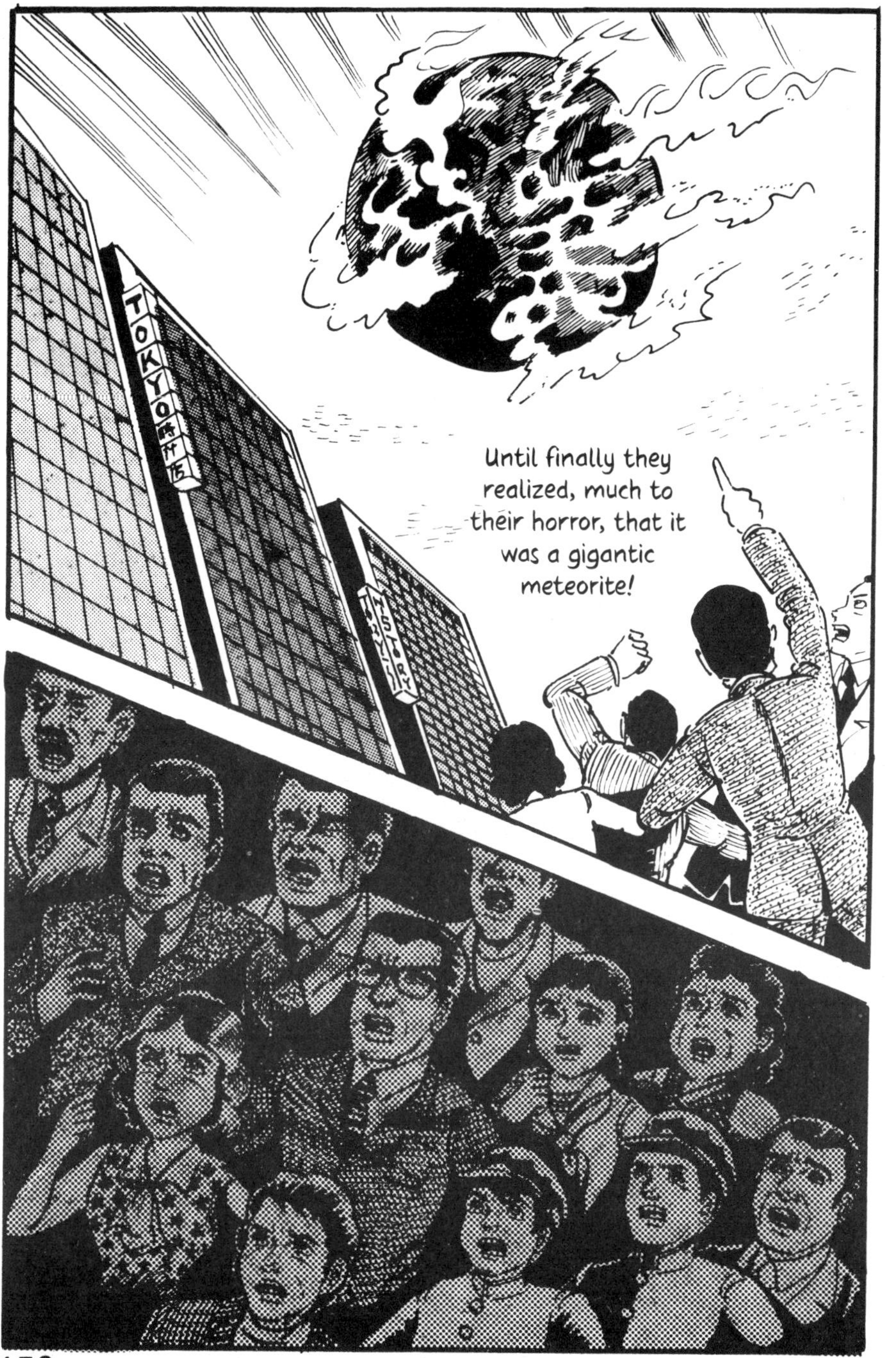
TOKYO
Until finally they realized, much to their horror, that it was a gigantic meteorite!

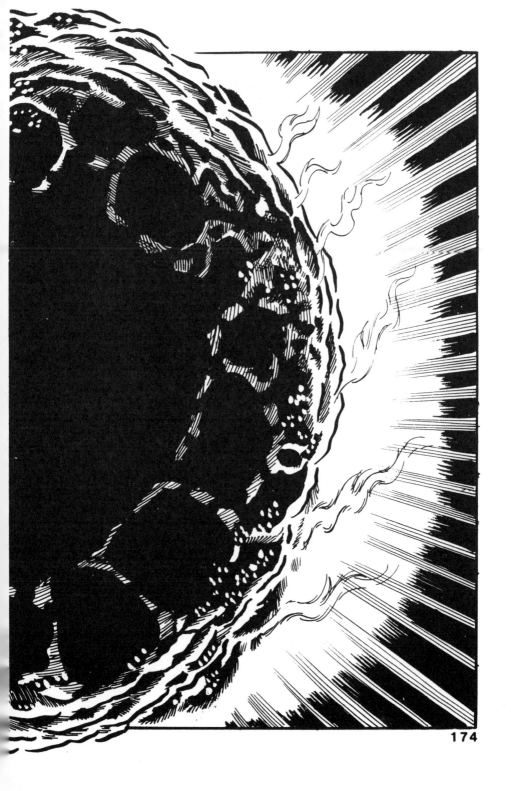

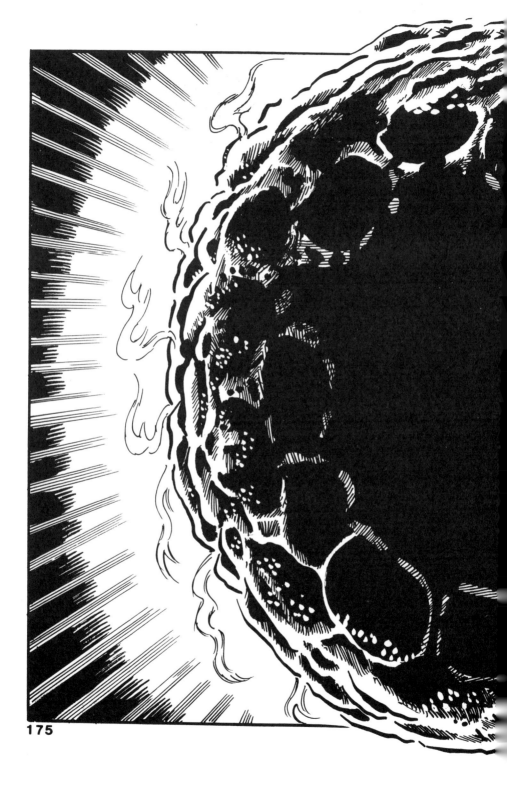

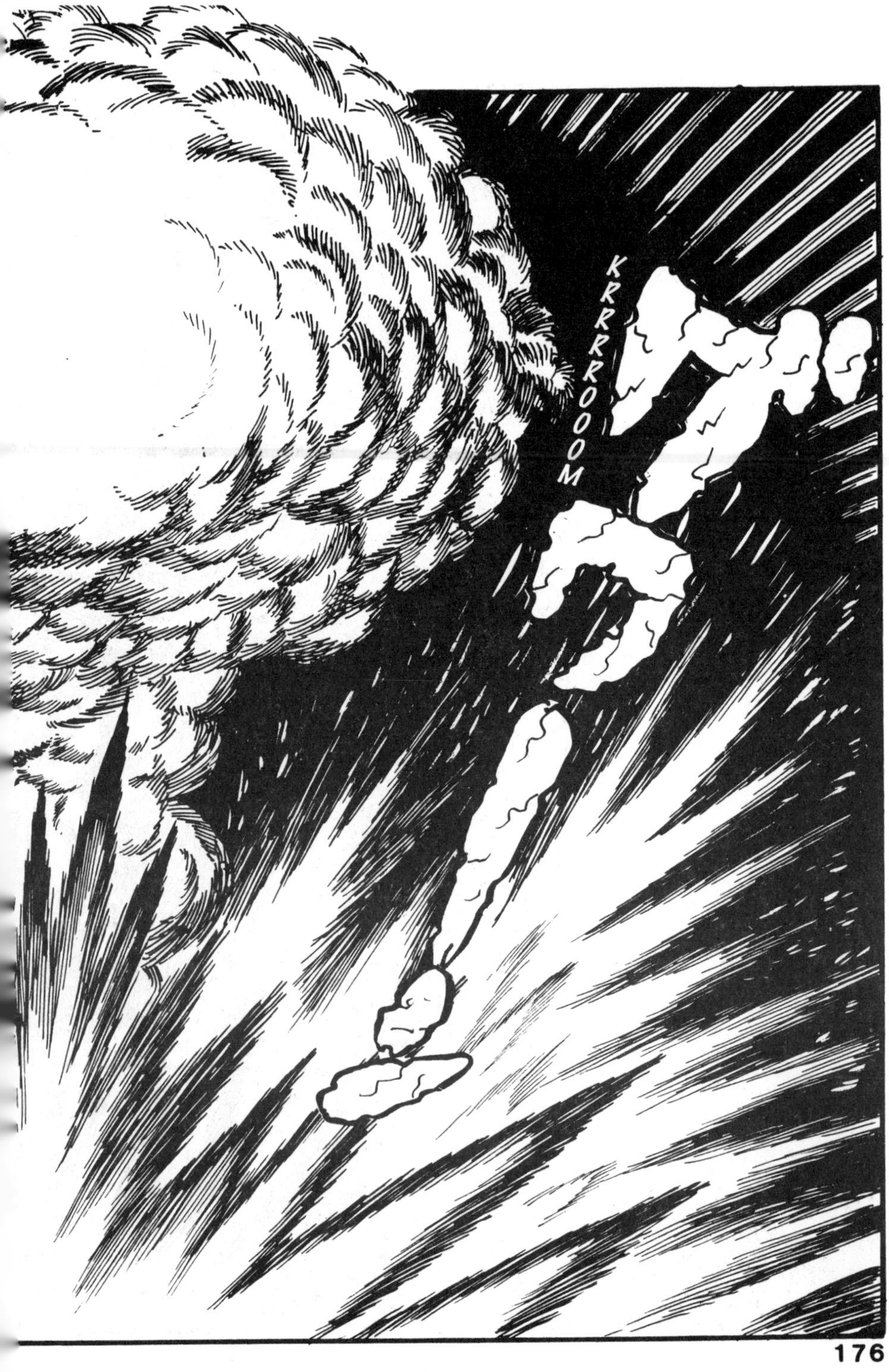
KRRRROOOM

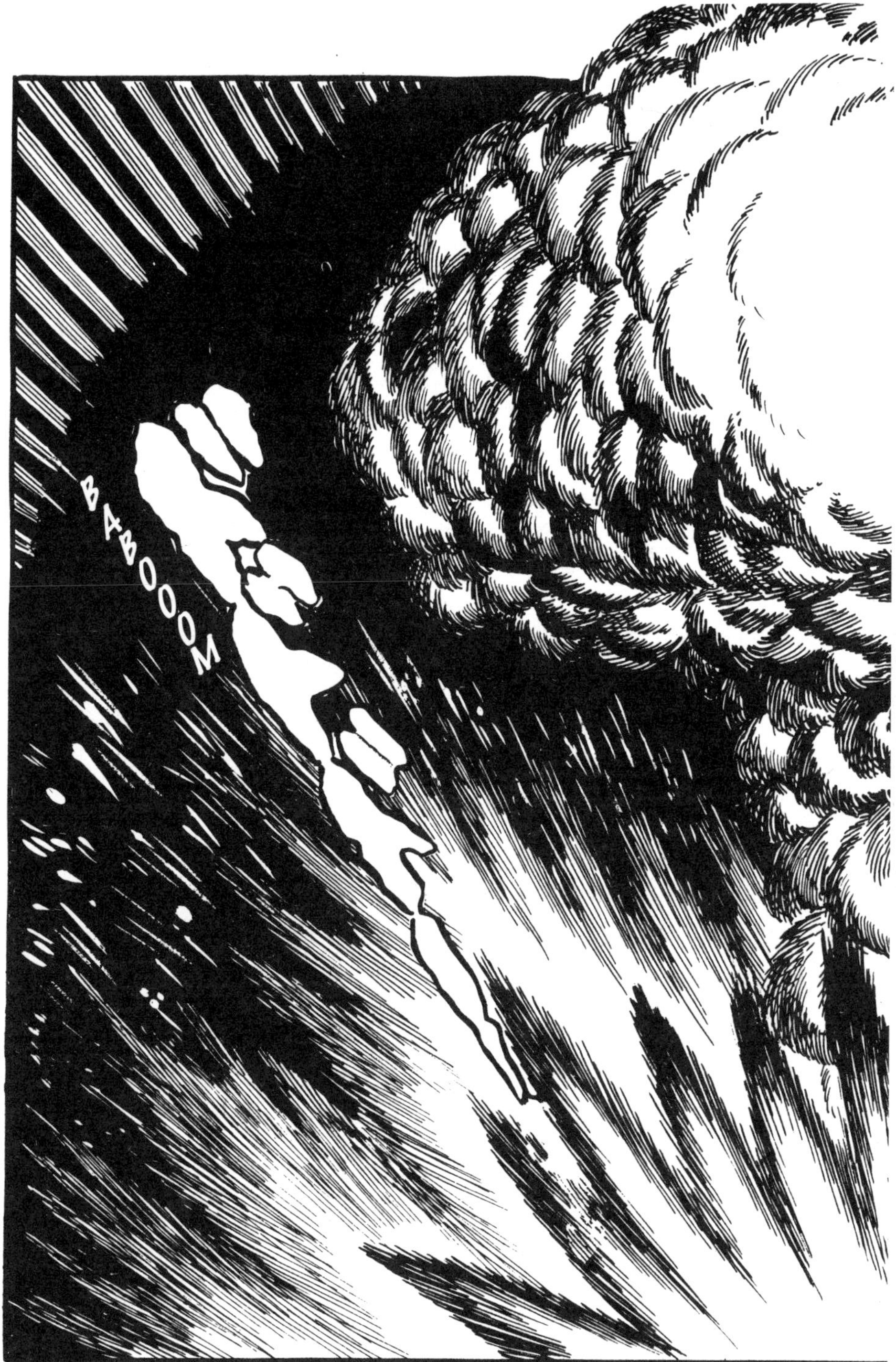
BABOOOM

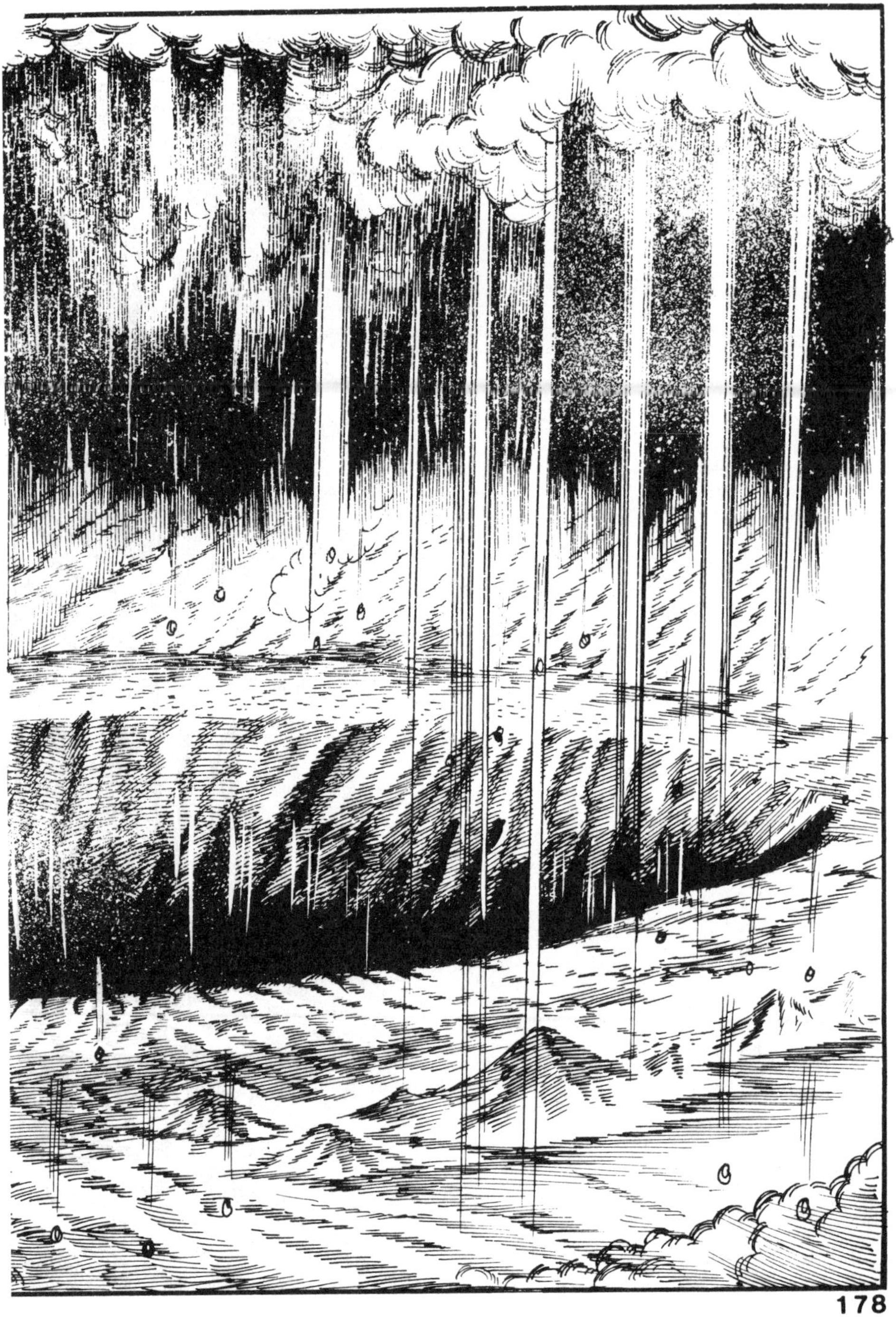

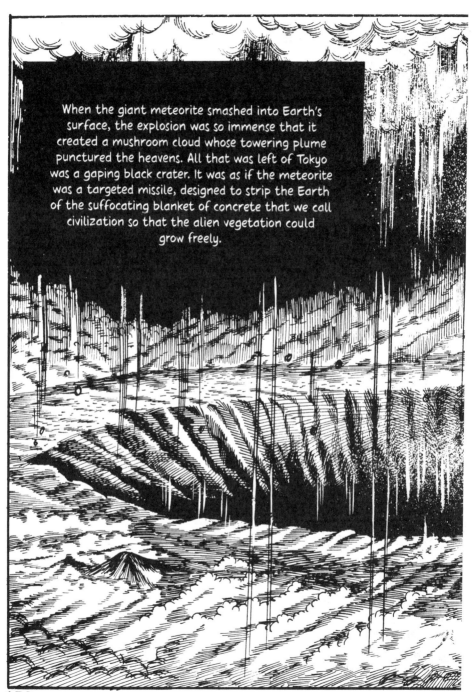

When the giant meteorite smashed into Earth's surface, the explosion was so immense that it created a mushroom cloud whose towering plume punctured the heavens. All that was left of Tokyo was a gaping black crater. It was as if the meteorite was a targeted missile, designed to strip the Earth of the suffocating blanket of concrete that we call civilization so that the alien vegetation could grow freely.

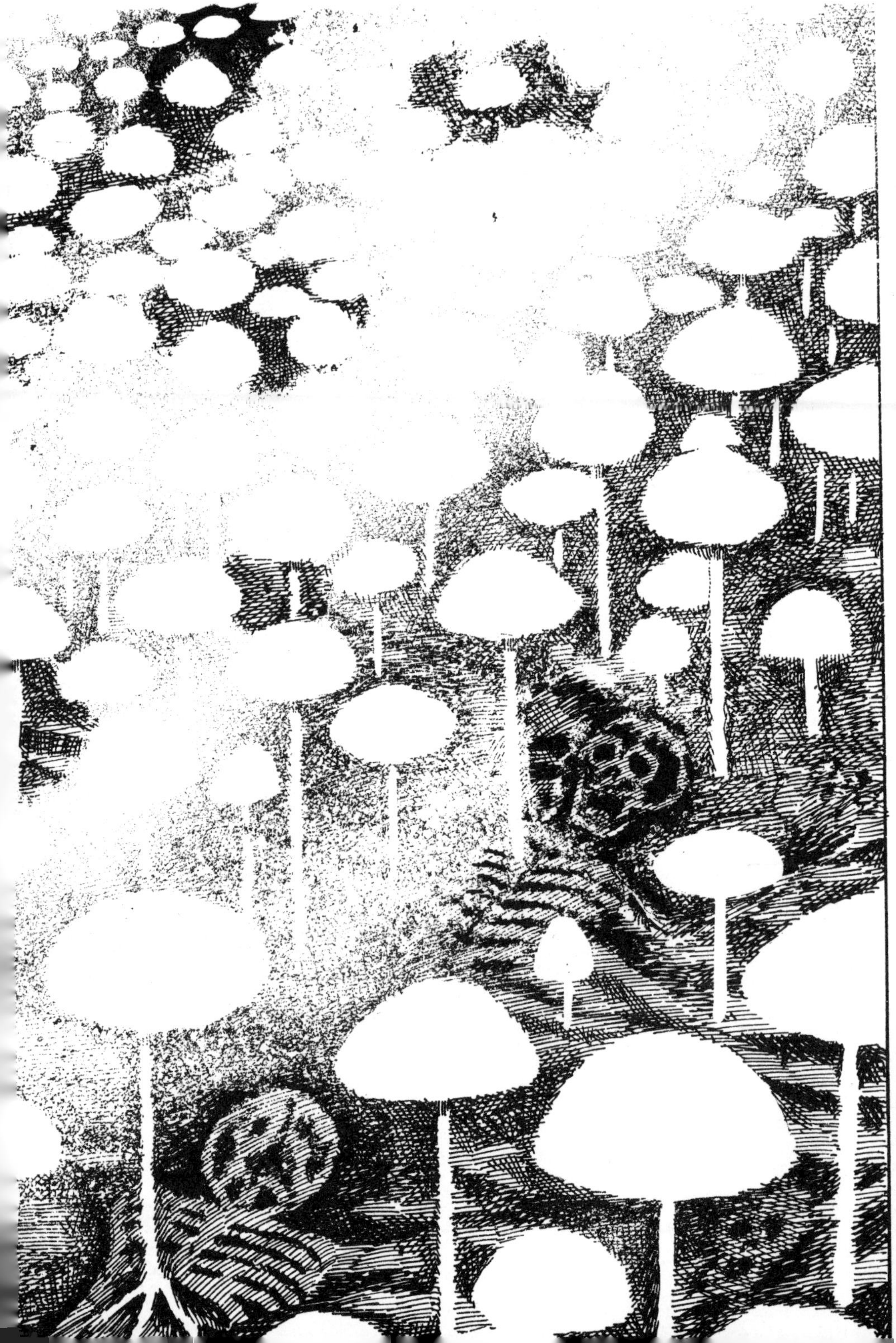

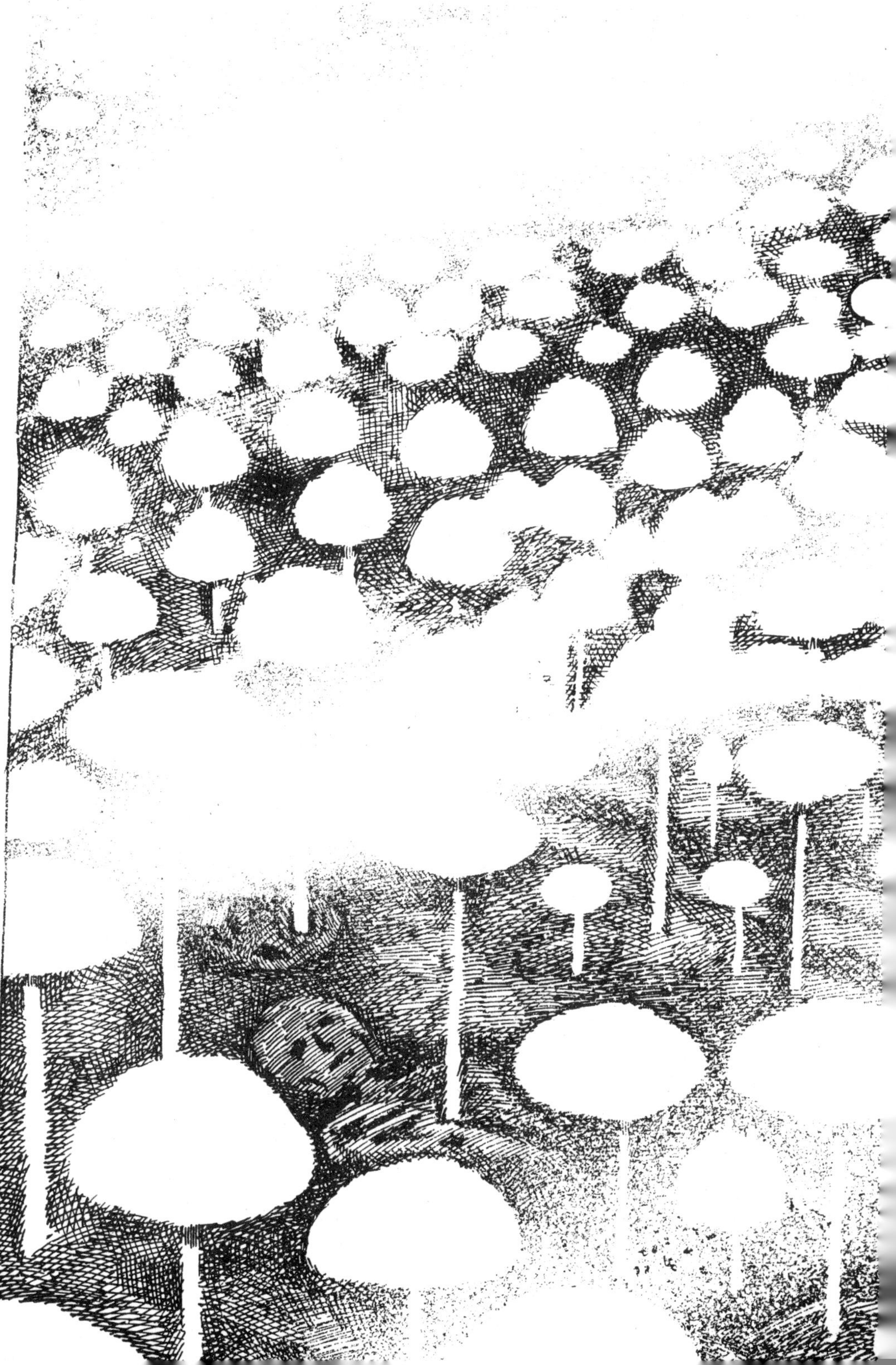

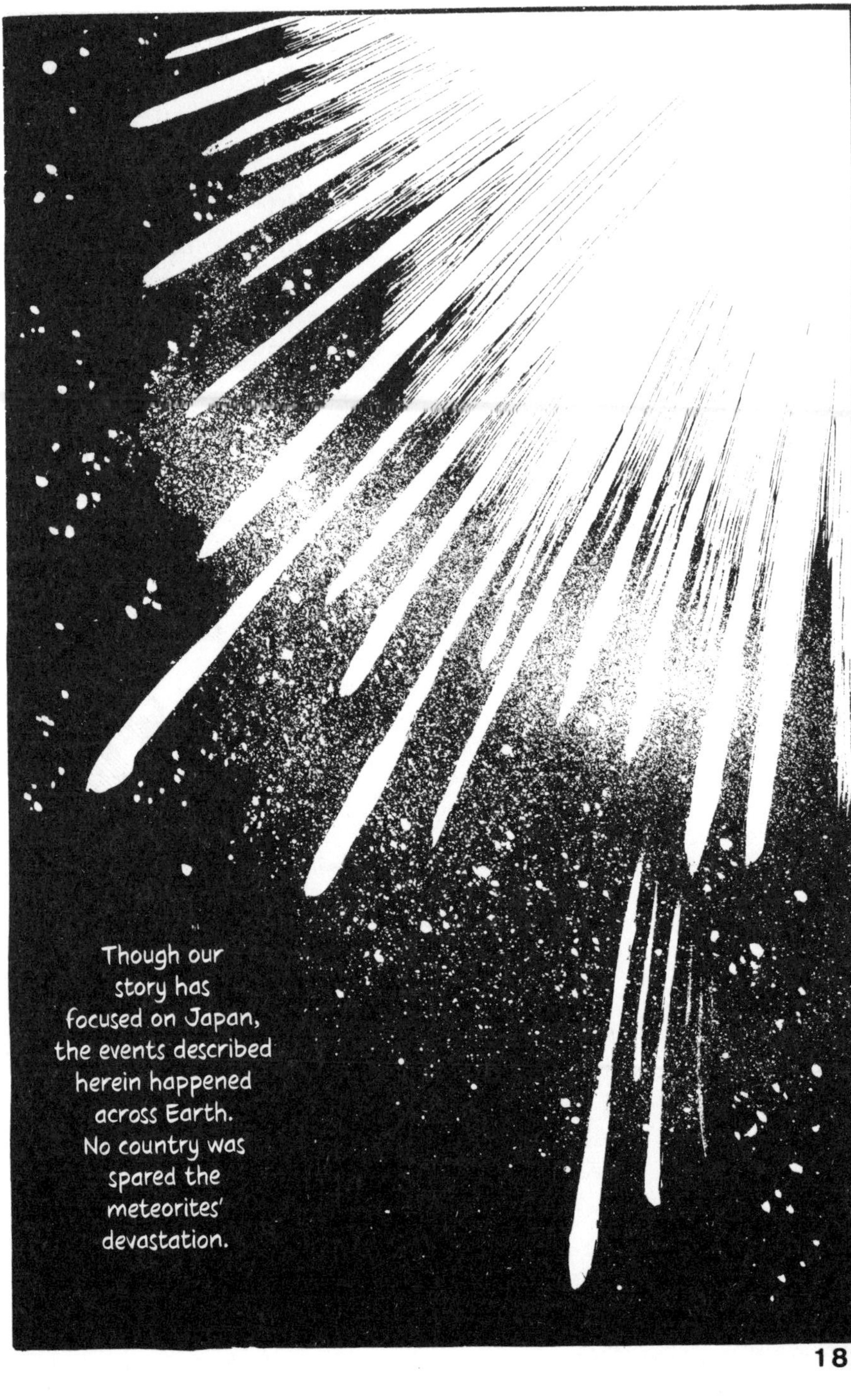
Though our story has focused on Japan, the events described herein happened across Earth. No country was spared the meteorites' devastation.

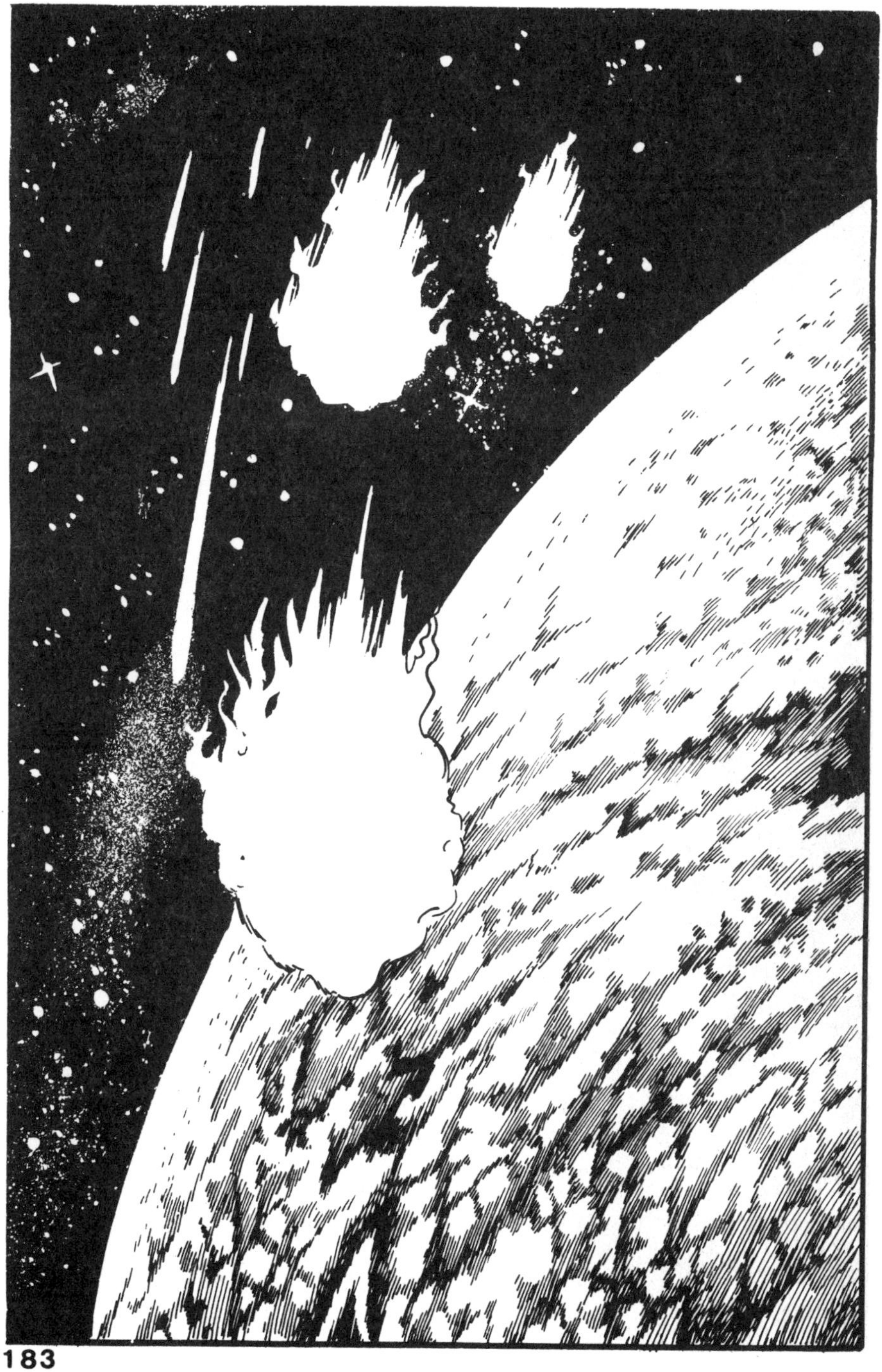

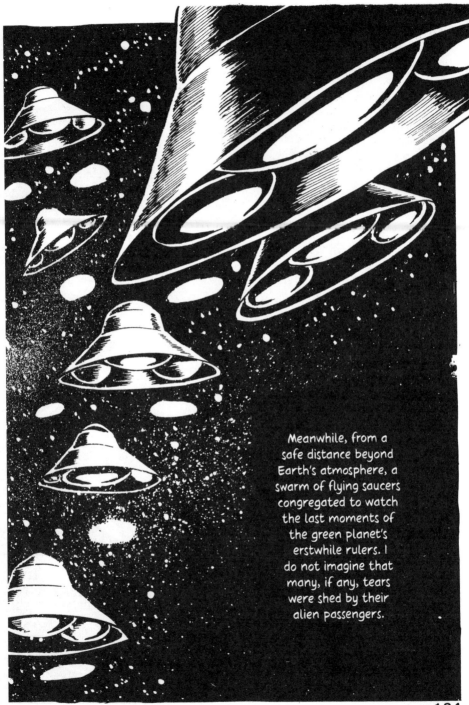

Meanwhile, from a safe distance beyond Earth's atmosphere, a swarm of flying saucers congregated to watch the last moments of the green planet's erstwhile rulers. I do not imagine that many, if any, tears were shed by their alien passengers.

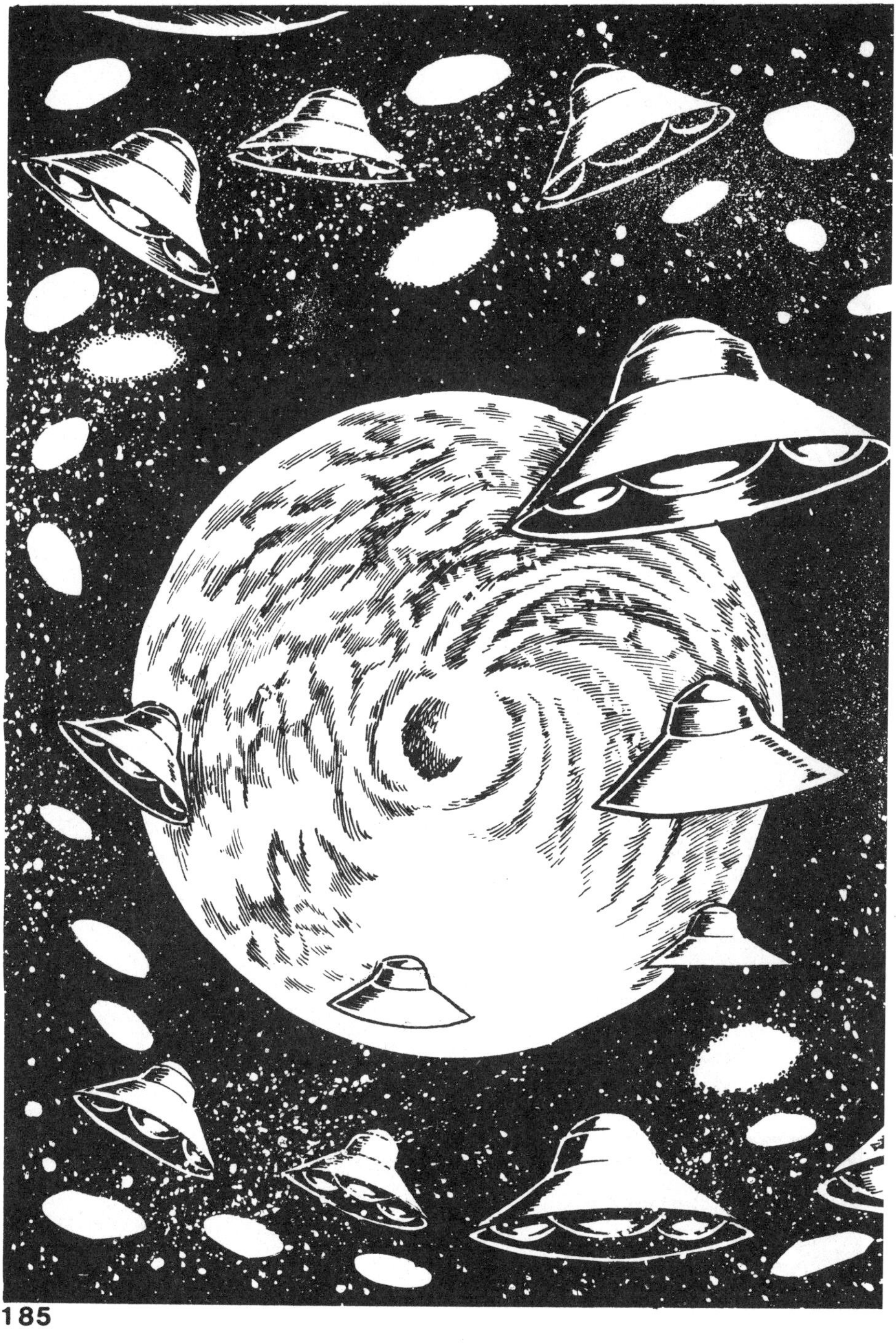

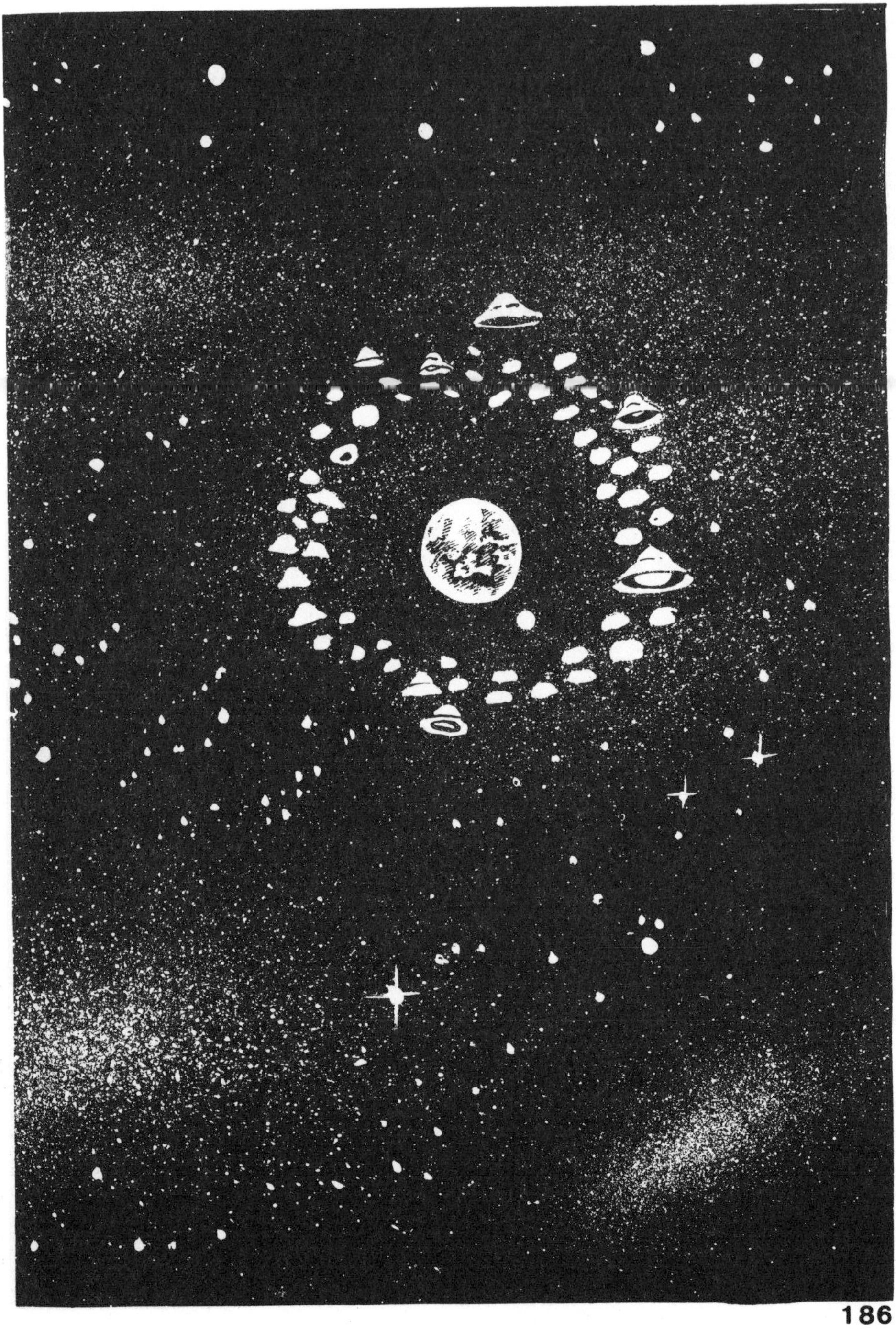

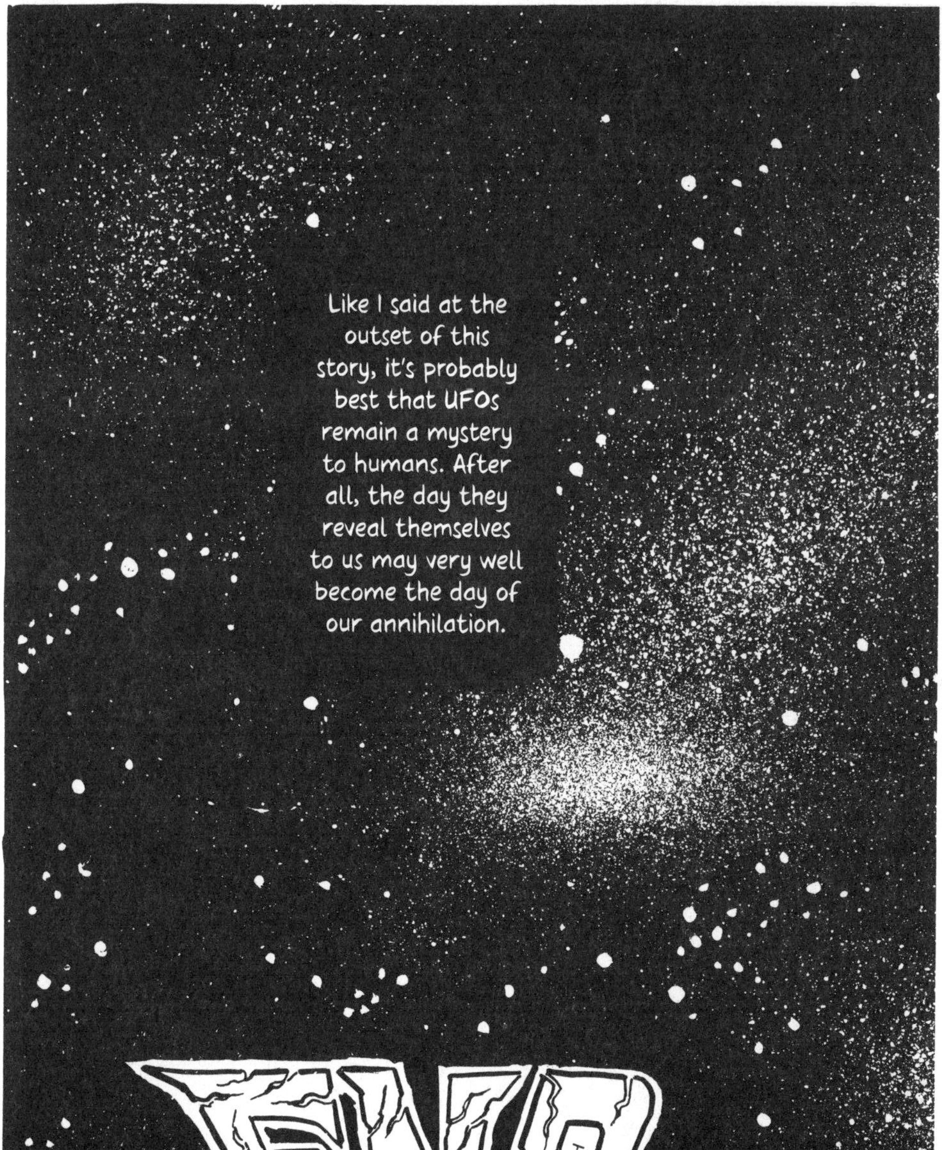
Like I said at the outset of this story, it's probably best that UFOs remain a mystery to humans. After all, the day they reveal themselves to us may very well become the day of our annihilation.
END

HOLD IT!

For the essays, turn to the
back of the book and read
left to right. To begin the
comic, turn to the front and
read right to left.

妖怪
天國
specter paradise
ようかい
ぱらだいす
新発見
化け物
集成
お化けの代表一つ目小僧は、顔の真ん中に大きい目が一つ。一本足で僧が化けたものだといわれている。しかし、この姿はずいぶん小型化され、可愛い存在に仕立てられたもので、昔は一つ目小僧が来ることを恐れ、それなりの撃退法も考えられていたほどだった。
「一つ目小僧」から「美少女河童」まで
妖怪ひとすじ三十余年の著者が解き明かす、愛すべきオバケたちのほんとうの姿。
ヴィジュアル満載!
白川まり奈
KKベストセラーズ

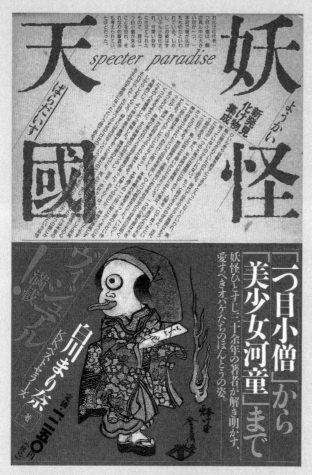

Yokai Paradise **(July 1994)**

Amidst renewed interested in yokai, urban legends, and the occult in the '90s, Shirakawa assembled this collection of entries about supernatural beings, monsters, and otherworldly visitors from the Japanese past. While the illustrations are culled from such famous historical sources as Tosa Mitsunobu, Toriyama Sekien, and Lafcadio Hearn, in addition to some newly produced images by illustrator Fujimoto Aoi, Shirakawa authored all the texts, demonstrating his chops as a researcher and folklorist for a non-manga audience. The author's bio reads: "First spurred on as a cartoonist, Shirakawa has spent the last thirty-some years obsessed with yokai, investing most of his free time researching these creatures he loves so much. Nothing, he says, could make him give up his blissful nightly hours buried beneath books and yokai goods, attempting to crack their mysteries with a drink in one hand." Posthumously, in 2016, P Vine Books published a collection of Shirakawa's own beautifully rendered drawings of yokai under the title *Yokai Picture Story*.

HIBARI HIT COMICS 怪談シリーズ

母さん
お化けを生まないで

白川まり奈 ホラー怪奇シリーズ

Mother, Please Don't Give Birth to a Monster (April 1988)

At the age of thirteen, pretty Miki, who mysteriously sweats blood when she's anxious, learns the shocking secret of her past: that she was born into a family of hereditary diviners who for centuries had relied on the prophecies of half-cow, half-human beasts known as *kudan* for their position and wealth, and that she herself had been born as one such monster, but had been saved by a mad genius surgeon who exchanged her cow body with her cow-headed twin sister's human body. Her sister now lives as a docile holy cow at a local shrine, while another cow monster scurries about in the old storehouse at the back of the family home. Too bad this was Shirakawa's last published manga, because he'd really gotten good again after some duds.

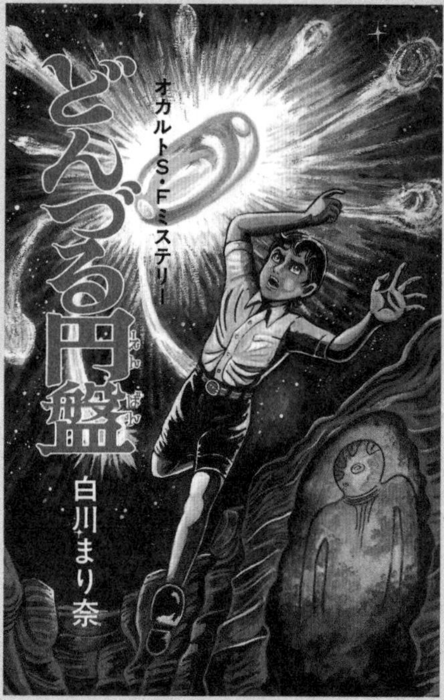
オカルトS・Fミステリー
どんづる円盤
白川まり奈

The Flying Saucer of Donzuru Peak (May 1975)

This one is summarized in Udagawa Takeo's text, so I won't recap it here. Shirakawa on the inside flap: "Hey kids, who do you think is actually riding in those flying saucers? Aliens? Humans? Gods? Or maybe the old man who lives next door…? The saucer passengers who appear in this manga are pretty strange. I know, you probably think this book is absurd. But I'm warning you! The minute humans let their guard down is when they allow things like the current environmental pollution crisis and open the door to humanity's annihilation." This is the only other Shirkawa manga that has been read widely, due to its inclusion in Ōta Shuppan's 1998 edition of *UFO Mushroom Invasion* as part of its legendary QJ Manga Select series.

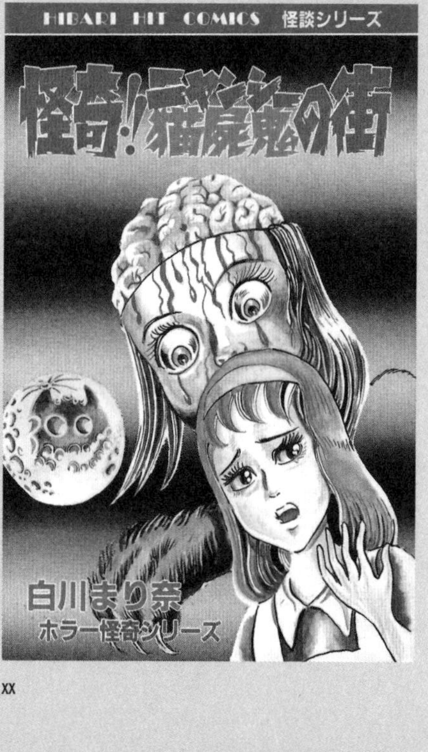
HIBARI HIT COMICS 怪談シリーズ
怪奇!!猫屍鬼の街
白川まり奈
ホラー怪奇シリーズ

Cat Zombie Town (November 1986)

The popular topic of *kaibyō* (supernatural cats) gets a modern, surrealistic update in this late work by Shirakawa, his first of three manga for Hibari Shobō in the latter half of the '80s. Shirakawa must've liked cats, as the finale reads like a public service announcement aimed at despicable brats who abuse our feline friends. If I were a kid reading this manga, the threat of getting lobotomized by a cat monster would certainly dissuade me from dissecting kittens live or shooting their eyes out with a toy gun. Shirakawa's drawing got pretty loose in the '80s, sometimes even sloppy, but he still knew how to spin a frightening yarn.

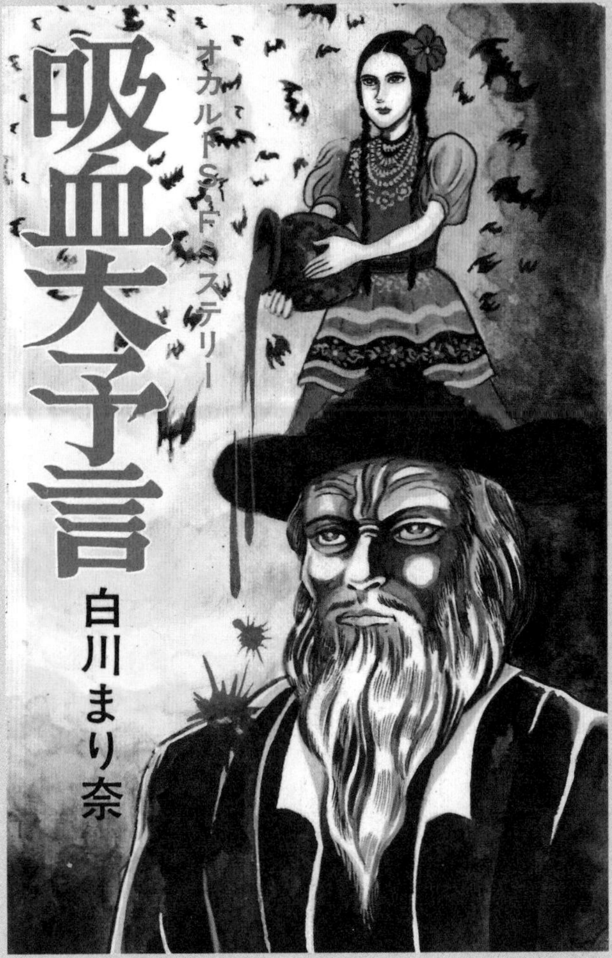
オカルトSFミステリー
吸血大予言
白川まり奈

***The Vampire Prophecy: The Vampire Legend, Part 4* (November 1975)**

Did Nostradamus really prophesize that the world would be taken over by vampires in 1999? By this point, Shirakawa had spun so much madness about vampires that even his earnest account of Count Dracula in fact and fiction reads like nonsense. There's some good gore and gothic scenery here, though the book's main purpose seems to be to offer a hypothesis about how vampires are actually a global phenomenon, appearing in non-European cultures throughout history under different guises and names. As Shirakawa's drawing improved, his stylistic debts to Nakazawa Keiji became more obvious, reinforced here by a shadowy view into the future of the Hiroshima A-Bomb Dome. Also, more flying saucers, first from the sketchbooks of Leonardo da Vinci, then swarming Earth eight years before the end of the world in 2010.

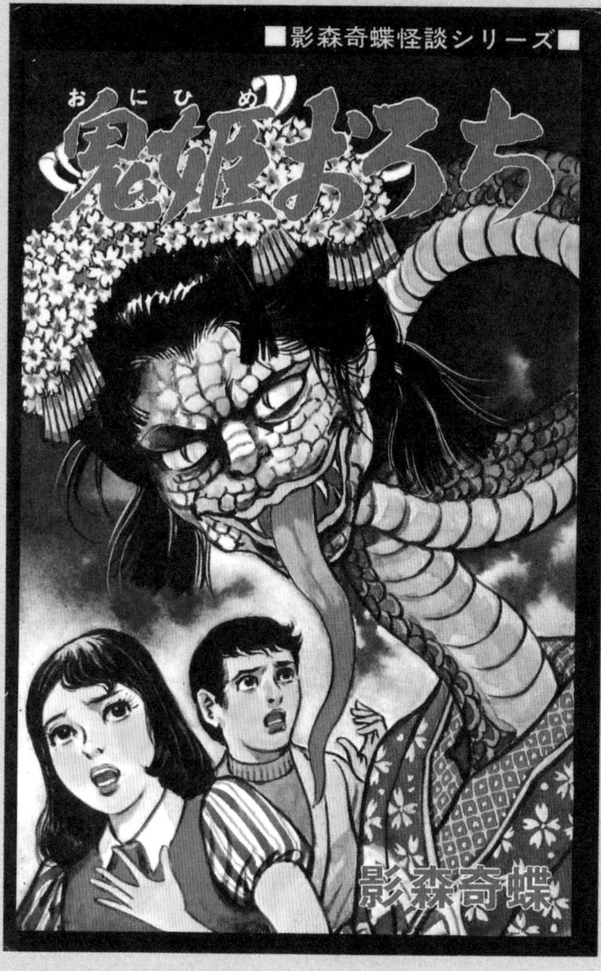
■影森奇蝶怪談シリーズ■
おにひめ
鬼姫おろち
影森奇蝶

The Demon Princess Serpent (December 1974)

Published under the penname Kagemori Kichō, this was Shirakawa's first book for horror manga powerhouse Hibari Shobō, and his only until the mid '80s. About a young warrior-class woman wronged by the patriarchy and exploited by legends of giant vengeful serpents, this manga is also the most conventional ghost and murder story the artist ever drew. "Behind all legends lie a hidden truth," writes Shirakawa in the manga's prologue, setting his occultist hat aside for a more rationalist and academic one for once. Trigger warning: this manga features a depiction of human teenager arm flesh sashimi!

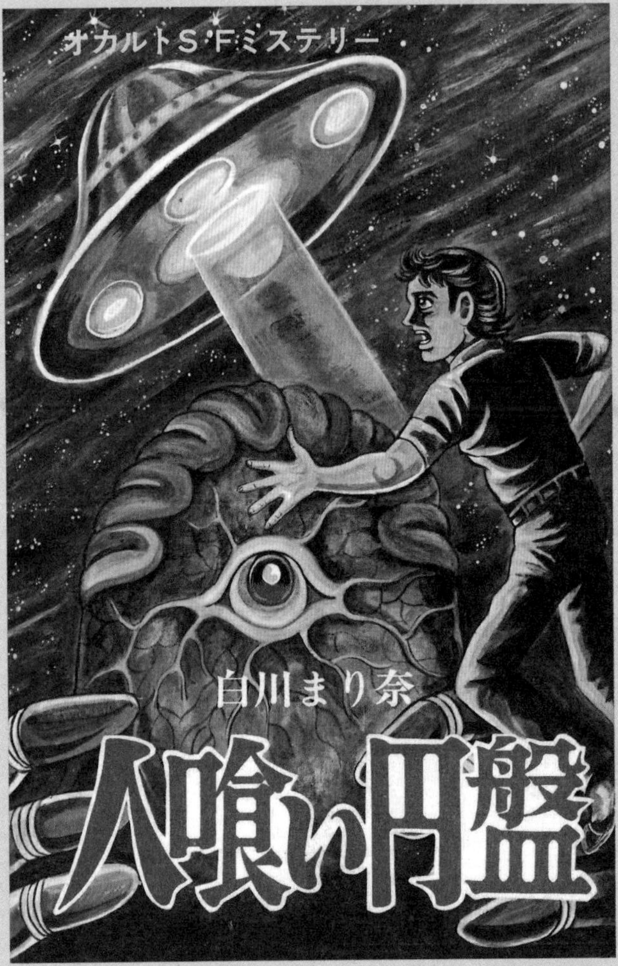
オカルトＳＦミステリー
白川まり奈
人喰い円盤

The Man-Eating Flying Saucer (September 1974)

While time-traversing spacecraft had featured in Shirakawa's vampire books, this was his first manga specifically about flying saucers and extraterrestrials. Ancient aliens and UFO religions feature front and center in this manga, which reads in parts like speculative nonfiction. What begins as a semi-serious inquiry into the possibility that medieval Japanese belief in *raigō* (the heavenly descent of the Buddha and bodhisattvas to whisk dying devotees away to the paradisical Pure Land) were actually contactee encounters ends in a dystopian vision of cannibalistic humans returning in time-traveling saucers to feast on gullible UFO believers. To answer the question at the end of Udagawa's essay: I suspect that Shirakawa did indeed believe in extraterrestrial visitors to Earth, but was doubtful of the reigning theories about their true identity and nature.

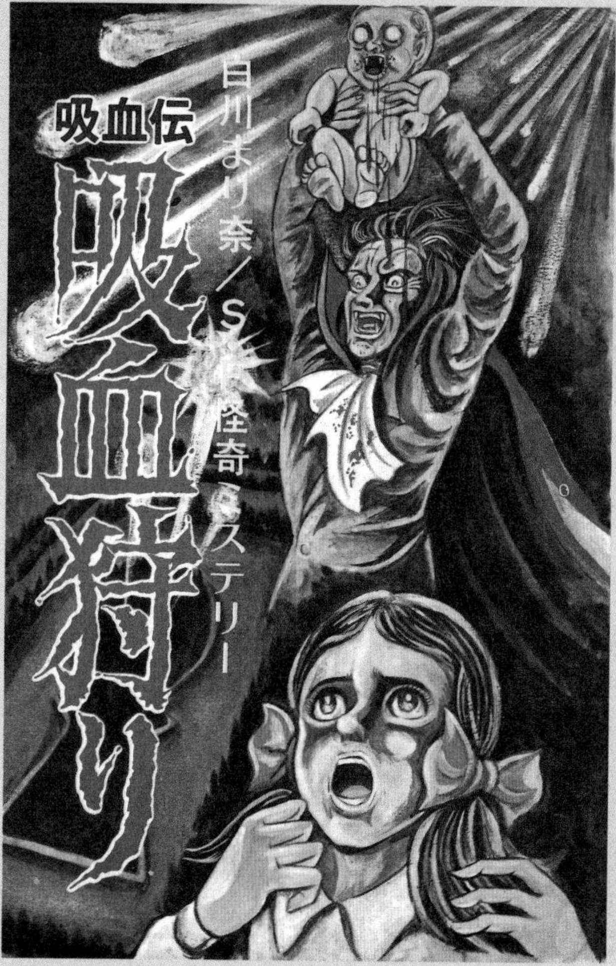
吸血伝
吸血狩り
白川まり奈／S
怪奇ミステリー

Vampire Hunter: The Vampire Legend, Part 3 (February 1974)

It's the 21st century. A white vampire hunter prowls New York City armed with a stake-loaded Gatling gun, looking for the black vampire priest who murdered his family. As the money-hungry Japanese government refuses to share its anti-vampirical vaccine with the world, a white supremacist scientist leads a mission to send an ark into space while Earth is nuked to eradicate the bloodsucker epidemic and all colored people along with it. A mysterious coffin races across space and time trying to undo the disaster. In another age, golden, egg-shaped time-capsules holding vicious vampire babies are found in an ancient Japanese tomb.

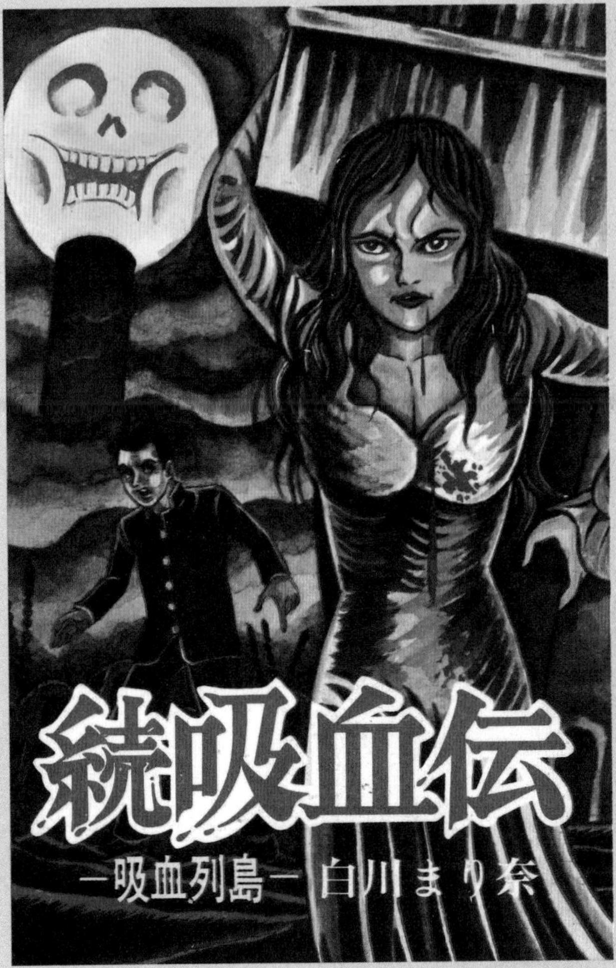

続吸血伝
―吸血列島― 白川まり奈

Bloodsucker Archipelago: The Vampire Legend, the Sequel (September 1973)

"No vampires are known to have existed in Japan," says Shirakawa on this manga's inside cover flap. "But that doesn't mean we should dismiss the possibility entirely." The result: bloodsucking Buddhist zombies in a remote Japanese village that is host to a secret biological warfare laboratory. The large amount of dialogue attests to how much Shirakawa enjoyed thinking through his crackpot ideas. Also, the first appearance of mushrooms in his oeuvre.

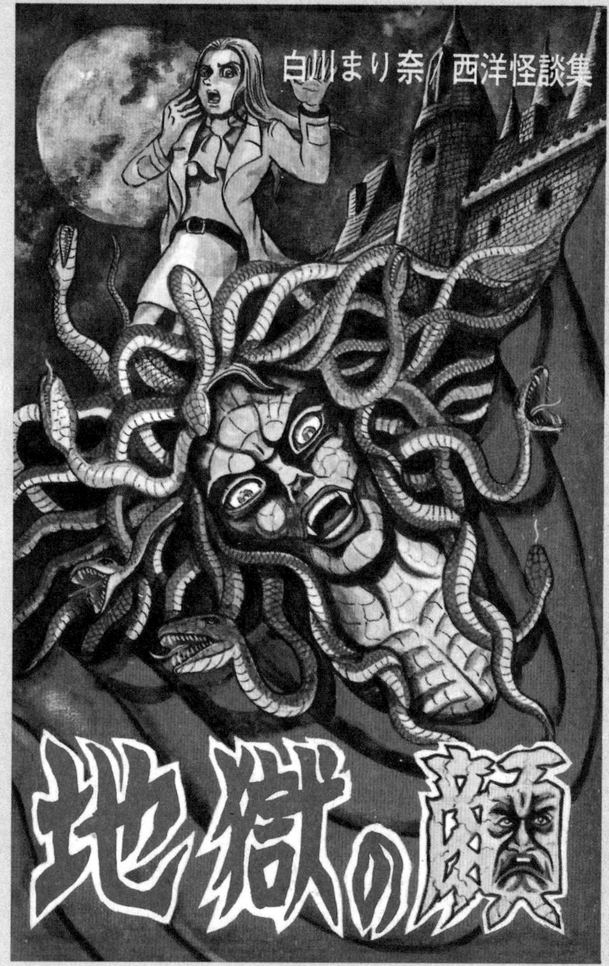
白川まり奈 西洋怪談集
地獄の顔

The Face of Hell (July 1973)

Subtitled "A Collection of Western Ghost Stories," this book begins with one Caroline of Scotland who became a werecat, then moves to her son Michael as he learns the harrowing truth about Gorgons after an ill-fated archaeological trip to Greece, before finishing with beautiful Madeleine who is beheaded and staked for supposedly being a vampire—woven together as a murder mystery around siblings battling over family wealth and haunted by a Medusa curse. The fashionable girl sleuth and fancy mansion setting suggest influence from Umezu Kazuo's *Orochi* (1969-70).

*dates of Shirakawa's manga are based on earliest known editions.

The Best of Shirakawa Marina

Ryan Holmberg

吸血伝

白川まり奈

The Vampire Legend (September 1972)

Vampires in an ancient French castle, vampires on the Riviera, vampires on the Moon—all courtesy of a lugubrious, tower-shaped tomb doubling as a time machine! From this, his very first book, Shirakawa's unique combination of bookwormishness and careening fantasy is already running wild. Stakes in the heart may mean death for vampires, but they sure beat an iron maiden to a pretty girl's face! This manga must have done decently well for Akebono Shuppan, because Shirakawa would go on to make it a series totaling four volumes, all from the same publisher, and all joyously insane.

The Vampire Legend (Akebono shuppan, September 1972)

Mother, Please Don't Give Birth to a Monster (Hibari shobō, April 1988)

about UFOs fall into four general categories. First, the "objective" type that aims to catalog, analyze, and explain sightings and related phenomena. Second, the "believer" type that accepts stories about the existence of aliens, their immanent invasion, or their role as planetary saviors at face value. Third, the "transcendental" type, which goes beyond the "believer" category with proclamations about alien-related spiritual realms that far exceed the known universe. Fourth, the "prisoner of conscience" type, which is forthright about the eccentricity of those whose experiences are documented in "objective" UFO literature, yet views them as victims of systematic censorship around the truth about extraterrestrials. If *Mundus Mysticus* falls into the fourth type and the CBA counts as type two,

what is *UFO Mushroom Invasion*? Is it pure fiction and fantasy? Is it speculation, or even perhaps prophecy? What would the artist say? While Shirakawa was still alive, I wish I had asked him the all-important question, "Sir, just how much of a believer are you?"

*This essay was originally published as a chapter in Udagawa Takeo's *Manga Zombie* (Ōta Shuppan, 1997), a cult classic survey of bizarre and forgotten manga artists. Changes to the original text have been made for the sake of clarity and accuracy, and to bring the text up to date. The entirety of *Manga Zombie* will be published in English by Ultra Gash Records in 2024, translated by Lorenzo Di Giuseppe. Thank you to Udagawa and Ultra Gash for allowing us to publish our own adaptation here.

is another classic in Shirakawa's UFO series for Akebono Shuppan. In the distant future, humans are starving due to the destruction of Earth's environment. Using flying saucers as time machines, they travel back in time to the present and begin devouring their ancestors, the evilness of which turns them into horned demons. Cockroaches, meanwhile, have grown gigantic due to radioactive contamination. They, too, travel back in time, in order to save humans in the present from their cannibalistic descendants in the future. The background plot is reminiscent of Nagai Gō's *Demon: The Rebellion of 2889 (Oni: 2889-nen no hanran,* 1970), while the idea of intelligent, predatory cockroaches reminds one of Umezu's *The Drifting Classroom (Hyōryū kyōshitsu,* 1972-74), yet the resulting synthesis could only have been the product of Shirakawa's idiosyncratic imagination. As a dedicated researcher of Japanese folklore and yokai, Shirakawa was able to take campy kitsch like flying saucers, on the one hand, and things familiar to daily life like vermin and fungi, on the other, and meld them into a uniquely vernacular brand of Japanese horror.

During the summer months, Akebono Shuppan published many shōjo horror titles by many unique but now largely forgotten artists. Most of them drew in a rather dry and anachronistic style, with numerous scenes that, though depicting the bizarre and scary, are nonetheless comfortably familiar, so much so that one wonders if they weren't sampled from other artists' work. Shirakawa's comics also have that quality. At the same time, as the artist himself once suggested, the "old-timey" style of his drawing contributes to and intensifies the atmosphere of mystery and terror. The existence of his work in a genre otherwise dominated by

unimaginative repetition is something of a minor miracle.

Shirakawa was born on September 20, 1940, in Sasebo in Nagasaki prefecture. After teaching himself how to draw manga, he moved to Tokyo and knocked on various publishers' doors before finding a willing party in Akebono Shuppan. His debut work, *The Vampire Legend (Kyūketsuden),* was published by Akebono in September 1972, followed by an assortment of ghost and other vampire manga, then his three UFO titles. While all of his other manga were published in a standard *shinsho* format (5 x 7 inches), *UFO Mushroom Invasion* alone was issued in a smaller, pocket paperback, *bunko* format (4 x 6 inches).

As a fan of both horror and science fiction, Shirakawa loved Ridley Scott's *Alien* (1979) as much as he did George Lucas's *Star Wars* (1977). Between 1986 and 1988, he drew three comics for the famous horror manga publisher Hibari Shobō, including his last published manga, *Mother, Please Don't Give Birth to a Monster (Kaasan, obake o umanaide,* April 1988). After that, he spent much of his time engrossed in research about yokai and Japanese folklore, resulting in the books *Yokai Paradise (Yōkai tengoku,* 1994) and the posthumously published *Yokai Picture Story (Yōkai emonogatari,* 2018). From his name, you might guess that he was a woman, though his sideburns begged to differ. Shirakawa was his actual family name. Marina was a penname, inspired by NASA's Mariner program, which sent interplanetary probes to Mars, Venus, and Jupiter in the '60s and early '70s. The artist passed away in July 2000, at the age of fifty-nine.

In his book *The Take-it-Easy Human Revolution (Nohohon ningen kakumei,* 1995), Ōtsuki Kenji argues that books

The Flying Saucer of Donzuru Peak (Akebono shuppan, May 1975)

all of humanity, but the entire animal kingdom, has been transformed into mushrooms. Earth returns to a state of peace and quiet, while an army of flying saucers watch patiently from space.

UFO Mushroom Invasion takes itself seriously as science fiction. In addition to the bleak story of planetary annihilation, there's also the many learned tangents about UFO lore and mushroom-related monster tales from the past. Shirakawa's drawing style, which at first glance reads like a lo-fi version of Umezu Kazuo (whose work was clearly an influence), gives the impression that the mushroom invaders come not from outer space, but rather somewhere deep in the jungle, as if they were tribal peoples. Indeed, the name used in the original Japanese version of the manga for the mushroom people, Kinokonga, combines the Japanese words

for "mushroom" (*kinoko*) and the exoticizing *konga*, which is the Japanese for conga drums, with echoes of "kong" from *King Kong*. The drawing is so powerfully fantastic at times that one almost wonders if Shirakawa didn't come up with the imagery while high on some kind of psychedelic, psilocybin trip. At the same time, the scenes of the mushroom men walking in the rain clearly evoke images of a-bomb survivors pelted by the black rain that followed the destruction of Hiroshima and Nagasaki, like those depicted in Nakazawa Keiji's *Barefoot Gen* (*Hadashi no Gen*, 1973-86), another likely influence. Shirakawa was skilled at taking the wonder around aliens and outer space and turning it into a form of horror—in a way that was particularly palpable for Japanese readers.

The Flying Saucer of Donzuru Peak

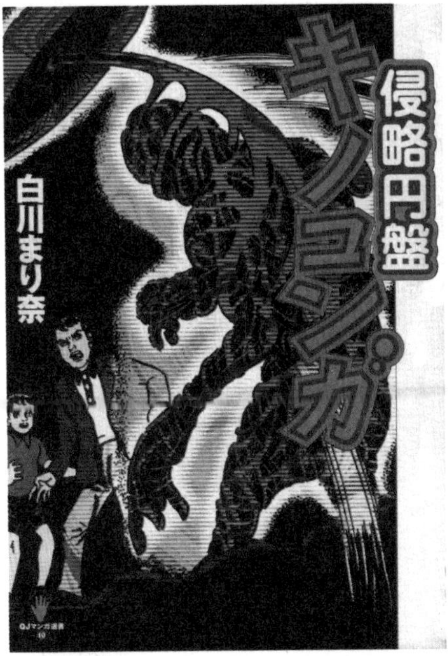
侵略円盤
キノコンガ
白川まり奈

UFO Mushroom Invasion (Ōta shuppan, November 1998)

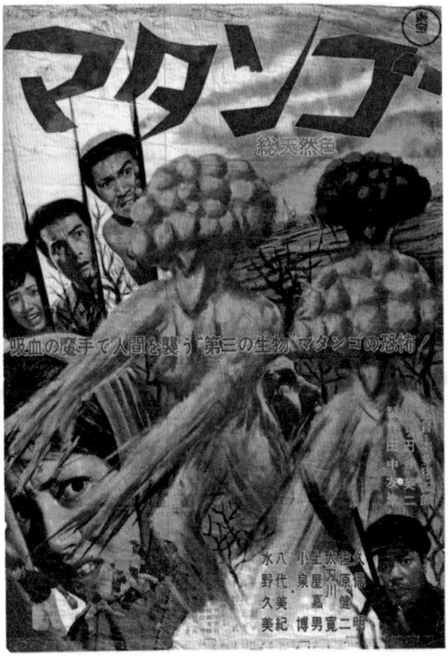
マタンゴ
総天然色
吸血の魔手で人間を襲う"第三の生物"マタンゴの恐怖!

Poster for *Matango* (1963), directed by Honda Ishirō

1971, and Tōhō Studio's sci-fi classic *Matango* (1963), which was directed by the same Honda Ishirō who made the original *Godzilla* (1954).

After escaping their captivity, Aoki and Sada sensei return to the crash site, where they discover that numerous scientists and an elderly man who lives in the mountains have been killed, buried, and turned into parasitic hosts that resemble "zombie funguses," a real-life phenomenon in which certain varieties of fungus invade the bodies of insect larvae. Suddenly the corpses wake up and attack them! Later they learn that the cause of this terrible transformation are the spores of a mushroom-like lifeform brought to Earth on the crashed spacecraft. One after another, humans are infected and killed by the spores. Aoki rushes home, worried about his family. He's too late, however. Not just his mother, father, and sister, but also his entire neighborhood, have been turned into mushroom people! In a gesture of mercy, Aoki sets fire to his family home. While watching the flames of this sublime funeral, he begins to cry. His tears don't last long, however, as his grotesquely transformed parents and sister emerge from the earth and threaten him with an otherworldly growl. He rushes to Sada sensei's home, only to find him infected too. In an unforgettable scene, Sada sensei implores Aoki to relinquish his attachment to humanity, give into mushroom consciousness, and join him in the warm embrace of Earth's soil.

And who could ever forget the climactic scene showing Aoki, fully fungalized, swaying eternally on that overgrown swing? At the end of the manga, not just

Shirakawa Marina, circa 1978

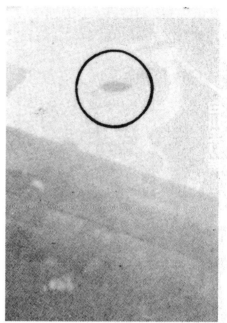

Photo of a UFO by the artist, Chofu city (May 15, 1974)

to speak.

Shirakawa Marina (1940-2000) drew multiple manga about Earth being invaded by strange lifeforms from outer space. Among them are *The Man-Eating Flying Saucer* (*Hitogui enban*, September 1974), the inside cover flap of which features a photo of a UFO taken by the artist himself, and *The Flying Saucer of Donzuru Peak* (*Donzuru enban*, May 1975). There's also his most famous book, *UFO Mushroom Invasion* (*Shinryaku enban kinokonga*, December 1976), which is well known among fans of freaky manga due to its reissuing in 1998 as part of the Quick Japan Manga Select (QJ manga sensho) series from Ōta Shuppan. All three were originally published by the former *kashi-hon* (rental book) publishing house Akebono Shuppan in Tokyo.

The story of *UFO Mushroom Invasion* goes as follows. Spoiler alert for those who haven't yet read the manga! One day, a large meteorite crashes into Earth. No one realizes it at the time, but this is the beginning of what quickly develops into catastrophic changes for life on Earth as we know it. While on a school hiking trip in the mountains, a boy named Aoki and his teacher Sada sensei discover that the meteorite is actually a UFO. After reporting the incident to the authorities, both the boy and his teacher are taken into custody by a team of shady scientists. They suspect that the body of a dead alien was discovered inside the spacecraft, but have no way to prove it while locked up inside the scientists' laboratory. So far, the story seems to follow famous incidents like those at Roswell in New Mexico. But then it swerves into a different universe, racing along a crescendo paved by the likes of Michael Crichton's *The Andromeda Strain* (1969), which was made into a movie in

I Believe in Shirakawa Marina!

Udagawa Takeo

Some people are simply possessed by UFOs.

Just to name a few of the most famous fanatics... In the United States there's George Adamski, who claimed to have made contact with visitors from outer space and been taken to the Moon, Mars, and Venus by them. There's also Claude Raël, founder and leader of the Raëlian Movement, which holds that aliens are actually gods. Swiss author Erich von Däniken, meanwhile, argued that the origins of human civilization are inconceivable without the help of extraterrestrials.

In Japan, there was once a group called the Cosmic Brotherhood Association (CBA), founded by one Matsumura Yūsuke in 1957. Dedicated to the study and pursuit of UFOs and extraterrestrial contact, the CBA counted among its supporters the novelist Mishima Yukio (for a short time, at least) and the emonogatari artist Yamakawa Sōji, who claimed to have witnessed UFOs multiple times. While many ufologists have prophesized planetary cataclysm and the salvation of humans at the hands of friendly aliens, the CBA turned this belief into something of a religious cult, with many of its members liquidating their property, quitting school and their jobs, running away from home, and moving into the mountains to hide. Their activities were something of a hot topic in the 1960s.

Of course, Earth did not perish. The CBA managed to survive its unfulfilled prophecy, turning its attention instead to

"ancient aliens." Inspired by the ideas of the American George Williamson, this thesis holds that alien contact has been part of human history since its very beginnings and was a major factor in human biological evolution. In the early '60s, the CBA got in trouble for messing with the ancient Chibusan Tomb (6th century CE), located in Kumamoto prefecture on the southern island of Kyushu. Believing that the colorful murals inside the tomb depicted alien contact, they erected a special gate and changed explanatory signage without permission, leading to police intervention and a lawsuit. In Biratori in southern Hokkaido, the association built a tiered pyramid into the side of a mountain for the purposes of honoring and summoning extraterrestrial divinities back to Earth. Known as the Haiopira (written "Hayopira" in Japanese and supposedly derived from local Ainu language meaning "armored cliff"), it was constructed by volunteer labor and completed in 1967, but was eventually closed due to a lack of funds. The CBA took their beliefs seriously, to say the very least.

In 1976, the magazine *Mundus Mysticus* (*Chikyū roman*) published a detailed chronology of the CBA in an issue titled "A Penchant for Heavenly Beings" (*tenkūjin shikō*). This is how I, a devoted reader of *Mundus Mysticus* in my youth, learned about the history of the CBA's shenanigans and began thinking about UFOs as simply a product of fantasy and delusion—as just another "urban legend," so

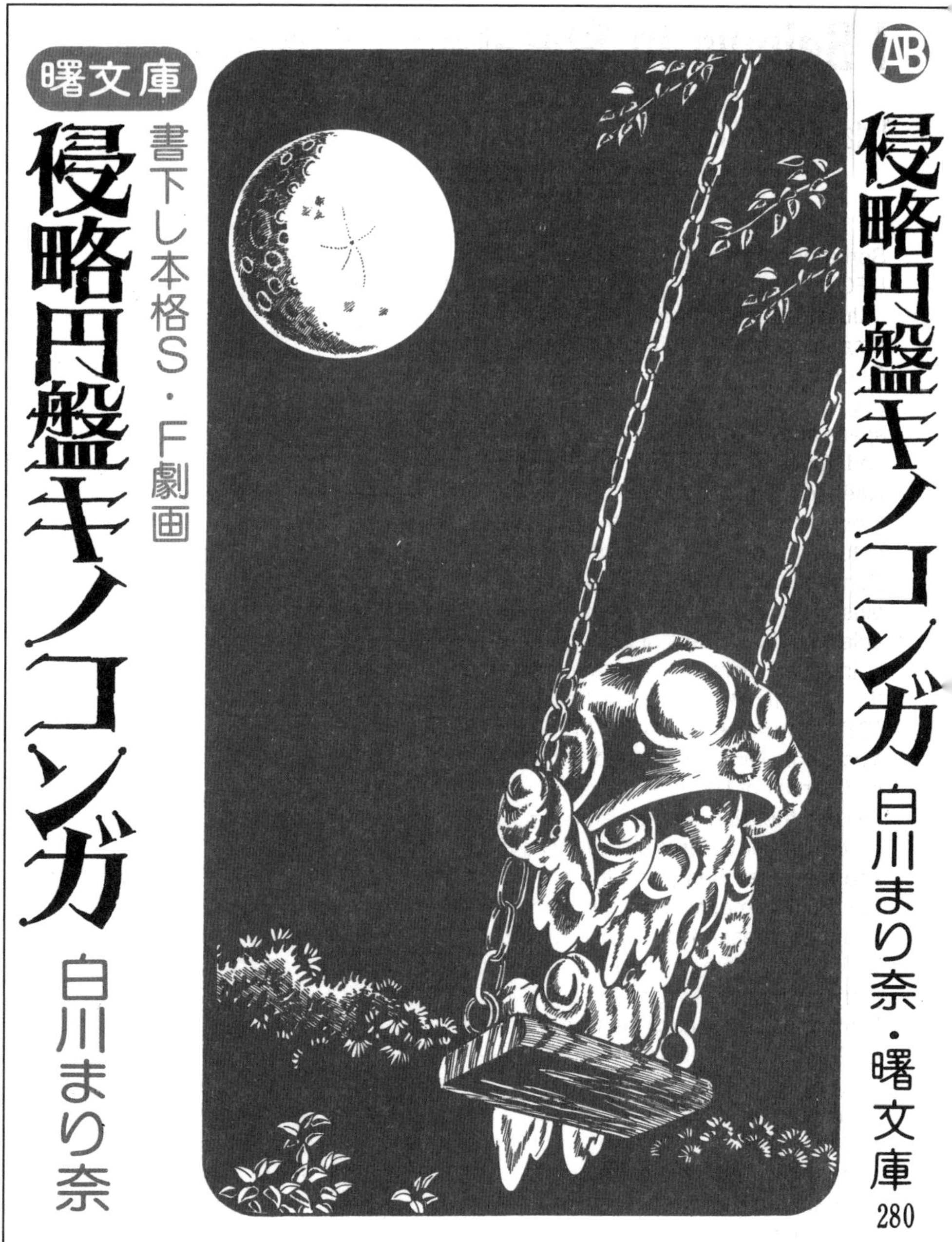
曙文庫
書下し本格S・F劇画
侵略円盤キノコンガ
白川まり奈
AB
侵略円盤キノコンガ
白川まり奈・曙文庫
280

UFO Mushroom Invasion (Akebono shuppan, December 1976), cover and spine

UFO
mushroom
INVASION

by Shirakawa Marina

Copyright 2024 © estate of Shirakawa Marina
Orginally published as *Shinryaku enban kinokonga*, 1976
English translation rights arranged through
Kunisawa Hiroshi and MANDARAKE, INC.

Translated and edited by Ryan Holmberg
Essays by Udagawa Takeo and Ryan Holmberg
Designed by Sean Michael Robinson
Lettered by Ozzy Von Eschen with Sean Michael Robinson

Published Fall 2024 by Smudge,
an imprint of Living the Line Books.

ISBN: 978-1-961581-01-2

PRINTED IN CHINA by
R.R. Donnelley Printing Associates